PERSPECTIVES ON THE
HISTORY OF ECONOMIC THOUGHT
VOLUME VIII

CONTRIBUTIONS TO THE
HISTORY OF ECONOMICS

Perspectives on the History of Economic Thought Volume VIII

Contributions to the History of Economics

Selected Papers from the
History of Economics Conference 1990

Edited by
S. Todd Lowry

Professor
Department of Administration and Economics
Washington and Lee University
Lexington, Virginia, US

Published for the History of Economics Society
by Edward Elgar

Published by
Edward Elgar Publishing Limited
Gower House
Croft Road
Aldershot
Hants GU11 3HR
England

Edward Elgar Publishing Company
Old Post Road
Brookfield
Vermont 05036
USA

A CIP catalogue record for this book
is available from the British Library

A CIP catalogue record for this book
is available from the US Library of Congress

ISBN 978 1 85278 448 5

Printed and bound by CPI Group (UK) Ltd, Croydon, CR0 4YY

Contents

v

Acknowledgements

I wish to express my appreciation to the participants in the 1990 History of Economics Society conference held here at Washington and Lee University in Lexington, Virginia for their scholarly efforts and patience in the process of negotiation and selection of papers reproduced in Volumes VII and VIII of this series. The authors of the selected papers have been most patient and helpful, responding to suggested revisions and in adapting their papers to the Elgar style.

I have also found the general editor of the series, Mark Blaug, pleasant to deal with, and the staff of Edward Elgar Publishing Limited has been very efficient and helpful.

Last, but not least, I wish to express my gratitude to Carolyn West Hammett for her initiative and services in organizing and hosting the meetings that gave rise to these papers and to Mary Hall Bobenia who worked up the printed programme, and the abstracts of the papers for the meetings and devoted many long and tedious hours to editing the selected papers for publication.

S. Todd Lowry
Washington and Lee University

Introduction

S. Todd Lowry

The papers collected in this volume are organized around the theme of the dual aspects of method in the development of economic thought. On the one hand, we can observe the development of a formal analytic method in economics and its application, currently or retrospectively. The formal study of such analytic systems constitutes the subdiscipline of methodology. On the other hand, we frequently find it sufficient to explore the emergence of economic perspectives and theories that raise provocative questions and provide insights into the ways and conditions under which economic ideas emerge. This latter may be characterized as a simple historical approach, but simple in the mathematical sense of elegance. It is, after all, out of the aggregation of insightful descriptions of the emergence and assimilation of ideas that we extrapolate a valid surmise about the physical and intellectual conditions, as well as the personalities that have promoted economic formulations. Of course, formal methodology purports to understand how to 'force' the gestation and birth of economic understanding while the simpler observational or descriptive approach presumes to enhance our recognition of the variety of contexts, personalities, institutions and material or intellectual forces that contribute to the development of ideas. The grand variety of an open historical method permits a greater openness to the breadth of problems and objectives that have concerned thinkers and policy-makers in the past. While this makes the study of the history of thought somewhat amorphous when contrasted with formal analytic methods, this very freedom from rigour incorporates a freedom from technical preconception and ideology that permits the study of the history of ideas to serve as a matrix for fresh insight into the foibles of human beings with their tendencies to cling to erroneous or irrelevant concepts and to perpetuate inappropriate values and spurious objectives. If nothing else, there is a sophistication that comes with the general study of the emergence of economic doctrine that provides the scholar with a certain scepticism and immunity to the promulgation of grandiose solutions or ultimate scientific methods.

The majority of these papers do not profess to be contributions to methodology. Some are studies of specific individual economic thinkers and their influence on others and on the public. Others study the genesis or transmission of concepts or systems of thought. They reflect the difficulty in defining a specific method appropriate for the study of the history of economic thought. The working consensus of the subdiscipline seems to be, of course, that it is this very ebullience of inquiry that provides the strength and merit of the field, offering an intellectual home for the pursuit of a type of open-ended curiosity into everything from formal research methods to the evolution of institutions that provide embedded bases for policy and clichés. One may well conclude that partisans should eschew the notion of an appropriate or correct method for the study of the history of economic thought. We may observe, however, that the variety of structure and perspective in this collection offers an illustration of the desirability of a provocative seedbed of heterodoxy. At the same time, it is probably desirable that we, as individual researchers, attempt to clarify in our own minds a method or system of investigation with which we are comfortable. We should value the provocative potential of contrasting or contradictory developments that make the history of the genesis of ideas a constant source of critical input into the formal refinement and application of ideas.

We may also note here that we choose to use the word *method* to refer to a broadly conceived analytic approach and the word *methodology* to mean the formal study of *method*. This distinction is, of course, implicit in the suffix *ology*, which means 'the study of' something. So when we refer to the application of a system of research principles, we refer to a *method*. When we refer to the reflective evaluation of systems of analysis or inquiry, we are dealing with *methodology*. When we discuss the ins and outs of the application of a particular method to a problem, we ought to be able to refer to the exposition as a 'methodical discussion', but the word *methodical* has been pre-empted into another nuance indicating *routine* or *systematic* with a non-scientific connotation. The result has been that the term *methodology* has been extended in usage to mean both the study of method and the application of a method, but this blurring of the clarity of discourse should be avoided. It is also useful to consider the distinction between the terms *technique* and *method*. This distinction parallels the difference between *tactics* and *strategy* in the military lexicon that, of course, has some application to the marshalling of intellectual resources to deal with challenges to our comprehension of economic problems. Despite the apparent pedantry of such definitional niceties, it is preferable to keep references to technique and method clearly distinguished from references to methodology. Thus, one does not apply a *methodology* to the analysis of a problem, but a *method*, while frequently employing specific analytic *techniques*.

The first paper, by André Lapidus, questions the effectiveness of appraising medieval economic ideas in terms of contemporary economic criteria. He finds that a retrospective method is inadequate for deciphering the intellectual nuances and institutional conditions of the times. However, we might add the caveat that, given a broader perspective on method, contemporary economic theory can be stated with sufficient generality of institutional flexibility and receptivity to nuance so as to embrace rather disparate economic problems in their own milieux.

The second paper, by Roger E. Backhouse, is a formal examination of a contemporary scientific method and the appropriateness of its applicability to economic research. As such, it is an inquiry dealing with methodology in the formal sense.

In contrast, the paper by Maurice Lagueux explores the use of metaphor in economic thought, specifically, the hydraulic metaphor. This exploration can be characterized as methodology in the broadest sense in that it inquires into the various types of image that contribute to analytic formulations in economics. A more sanguine extension of this inquiry could include Quesnay's, Hobbes's and Oresme's observations of the circulation of the blood as a hydraulic process. In a specific instance, the use of an illustrative metaphor would be considered an expositional technique, but when examined as a general category of comprehensive images, the study takes on the character of methodology.

In her paper on Simon Kuznets, Vibha Kapuria-Foreman analyses the interplay of empiricism and institutional considerations in the research method of one of our more independent and original economists.

In a somewhat parallel study of the ambivalent efforts of a major thinker, Annie L. Cot brings out the heavy administrative commitment of Jeremy Bentham, who offered codes and institutions for the reform of human society. Despite this aspect of his work, his felicific calculus was embraced as the basis of a participative subjectivism and Bentham was made a part of the liberal utilitarian tradition. We are left to wonder whether the felicific calculus is a technique for expert administrators to use in making efficient decisions or a method by which one can better predict the expression of natural rationality in human behaviour.

Another instructive aspect of the study of the writings of individual economists is Anastassios D. Karayiannis's presentation of the work of Rowland Hamilton on risk, uncertainty and profit. This is basically a study of intellectual default, which is quite pertinent to an understanding of the history of thought. It is important for us to understand why some ideas or the individuals who promulgate them are completely ignored at a given time or place. It would be rather strained to assert a negative method to study the hows and whys of the failure of society or an active discipline to receive or accept ideas in a variety of circumstances, but it does happen, and the ideas, in retrospect, are essentially identical to those that were received with enthusiasm from someone else, or at a later date. Such instances raise serious questions about both the formal and the natural processes of intellectual growth and progress and are fit subjects for study with rhetorical overtones. One is probably confined in such cases to using a comparative method.

The two ensuing papers deal with the reception and influence of Léon Walras on the political and economic front. Pierre Dockès recounts the fortuitous reception of Walras's writings by a few very influential students at the equally influential Ecole Normale Supérieure in Paris in the late nineteenth century, which led to the widespread acceptance of Walras's writings.

Richard Arena continues the examination of Walras's influence, but on another famous economist: J.A. Schumpeter. This chapter combines the influence of a hagiographic commitment to Walrasian analysis with a record of adaptation to the realities of a dynamic system.

The next two papers deal with the emergence of different types of economic ideas in what seemed to have been inappropriate and appropriate socioeconomic milieux. J.-Michel Servet chronicles the surprising emergence of a body of liberal socioeconomic thought during the first five years of the French Revolution when one would have expected a very strong protomilitary authoritarian philosophy.

By contrast, the study by Arnaldo Canziani and Paolo Rondo Brovetto analyses the institutional and technical commercial environment in which the continental European analysis of the firm and its particular method were developed in the 1920s. Such studies as these last four sharpen our focus on the interaction between the history of thought as a broad-gauge method for formulating questions and problems about how economic ideas emerge, on the one hand, contrasting on the other with the specific history of how specific formal methods of investigating and elucidating economic phenomena are promoted by individuals.

R.S. Hewett demonstrates the continuing validity of one of the premium methods employed by historians of economic thought: the tracing of the development of an analytic perspective and identifying its subtle shifts and dilution over time. Such a system of temporal comparisons or an evolutionary method permits the researcher to identify shifts and blurrings of precision in theory that are not readily apparent when confronted with a formal, detailed and elaborate theory in contemporary vogue.

Vincent J. Tarascio and Ronald Bird offer us a thorough systematic investigation, delving into the work of Wilfredo Pareto to clarify his scarcity-oriented rent theory in a general equilibrium analysis of primarily capital rents. This is one of the ongoing services of historians of thought – the analysis and reformulation of the work of past theorists in order to make it accessible to researchers on the contemporary economic scene.

The final two papers in this collection deal with Keynesian monetary theory and apply specific analytical techniques that are not necessarily limited to historical inquiry. First, Hansjoerg Klausinger uses a model as a reference base for evaluating the internal consistency of Keynes's theories on money and interest. By contrast, Ivo Maes uses the comparative method to examine the views of Keynes and Hicks while specifically examining the forms taken by their equilibrium analysis of monetary processes. Although equilibrium can be considered an ideological assumption in some contexts, it is also a technique for examining quantitative consistency.

It is, of course, not to be presumed that the authors of these papers all had methodological motives in mind when they prepared them, but the consideration used in correlating them in this volume has been the various types and aspects of method that they illustrate. The great variety of method, technique and conceptual orientation that characterizes the subdiscipline of the history of economic thought offers this unifying theme when others fail. Nevertheless, the chronology of these papers, from the Middle Ages to the present and their variety of comment on the provocative circumstances that do, or do not, give rise to established economic ideas provide an instructive survey of the history of economic perspectives.

Contributors

Richard Arena, LATAPSES, Université de Nice-Sophia Antipolis and CNRS, France

Roger E. Backhouse, Department of Economics, School of Social Sciences, The University of Birmingham, United Kingdom

Ronald Bird, Kensington, Maryland

Paolo Rondo Brovetto, Università Commerciale 'L. Bocconi', Milan, Italy

Arnaldo Canziani, Università di Brescia, Dipartimento di Economia Aziendale, Bresci, Italy

Annie L. Cot, Groupe de recherches épistémologiques et socio-économiques, Université de Paris-I Panthéon-Sorbonne, Paris, France

Pierre Dockès, Department of Economics, Université Lumière-Lyon 2, Lyon, France

R. S. Hewett, Department of Economics, Drake University, Iowa, US

Vibha Kapuria-Foreman, Department of Economics and Business, The Colorado College, US

Anastassios D. Karayiannis, Department of Economics, University of Piraeus, Greece

Hansjoerg Klausinger, Institute of Economic Theory and Policy, Vienna University of Economics and Business Administration, Austria

Maurice Lagueux, Département de philosophie, Université de Montréal, Montréal, Québec, Canada

André Lapidus, Centre d'Histoire de la Pensée Economique, Université de Paris I-Panthéon-Sorbonne, Paris, France

Ivo Maes, National Bank of Belgium and University of Antwerp (UFSIA), Belgium

J.-Michel Servet, Centre Auguste et Léon Walras, Faculté de Sciences Economiques et de Gestion, Université Lumière Lyon 2, France

Vincent J. Tarascio, Department of Economics, The University of North Carolina at Chapel Hill, North Carolina, US

1 The limits and extent of a retrospective approach in the history of economics: the case of the Middle Ages

André Lapidus

Introduction

The question of the retrospective approach has a special flavour when applied to the history of economics. During the fifth century BC, Zeno expounded some mathematical and physical paradoxes which, according to Bertrand Russell, anticipated in several points the birth of differential calculus. To remember this could challenge our understanding of the evolution of knowledge or of ancient Greece's perception of nature. It is not supposed to challenge our conception of modern mathematics.

There is nothing similar to this in the history of economic thought. When for instance, reading Quesnay through an input–output framework, the *Essay on Profits* by D. Ricardo through a Sraffian model, Marx as an exercise in linear algebra or Walras as a mere precursor of the utilization of fixed-point theorems in demonstrating the existence of general equilibrium, we all know that the works of Quesnay, Ricardo, Marx or Walras vanish when confronted with modern economics. A recent book tried to explain this phenomenon by stressing the specificity of the production of knowledge in economics by means of rewriting (Schmidt, 1985). This involvement of modern economics in the reading of past authors is also attested by the dedication of Mark Blaug's well-known *Economic Theory in Retrospect*. The book is dedicated 'To my son, David Ricardo' (Blaug, 1985, p. vi). I am indebted to Mark Blaug for this doubt: did he really call his son David Ricardo? Of course the question is more important than the answer – except for Mark Blaug's son – for it points to the singularity of the retrospective approach. It is a rational inversion of time, in which the past actually becomes the future. This means that our ignorance is transformed: instead of considering the past as something that escapes our understanding only because we cannot succeed in extracting it from our memories, it moves into a figure which, like the future, simply cannot be thought of in other terms than present ones – these terms remaining a part of our present knowledge.

Hence the historian of economics becomes a translator. Basically, as long as the past is treated like the future, it cannot have a lexicon different from the present one. Of course the world described does not meet ours exactly. But it remains a possible world. Usually, this world is ruder – and ours is the better one – when, for instance, we grant that David Hume never read Frenkel and Johnson before laying the first stone of the price-specie flow mechanism. Sometimes, on the contrary, the world is better than the one we know, even if it is built with the same materials; such was, for instance, Keynes's reading of Scholastic or mercantilist authors when compared with mainstream economics in the 1930s.

Clearly, this approach has proved to be fruitful; at least it is a powerful device for training in modern economic theory. But, still more, it is imperative as a set of figures of what we think economic theory – our economic theory – could be, just as science fiction depicts not our future but our fears and our knowledge of the potentialities of contemporary societies.

No wonder, then, that it is not so easy to put the retrospective approach in the history of economics on trial. Nevertheless the offence – if offence there be – seems obvious to establish since the border between a retrospective approach founded on modern topics and, let us say, a reasoned chronicle that would exclude them can be identified without requiring too much exertion. This paper, which focuses on medieval economic thought, aims at showing that if the retrospective approach is characterized by an extensive use of present knowledge about economic theory it becomes difficult even to imagine what a non-retrospective approach would be (part 1). More exactly, it will be argued that the demarcation between retrospective and non-retrospective approaches lies not in the involvement of contemporary economic theory, but in the particular way in which it is involved (part 2).

1.   Retrospective approach without limits: readings of the just price
The Middle Ages seems to supply a sharp difference between retrospective and non-retrospective analysis, this time easy to distinguish. The Thomistic concept of just price constitutes a good example for which retrospective approaches abound.[1]

1.1   Two ideal types of retrospective approach
Such was, for instance, Raymond De Roover's interpretation of the just price (see De Roover, 1951, 1958, 1971). The works of De Roover were written in a persisting debate about the retrospective meaning of the just price: cost of production or market price? In spite of – or because of – his great historical erudition, De Roover did not try to escape this question:

> The purpose ... is to demonstrate that the generally accepted definition is wrong and rests on a misinterpretation of the Scholastic position on the matter. According to the majority of the doctors, the just price did not correspond to cost of production as determined by the producer's social status, but was simply the current market price. (De Roover, 1958, pp. 420–1)

At issue is first the strange idea that a definition could be wrong: a definition is nothing but itself and is neither right nor wrong. Most authors whose theses are challenged by R. De Roover carefully presented the definitions given by Albert the Great, Thomas Aquinas or John Duns Scotus. And those definitions could not be wrong: they were their respective definitions of a just price. So if a 'generally accepted definition' can be said to be wrong, it is not owing to its original formulation, but to its restatement by contemporary commentators, in congruence with modern economic theory. Thus, when asserting that a definition was wrong, De Roover obviously meant that the just price was not retrospectively read through the right modern economic theory.

In this connection, cost of production value theories appear as De Roover's repulsive pole. This last is then reduced either to a price level under which 'the market price could not fall permanently' (De Roover, 1958, p. 422) or to a particular Scotist theory of price (De Roover, 1971, p. 52). But, strictly speaking, this meant that Schoolmen in general (or J. Duns Scotus, in De Roover, 1971) knew that a price was a sum of incomes; that each income appeared as a part of a cost; that this relation was made possible because both income and cost were linked to specific functions determining production; that production itself was already an autonomous concept, distinct, for instance, from handling, consumption or distribution. It is worth checking that De Roover never argued this simple fact: no theologian of the thirteenth or fourteenth century ever dared the outline of a theory of production and distribution that would have looked like the very conception that he himself criticized. Instead, while minimizing the role of the cost of production he assumed that, had Thomas Aquinas been trained enough in the microeconomic theory of the producer, he would surely have shared De Roover's view and concluded that costs of production ought to have played a limited role in the theory.

The utility theory of value constituted the attractive pole of De Roover's general perspective. It is perhaps best examined in *The Schoolmen's Economic Doctrines* (1971). However great his familiarity with medieval thought, he nonetheless claimed that 'Schoolmen had indeed a value theory founded on utility and rarity' (De Roover, 1971, pp. 49–50). But when discussing the role of utility, R. De Roover not only quoted Albert the Great, Thomas Aquinas, Buridan or Olivi; he also studied the meaning of 'utility' in relation to the modern understanding of this term, quoting J.B. Clark as well. It could have been a figure of speech. It was much more. The reference to modern utility helped De Roover contrast subjective with objective utility, the latter leading to a 'social value', close to the concept of 'just price'. But it also helped him consider that the meaning of the Latin terms *indigentia* and *complacibilitas* belongs to the lexical field of utility. We might be of another opinion[2] – and I am – but we must recognize that it would make no sense if the modern conception of utility were dismissed.

A second example was given by David Friedman's analysis of the just price (Friedman, 1980). Yet here the purpose appears to have been different. Friedman's paper was an attempt to show the mutual consistency of the free bargaining process which led to legal contracts in Roman or canon law and of the Scholastic theory of the just price. As the just price takes place in the context of bilateral exchange, it can be viewed as supplying an answer to the indeterminacy raised by a bilateral monopoly: if a set of rules fixes the price as distributive justice and commutative justice do, a general agreement on these rules eliminates the transaction costs generated by the negotiation process. The just price then expresses the rationality of the rule when equilibrium is not unique and when exchange is submitted to transaction costs. Were Scholastic authors as aware of this as we, as modern economists, now are? To my knowledge, there is no textual evidence to support this position;[3] and nor did Friedman really try to find any. He just argued that 'both the medieval legal doctrine of freedom of contract and the Scholastic ethical doctrine of just price may have been desirable institutions' (Friedman, 1980, p. 234). Consequently, Friedman's argument was not the discovery of a hidden piece of Scholastic reasoning. It was just a possible missing piece that makes such reasoning intelligible today. And the presumed unintelligibility, for Scholastic authors, of this missing piece obviously did not matter. So that, in spite of the blatant ignorance of medieval times about imperfect competition, it was a way to go about determining just price.

De Roover's and Friedman's approaches to the just price both rest on contemporary knowledge: the theory of the producer and of the consumer on the one hand, the bilateral monopoly theory on the other. But these two lines of contemporary analysis yield different results. In the first case, modern theory is only a refinement testifying that if we now think in a better way, we do not think anything else than our ancestors did. In the second case, the bilateral monopoly argument is not assumed to be present, even as a mere outline, in thirteenth-century writings, but to reveal a non-expected function – the elimination of transaction costs – associated with an ancient theory.

1.2 Non-retrospection as a particular case of retrospection

By way of contrast, a non-retrospective approach is thought to pay tribute to historical faith by withdrawing any attempt to read medieval contributions through the prism of modern economic knowledge. The point is that, when dealing with elements of economic thought, such an approach has probably never existed. Now, if we pay enough attention to the secondary literature concerning the just price, it becomes clear cut. When a non-retrospective position was assumed, it never prevented the author from following the same paths as De Roover or Friedman. So non-retrospection happens to be nothing more than an intention.

James Baldwin (1959) is generally considered by historians of economics as representative of attempts to give a non-retrospective account of the Middle-Ages economic thought, through one of the most exhaustive texts devoted to the theories of the just price during the twelfth and thirteenth centuries. However, his treatment of Thomas Aquinas's theory of the just price remained structured by a retrospective approach, borrowing its figures from the two ideal types studied above.

As Hollander (1965) was later to do, Baldwin identified a break within Thomas's conceptions. He rightly pointed out that the commentaries on the *Ethics* insisted on the role of labour and expenses, while in the *Summa Theologica* (II–II, q.77, a.1, resp.), the argument had evolved in a more Aristotelian fashion, such as to explain that 'the value of goods is that which comes into human use and is measured by a monetary price'. Not surprisingly, then, Baldwin concluded that 'Thomas definitely accepted the Aristotelian theory of value of want, satisfaction or utility and offered a psychological theory consonant with the theoretical demands of the current price' (Baldwin, 1959, p. 77). Let us neglect the question of knowing whether this was a good or a faithful picture of the Thomistic concept of the just price. It remains that it could hardly be viewed as non-retrospective. In fact, it was a retrospective picture, just as De Roover's picture was.

But Baldwin's presentation was also retrospective in another sense. As attested in the index of his book, he used the terms 'current price' and 'market price' as synonyms. His fight for an interpretation of the just price was also a fight inside what he considered as the economic debates of his time, still stamped with the opposition between the utility and labour theories of value, between market and cost prices. His challenge was then directed against previous presentations of the just price, like Ashley's (1920) or Tawney's (1937). When vindicating a Scholastic utility theory of value, Baldwin paved the way for understanding the just price as the outcome of a market process, as a market price. But was there anything like the intuition of a market price during the thirteenth century that would allow such an interpretation to avoid the retrospective bias?

Surely the answer is no. Market price is a rather sophisticated concept. It assumes (1) that individual behaviours involved in transactions are founded on subjective appreciations; (2) the intuition of a functional relation between prices and quantities supplied or demanded; (3) a notion of equilibrium, in order that market price be seen not as directly determined by other variables, but as the particular value of a variable which equalizes quantities supplied and demanded; (4) even as a rough approximation, a process explaining how price would respond to a possible gap between supply and demand.

Now it may be shown (Lapidus, 1986, chs 1, 2) that, if the first condition was sometimes approached during the thirteenth and fourteenth centuries, mainly by nominalist or Scotist theologians, the second condition constituted an insurmountable impediment before the sixteenth century, in Salamanca. Still more, the third condition did not definitely triumph before Adam Smith, and we should not underestimate the weight of the fourth condition in early economic thought: for a long while it belonged more to merchants' practical knowledge than to scholars' knowledge.

Of course, J. Baldwin never argued that Scholastics had built up the concepts of demand function, of equilibrium or of market process. But, when asserting that the first condition was more or less fulfilled, he felt able to behave as if the other conditions happened to be satisfied: 'utility, as it may be called, presents a psychological explanation that supports the *function of demand* of buyers in the general *process of supply and demand*. Both Albert and Thomas were not only aware of this Aristotelian theory of value, but they also advocated emphatically its fundamental principles' (Baldwin, 1959, p. 77; my italics). To some extent, perhaps, this prompt conclusion was true: for if we have enough data at our disposal about fairs in Champagne, if these are reliable enough, we could estimate supply and demand functions and conclude that prices behave *as if* they were competitive market prices. But this does not mean that the actors at the fair had precisely this theory of their commercial practice. The opinion of the theologian is no more conclusive: to support his interpretation, Baldwin (ibid., p. 77) mentioned a case where Thomas Aquinas considered as just the price of cloth currently observed in Tuscany. Nonetheless, this does not imply that the theologian's explanation of this price was a market price theory but that his explanation, if he had any, did not contradict this theory.

Finding, with J. Baldwin, a market price behind the just price hence belongs to the same thought process as D. Friedman's, when he considered the just price as solving a bilateral monopoly problem. The point is that a typical non-retrospective approach appears as a combination of two retrospective approaches in De Roover's and in Friedman's guise. But was it possible to do away with retrospection?

2. The involvement of present economic knowledge in retrospective and non-retrospective approaches

If this means doing away with present economic knowledge, surely not. Moreover, it would not be desirable to do so; and, as far as I know, no historian of economics has ever achieved this. In the sense used in the preceding section, non-retrospection in no case existed. If we intend, as economists, to learn something from the past of our discipline we ought, in some way, to relate this past state to its present state. Henceforth the distinction between retrospection and non-retrospection can no longer be founded on the presence or absence of contemporary knowledge. The main issue is no longer to understand how it would be possible to avoid retrospection in order to reach the genuine lessons from the past, but to understand what is missed or learned from this past through the specific involvement of present knowledge both in the retrospective and in the non-retrospective approaches.

To put it briefly, the point is that the retrospective approach uses contemporary economics as a prescriber. It prescribes: (1) the borders which are presumed to close an autonomous field of explanation; (2) the principles of explanation; (3) the identity of economic categories.

Obviously, when a past author is supposed to deal with the same field as we do, when we can recognize his problems as ours and when his categories meet ours, we can hardly learn from his work anything which could challenge our discipline from the standpoint of its borders, principles of explanation and categories. This could be of minor importance if one is studying, for example, the theory of interest during the first half of the twentieth century, for the emphasis is on alternative determinations of interest about which the attempt is to identify the outlines of modern conceptions or shortcomings. On the contrary, the exercise becomes perilous when it takes place within a period, like the Middle Ages, in which it is suspected that interest could have a different content, that its explanations aimed at solving other problems, that it entered principles of reasoning that hurt ours all the more so since something like political economy did not even exist.

Presumably this explains the puzzling status of Scholastic economic thought in the history of economics. Either it keeps a historical appeal or a philosophical one; the latter, however, leaves the economist as such disarmed, balancing between the fascination of exoticism and a polite disinterest; or it gives rise to its simplest reading, based on the questions 77 and

78 of Thomas Aquinas's *Summa theologica*, II–II – but the materials gathered in these few pages then appear so thin that it now proscribes retrospection for lack of analytical content, now allows an incredibly wide spectrum of retrospective interpretations. However, this makes it easier to highlight the questions a strictly retrospective approach misses through the three types of above-mentioned prescriptions. Until now, we have used the theory of the just price in order to dismiss the usual understanding of retrospection based on the *presence* of contemporary economics. In the following, the doctrine of usury will illustrate the idea that the difference between retrospection and non-retrospection rests on the *type of involvement* of contemporary economics.

2.1   The borders: usury as a sin

Retrospectively, the doctrine of usury combines two kinds of development: first, a positive explanation of interest; second, normative propositions forbidding some transactions implying interest to be paid. The overlapping of these two kinds of development within the writings of the same authors already makes it difficult to distinguish them, so that a current interpretation would suggest that, as Scholastics condemned interest loans, they had no theory of interest. But, on second thought, to condemn something has never meant that it could not be explained. If both the explanation and the condemnation remain inside the limits of an economic debate, they will not give rise to interpretations other than retrospective ones – in De Roover's or in Friedman's guise – as in Keynes (1973, pp. 351–2) or Schumpeter (1954, p. 105). Keynes, for instance, argued that the medieval doctrine of usury led to the understanding that lowering interest increases the incentive to invest and thus helps fight underemployment. This could be true, exactly as Friedman's interpretation of the just price is. But there is hardly any evidence that Schoolmen were aware of the links between investment and employment level or between the interest rate and investment; and still less evidence that underemployment in the Middle Ages was of a Keynesian type rather than caused by foreign and civil wars, fires and epidemics. However, although it remains possible to build a strictly economic explanation that would not contradict the main theses about usury, the simple recognition of the fact that *usury was a sin*, that it was rejected not only on legal but on theological grounds, decidedly constrains its economic meaning.

In patristic literature, usury was a sin because, in spite of the agreement of both parties, a harm is inflicted on the borrower by the lender.[4] From an economic standpoint, the combination of the agreement and the harm implies (1) that both the creditor and the debtor prefer the transaction to be processed rather than refrain from lending and borrowing; (2) that after the loan is granted to the debtor, his situation is the worse while the creditor's is the better. In other words, the creditor appropriates the whole surplus of the transaction (Lapidus, 1987, pp. 1097–8). Hence, it is because economic problems were opened on a religious context that usury was considered a sin; and it is because usury was a sin that we could in turn, as economists, identify interest with a surplus in exchange and usury with the appropriation of this surplus.

Later on the nature of the sin became more precise. Since the early thirteenth century, for William of Auxerre[5] or Robert of Courçon,[6] usury appeared mainly as a *sin of intention*. This had far-reaching consequences (see Lapidus, 1991), as usury happened to be not a matter of fact, but a matter of intention. Usually this created no difficulty: when a fact was sinful, such was its intention. But usury was a special case, in which the link between the intention and the fact was tenuous: all the intentions did not lead to the fact – which justified frequent comparisons with the sin of lust – and all the facts were not the proceeds of an usurious intention – the analogy, this time, was with the sin of simony. This particularity prevents us from treating the prohibition of usury as foreshadowing, for example, Becker's economics of crime: in Beckerian fashion, only the materiality of the fact matters; conversely, within the doctrine of usury, it is the intention that matters.

So the often confused and sometimes contradictory pictures given by Schoolmen all through the Middle Ages do not reveal the numerous failures of a thought too close to religion for it is not to be far from science. Instead, in a context where the creditor is usually alone in possessing complete information on his private intention, they reveal the tremendous difficulties which arise while setting the rules and incentives that would first, allow transactions based on a non-usurious intention; and second, condemn or prohibit other transactions, sometimes very similar, but founded on a usurious intention. This explains (Lapidus, 1991) the successive devices, based on property, then on risk, the aim of which was to distinguish the intentions of potential creditors.

Again, it is because propositions now considered as economic were not sufficient to give a proper account of the doctrine of usury that we become able to draw upon its wider economic significance.

2.2 The principles of explanation: the reason for interest; alternative views

At first sight, one of today's dominating forms of understanding interest would identify it as the difference between the present prices of a present and a future commodity, whatever the commodity: consumption goods, physical or financial assets, or money. It is only at a second stage that, as a consequence, interest turns out to be an income paid by the demander of the present commodity and received by its supplier. So investigating the reason for interest does not primarily concern the income it generates but the prices of present and future commodities. The not so old-fashioned debate about the Böhm-Bawerkian 'three reasons for interest' still illustrates this approach. The works of Irving Fisher, for instance, coming after the rejection of Böhm-Bawerk's second reason by Menger or Wieser, showed that it was not so obvious to draw a rational statement justifying the underevaluation of the future – in this case the rationality shifted to alleged differentiated behaviours rooted on the social, cultural or racial origins of the agents (Cot, 1989). But, once some reasons are found to establish a difference between the prices of present and future commodities, interest is explained together with the income it represents.

Applied to the medieval theory of interest, this way of reasoning would be as retrospective as it is damaging. Within the Scholastic tradition interest was first an income arising from the difference between the capital paid back and the capital lent. Henceforth, canon law understood usury as 'that which exceeds capital' (*Decretum*, c.14, q.3, can.1). The difficulty stems from the fact that the loan has an opportunity cost: at its beginning, the commodities the creditor renounces buying and, at the expiry date, those that the debtor, in turn, cannot buy to pay back his debt. Now, most Schoolmen, following Thomas Aquinas (*Summa Theologica*, II–II, q.62, a.4, resp.2) or Giles of Lessines (*De Usuris*, c.9), acknowledged that future goods have lower present values than do present ones. The problem was twofold: (1) to find reasons – if any – for interest as an income; (2) to understand how interest, whatever its value, could be made compatible with differences between prices of present and future goods.

Of course the retrospective approach is quite inaccurate to give an account of this representation of interest: if we seek evidence in Scholastic writings that interest, as an income, is derived from a difference between the prices of present and future goods, we hardly find any. So that retaining retrospection would lead to the disenchanted report that we do have a theory of interest while Schoolmen had none, although they were conscious that a present good is worth more than a future one. Retrospection acts then in Friedman's fashion: Schoolmen 'were tied up by a dogma which did not allow any discussion' (De Roover, 1971, p. 76) and, as they set various devices – the extrinsic titles – to turn the rule and authorize interest, our explanation could substitute for their lack of explanation.

On the contrary, if we give up the retrospective approach, Scholastic attempts to build a theory of interest appear to have inverted our thought processes: instead of starting from prices to reach income, they started from income to reach prices. And, just as the reason for interest is now rooted in prices, it was then rooted in income. Besides, it was probably as tedious for Thomas Aquinas, Giles of Lessines or Alexander Lombard to identify the source of income to make the difference between prices possible, as for Böhm-Bawerk, Wieser or Fisher to find the difference between prices from which interest, as an income, is derived.

But, if we are open-minded enough to accept the idea that the medieval starting point denotes another way of explaining interest, the complicated debates we are rediscovering seven centuries later do not compel us to consider the authors of the Middle Ages as guilty of insufficient analytical power.

The history of this debate is that of a meticulous examination of the reasons that would permit a stock to be a source of income. It began with Gratian's collection of canon law in the mid-twelfth century. A decret called '*Ejiciens*', wrongly attributed to John Chrysostom, asked whether 'the one who rents a field to receive its fruits or a house to receive an income is not similar to the one who lends money at usury' (*Decretum*, dist.88, can.11). 'Certainly not', answered the author, giving three reasons:

> First, because the only function of money is the payment of a purchase price. Then, because the farmer makes the earth fructify, the tenant takes advantage of inhabiting the house: in both cases, the owner seems to give use of his thing to receive money and, in a certain way, he exchanges gain for gain, whilst from money which is stored up, you make no use. At last, its use gradually exhausts the earth, deteriorates the house, whilst the money lent suffers neither diminishing nor ageing. (Ibid.)

The first reason advocated recalls the Aristotelian argument about the sterility of money. The second one – not so definite if separated from the first – bypasses the problem: a stock is a source of income for somebody if it is already a source of income for somebody else. The third reason is far more interesting: it asserts that a stock is a source of income from the moment that stock depreciates. It is then defined as the counterpart of this depreciation. But, consistent as this treatment seems to be, it does not give rise to any explanation of interest on money loans: if interest is a difference between capital paid back and capital lent, it cannot be an income, for money capital never depreciates. To receive interest on a loan is then to receive something that simply ought not to exist as an income. This shows the limits of the argument developed by *Ejiciens*. If there are some reasons for the capital paid back to be greater than the capital lent, either those reasons are violated if no interest is paid or the requirement that the stock depreciates is not fulfilled.

The great skilfulness of Thomas Aquinas was to solve this problem by reversing *Ejiciens*' third reason.[7] Thomas Aquinas's argument is expounded in *De Malo* (q.13, a.4c) or in the *Summa Theologica*:

> One must know that the use of certain things is identical with their consumption . . . . In such [exchanges], one must not count the use of the thing apart from the thing itself but, as a result of conceding the use, the thing itself is conceded. And this is why, for such things, the loan transfers property. Thus, if someone wanted to sell wine on the one hand and the use of wine on the other hand, he would sell twice the same thing or sell what is not . . . . Conversely, there are things the use of which is not their consumption. So, the use of a house is to live in, not to destroy it. Therefore, one can concede separately use and property. (*Summa Theologica*, II–II, q.78, a.1, resp.)

This statement is close to the Roman law argument about the *mutuum* – a free loan contract transferring property – (see *Digesta*, 44, 7, f.1, n.2, 4). But the *mutuum* only supplied a legal framework for the prohibition of usury. It just stipulated that, if a loan is a *mutuum*, nothing above the principal can be paid to the creditor. This does not imply that, if another contract is adopted, the thing and its use cannot be charged for separately, thus giving birth to interest. Thomas Aquinas added something more: there are things the nature of which is being destroyed – consumed – by use, so that the thing itself cannot be distinguished from its use.

The argument is a philosophical one. It was challenged all through the Middle Ages, and condemned by Pope Nicholas III in a decretal incorporated in canon law (*Decretales*, Liber Sextus, V, tit.11, c.3, *Exiit qui seminat*), thus supporting non-Thomistic interpretations of usury (Lapidus, 1987, pp. 1101–2). As an economist, I have nothing to say about it. But I can appreciate its economic consequences. On the one hand, interest as an income no longer proceeded from the depreciation of a stock but from the possibility of separating property from use – the sale of the latter producing the income. Therefore, a house or a field could – as in *Ejiciens*, but for other reasons – be the source of an income, whilst bread, wine and, of course, money could not. On the other hand, Thomas Aquinas's construction solved the problem of the incompatibility of interest as an income with the differences of prices between present and future commodities. The key is that if this difference was actually filled in, it was not by an income resulting from the sale of the use of money, but by a compensation for its indisponibility (this grounded the existence, besides the main loan contract, the *mutuum*, of extrinsic titles): 'One harms one's neighbour when preventing him from collecting what he legitimately hoped to possess [which *could* be the case for the creditor]. And then, the compensation should not be founded on equality because a future possession is not worth a present possession' (*Summa Theologica*, II–II, q.62, a.4, resp.2). Strictly speaking, it is noticeable that this 'interest' is not truly an income: it is an intertemporal transfer which leaves the ex-post situation of the lender unchanged, had he contracted or not.

So, to the question of knowing whether it was possible to found interest to be an income which would compensate the difference between prices of present and future commodities, Thomas Aquinas gave a most elegant answer: interest cannot be founded as an income from a money loan; but the money loan can found transfer payments preserving the situation of the creditor. As can be seen, this formulation uses contemporary economic knowledge without taking the precautions of clothing it in a medieval fashion. Nevertheless, a retrospective approach would have been deprived of the means to acknowledge this.

2.3　Identity of economic categories: commodities, time and substitution
Up to a certain point, we are immune to identity change of economic categories. We all know, for example, that when we read the word 'profit' in a classical text, it often refers to the value counterpart of a physical surplus; that a neoclassical text from Cambridge in the 1920s often teaches that a zero profit rate prevails in long-term equilibrium; that profits, in a Schumpeterian text, are the outcome of an innovation process. Such identity shifts are familiar enough to avoid retrospective approaches that would prescribe a conception of profit to the reading of writings in which profit has moved to another identity. The intellectual mechanism is hardly conscious. For instance, from a (modern) neo-Ricardian point of view, we never conclude from the reading of the above mentioned text of the 1920s that its author failed to recognize that a method of production involving zero profits would be given up; instead we underline the fact that he assumed the capital to be borrowed, that interest ought to be paid for, and that if something escaped the author's attention, it is the possibility of considering interest as a withdrawal from profits. This intellectual mechanism remains efficient as long as the identities of economic categories are still competing in modern economic theory. But it becomes less and less efficient when dealing with economic categories, some of whose identities have disappeared from contemporary knowledge. Again, such examples abound in Scholastic writings.

In a money loan, a *mutuum*, the prohibition of interest was linked to the fact that the money lent and the money paid back were not, physically, the same commodity, so that the ownership of the lender had to be interrupted at the beginning of the loan. Conversely, if they were the same commodity, interest could have been charged on it because the lender would have kept his ownership all through the loan while selling the use of it. This case was known as *mutuum ad pompam*. For Thomas Aquinas, the argument ran as follows: 'silver money could have a secondary use: for instance, if money is conceded to somebody in order to make a display of it or to pawn it. And one can licitly sell such a use of money' (*Summa Theologica*, II–II, q.78, a.1, ad 6).

Through a retrospective approach, the comparison of the *mutuum* with the *mutuum ad pompam* is quite puzzling. This prompts us to consider the *mutuum ad pompam* as similar to the *mutuum* for, in both cases, the money lent and the money paid back *are not* the same commodity (which would imply that interest is, in both cases, possible today and impossible in the Middle Ages). The reason is that, trained as we are in the general economic equilibrium tradition, we adopt a conception of time internal to commodities, so that two commodities available at two different dates are themselves different, whatever their physical similarities. But, as the money lent and the money paid back in the *mutuum ad pompam* were said to be the same commodity, this reveals that time remained external to commodities. Already such an analysis denotes a shift in the identity of the commodities, though this shift is still obvious to control: after all, classical economists usually also had an external conception of time, which we spontaneously share when we forget the lessons of general equilibrium.

Let us admit that the retrospective approach has bypassed the trap and therefore accepted the externality of time. It should be – retrospectively – clear, then, that Schoolmen did not succeed in recognizing that the money lent and the money paid back in the *mutuum* are the same commodity, exactly as in the *mutuum ad pompam* (which would mean that in both cases interest could be perceived). The reason is, now, that in contemporary economics, two commodities are alike when they are perfect substitutes, whatever their physical differences may be: in an economy consisting of colour-blind agents, green gloves are rigorously the same commodity as red ones, and no one will care what the results of a spectrographic analysis are. Once again, it is clear that the retrospective approach would have failed. It is on the grounds of an economic argument – perfect substitutability – that two commodities are said to be the same. But in a Thomistic perspective two commodities cannot be the same if they are not the same being. A convenient way to check this is the possibility of keeping ownership of the commodity in question. As could already be seen, this was the case with the *mutuum ad pompam*, but not with the *mutuum*. The shift in identity is achieved: the idea of 'same commodity' has ontological rather than economic roots.

Nonetheless, this does not mean that the idea of 'perfect substitutability' plays no part. In a money loan, the money lent and paid back could be called 'perfect substitutes' for they are equivalent in the loan and intrinsically identical. But this does not imply – as we would again have retrospectively imagined – that these two different commodities composed of the same amount of money give rise to subjective indifference for every agent – obviously it does not, particularly for the lender and for the borrower. That is, the same nature is actualized in two different beings.[8] What then is this nature shared by the money lent and paid back?

Chiefly in his commentaries on Aristotle's *Politics*, Thomas Aquinas stressed the conventional dimension of money (see *In VIII Libros Politicorum*, I, 7). For the theologian, this meant that apart from its material existence, justifying its secondary use as already noted about the *mutuum ad pompam*, it was a product of human reason, as the most complete form of exchange. It is then through the study of exchange that the nature of money can be found. In this respect, Thomas Aquinas pointed out two functions of money, which he discussed at length when commenting on the *Sentences*, the *Politics* or the *Ethics* and, of course, in the *Summa*. The first function of money stood in the Aristotelian tradition – it is a means of exchange: 'But money, according to the Philosopher [Aristotle] in the *Ethics* (V, 5) and in the *Politics* (I, 3), was principally invented to facilitate exchanges: and so, the proper and principal use of money is to be consumed without diversion, because it is spent in exchanges' (*Summa Theologica*, II–II, q.78, a.1, resp.). In spite of a similar reference to the authority of Aristotle, Thomas Aquinas was not so faithful to the Philosopher when introducing the second function of money – the unit of account:

> All other things have from themselves some utility: however, this is not the same for money. But it is the measure of the utility of other things, as it is clear from the Philosopher in the *Ethics* (V, 9). And therefore the use of money does not hold the measure of its utility from this money itself but from the things which are measured by money according to the various people who exchange money for goods. Hence, receiving more money for less seems nothing else than differentiating the measure in giving and receiving, which obviously brings inequity. (*In IV Libros Sententiarum*, 1.III, dist.37, a.1, q.16)[9]

Therefore the identity of nature that makes perfect substitutes of the money lent and of the money paid back rests on their ability to be considered a means of exchange and a unit of account. These correspond to the final and to the formal cause of money respectively. The Aristotelian argument that in a loan money cannot stand in for exchange as its final cause is well known. Thomas Aquinas, in his commentaries on the *Sentences* quoted above, added something more. He argued that in a money loan, if interest is paid to the creditor, the formal cause of money would also be perverted. Consequently, the money lent and the money paid back are together perfect substitutes identical in quantities (nature of money) and different commodities (consumptible goods; external time) when no interest is paid. A retrospective approach that would have missed the identity changes of the economic categories would, also, have missed this result.

If the retrospective approach has been shown to have a much wider compass than was expected, it also shares with the non-retrospective approach the necessity of being rooted in modern economic knowledge. But a common root does not prevent the two approaches from displaying competing fidelities to this modern economic knowledge. The fidelity of the retrospective approach is the most comfortable: every investigation in the past constitutes an opportunity to discover, among the awkwardness of ancient texts, the beloved features of some appealing contemporary economic theory. Conversely, the kind of fidelity of the non-retrospective approach is the most demanding: it is the fidelity of economics always seeking itself, accepting in advance the odd figures it is to meet if its borders, principles of explanation or categories vanish in turn. It is receptive enough to have been defined only negatively in relation to the retrospective approach. Perhaps it is nothing else than an economic approach in the history of economic thought.

Notes

1. Most of them now appear as variations around the theme of competitive market prices. Nonetheless, some authors, like Wilson (1975), tried to show that such interpretations miss the essential of the social process which, in Thomas Aquinas's writings, determined the just prices. For a discussion of this question, see Worland (1977).
2. This point is interestingly discussed by Odd Langholm (1987, pp. 122–5).
3. However, it can be noticed that, for Thomas Aquinas at least, as civil laws do not repress all the vices and thus allow mutual deceit (*Summa Theologica*, II–II, q.77, a.1, obj.1) the rate of exchange in a transaction depends on the ability of the parties. It follows that, if the just price dismisses neither the vices nor the abilities to bargain, it cancels out their effects.
4. This interpretation was long-lasting. Thomas Aquinas, for instance, wrote that 'the one who pays interest does not pay it absolutely voluntarily, but owing to some necessity: he needs to receive the money of the loan whilst the one who has this money does not want to lend without interest' (*Summa Theologica*, II–II, q.78, a.1, ad 7).
5. 'Usury is the intention to receive something more in a loan than the capital' (*Summa Aurea*, t.48, c.1, q.1).
6. 'Usury is a sin resulting from the fact of receiving or aiming at receiving something above the principal' (*De Usura*, p. 3).
7. On the comparison between *Ejiciens* and Thomas Aquinas, see Noonan (1957, pp. 54–5).
8. The opposite case is also studied by Thomas Aquinas. When discussing the respective values of 'artificial' and natural gold (*Summa Theologica*, II–II, q.77, a.2, ad 1), he took up the question of the substitutability of two goods the nature of which is definitely different.
9. It is worth noting that, as regards this second function of money, Thomas Aquinas moved away from Aristotle. For this latter, the value of money, in contrast with his commentator, was determined by the goods it is exchanged for. So that, always in contrast with Thomas Aquinas, 'money itself is submitted to depreciations, for it has not always the same purchasing power' (*Ethics*, V, 5:14).

References
Ashley, W. (1920), *An Introduction to English Economic History and Theory* (4th edn), London: Longman.

Baldwin, J. W. (1959), 'The Medieval Theories of the Just Price', *Transactions of the American Philosophical Society*, **49** (4), July.

Blaug, M. (1985), *Economic Theory in Retrospect*, 4th edn, Cambridge: Cambridge University Press.

Corpus Juris Canonici (1879–81), 2 vols, Leipzig: B. Tauchnitz.

Cot, A. L. (1989), 'Le gène et l'intérêt: L'anamorphose d'Irving Fisher', *Oeconomia (Economie et Société – serie PE)*, **11**.

Decretales, in *Corpus Juris Canonici*, Vol. II.

Decretum, in *Corpus Juris Canonici*, Vol. I.

De Roover, R. (1951), 'Monopoly Theory Prior to Adam Smith: a Revision', *Quarterly Journal of Economics*, **65**, pp. 492–524.

De Roover, R. (1958), 'The Concept of the Just Price: Theory and Economic Policy', *Journal of Economic History*, **18** (4), December, pp. 418–34.

De Roover, R. (1971), *La Pensée Economique des Scholastiques*, Montreal and Paris: Vrin.

Digesta (1968), in *Corpus Juris Civilis*, Vol. I, Dublin and Zurich: Weidmann.

Friedman, D. D. (1980), 'In Defense of Thomas Aquinas and the Just Price', *History of Political Economy*, **12** (2), Summer.

Giles of Lessines *De Usuris*, in Thomas Aquinas, *Opera Omnia*, Vol. XXVIII.

Hollander, S. (1965), 'On the Interpretation of the Just Price', *Kyklos*, **18**.

Keynes, J. M. (1973), *General Theory of Unemployment, Interest and Money*, in *Collected Writings*, Vol. VII, London: Royal Economic Society.

Langholm, O. (1987), 'Scholastics' Economics', in S. T. Lowry (ed.), *Pre-Classical Economic Thought*, Boston, Dordrecht and Lancaster: Kluwer.

Lapidus, A. (1986), *Le Détour de Valeur*, Paris: Economica.

Lapidus, A. (1987), 'La Propriéte de la monnaie: doctrine de l'usure et théorie de l'intérêt, *Revue Economique*, **38** (6), November.

Lapidus, A. (1991), 'Information and Risk in the Medieval Doctrine of Usury during the Thirteenth Century', in W. Barber (ed.), *Perspectives on the History of Economic Thought*, Vol. V, Aldershot: Edward Elgar.

Noonan, J. T. Jr (1957), *The Scholastic Analysis of Usury*, Cambridge, MA: Harvard University Press.

Robert of Courçon (1902), *De Usura*, in G. Lefevre (ed.), *Le Traité 'De Usura' de Robert de Courçon*, Travaux et Mémoires de l'Université de Lille, Vol. X, memoir 30.

Schmidt, C. (1985), *La Sémantique Économique en question*, Paris: Calmann-Lévy.

Schumpeter, J. A. (1954), *History of Economic Analysis*, London: Allen & Unwin.

Tawney, R. H. (1937), *Religion and the Rise of Capitalism*, New York: Harcourt, Brace.

Thomas Aquinas (1871–80), *Opera Omnia*, ed. P. Mare and S. E. Frette, Paris: Vivès.

Thomas Aquinas, *De Malo*, in *Opera Omnia*, Vol. XIII.

Thomas Aquinas, *In IV Libros Sententiarum*, in *Opera Omnia*, Vol. X.

Thomas Aquinas, *In VIII Libros Politicorum*, in *Opera Omnia*, Vol. XXVI.

Thomas Aquinas, *In X Libros Ethicorum ad Nichomachum*, in *Opera Omnia*, Vol. XXV.

Thomas Aquinas, *Summa Theologica*, in *Opera Omnia*, Vol. III.

William of Auxerre (1986), *Summa Aurea*, Paris: CNRS.

Wilson, G. (1975), 'The Economics of the Just Price', *History of Political Economy*, **7** (1), Spring, 56–74.

Worland, S. G. (1977), *Justum Pretium*: One More Round in an Endless Series', *History of Political Economy,* **9** (4), Winter.

2   Lakatos and economics*
Roger E. Backhouse

1.   Introduction

Aims

In the past 15 years there has been much debate over the relevance of Lakatos's methodology of scientific research programmes (MSRP) to economics. However, although economists have continued to find the concept of a scientific research programme valuable in interpreting the history of economic thought, Lakatos's methodology has recently been subjected to a number of very severe criticisms. The aim of this paper is to survey these and to make some tentative suggestions as to what we should, and should not, retain from Lakatos's methodology.

In this paper our prime concern is with general issues, concerning the relevance of Lakatosian ideas to economics as a whole. Many of the examples, however, will be taken from contemporary macroeconomics. There are two reasons for this. The obvious one is my own interests (e.g. Backhouse, 1991). The second is that some of the most interesting papers, to which I wish to respond (notably Hands, 1985, 1990; Maddock, 1991; Hoover, 1991), deal with macroeconomics.

Before venturing into a discussion of Lakatos's methodology it is important to note that there are two reasons why we may be interested in methodology. We may be searching for a methodology which does no more than describe what economists actually do. Alternatively, we may be concerned with appraisal: with comparing what economists actually do with what they ought to do. This paper is based on the assumption that we should be concerned with appraisal. It is important to make this clear, because it limits the range of conclusions we can accept. In particular, it means we cannot simply say that Lakatos's MSRP applies to some areas but not to others. If we were concerned merely with description there would be nothing inherently wrong with such a conclusion (though we might wish to ask 'Why?'), but if we are concerned with appraisal we cannot stop there. It may be that the MSRP does not fit one area of economics because, for some reason, it is an inappropriate methodology to adopt in that area; or it may be that economists working in that area are guilty of bad practice – that they should be following the methodology but, for some reason, they are not doing so. The difference between these two cases is of vital importance.

The main issues
Lakatos's MSRP comprises three main elements.

1. *The research programme*, made up of a hard core and sets of positive and negative heuristics, as the object of appraisal.
2. *An appraisal criterion*, of corroborated excess empirical content.
3. *A criterion by which the MSRP can be appraised* (which has been termed 'the methodology of *historical* research programmes', or MHRP) based on the thesis that if the MSRP is appropriate, economists will abandon degenerating research programmes in favour of progressive ones.

Though they are sometimes grouped together, as though forming part of an indivisible package, these three elements must be considered separately, for different issues arise in respect of each of them.

2.   The concept of a scientific research programme
Problems which arise in identifying SRPs
Many economists have tried to identify Lakatosian SRPs in economics, but though there have been successes, the verdict has in many cases been that Lakatos's categories are at the same time too rigid and too imprecise.

The first problem to arise is that of whether SRPs are to be defined on a large scale or a small scale. At one extreme we can view neoclassical economics as one SRP, ranged against various heterodox programmes (institutionalism, post-Keynesianism and so on). At the other extreme we can define research programmes at a micro level, each encompassing a small, well-defined section of the literature. For example, microeconomics can be analysed in terms of a neo-Walrasian SRP (Weintraub, 1985) or in terms of smaller programmes: human capital theory (Blaug, 1980, ch. 13); the economics of the family (ibid., ch. 14). In macroeconomics we might argue in terms of a neo-Walrasian SRP (Weintraub, 1979; Backhouse, 1991) or we might distinguish monetarist and Keynesian SRPs (Cross, 1982). Within 'monetarism' we might distinguish between the new classical SRP (Maddock, 1984, 1991) and the earlier SRP associated with Milton Friedman. Within Keynesian economics there is a strong case for distinguishing the literature on rationing models as a distinct research programme, set against, for example, the later literature which rejects the fixed-price assumption in favour of imperfect competition (such as Hart, 1982; Blanchard and Kiyotaki, 1987; Marris, 1991). Alternatively, we might distinguish even more micro-level SRPs (such as the literature on the implications of rational expectations for the theory of the consumption function, or attempts to test the efficiency of foreign exchange markets). Lakatos's MSRP is sufficiently elastic that none of these different interpretations can, *a priori*, be ruled out. Each has some merit.

Once we have decided how we are going to apply the MSRP, a further set of problems arises.

1. Programmes may overlap, with some theories apparently fitting into two different programmes.
2. Different programmes may be related to each other.
3. It is sometimes difficult to identify a hard core that is unchanged over the life of the research programme, and which is common to all the theories that are considered to form part of the programme.

To illustrate these problems we shall consider two examples: the use of a neo-Walrasian SRP to interpret macroeconomics since Keynes; and the characterization of the new classical macroeconomics as a SRP. These two cases are chosen because they seem relatively strong examples where Lakatos's methodology appears to work rather well. In both cases, however, all three problems arise.

Example I: neo-Walrasian macroeconomics Weintraub (1985) has defined the hard core and heuristics of a neo-Walrasian programme which can be used to interpret the literature on the existence of general competitive equilibrium. Only minor modifications are required for it to be possible to use this SRP to make sense of the history of macroeconomics since Keynes (this is discussed in detail in Backhouse, 1991, on which this and the following three paragraphs are based). Two features are central to this programme: the assumption of individual optimizing behaviour and the construction of fully specified, consistent models. This means that the SRP is defined in terms of a modelling technique, rather than a set of beliefs about the economy, a point to which we shall return.

Given the undoubted importance of the assumption of rational behaviour in postwar economics it is, at first sight, hard to see how such an interpretation of Lakatos's MSRP could fail to fit. It would seem simply to demarcate neo-Walrasian economics from various heterodox approaches (institutionalism, post-Keynesianism and so on). Yet even this application of Lakatos raises some serious problems. Consider the example of Milton Friedman. His aversion to complex, formal modelling, together with his approach to empirical work, especially on money, place him outside the neo-Walrasian SRP as we have defined it here. To accommodate Friedman we might wish to define a 'Chicago' research programme (say as defined by Reder, 1982). This, however, raises the question of overlap between the neo-Walrasian and Chicago SRPs, for some work (notably Friedman's AEA presidential address) is important to the evolution of both programmes.

There are also problems with the early phase of Keynesian economics, for Keynes's *General Theory* and much of the early work interpreting it fell outside the neo-Walrasian SRP. (Keynes, for example, reasoned in terms of 'propensities' rather than optimizing behaviour, in a manner more reminiscent of Adam Smith or Alfred Marshall than of neo-Walrasian economics.) We thus have to tell the story in terms of neo-Walrasian economics' encompassing theories which previously lay outside its domain. In so far as this just represents the victory of one SRP over another, it presents no difficulties. But what we have is not so much a competition between programmes as the taking over by one programme of theories developed within another programme. In other words, we have to explore the nature of the relationship between competing SRPs in a way that goes beyond simple competition.

Finally, there is the problem of defining the hard core. The main reason why we do not have more problems is that the hard core has been defined so as to have very little definite economic content beyond the assumption of individual optimizing agents operating in interlinked markets. This means that the positive heuristics, requiring the construction of fully specified, consistent models, are important in defining the character of the programme. They do more than simply protect the hard core, for they are important in defining the programme's modelling strategy. Even with such a restricted hard core there are problems. Those associated with the work of Keynes and that of some of his early followers have already been discussed. Another problem concerns information. Prior to the 1960s little attention was paid to the information available to agents, but since then it has acquired great significance. In contemporary neo-Walrasian economics it is important that individuals are assumed to have a well-defined set of information, whereas in the 1950s this was not the case.

Example II: new classical macroeconomics   The same problems arise when we try to distinguish SRPs on a smaller scale and with a more definite economic content. As our example, consider the case of the new classical macroeconomics. It is possible to characterize the new classical macroeconomics as a Lakatosian SRP, the hard core of which comprises the 'Lucas' aggregate supply function, the natural rate hypothesis, and rational expectations. Maddock (1991) has persuasively argued that such a programme was well established by around 1972, and that such a programme provides an adequate framework with which to explain the sequence of literature associated with the new classical tradition. Even so, all three of the problems listed above arise.

Consider first the general equilibrium component of the new classical macroeconomics. This could be viewed as a component of different SRPs, in each of which it plays a different role. Within the new classical SRP it forms part of the negative heuristic: it allows research to proceed without being distracted by a series of microeconomics-based critiques. Within the neo-Walrasian programme, however, it forms part of the positive heuristic.

Problems involving the relationship between different programmes are emphasized by the fact that important parts of the new classical literature are directed at competing research programmes, rather than contributing towards the development of the new classical programme itself. Lucas (1972), for example, was concerned with the weaknesses of standard (non-new classical) testing procedures. From the viewpoint of Lakatos's MSRP such arguments were superfluous. An even stronger example is Lucas's critique of econometric policy evaluation, which sought to point out a major internal inconsistency within an alternative research programme (Lucas, 1976). This is arguably the most influential paper Lucas has ever written, and yet it is hard to see a role for it if we adopt a strict Lakatosian approach.

The difficulties involved in defining a clear hard core, even for such a seemingly well-defined programme as the new classical macroeconomics, can be illustrated by citing examples of papers that violate parts of what would normally be thought of as the new classical hard core. Lucas and Rapping (1969), considered by one commentator to be the first paper of the new classical macroeconomics (Hoover, 1988, p. 27), uses adaptive, not rational expectations. Sargent and Wallace (1975) used a modified IS–LM model, not a model based on maximizing behaviour. Sargent and Wallace (1982) present a model incorporating the real bills doctrine, according to which changes in nominal money balances affect real consumption decisions, violating the 'hard core' assumption that real magnitudes are determined independently of nominal magnitudes. There are, of course, explanations for all these 'aberrations'. Lucas and Rapping wrote before the SRP had been fully articulated. Sargent and Wallace used the IS–LM model in order to attack their opponents on their home ground. When they adopted the real bills doctrine they reinterpreted the notion of 'neutrality of money'. Yet these explanations do not get rid of the problem, for if the concept of the hard core is to have its full meaning, work within the programme should not conflict with it.

3.   The appraisal criterion

'Rhetorical' perspectives

Some of the most thorough going critiques of Lakatos's appraisal criterion come from those economists who advocate replacing economic methodology, at least as it is traditionally understood, with an analysis of economists' rhetoric. McCloskey has argued that *any* prescriptive methodology (of which Lakatos's is one) is presumptuous and laughable: how can an outsider (the methodologist, or philosopher of science) tell a practitioner (the scientist) the best way to conduct his or her research? According to McCloskey, 'Einstein remarked that "whoever undertakes to set himself up as a judge in the field of Truth and Knowledge is shipwrecked by the laughter of the gods". . . . Any methodology that is lawmaking and limiting will have this risible effect' (McCloskey, 1986, p. 104). If methodological prescriptions were made without any reference to economists' practice, McCloskey's criticism would have some force. An important aspect of Lakatos's MSRP, however, is that there is an interaction between prescriptive methodology and scientific practice, which comes about through the methodology of *historical* research programmes. If the MSRP succeeds in making explicit the methodology underlying the best practice of economists (which is what the MHRP is about) McCloskey's criticism is avoided.

A more direct, and very different attack on Lakatos is provided by Colander, who claims that,

> Most mainstream economists who are satisfied with the state of economics [how many of these are there?] follow (probably implicitly, because few study methodology) some brand of Popperian or Lakatosian methodology of science, both of which are refinements of logical positivism. [!] A principle of these scientific methodologies is that economics (or any other science) is advanced by the empirical testing of well-specified propositions. (Colander, 1990, p. 189)

He equates 'well-specified' with formal mathematics, and empirical testing with formal econometrics, with the result that he has little problem in showing that there is more to economic analysis than this. Though it *may* be true that many economists (and in particular many graduate students, who are the main focus of Klamer and Colander's book) do interpret theory formulation and empirical testing in this restrictive way, there is no need to do so: precision does not necessarily imply mathematics (though for some problems it may do) and empirical testing does not necessarily involve quantitative data. Good historical research (and I have in mind 'traditional' history, not simply cliometrics) can legitimately be seen as involving the formulation of clear hypotheses which are tested against empirical data (cf. Blaug, 1980, p. 127). Provided that we avoid falling into the traps indicated by Colander, therefore, we need not abandon a methodology based on empirical testing. (I leave on one side the question of whether or not Colander is justified in describing Popper and Lakatos as 'positivist'.)

Eclecticism, relativism and critical pluralism

A similar, though not identical, position towards Lakatos is adopted by economists who explicitly endorse an eclectic approach to methodology. A clear example here is Dow's endorsement of what she terms 'Babylonian' methodology (Dow, 1985). Dow's position is that economists should be using a variety of approaches, not a single, internally consistent one. This may indeed be a fair account of the situation in which we find ourselves, in that it may in practice be impossible to find a single, adequate methodology. To say this, however, is not the same as showing that we should not *seek* a consistent methodology.

A similar refusal to choose between methodologies emerges from parts of the literature on the sociology of knowledge. Knowledge is seen as the product of a particular community, without meaning outside that community. From such a perspective the search for a single methodology is misguided. The response to this is twofold. First, we do not have to be positivists to accept that there are empirical data which constrain knowledge, and which cause different communities to have certain things in common. Secondly, in the literature on economic methodology we are concerned with a particular, albeit somewhat extended, scientific community. It is thus reasonable to assume that shared knowledge and beliefs are sufficiently great to make communication within this community possible.

Though he has been accused of this, Caldwell's 'critical pluralism' is not the same as eclecticism, but if it is (wrongly) presented as an *alternative* to Lakatos's MSRP, its implications sound very similar. Loosely, Caldwell's position (see Caldwell, 1982, 1988, 1990) is that we should not confine our attention to any one single methodology (whether Lakatos's or any other), for there are, at least at present, no grounds for claiming that any one methodology is superior to all others. This position is differentiated from eclecticism by the contention that all methodologies should be critically appraised. Critical pluralism is, therefore, not an alternative to Lakatosian methodology, but a meta-methodology according to which alternative methodologies are to be appraised. Thus the arguments presented here, which are aimed at evaluating one particular methodology, are consistent with a critical pluralist position.

Specific criticisms of excess content

Lakatos's appraisal criterion of corroborated excess content, or 'novel facts', has also been criticized by Hands, an economist who is sympathetic towards many other aspects of Lakatos's methodology (see below). He has two distinct lines of criticism to offer. The first is that good economic theories involve much more than simply the successful prediction of novel facts:

> Why would we want to accept the position that *the sole necessary condition for scientific progress is predicting novel facts* not used in the construction of the theory? Surely humankind's greatest scientific accomplishments have amounted to more than this. We in economics and those in every other branch of science choose theories because they are deeper, simpler, more general, more operational, explain known facts better, are more corroborated, are more consistent with what we consider to be deeper theories: and for many other reasons. Even if we can find a few novel facts here and there in the history of economics, and even if those novel facts seem to provide an occasional 'clincher', the history of great economics is so much more than a list of these novel facts. (Hands, 1990, p. 78)

He goes on to cite Smith's invisible hand, Walras's notion of multimarket interdependence, Marshall's welfare economics and Keynes's notion that aggregate demand determines the level of output and employment as constituting great economics. These, he argues, have given insight and progress, not just 'an occasional novel fact' (ibid.).

The response to this is that the prediction of novel facts is important because it enables us to be sure, in a way that the other criteria cited by Hands do not, that we are making progress in understanding the real world. As Blaug has put it, '"scientific progress" is progress in achieving "objective knowledge" and the only way we can be sure that we have achieved objective knowledge is to commit ourself to the prediction of novel facts' (Blaug, 1991, p. 102).

It is here that the second strand of Hands's criticism is relevant, for such a statement has to be based on some epistemology. Hands argues that Lakatos's appraisal criterion is based on the Popperian notion of empirical content (Hands, 1985, pp. 5–8). Furthermore, the emphasis on novel facts rather than falsification (characteristic not only of Lakatos, but also of certain of Popper's writings) was an attempt to move away from Popper's original emphasis on falsificationism to a position more consistent with Popper's view of verisimilitude as the aim of science. Popper's theory of verisimilitude, however, has been subjected to extensive criticism. Hands thus argues that because Lakatos completely abandoned falsificationism in favour of the prediction of novel facts, he was left with an appraisal criterion that lacked any firm epistemological basis (see

Hands, 1991). Hands thus concludes that we should abandon the prediction of novel facts as our appraisal criterion, even if we retain other elements in the MSRP.

4. The 'methodology of historical research programmes'
Appraising the best gambits
Lakatos's contention is that 'a rationality theory – or demarcation criterion – is to be rejected if it is inconsistent with an accepted "basic value judgement" of the scientific élite' (Lakatos, 1978, p. 124). He compares this criterion with Popper's methodology, arguing that the latter depends on the existence of '(relatively) singular statements on whose truth-value scientists can reach unanimous agreement' (ibid.). He defends his meta-methodology against the charge that differences of opinion are too great to permit its use:

> While there has been little agreement concerning a *universal* criterion of the scientific character of theories, there has been considerable agreement over the last two centuries concerning *single* achievements. While there has been no *general* agreement concerning a theory of scientific rationality, there has been considerable agreement concerning whether a particular step in the game was scientific or crankish, or whether a particular gambit was played correctly or not.

He then draws the conclusion that 'an acceptable definition of science (methodology) 'must reconstruct the acknowledgedly best gambits as "scientific": if it fails to do so it must be rejected' (ibid.).

This meta-criterion for appraising methodologies is crucial because it provides the necessary link between methodology and the judgements of working scientists. Lakatos's exposition of it has been quoted at length in order to make the point that applying it to economics is less straightforward than it might appear. A necessary condition for it to work is that we can define both a 'scientific élite' and a set of scientific gambits in such a manner that there is *unanimity* amongst this elite on both whether these gambits were 'scientific' and whether they were 'applied correctly'. In the sciences with which Lakatos was concerned this condition is easily satisfied, but in economics the case is far less clear cut.

To see this, consider Hands's attempt to apply this meta-criterion (Hands, 1985, 1990). To avoid unnecessary controversy he considers only two major achievements: Keynes's *General Theory* and general equilibrium theory. But do even these satisfy Lakatos's condition? Surely a major issue underlying, implicitly if not explicitly, the methodological debates of the past two decades has been the question of whether the general equilibrium paradigm has led economists astray. While Hands may be right in working on the assumption that the answer to this is 'No', it is important to be clear about what is being assumed.

Sociological factors
Implicit in Lakatos's MHRP are three assumptions: that 'truer' theories will be more successful than 'less true' theories in predicting novel facts; that scientists believe (know) this; and that scientists are motivated to search for the truth. The first of these is discussed elsewhere in this chapter. If we assume that it is correct, then it is not difficult to argue for the second assumption. Problems arise, so it has been argued, with the third assumption. Colander (1990), for example, argues the following:

> Unlike the Popperian and Lakatosian methodologies, a sociological approach does not assume that scientists are searching for the truth. Truth is one of their goals, but only one; professional advancement, recognition, and wealth are others of perhaps equal or more importance. *Good science is made possible by institutional conventions that make it in scientists' interests to follow reasonable conventions that are most likely to limit subjectivity and bias.* (Colander, 1990, p. 191)

This leaves open the possibility, to which attention was drawn long ago by Leontief (1971), that the structure of incentives in the profession may be such that the economics as a whole (i.e. not just the work of a few 'perverse' individuals) may move in the wrong direction. If this is so then we have to be careful before applying Lakatos's MHRP. For example, a Lakatosian interpretation of the new classical macroeconomics required that, at least in the early stages when it was attracting adherents from Keynesianism, it appeared progressive. If this were not the case, this would, according to Lakatos's meta-criterion, undermine Lakatos's MSRP. If, on the other hand, we can establish that the structure of incentives in the profession during the 1970s was such that searching for truth was pushed aside in favour of lines of inquiry, we could not draw any useful conclusions concerning the validity of progressivity as an appraisal criterion.

5.   Where do we go from here?
The argument so far
In reviewing the problems various economists have found with Lakatos's methodology a number of criticisms have already been answered. There remain, however, some serious problems which need to be dealt with.

1.   The concept of a scientific research programme, as defined by Laka-
     tos, captures important aspects of economic inquiry, but it appears to

be inadequate in that it fails to account for the diversity of interrelationships between theories that we observe.

2. We lack a firm epistemological foundation for the use of novel facts as an appraisal criterion.
3. The conditions required for rational reconstructions to provide unambiguous appraisals of Lakatos's MSRP are so restrictive that they are unlikely to be satisfied in economics. Rational reconstructions of the history of economic thought, however successful, are thus unlikely to provide a clear-cut answer as to the relevance of the MSRP.

Alternative responses

How should we respond to these criticisms of Lakatosian methodology? The easiest would be to abandon Lakatos's MSRP. There are two major problems with this. The first is that if we want to understand economics we need to find an alternative methodology, and it is not clear that anything better is available. If we abandon methodology altogether, we have to give up the important task of appraisal. As an example, consider Hoover's (1991) response to the difficulties of applying Lakatos's MSRP to the new classical macroeconomics. He proposes that we should view economic theories much as an anthropologist might view a society, basing his analysis on a 'kinship table' showing the relationships between members of the society: there are several families, with relationships between individuals also extending across family boundaries. The problem is whether such an approach, however well it may describe the multifarious links between various parts of the literature (and Hoover's table is excellent in this respect), can ever go beyond description. Any appraisal of theories must be on an *ad hoc* basis.

An alternative is to modify Lakatos's methodology. Remenyi (1979) has proposed modifying Lakatos's concept of the SRP by allowing for what he terms 'demi-cores': sets of assumptions which constitute a hard core for parts of the research programme. We thus have a structure of programmes and sub-programmes. Though this may work in some contexts, it is not clear that such an approach is an adequate response to the problems discussed above. It does not get us very far, for example, in understanding the complex set of relationships within the new classical macroeconomics that we find in Hoover's kinship table. By weakening the metaphor of the hard core, Remenyi's scheme loses much that is attractive in Lakatos's MSRP, without bringing us much by way of compensation.

Not surprisingly, in view of the nature of his criticisms, Hands chooses to modify Lakatos's MSRP by abandoning novel facts as the appraisal criterion in favour of a broader range of criteria (such as those cited earlier). As regards the concept of a research programme, he is open-minded about whether a 'substantially modified version' of the MSRP might be successful, citing Remenyi's and Weintraub's work as examples. He is definite that to be successful such a modified version 'must be written with the actual history of economic thought (at least the best gambits) squarely in sight' (Hands, 1985, p. 13). Putting aside the difference over the appraisal criterion, this conclusion is compatible with the following suggestion as to where we might go from here.

Given the arguments against completely abandoning Lakatos's MSRP, and given the problems involved with applying it unchanged, we are faced with the problem of how to modify it. Remenyi's strategy of complicating it seems unlikely to work, for it fails to allow for the diversity of structures we find within economics. This suggests that we should perhaps be moving in the opposite direction: that of radically simplifying Lakatos's MSRP. The suggestion offered here is the following: (1) that we should retain Lakatos's appraisal criterion; but (2) that we should replace his concept of a scientific research programme with something much broader.

The appraisal criterion
What justification is there for retaining Lakatos's appraisal criterion? The main one is that it seems to be the criterion which economists use when asked to justify the theories they use. When a neoclassical economist claims that his or her theories 'work', what they mean is something very close to Lakatos's novel facts. It is thus an appraisal criterion based on the judgements of practising economists.

There is also a strong 'common sense' argument in favour of novel facts as an appraisal criterion. Such a criterion is widely used in econometrics where, despite a large battery of statistical tests, it is considered necessary to do more than test a model against the data set on which it was estimated. It is thus common practice for econometricians to reserve data in order to conduct out-of-sample tests, and to test models on data sets other than those on which they were originally estimated. The defence of such procedures is that if an estimated model is a true representation of the model generating the data, its predictions will be correct (subject, of course, to random elements). If the estimated model differs from the true model we would expect there to be some set of data that it will fail to predict correctly. Out-of-sample predictive success, a criterion similar to 'novel facts', is thus a necessary condition for a model to be correct. Do the arguments that have been used against 'novel facts' as an appraisal criterion also invalidate such out-of-sample tests in econometrics? It could be argued that when we compare two models, neither of which is the true model (presumably this is almost universally the case in economics), we come up against 'second-best' problems: a 'less correct' model may perhaps predict better than a more correct one, but this raises the problem of how we measure the correctness of a model.

These arguments are not intended to deny the desirability of a more secure epistemological foundation for any criteria – that is not in dispute. The point is rather that the failure of philosophers to provide an acceptable epistemological foundation does not *necessarily* mean that it is wrong to use Lakatos's appraisal criterion.

The unit of appraisal

If we are to retain Lakatos's appraisal criterion without accepting his definition of a research programme, what should be appraised? The simplest answer would be to abandon the concept of a research programme in its entirety. Such a response would take us back to Popper, who presented an appraisal criterion very close to Lakatos's (Popper, 1972, ch. 10, esp. pp. 240–8). A better solution is to retain Lakatos's insight that it is not individual theories but *sequences* of theories that should be appraised. The theories in such a sequence must be related to each other in some way if the object of appraisal is not to be completely *ad hoc*. The relationship between theories that Lakatos specified was that of sharing a common set of hard-core assumptions (the heuristics of a research programme being concerned simply with protecting this hard core), but there is no reason why some other relationship should not be specified. For example, the interpretation of the 'neo-Walrasian research programme' offered in Backhouse, 1991, is further from Lakatos's methodology than it might appear to be. The reason is that the programme's positive and negative heuristics (as defined there) do more than protect the hard core: the neo-Walrasian research programme is thus an example of a research programme defined by its heuristics as much as by its hard core.

The suggestion is that we should apply Lakatos's appraisal criterion, and use it to appraise research programmes, where research programmes are *not necessarily* defined in terms of their hard cores. The function of the hard core in Lakatos's MSRP was to eliminate *ad hoc* sequences, but there is no reason why *ad hoc* sequences cannot be eliminated by other means. This is not to say that Lakatos's criterion of a common hard core will never be appropriate: sometimes it will be. The point is that it is not a *necessary* condition for a coherent research programme. In other words, Lakatos has provided us with just one example of what a research programme might look like.

It is natural to argue that Lakatos's methodology of historical research programmes should be used to appraise this revised version of the MSRP. The problem here is that our revised MSRP cannot possibly perform worse than Lakatos's, the reason being that any history that is compatible with Lakatos's MSRP is *a fortiori* compatible with ours. Using Popperian language, the revision we have introduced is content-decreasing, in that the set of possible histories that would lead us to reject the MSRP has been reduced. So the most effective way to defend our modification is to argue that defining research programmes in terms of sets of hard-core assumptions was *ad hoc* and that all we have done is to remove this *ad hoc* element.

6.   Concluding remarks

Lakatos's MSRP has been subjected to many criticisms, but these are not fatal. The most telling criticism would seem to be the failure of the history of economic thought to fall into the simple categories implied by Lakatos's framework. Rather than taking this as a reason for abandoning Lakatos altogether, it seems preferable to modify his MSRP to allow for a greater variety of types of research programme, retaining his appraisal criterion intact. If this suggestion were accepted, it would be natural to regard one of the major tasks facing historians of economic thought as being to discover the defining characteristics of research programmes in economics. These programmes could then be appraised according to their success in predicting novel facts. This suggestion strengthens the connection between methodology and the history of economic thought that was already a feature of Lakatosian methodology.

Note
*   I am grateful to several colleagues and to participants in the History of Economics Society meeting for helpful comments on an earlier draft of this paper. Particular thanks should go to Richard Davies, Crauford Goodwin, Chris Hookway, Kevin Hoover, Andrea Salanti and Jeremy Shearmur. Needless to say, I alone remain responsible for any remaining errors or confusions.

References
Backhouse, R. E. (1991) 'The neo-Walrasian Research Programme in Macroeconomics', in Blaug and De Marchi (1991).

Blanchard, O. and Kiyotaki, N. (1987), 'Monopolistic Competition and the Effects of Aggregate Demand', *American Economic Review*, 77 (4), pp. 647–66.

Blaug, M. (1980), *The Methodology of Economics*, Cambridge: Cambridge University Press.

Blaug, M. (1991), 'Reply to D. Wade Hands' "Second Thoughts on Second Thoughts: Reconsidering the Lakatosian Progress of *The General Theory*" ', *Review of Political Economy*, 2 (1), pp. 101–3.

Blaug, M. and De Marchi, N. B. (eds) (1991), *Appraising Modern Economics: Studies in the Methodology of Scientific Research Programmes*, Aldershot: Edward Elgar.

Caldwell, Bruce (1982), *Beyond Positivism: Economic Methodology in the Twentieth Century*, London: Allen and Unwin.

Caldwell, Bruce (1988), 'The Case for Pluralism', in Neil De Marchi (ed.) *The Popperian Legacy in Economics*, Cambridge: Cambridge University Press.

Caldwell, Bruce (1990), 'Does Methodology Matter? How Should it be Practiced?' *Finnish Economic Papers* **3** (1), pp. 64–71.

Colander, D. (1990), 'Workmanship, Incentives and Cynicism', in A. Klamer and D. Colander (eds), *The Making of an Economist*, Boulder, CO: Westview Press.

Cross, R. (1982), 'The Duhem-Quine Thesis, Lakatos and the Appraisal of Theories in Macroeconomics', *Economic Journal*, **72**, pp. 320–40.

Dow, S. C. (1985), *Macroeconomic Thought*, Oxford: Basil Blackwell.

Hands, D. W. (1985), 'Second Thoughts on Lakatos', *History of Political Economy*, **17** (1), pp. 1–16.

Hands, D. W. (1990), 'Second Thoughts on "Second Thoughts:" Reconsidering the Lakatosian Progress of *The General Theory*', *Review of Political Economy*, **2** (1), pp. 69–81.

Hands, D. W. (1991), 'The Problem of Excess Content: Economics, Novelty and a Long Popperian Tale', in Blaug and De Marchi (1991).

Hart, O. (1982) 'A Model of Imperfect Competition with Keynesian Features', *Quarterly Journal of Economics*, **97**, pp. 109–38.

Hoover, K. (1988) *The New Classical Macroeconomics: A Sceptical Inquiry*, Oxford: Basil Blackwell.

Hoover, K. (1991), 'A Scientific Research Program or Tribe: a Joint Appraisal of Lakatos and the New Classical Macroeconomics', in Blaug and De Marchi, (1991).

Lakatos, I. (1978), 'History of Science and its Rational Reconstructions' (1971), reprinted in *The Methodology of Scientific Research Programmes: Philosophical Papers, Volume I*, Cambridge: Cambridge University Press.

Leontief, W. (1971) 'Theoretical Assumptions and Non-observed Facts', *American Economic Review* **61** (1), pp. 1–7.

Lucas, R. E. (1972) 'Econometric Testing of the Natural Rate Hypothesis', in O. Eckstein (ed.), *The Econometrics of Price Determination*, Washington, DC: Board of Governors of the Federal Reserve System.

Lucas, R. E. (1976), 'Econometric Policy Evaluation: a Critique', in K. Brunner and A. Meltzer (eds), *The Phillips Curve and Labour Markets*, Supplement to *Journal of Monetary Economics*, **1**.

Lucas, R. E. and Rapping, L. A. (1969), 'Real Wages, Employment and Inflation', *Journal of Political Economy*, **77**, pp. 721–54.

Maddock, R. (1984), 'Rational Expectations Macrotheory: a Case Study in Program Adjustment', *History of Political Economy* **16** (3), pp. 291–310.

Maddock, R. (1991), 'The Development of New Classical Macroeconomics: Lessons for Lakatos', in Blaug and De Marchi (1991).

Marris, R. (1991), *Reconstructing Keynesian Macroeconomics with Imperfect Competition*, Aldershot: Edward Elgar.

McCloskey, D. M. (1986), *The Rhetoric of Economics*, Brighton: Wheatsheaf Books.

Popper, K. R. (1972), *Conjectures and Refutations*, 4th edn, London: Routledge & Kegan Paul.

Reder, M. W. (1982) 'Chicago Economics: Permanence and Change', *Journal of Economic Literature*, **20** (1), pp. 1–38.

Remenyi, J. V. (1979), 'Core Demi-core Interaction: toward a General Theory of Disciplinary and Sub-disciplinary Growth', *History of Political Economy*, **11** (1), pp. 30–63.

Sargent, T. J. and Wallace, N. (1975), 'Rational Expectations, the Optimal Monetary Instrument and the Optimal Money Supply Rule', *Journal of Political Economy*, **83**, pp. 241–55.

Sargent, T. J. and Wallace, N. (1982), 'The Real Bills Doctrine versus the Quantity Theory: a Reconsideration', *Journal of Political Economy*, **90**, pp. 1212–36.

Weintraub, E. R. (1979), *Microfoundations*, Cambridge: Cambridge University Press.

Weintraub, E. R. (1985), *General Equilibrium Analysis: Studies in Appraisal*, Cambridge: Cambridge University Press.

3 What's wrong with metaphors in economics: the case of hydraulic metaphors[1]

Maurice Lagueux

In discussing the characteristics of certain hydraulic metaphors in economics, I obviously do not intend *to promote the use* of hydraulic models by economists. It is clear that hydraulic models are completely inadequate for dealing with the complex relations that are analysed in modern mathematical economics. Nevertheless, since many economists occasionally turn to these models – or to these metaphors – in order to clarify their theories, it would be worth while to have a look at their surprising attempts to express their views with the help of pipes and cisterns. Of course, these economists usually consider their reference to hydraulics as a purely pedagogical device which cannot be accorded the same status as a standard model described in either ordinary or mathematical language. However, since hydraulic models have the advantage of clarity, an examination of them may help to clarify the question of the role of metaphors in economics, a question which, since the works of McCloskey, Klamer, Mirowski and some others, increasingly interests methodologists.

Before discussing this methodological question, let us briefly review the unusual history of hydraulic models and metaphors in economics. It is an unusual history because it mainly consists in a few cases of the almost eccentric use of an imagery which is not taken very seriously by contemporary economists. As a rule, hydraulic metaphors are not listed in the indexes of relevant economics books. One merely finds reference to the economic phenomena that such metaphors are used to describe, so it is not easy to locate the curious passages where these metaphors are found. In any case, it is useful to distinguish two periods in this history. The first period reaches its peak at the end of the eighteenth century and terminates somewhere in the mid-nineteenth century, once classical economics had been fully developed. During this period, references to hydraulics are perceived as if they contribute to the status of economics by showing that it has to do with mechanisms that have exactly the same structure as those hydraulic mechanisms which are satisfactorily analysed in physics and even in biology. The second period corresponds roughly to the last hundred years, a period during which some rather unexpected and colourful references to hydraulics have sometimes been made by exponents of modern micro- and macroeconomics. In this more recent period, the goal of these references is no longer to show that economics is just as 'scientific' as physics; they seem instead to serve a merely pedagogical purpose. Nevertheless, underlying these references there is still the assumption that economics has to do with mechanisms which are very similar to those studied in physics.

Let us begin by considering hydraulic metaphors of the first period. Two very well-known contributions, Hume's essay 'Of the Balance of Trade', written in 1752, and Turgot's 'Réflexions sur la formation et la distribution des richesses', written in 1766, explicitly referred to the equilibrium of liquid in a communicating vessel. Hume suggested that an equilibrium mechanism would automatically prevent any haemorrhage of gold resulting from free trade (Hume, 1970, pp. 63–4). Similarly, Turgot suggested that the respective levels of rent, interest and profit must be systematically related and that there must be 'a kind of equilibrium' between them, just as there is between the respective levels of 'two liquids of different weight'[2] each contained in a branch of a communicating vessel. In both cases the metaphors have to do with the counterbalancing forces which act on the liquids rather than with the liquids considered as physical substances. Naturally, liquids have to be substances in order to be subject to the relevant force, that is to say to gravitation; but when it comes to the economic phenomena described by Hume and Turgot, the relevant force is self-interest, a 'force' which influences the level of gold in a country, or the level of revenue in a particular use, by reacting to the level of prices or to the rate of return from capital (rent, interest or profit) in a way which does not imply, at least not directly, that these economic 'entities' have to be considered as substances. For Hume and for Turgot, the only crucial point is that self-interest acts automatically, just like gravitation in the case of liquids, to restore equilibrium.

The situation is very different when it comes to what seems to be the most systematic reference to hydraulics during this early period. We find it in Canard's *Principes d'économie politique*, published in 1801. Canard's metaphor – which is apparently a development of some more timid suggestions of Cantillon (1952, pp. 90, 102) – also implies that certain economic mechanisms operate in exactly the same way as similar mechanisms in hydraulics. However, far from being considered in isolation, these mechanisms are considered to be part of the whole economic system. And this system itself, interpreted in an almost organic way, is seen as a complex network of channels in which money and goods circulate continuously in a process which functions in exactly the same way as the circulation of blood through the network of arteries and veins in the human body (Canard, 1969, pp. 20, 61, 69–70, 74–5, 109, 122–4 etc.).

When we compare Canard's metaphors with those of Hume and Turgot, many things become noteworthy. Canard's metaphors have a general character. They relate to hydraulic phenomena which are natural and even organic, instead of being associated with laboratory apparatuses. They refer to hydraulic and economic phenomena as if they were essentially the same sort of phenomena. This last point is illustrated by the fact that blood circulation is supposed to be clarified with reference to the circulation of money and goods as much as the latter is clarified with reference to blood circulation. Money and goods literally 'flow' like liquids and both obey similar laws. More crucially, money and goods are treated like liquids because they are considered to be *substances* which are conserved throughout their circumvolution in the economic system. For Canard, it was natural to consider them as substances because, for him as for most economists of this period, value itself *was* a kind of substance originating in labour. Any amount of value, whether it takes the form of goods or of money, is expected to behave like a liquid when it flows along the channels of consumption or of production. It was this circulatory scheme, anticipated by Boisguillebert and analysed in a more abstract way by Quesnay, which was still central in Marx's theory, even if, by this time, an explicit hydraulic imagery was no longer a source of scientific credibility for economics.

However, with the so-called marginalist revolution, this substantialist way of characterizing economic processes was rejected. As a consequence, hydraulic metaphors became much less attractive to economists. Since it is difficult to conceive of utility as a substance, one might doubt whether microeconomic price levels based on marginal utility could ever be usefully compared to water levels. Oddly enough, it was precisely in this context that Irving Fisher devised what is probably the most sophisticated hydraulic model of economic theory ever conceived. Fisher built an ingenious apparatus capable of simulating the alternative mathematical model which depicts the mechanism involved in a self-equilibrating market (Fisher, 1925, p. 24ff). This second life given to hydraulic metaphors corresponds to what I called the second period of their history.

Before discussing the significance of the important differences between Fisher's complex hydraulic metaphor and the previous ones, let's consider a few of the unique characteristics of his apparatus. The basic structure remains the same: a system of cisterns which communicate with each other from the bottom ends. The differences in the shape of these cisterns corresponds roughly to differences in the tastes of different individuals with respect to a particular good. Fisher postulates that the distance from

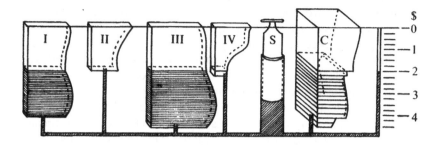

Source: Fisher (1925, p. 28)

Figure 3.1

the actual level of the liquid to a satiety level is an analogon of marginal (decreasing) utility, since this distance always decreases with the addition of more liquid. However, a microeconomical model of the market must be able to account not only for the distribution of any single *good* between many consumers, but also for the distribution of the *revenue* of any single consumer between many goods. In the first case, the volume of the liquid will have to correspond to the quantity of the good, but in the second case to its monetary value. Far from being impeded by this problem, Fisher decided to use two different liquids which were strictly isolated from one another. But as the one liquid had to correspond to the quantity and the other to the monetary value of *the same* goods, Fisher was forced to associate each cistern containing the first type of liquid with a cistern containing the second type. Thus he constructed double cisterns having a front compartment for the first type of liquid and a back compartment for the second. Although the two liquids were strictly isolated from one another, it was essential that their respective levels were interdependent. Fisher made sure that the levels were interdependent by constructing a very ingenious system of levers. He described this system in detail in order to show that it made his hydraulic model equivalent to a typical mathematical model of the market. However, this system would not have been able to simulate the multiple transactions of a theoretical market in the process of readjusting towards equilibrium without the presence of a large tank in which all of the cisterns were floating and moving vertically (because of the weight of their content and the constraint of the levers) until the liquid in each cistern reached its equilibrium level. As the monetary value of a good is capable of variations which are unrelated to its quantity, it is also important to mention that the walls of back compartments had to be

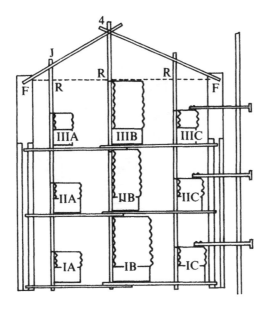

Source: Fisher (1925, p. 39)

Figure 3.2

made of flexible leather in order to accommodate an increase in the volume of a liquid which did not change the other liquid's level.

If this model appears complex and artificial by contrast with the communicating vessels of Hume and Turgot, which were based on an apparatus found in any laboratory (or even in nature), it is largely because Fisher had not only to simulate a mechanism – a task for which hydraulic models are clearly appropriate – but also to take account of the fact that in this mechanism no real substance is involved. As Philip Mirowski (1989, ch. 5) has emphasized, the marginalist theory of value, by contrast with the classical theory of value, is *not* substantialist, and the mathematical model that Fisher was translating into hydraulic terms was a model derived from a physical theory in which the concept of a field had superseded the concept of a substance. However, as a liquid *is* a substance. Fisher had to find very artificial ways of coping with this situation. The 'flexible leather' walls of the compartments and the total separation of the liquid-value from the liquid-quantity of goods were the devices he used to free his liquids from the limits imposed by their substantiality.

In devising his apparatus it is clear that Fisher had no intention of

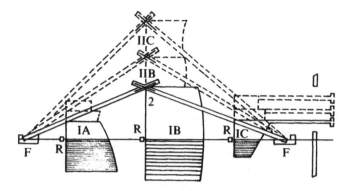

Source: Fisher (1925, p. 39)

Figure 3.3

promoting the scientific character of economics. Indeed, he had instead to defend the usefulness of his gadget against sceptics. The sophisticated mathematical model he provided in the same book represents a much more serious scientific undertaking and is far more effective for problem-solving. Given its complexity and its artificiality, it is even doubtful that such an apparatus was a very helpful pedagogical device. Moreover, even if Fisher was sincere when he suggested that it could be an instrument of research permitting economists to literally observe some of the puzzling effects of exogenous intervention in such a system (Fisher, 1925, pp. 65–6), one may remain unconvinced.

More importantly, Fisher's undertaking was a remarkable attempt to make clear the similarity between hydraulic and economic mechanisms. Before discussing the significance of the metaphorical character of such an apparatus, it may be worth while to say a few words about some other hydraulic apparatuses devised by economists. About two years later, Fisher, who was obviously convinced of the analytic virtues of hydraulic apparatuses, devised a simpler hydraulic model for analysing bimetallism by adapting some of the techniques used in his complex microeconomic model (Fisher, 1894). Shortly afterwards, he was followed by Edgeworth, who adapted Fisher's hydraulic model to symmetalism, another theory of currency (Edgeworth, 1895).

In the twentieth century another sophisticated hydraulic apparatus was devised by A.W. Phillips, the inventor of the well-known curve of the

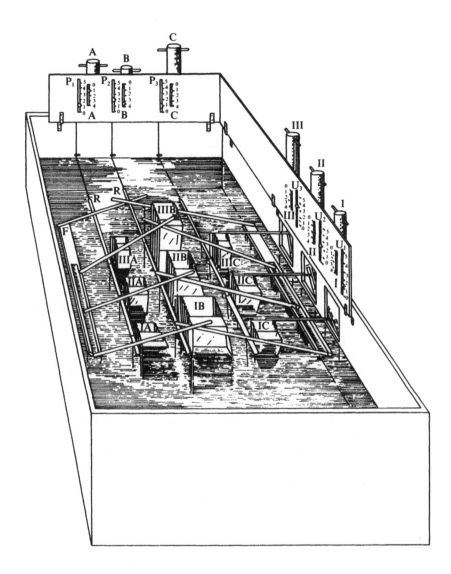

Source: Fisher (1925, p. 38)

Figure 3.4

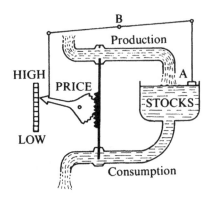

Source: Boulding (1966, p. 169)

Figure 3.5

same name (Phillips, 1950). This time, however, a *macroeconomic* phenomena was simulated. Phillips integrated into his model a simpler one used
by K. Boulding in order to illustrate the equilibrium mechanism of a
market in his microeconomic textbook. The central component of Boulding's apparatus is a tank containing water (Boulding, 1966, Vol. I, p. 169).
Water flows in and out of the tank and a float at the surface is connected,
through a system of levers, to a rod which automatically pushes or draws
on a set of valves so that the level of the water in the tank is maintained at
an equilibrium level.

For Boulding, this mechanism simulated a goods market. Phillips took
over this hydraulic model and used it to illustrate the working of a *money*
market in a manner consistent with the views of those 'orthodox' Keynesians whom, incidentally, Coddington (1976, pp. 1263–7) has labelled
'hydraulic Keynesians'. As is well known by economists, who are familiar
with the cruder hydraulic representation found in many textbooks, in such
a view the demand for money is normally divided between the demand for
liquidity and the demand for transactions. Actually Phillips only used
Boulding's market mechanism for the simulation of the demand for liquidity with interest rates corresponding to price levels. Although it commu-
nicates freely with the water representing the demand for liquidity, the
water representing the demand for transactions was treated as a part of a
circulatory system conceived in a manner similar to Canard's network of
channels. It is noteworthy that with Phillips's hydraulic apparatus, we are

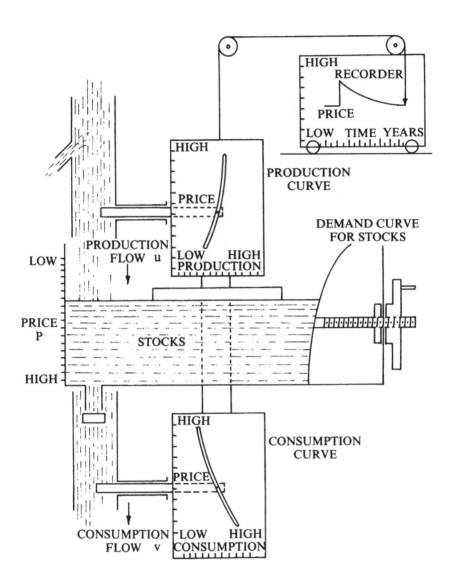

Source: Phillips (1950, p. 285)

Figure 3.6

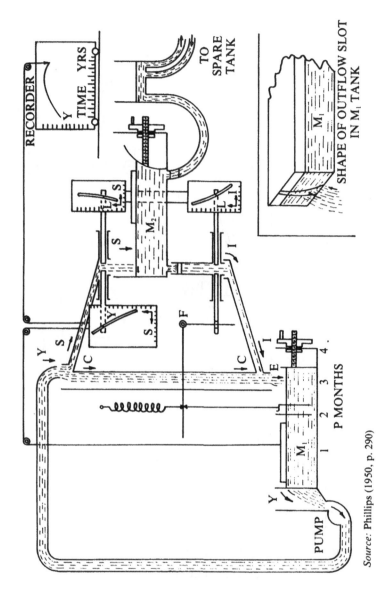

Source: Phillips (1950, p. 290)

Figure 3.7

44

back to a model in which the liquid is considered as a conserved substance, which is precisely the reason Mirowski would refuse to consider the so-called 'hydraulic' interpretation of Keynes as a 'neoclassical' interpretation. Indeed, for Mirowski, the concept of 'neoclassicism' is coextensive with the application to economics of a mathematical formalization borrowed from thermodynamics where the basic entities are interpreted as fields and not as substances (see Mirowski, 1989, ch. 6).

In any case, during the last hundred years certain famous economists have found it worth while to design sophisticated hydraulic apparatuses and they have done so with the utmost care and attention. It is time now to underline a few of the essential characteristics of such apparatuses. We have seen that they were totally artificial devices designed to simulate an economic mechanism. This explains why they often included components like pointers on graduated scales, Cartesian graphs, charts drawn by pencils fixed to moving arms, etc. These components, which I shall describe as 'epiphenomenal', are totally inessential to the actual working of the mechanism. Their only function is to translate the hydraulic mechanism into the appropriate economic language.

By contrast with Hume's, Turgot's or Canard's metaphors, these carefully designed apparatuses can be considered as genuine *theoretical models*. Designed during a period characterized by mathematical modelling in economic theory, these hydraulic apparatuses are models of an alternative type. We have seen that Fisher goes so far as to consider them instruments of theoretical discovery, but it is clear that they suffer from severe limitations when competing with mathematical models on this ground. It is perhaps more appropriate to point out with Edgeworth (1895, p. 444) that these two types of model are complementary in the way that a magnifying glass and a microscope are complementary. If a mathematical model can help to dissect an economic mechanism, to analyse the way it works under any theoretical circumstances and to make clear, at least in principle, its less visible implications, an hydraulic model can help to show how the system works as a whole.

Such seems to be Edgeworth's view, but such a comparison could be misleading if it were taken too literally. Microscopes and magnifying glasses are not models, they are instruments used to increase the power of our senses. It is clear that the models of cells displayed in museums are different from the microscopes instrumental to the research through which they were designed. But since mathematical or hydraulic models of economic phenomena *are* models, it might be interesting to raise the question of how these two types of model compare with one another. Besides their superior analytic power, is there any reason to consider mathematical models as more acceptable than hydraulic models? Are they less metaphorical than hydraulic models? At first glance this may seem to be so for, unlike hydraulics, mathematics is a universal language. It may be tempting to conclude that, unlike the construction of hydraulic models in economics, the construction of mathematical models in economics does not involve a *comparison* of economics with another domain. When the economist constructs a mathematical model he or she merely uses mathematical language to *describe* an economic phenomenon.

But is a mathematical model really descriptive? The description of an atom as a miniature solar system would be considered to be completely metaphorical. But why should the description of an atom as a structure whose characters are defined by some mathematical model, let's say by the Rutherford model, be considered less metaphorical? It is true that an atom is far from actually being a solar system, but does Rutherford's model describe *exactly* what an atom is? Given the existence of different competing theoretical models, most philosophers of science would not accept such a characterization. More radically, Nancy Cartwright does not hesitate to conclude that the theoretical laws of physics – those on which explanatory models are based – are simply false.[3] If the criteria for not being a simple metaphor is the exactness of the description provided by the candidate, it seems that the models of physics can still be considered as metaphorical.

In any case I am concerned with models in economics, not with models in physics. It is true that an actual market is far from being a Fisher's apparatus, but does a general equilibrium model describe it *exactly*? It would be very difficult to uphold the claim that such a model is an exact description of actual markets, so on what basis could one maintain that it is less metaphorical than Fisher's apparatus? Neither can be considered an accurate description of an actual market, but both help us to understand the mechanism which is responsible for the attention given to the market by economists. To see clearly that there is no real rupture of continuity between these two types of model when it comes to their metaphorical character, let's consider the case of geometrical models, which are a particular kind of mathematical model. It is difficult to see why the 'well-behaved' indifference curves, the 'frontiers' and the 'paths' of geometrical models should be considered as pure descriptions of economic phenomena in a sense which is not applicable to Canard's channels or to Boulding's moving rod. And if geometrical models are metaphorical, it will be difficult to argue that the algebraic relations used to describe economic phenomena have a different status. Obviously, mathematical language can be used to *measure* a phenomenon; but to maintain, for example, that, in a particular market, the price of good A is twice the price of good B – a measurement of A's price which may be descriptively accurate – is very different from implicitly *comparing* the process by which economic prices are fixed with the solution of a system of equations.

There is no doubt that an adequate response to this question would require a much more detailed discussion than it is possible to provide here. Nevertheless, let us admit that both mathematical and hydraulic models are metaphorical, and let us try to clarify what it is that makes mathematical models so much more popular with economists. As already stated, the superior analytic power of these models is largely responsible for economists' preference for them, but this is not the whole story. After all, even though they are not much more analytically powerful than hydraulic models, geometrical models have not been discredited by economists to the same extent. Clearly there are other reasons which explain why economists do not accord the same status to hydraulic as to mathematical models. I shall suggest two reasons for this, both of which have to do with the fact that hydraulic models are *less abstract* than mathematical models.

The first reason concerns the fact that hydraulic models involve a physical substance, a liquid, as their essential element. In contrast, mathematical entities are not substances and, while they are defined with the help of some invariants, they are not committed to respecting any principle of conservation. We have seen that this is responsible for the introduction in Fisher's hydraulic apparatus of cumbersome gadgets like compartmentalized cisterns with flexible leather walls. It also explains why, after Fisher's heroic attempt, hydraulic models have been restricted to areas like orthodox Keynesian macroeconomics where, as noted by Mirowski, the theory does not clash with a substance theory of value in the way that neoclassical microeconomics does. The need for metaphors less associated with physical substances was clearly emphasized by Frank Knight when he suggested that economists refer to the 'flow of light' rather than to the 'flow of water',[4] in order to describe what consumers buy, because consumers tend more and more to purchase 'services' which cannot be embottled and which are not destroyed by consumption. In any case, according to the present view, mathematical models are no less metaphorical than hydraulic models; it is just that mathematical metaphors refer to entities which are uninterpreted and more abstract, which is why these entities can be freely interpreted either as substances or otherwise, according to the sensibility of the economist and to the constraints of the theory or of the actual world.

A second source of economists' uneasiness with hydraulic metaphors has to do with their mechanistic and deterministic character. Given the subjective basis of modern microeconomics, the idea that economic phenomena have the same regularity as hydraulic phenomena seems unacceptable. No one would deny the existence of social mechanisms; but such mechanisms are usually interpreted as 'unintended results' of a large number of independent human actions and not as deterministic mechanisms like those involved in hydraulic models. The characteristics of what I have called the epiphenomenal components of hydraulic apparatuses suggest that any specifically economic interpretation of the mechanism involved leaves only a very superficial role for this subjective basis. However, this does not mean that mathematical models are less mechanistic than hydraulic models. If Mirowski is right when he says that the economist just reinterprets a formalization which was devised for the analysis of physical phenomenon, then the epiphenomenal character of an economic interpretation of a hydraulic machine should not appear very peculiar to economists. If the shape of Fisher's cisterns is such that they can be added up to obtain the *equivalent* of a demand curve, as Fisher himself pointed out (1925, p. 30), then why should such a demand curve be considered a more appropriate metaphor than a flexible cistern for characterizing the changing tastes of consumers? Again, the difference in the degree of abstraction of these two metaphors seems crucial in explaining the preference of economists for mathematical models. Geometrical curves and algebraic functions (to an even greater extent) are capable of unlimited variation. By contrast, it is difficult to imagine a cistern whose shape would be variable enough to mirror the flexibility of consumers' tastes. So it seems possible to argue that an indefinitely adjustable demand function (or even a moving demand curve) genuinely *describes* the subtly changing taste of a consumer, while an elastic cistern would not be a simple description, but instead a bold and somewhat ridiculous metaphor. But if, for the sake of methodological analysis, we were to suppose that cisterns were able to transform themselves just as easily as algebraic functions (or geometrical curves) in order to accommodate a spontaneous change in taste, then *in what sense* could we say that they were less descriptive and more metaphorical than these algebraic functions and geometrical curves? The only sensible answer to this question seems to be that, in principle at least, a mathematical function could empirically measure any possible change in the taste of a consumer, as unpredictable as this change may be, whereas such a measure could not be provided even by extensible cisterns, not to mention actual cisterns. But such a flexible empirical function has nothing to do with the functions that are used in explanatory models. Mathematical explanatory models function in a way which is just as predeterminate and removed from genuine description as hydraulic explanatory models, otherwise it would be difficult to see how they could be considered explanatory. In a Walrasian system the demand functions are equations whose solution is just as strictly determined as the level of water would be in a well designed hydraulic machine. So, if mathematical models appear to be more realistic, it is largely because moving curves or, better still, algebraic functions are tools which are *potentially* more descriptive of human tastes than extensible cisterns. But as far as the deterministic character of an explanatory model is concerned, the final result is the same in both types of model.

Thanks to their relative simplicity, hydraulic metaphors may help us to understand the role of metaphors in economics and possibly in science in general. And there is no reason to be disturbed by the fact that metaphors are pervasive in science. They are not a licence to logical anarchy. To recognize their importance is not to vindicate McCloskey's thesis about rhetoric. The assertion that all theories are to some extent metaphorical does not entail that all metaphors are of equal value for scientific purposes. Some metaphors provide better explanations or predictions than others, and some are more successful than others when the descriptive relevance of their components is put to the test. The rhetorical 'school' in economics was right to remind us of the importance of metaphors, but metaphors are important merely because they are an inevitable part of any language. There is surely nothing new in saying that mathematical language is metaphorical: Plato and Aristotle used the example of a *line* in a metaphorical way. Just as for these philosophers, the crucial point is to distinguish what a metaphorical language says about the object analysed from what is just a consequence of the metaphorical character of this language. The advantage of straightforward metaphors like hydraulic metaphors is that this distinction is relatively easy to make. When a more abstract and mathematical language is used metaphorically the distinction becomes dangerously obscure. Whatever other results it might achieve, a short critical review of hydraulic metaphors in economics would be justified if it helped to make clear the danger of forgetting the very existence of such a crucial but easily forgotten distinction.

Notes

1. The author is grateful to SSHRCC for financial assistance and to Daniel Desjardins, E. Forget, B. Ingrao, B. Jurdant, G. Lafleur, S. T. Lowry, J. Magnan de Bornier, W. Milnes, P. Mirowski, R. Nadeau, M. Rosier, R. Weintraub and A. Zylberberg for suggestions and comments.
2. Turgot (1970, p. 178): 'deux liqueurs inégalement pesantes'.
3. Cartwright (1983); see Introduction and Essay 3.
4. Knight (1950, pp. 26–7). This passage was drawn to my attention by Robert Nadeau.

References

Boulding, K. E. (1966), *Economic Analysis*, Vol I: *Microeconomics* (1941), 4th edn, New York: Harper & Row.

Canard, N.-F. (1969), *Principes d'économie politique* (Buisson, Paris, 1801), Rome: Edizioni Bizarri.

Cantillon, R. (1952), *Essai sur la nature du commerce en général*, Paris: Institut National d'études démographiques.

Cartwright, N. (1983), *How the Laws of Physics Lie*, Oxford: Clarendon Press; New York: Oxford University Press.

Coddington, A. (1976), 'Keynesian Economics: the Search for First Principles', *Journal of Economic Literature*, **14** (4), p. 1258–73.

Edgeworth, F. Y. (1895), 'Thoughts on Monetary Reform', *Economic Journal*, **5**, pp. 434–51.

Fisher, I. (1925), *Mathematical Investigations in the Theory of Value and Prices* (1892), New Haven, CT: Yale University Press.

Fisher, I. (1894), 'The Mechanics of Bimetallism', *Economic Journal*, **4**, pp. 527–37.

Hume, D. (1970), 'Of the Balance of Trade', in D. Hume, *Writings on Economics*, ed. Eugene Rotwein, Madison: University of Wisconsin Press.

Knight, F. H. (1950), 'Introduction' to C. Menger, *Principles of Economics*, Glencoe, IL: The Free Press.

Mirowski, P. (1989), 'More Heat than Light', New York: Cambridge University Press.

Phillips, A. W. (1950), 'Mechanical Models in Economic Dynamics', *Economica*, **17**, pp. 283–305.

Turgot, A. R. J. (1970) 'Réflexions sur la formation et la distribution des richesses' (1766), in A. R. J. Turgot, *Écrits économiques*, Paris: Calmann-Lévy.

4 The empiricism of Simon Kuznets
Vibha Kapuria-Foreman

This chapter examines Simon Kuznets's approach to economic analysis. Much of the current work in national income accounting, the economics of growth and development and income distribution finds its origins in the empirical and theoretical contributions of Simon Kuznets. His methodological approach and philosophical vision of the purposes of economic inquiry were the sources of these contributions but these roots have not been investigated.

This chapter examines this dichotomy. It demonstrates that Kuznets employed an empirical method derived from his perception of the proper roles of economic investigation and the goals of productive activity. These perceptions determined the subjects to be investigated, the manner in which such examinations would proceed and even the structure of the categories devised to aid his inquiries.

An initial discussion of Kuznets's approach to economic data and his understanding of the goals of quantitative research is followed by a description of the manner in which this view caused a severe disagreement between Kuznets and the creators of the official US national income accounts. The origins of Kuznets's empirical approach and his view of the proper role of economic theory and modelling during economic investigations are then explored in order to highlight his novel approach to national income accounting. I conclude with a discussion of how Kuznets's understanding of the role of economic inquiry can explain several recent attempts at reformulation of the national income accounts.

Kuznets's research interests progressed from business cycles to national income to economic growth. His initial research dealt with the money wages of factory workers in Kharkov in the USSR. His earliest efforts in the United States related directly to the research interests of his teacher and mentor, Wesley Clair Mitchell. Thus, Kuznets's doctoral dissertation investigated cyclical fluctuations in retail and wholesale trade.

These efforts and all succeeding inquiries were characterized by the same approach – the empirical analysis of economic phenomena. But as one might expect from an innovative pioneer influenced by Mitchell's tutelage, Kuznets's empiricism involved a subtle and sophisticated awareness of the nature of data. He wrote often of the subjectivity of the process of data collection and analysis – the classification of items, the choice of units, the level of aggregation; Kuznets viewed each as involving choices that could only be made in light of the known goals of the inquiry.

Kuznets envisioned three roles for quantitative economic research: interpretive, generalizing and predictive. He asserted that each of these goals was to be pursued under known basic assumptions about the goals of economic life and the economic relationships embodied in existing theory. This meant quantitative research must be conducted in accord with accepted economic theory and the institutional realities within which economic events occurred. Who is classified as a producer for national accounts purposes depends upon the economic definition of production. Even then, however, categories employed in economic research are necessarily institutional categories and therefore subject to change. Thus, the treatment of unpaid household efforts as non-market productive activities to be excluded from national income accounts flowed from institutional and practical rather than theoretical considerations. Similarly, what was to be included or excluded as productive activity was determined by how society views such activity. For example, drug dealing is illegal and is therefore not a productive activity. Kuznets viewed such categories as determined by culture and society and varying across both time and space.

To state that Kuznets used theoretical constructs while assembling and organizing his data is to belabour the obvious. All economic research involves a complex interplay of deductive and inductive reasoning. Theoretical and empirical elements are necessary for preliminary classification and appraisal, the formulation of hypotheses and the production of predictions. 'There is no such thing in economic research as a simple fact' (Kuznets, 1972, p. 25). According to Kuznets, no data are independent of basic assumptions and extant hypotheses. Each step in economic research must be undertaken with respect to either explicit or implicit assumptions about the goals of economic activity and the institutions that define these goals. Examples of the institutional fluidity of judgements made during the conduct of quantitative economic research have already been provided. Since the categorization of human activities must be determined on the basis of social and institutional constructs, that classification will necessarily vary across time and space. While such delicacy is laudable in an empiricist it often delays the national accountant. So the same methodology that made Kuznets's work meticulous and admirable when applied to economic growth led to a serious dispute when employed in constructing the national income accounts.

Kuznets's insistence on the necessity of employing explicit or implicit assumptions about the goals of economic activity was directly responsible for his repudiation of the official US national income accounts in 1947.

Kuznets had joined the National Income Division of the National Bureau of Economic Research in 1931. Over the succeeding decade he wrote a series of articles and several books detailing the national income and national product of the US. He defined national income as the net contribution of the productive resources of an economy flowing to ultimate consumers, capital stock and the balance of international payments.

National income excludes the net value of certain goods and services whose production is classified as outside the field of economic activity. Primary among the items excluded are those produced and consumed within the family. Kuznets argued repeatedly that all national income estimates are appraisals because they are based on some widely accepted criterion of social productivity. In the absence of such a concept, national income would be a meaningless total from which there would be no justification for excluding gifts, transfers and income from theft and robbery. Therefore, some notion of a socially accepted definition of productive activity must be antecedent to any definition of national income and must guide all subsequent choices regarding the treatment and valuation of particular entries. Because of this conditional character, Kuznets was insistent upon the consistent and explicit treatment of all questions of scope and presented several variants of national income estimates to accord with alternative definitions.

Kuznets defined economic goods and services as those that are a source of satisfaction, relatively scarce, disposable (appearing on markets of a certain kind) and legal. National income was derived as the sum of goods and services exchanged on all markets for money or for barter. Also included were products retained by producers for their own consumption as well as the services of owner-occupied houses. This was seen by him as the best mechanism for appraising the final net product of the business and public sectors of an economy (Kuznets, 1941, pp. 3–50).

In an essay in the *Review of Economics and Statistics* published in August 1948, Kuznets detailed his criticisms of the national income accounts originally presented in July 1947 (Gilbert *et al.*, 1947). They were based on his perception of the changing institutional nature of a money economy over time and across space. In this and subsequent articles he argued that the accounts dealt with questions regarding scope, netness and valuation in a manner that was subject to censure on myriad grounds. He maintained that the accounts did considerable injustice to our concept of national income as an estimate of the net contribution of an economy to the welfare of its citizens and were thus a deviation from the historically established concept of national income.

In this matter Kuznets was less than precise. Although the version of the accounts adopted in 1947 abandoned any pretence of employing the accounts to measure economic welfare, this departure was in the spirit of the guidelines laid down by Alfred Marshall and A. C. Pigou.[1] What upset Kuznets was the change in direction from the pioneering work of Spahr and King;[2] they had been interested in the impact of economic growth on the welfare of the working classes.

Kuznets was even more disturbed by the absence of any consensus regarding the end result of economic activity. If the purpose of economic activity is production then decisions regarding the treatment of housewives' services, the government sector and illegal activities would differ from the decisions made if the accepted end purpose of economic activity is consumption.

Kuznets maintained that the decisions on inclusion or exclusion had been made solely on the basis of expediency. Such solutions might have been appropriate if the institutional character of the economy remained frozen but he felt that such solutions distort our view of the economy since these items are themselves subject to change. Thus the exclusion of the services of housewives constitutes a large and variable omission from national income. Similarly, the inclusion of all costs of business activity and all government services as part of the final product introduces an element of double counting – an element that makes a mockery of 'national income' as that term has been employed by past investigators and also renders impossible attempts at comparison over time.

Kuznets's definition of national income differed from that employed by the Department of Commerce mainly with regard to the treatment of government. Kuznets had chosen to evaluate the contribution of the public sector in terms of the payments made for its services. This method was adopted in order to ensure consistency with the valuation of output of the private sector and because of its sensitivity to short-term fluctuations. Further, in deriving the net value of production, the value of all services 'sold' by government to business was deducted as being intermediate in nature.

However, Kuznets's major objection to the Department of Commerce version of the accounts was a matter of approach. His definition of national income had been guided by the perception that the end result of economic activity is the fulfilment of the needs of ultimate consumers. National income was to be measured in a manner suggested by theoretical considerations and constrained by practical limitations. Choices were guided by three principles: the distinction between economic and other activities, the disparity between productive and non-productive endeavours and the accountant's perception of the social philosophy guiding society.

Although Kuznets was willing to assess society's basic assumptions about the goals of economic activity and use that assessment as the basis for his definition of national income, making such a judgement was most difficult for Gilbert *et al.* when creating the Department of Commerce series. They chose not to constrain their inquiry in this manner. Similarly, a determination of the economic relationships embodied in existing theories is a complex task. Kuznets never explicitly stated how he made choices regarding the relationships to be accepted and investigated.

One could argue that these differences arose from very different conceptions of the proper role of national income accounts. The official accounts were comprised of pragmatic choices undertaken in order to construct a series calculated consistently over a long period which would therefore allow straightforward comparisons. Kuznets envisioned the structure of the accounts as much more fluid and flexible, changing with the constant redrawing of the lines between economic and non-economic, market and non-market activities. He asserted that the official national income accounts were not consistent for two reasons. First, they were derived from an inconsistently applied definition of productive activity. Second, the application of an unchanging concept of income to a changing economy would necessarily yield results that were not directly comparable.

Kuznets's empirical bent derived from his perception of the nature and purpose of economic inquiry. His inclination toward empiricism as well as his particular practice of quantitative inquiry[3] reflect his philosophical understanding of its role in research. Although he repeatedly affirmed the need for theory in conducting empirical research, he was even more vocal regarding his distrust of theory. This misgiving arose from unsuccessful attempts to employ theoretical constructs to guide his empiricism.

Whereas one can operate efficiently with a representative unit in deductive theory, this useful theoretical device leads only to confusion when employed in empirical research. For example, the representative unit in agriculture differs substantially in size and responsiveness from the representative unit in industry and trade; the impact of changes in technology, resource availability and institutions will also differ. Quantitative economic research is required to determine if behavioural assumptions change and, if so, to determine the size and direction of these changes (Kuznets, 1972, p. 6). Thus, although quantitative research could certainly aid further theoretical work the relationship was clearly not reciprocal.

Robert Fogel (1987, pp. 28–9) argues that Kuznets preferred economic theory in its descriptive and generalizing function. Fogel distinguishes between theories explaining observable economic behaviour in the following manner: on one hand are theories based on simple assumptions and weak functional relationships; on the other are demonstrations that prior generalizations about economic events could be derived from a certain set of *a priori* assumptions. Thus, Fogel distinguishes between *a priori* assumptions as a first step in analysis and as shorthand to describe empirically observed behaviour. He argues that Kuznets was largely uninterested in the former while finding the latter a fruitful source of ideas for empirical research.

Kuznets made these misgivings clearer while discussing trends and problems in quantitative economic research. He argued that simplifying assumptions could lead to the removal of a large number of important factors from the list of endogenous variables. Later those variables which are now accepted as exogenously determined may disappear entirely from the investigator's consideration (Kuznets, 1972, p. 63).

Yet clearly Kuznets was a theorist. His empirical research would have been much less valuable had he restricted himself to reporting data without searching for explanations of the relationships discovered. There are major theoretical contributions in his analyses, among others, of population changes and economic growth,[4] productivity changes and the pace and pattern of growth, and the impact of economic growth on income distribution.

A partial explanation of Kuznets's dual vision of economic theory may be derived from an examination of the kinds of theory he derided and the evolution of his opinions. Most of his criticism of theory related to the subjects he investigated. He was critical of business cycle theories in the 1930s because of their reliance on equilibrium economics (Kuznets, 1930). Since Kuznets analysed the economy as dynamic, kinetic and changeable, he found the concept of equilibrium too rigidly static and predetermined (non-anarchic) to describe the processes he observed.

Similarly, general theories of economic growth tended to omit crucial factors and thus yielded misleading conclusions. Here his criticism focused on the sterility of such theories. He asserted that theoretical inquiry as well as empirical analysis must be conducted with due consideration of their eventual role in determining policy. However, he argued in favour of a continuing search for a general theory of economic growth while admitting that the data necessary for its formulation would probably never be assembled in his lifetime.

By the 1960s Kuznets tended to be much less critical of economic theory. He clearly found some theory useful as a source of relationships to be investigated and as a mechanism for categorizing data and classifying activities. He considered most growth theories too narrowly constructed and lacking in historical and institutional detail to provide a full understanding of the process of economic growth but nevertheless thought the search worth while. Not only did Kuznets's view of theory become less critical but he also began to define and describe it less narrowly. From an early perception of theory as formal conclusions drawn from *a priori* assumptions, Kuznets began to employ a wider definition that encompassed an understanding of economic relationships and was necessary and useful for each step in research.

Kuznets was hesitant to employ mathematical and econometric models. This reluctance arose not from any distrust of theory *per se* but from an awareness of its historical relativity (Easterlin, 1987, p. 71); data are shorn of their validity when separated from a specific temporal and institutional reality. In like manner, Kuznets preferred numerical examples over mathematical models. The numerical examples were more easily understood and less likely to be stretched beyond their limits (Fogel, 1987, pp. 25–6). Yet Kuznets did employ mathematical models to illustrate a theoretical argument. When discussing the impact of high rates of population growth on per capita income, he chose to illustrate the discussion of alternative trends and prospects by a series of models. Each version assumed different values for the population growth rate, incremental capital–output ratio, government consumption, age structure of the population, etc., to illustrate his earlier theoretical conjectures and to demonstrate the deficiencies in the crude analytical relationships embodied in the mathematical model.

Some understanding of the evolution of Kuznets's methodology may be obtained from a comparison of his approach with that of Wesley Clair Mitchell. Kuznets, like Mitchell, chose the empirical approach because of his percepetion that the questions he posed were more amenable to statistical analysis. Both scholars eschewed the theoretical approach and expressed distrust of deductive theory and both argued that neoclassical theory, steeped as it is in equilibrium analysis, was inadequate for their purposes. Instead, Mitchell and Kuznets focused on the role of institutions in enhancing and limiting the processes they were studying. Finally, each emphasized the relevance of economic investigation to policy-making. Kuznets in particular concentrated on the need to shape institutions to facilitate the advancement of society's objectives.

Kuznets was particularly interested in the welfare implications of the changes he was analysing. His early interest in national income related to the distribution of the burdens and benefits of change. Similarly, in his discussions of modern economic growth the key question relates to the economy's success at supplying a growing volume (per capita) of goods and services to its population.

This perception of the goal of economic inquiry as a guide to enlightened policy-making illuminates the subjects he investigated and the approach he adopted. To Kuznets, economic activity has validity if it provides goods and services to the current and future residents of a nation. The frequency, certainty, volume and distribution of these goods and services were thus the object of his lifetime study. Since these characteristics of the production process could not be determined by theoretical inquiry, the empirical approach was necessary.

However, Kuznets's interest was not limited to enumeration and evaluation. He was also profoundly interested in obtaining an understanding of the processes that produced these results. Such an understanding was essential if the processes of growth and distribution were to be guided in welfare-enhancing directions.

In his Nobel Memorial Lecture (Kuznets, 1971), Kuznets defined modern economic growth as a long-term rise in a country's capacity to supply an increasing volume and variety of economic goods to its population. He focused on advancing technology as well as institutional and ideological adjustment to technological change as the key variables encouraging or inhibiting growth. Kuznets emphasized the need to investigate the sources of inflexibility in social and political institutions and their role in inhibiting the adoption, adaptation and spread of modern technology. He believed the absence of modern economic growth in many less developed countries flowed not from the unavailability of modern technology but from the slowness of its absorption (which was ultimately a problem with the institutional structure). He therefore perceived that this area of research would be the most productive for the guidance of policies to facilitate modern economic growth and improvements in welfare.

Since 1947 there have been numerous attempts to recast the national income and product accounts to solve some of the conceptual problems associated with the definition of production, the distinction between final and intermediate activities, the ultimate uses of final output and difficulties of valuation. In 'Extended Accounts for National Income and Product', Robert Eisner (1988) describes several such attempts, including his own, and outlines some of the results derived from recent re-evaluations of national income and output.

What is particularly notable about these attempts at reformulation are the ways in which they flow from Kuznets's original criticisms of the official national income and product accounts. Most extended accounts attempt a more consistent treatment of production, identify a portion of government activity as intermediate in nature and broaden the concept of capital formation to include investment in intangibles. From a comparison of these revisions, Eisner draws the following conclusions about the nature of the US economy. First, net investment appears as a much larger share of national income than in the Bureau of Economic Analysis measures. Second, labour's share of income is greatly expanded in the extended accounts. Third, it is probable that the distribution of income becomes very different when non-market activity is accounted for since the poor and aged appear to engage in much less market production than do the rich and/or the young. Finally, the movement of certain activities between the market and non-market spheres of the economy appears to vary with the business cycle.

The most interesting results relate to the quintessential Kuznetsian questions: current and future growth; the contribution of the economy to consumption and capital formation; labour's share of national income; the changing burdens of economic growth and the distribution of income.

Recent attempts at reformulation embody the spirit of Spahr, King and Kuznets. Even more, we appear to have travelled full circle to rediscover the importance of the questions asked in shaping the collection and classification of data. The questions that motivated Kuznets in the 1930s did not inspire Gilbert *et al.* Some of those questions had been answered while others had become irrelevant as some goals were achieved and others abandoned. The structure of the national accounts had to change to answer the new questions being posed because of the changing needs of policy-makers and of society.

The overlap between the recent reformulations of the national income accounts and the definition and structure formulated by Kuznets arises from attempts to address a common set of concerns. Questions about the effectiveness of a nation's productive apparatus at providing for the needs of its population necessarily require collecting certain kinds of data and arranging them in specific ways. The scheme of arranging data designed by Kuznets may be the best way of defining national income and formulating national accounts if an answer is sought to the question described. This approach is superior because all Kuznets's choices regarding definition, inclusion and valuation were guided by a desire to determine the effectiveness of an economy at satisfying the needs of current and future consumers.

Notes

1. In *The Economics of Welfare* (Pigou, 1932, p. 34) Pigou cites Marshall in support of identifying national income with goods and services that are purchased in markets plus the imputed rent on owner-occupied houses as well as its valuation at the point of production.
2. Charles B. Spahr (1896). Spahr argued that the distribution of wealth and income had become more unequal as a result of industrialization. Willford Isbell King (1930). This study focused on the point of view of the individual income recipient (p. 43) in order to discover changes in the income share of labour.
3. Each of Kuznets's monographs is a lesson in economic research. Whether discussing national income in the *Encyclopedia of the Social Sciences* (1933), economic growth in 'Toward a Theory of Economic Growth' (1955) or income distribution in 'Demographic Aspects of the Size Distribution of Income' (1976), he explained what he intended to investigate and why, defined his concepts and described the practical problems associated with each analytical definition. After warning of the difficulties that arise due to the contrast between the absolute categories constructed in economic analysis and the absence of such pure forms in reality, Kuznets presented his results. These results, he admitted,

were tentative because he had been sailing uncharted seas – the data available were not always of high quality and often had been collected by an investigator in pursuit of the solution to a different problem, they were just as often not comparable because of differences (especially between countries) in definition and classification, and they had gaps. Employing these results, he offered tentative hypotheses about correlations. But these hypotheses were comprehensive – each possible explanation was investigated.

4. For example, in *Modern Economic Growth* (Kuznets, 1966, pp. 34–85) Kuznets explored the reasons a high rate of population growth had become a burden on per capita income growth in recent times although it had been a source of increased growth in the past.

References

Easterlin, Richard (1987), 'Kuznets, Simon', in John Eatwell (ed.), *The New Palgrave: A Dictionary of Economics*, Vol. III, New York: Stockton Press.

Eisner, Robert (1988), 'Extended Accounts for National Income and Product', *Journal of Economic Literature*, **26** (4), December, pp. 1611–84.

Fogel, Robert (1987), *Some Notes on the Scientific Method of Simon Kuznets*, New York: National Bureau of Economic Research, no. 2461.

Gilbert, Milton, *et al.* (1947), 'National Income and Product Statistics of the United States 1929–46', *Survey of Current Business* (Supplement), **27** (7), July.

King, Willford Isbell (1930), *The National Income and Its Purchasing Power*, New York: National Bureau of Economic Research.

Kuznets, Simon (1930), 'Equilibrium Economics and Business Cycle Theory', *Quarterly Journal of Economics*, **44**, May, pp. 381–415.

Kuznets, Simon (1933), 'National Income', *Encyclopedia of the Social Sciences*, New York: Macmillan, pp. 205–24.

Kuznets, Simon (1941), *National Income and Its Composition, 1919–38*, New York: National Bureau of Economic Research.

Kuznets, Simon (1948), 'Discussion of the New Department of Commerce Income Series', *Review of Economics and Statistics*, **30** (2), August, pp. 151–79.

Kuznets, Simon (1955), 'Toward a Theory of Economic Growth', in Robert Lekachman (ed.), *National Policy for Economic Welfare at Home and Abroad*, New York: Doubleday, pp. 12–85.

Kuznets, Simon (1966), *Modern Economic Growth*, New Haven, CT: Yale University Press.

Kuznets, Simon (1971), 'Modern Economic Growth: Findings and Reflections', *Nobel Lectures, Including Presentation Speeches and Laureate's Biographies*, Amsterdam, New York: Elsevier.

Kuznets, Simon (1972), *Quantitative Economic Research: Trends and Problems*, New York: National Bureau of Economic Research.

Kuznets, Simon (1976), 'Demographic Aspects of the Size Distribution of Income', *Economic Development and Cultural Change*, **25**, pp. 1–94.

Pigou, Arthur C. (1932), *The Economics of Welfare*, London: Macmillan.

Spahr, Charles B. (1896), *The Present Distribution of Wealth in the United States*, New York: Thomas Y. Crowell.

5 Jeremy Bentham between liberalism and authoritarianism: the French mirror

Annie L. Cot[1]

History of economic thought traditionally regards Jeremy Bentham as a *Janus bifrons*: on the one side, Adam Smith's faithful disciple, inventor of the *felicific calculus*, the calculus of pleasures and pains on which two centuries of political economy rest; on the other, the passionate social reformer who devoted twenty years of his life to the Panopticon, which he viewed as the best means to achieve 'the greatest happiness of the greatest number' principle. An examination of Bentham's activities and writings during the years of the French Revolution, however, compels us to merge these opposing profiles. Such an undertaking also calls into question the idea, inherited from the end of the nineteenth century, that the utilitarian doctrine originated in complete consistency with the economic and political principles attached to Enlightenment liberalism.

In that sense, Bentham's dissensions with Smith in the early 1790s established the foundations of the two main theoretical lines that would define social thought during the first half of the nineteenth century. The first line, which inherited the legacy of the modern natural law school, is centred around the rational individual, designed as an autonomous social entity, and, therefore, as an atomistic unit of decision in society. The nature of the bonds between these autonomous individuals is revealed in Smith's work: sympathy on the ground of 'moral sentiments' and harmonization of private interests through the invisible hand on the market. The second line is defined by the utilitarian tradition. Although based in the same way on individual autonomy, it incorporates neither the idea of contract, nor the legacy of natural law. Consequently, the horizontal bond of the market is replaced by a double structure: the individual level, defined as totally autonomous through the *felicific calculus*; and the global level, where government intervention is supposed to produce harmony between potentially conflicting private interests – the 'greatest happiness of the greatest number' principle.

The parallel between the two constructions points out the major differences between the two meanings of the liberal idea in the nineteenth century. The first one is based on a narrow link between economic and political liberalism; the second on a separation between economic liberalism on the one hand, legislative and political centralization on the other.

These two traditions, with their common roots in the Enlightenment, remained entangled until the coming of the French Revolution, when three major cross-currents found expression: the opposition between the natural law tradition and the positive law tradition; the opposition between private interest and public duty as the logical unit of both morals and politics; and, as a consequence of the latter, the opposition between the market and the state as the means to produce harmony between private interests, that is between the invisible hand and the visible hand, or, to use Bentham's words, between state 'agendas' and 'non-agendas'.

France became Bentham's central concern quite early, by the fall of 1788.[2] As he later wrote, 'France is the country, above all others, in which any new idea – provided it be a useful one – is most readily forgiven. France, towards which every eye is turned, and from which models are exported for the various branches of administration . . .'.[3] In November 1788 he responded to a question published in *The Times* about the means of organizing the Etats Généraux and began to write an essay on *Representation*.[4] 'What would France . . . do, if I were to desert [it]?' was Bentham's emphatic answer in March 1789 to an invitation from Lord Lansdowne to visit Lisbon. 'You are to know', we can read in the same letter addressed to Lansdowne's son,

> that, for these five or six months past, my head and my heart have been altogether in France; our own affairs I think no more of them than of those of the *Georgium Sidus*. I am working as hard as possible on a treatise on the conduct and discipline of political assemblies, under the short title of *Political Tactics*; dissecting the practice of our two Houses, for the instruction of their newly created brethren; having taken out a license from your father for cutting and hacking without mercy. I am labouring might and main to get out some of the most essential parts at least time enough for their meeting.[5]

And in a letter to Mirabeau: 'I think only of France, I think only for France.'[6]

France already knew Bentham as an economist. Shortly after its English publication, his *Defence of Usury* was translated into French – with two different versions, *Apologie de l'usure* and *Lettres sur la liberté du taux de l'intérêt et de l'argent*[7] – and passionately discussed in the first revolutionary clubs. His interest in the Revolution lasted until 1796. Together with Samuel de Romilly, and with the help of Mirabeau (whose secretary was then Dumont of Geneva, Bentham's French editor) he set himself up as an adviser to the Constituent Assembly and corresponded with Morellet, Mirabeau and La Rochefoucauld – all longstanding friends of Lord Lansdowne.[8] His commentaries, interventions, advice and projects concerned judicial organization, the foundations of parliamentary procedure, the confiscation of Catholic properties and the restoration of Protestant goods, the emancipation of the colonies, and the abolition of law taxes. He also considered different means to help the Constituent Assembly financially: a tax reform on escheat (inheritances to be returned to the state); a proposal of annuity-note paper; and a criticism of Sieyès' position on the right to assistance for the poor.

All these propositions are crucial to an understanding of Bentham's theoretical project. But three among them are worth examining more carefully: not so much for the influence they could have had on French affairs, but for what they reveal of the essential opposition in Bentham's social thought between radical economic liberalism and the claim for the necessity of state control over society.

In this regard, we shall examine first Bentham's advocacy of emancipation for the French colonies, then his criticism of the French *Déclaration des Droits de l'Homme et du Citoyen* and finally his Panopticon project, sent to the Constituent Assembly in 1791.

1. 'Trade is the child of capital'

'Emancipate your colonies!' is one of the great watchwords Bentham offers French Revolutionaries.[9] In the theoretical tradition of his *Defence of Usury*, Bentham advocated the emancipation of all colonies on the basis of what appears to be an economic liberalism much more radical than that of Adam Smith in *The Wealth of Nations* – more radical and, most of all, based upon different principles.

Smith linked colonial trade with the basic framework defined at the beginning of *The Wealth of Nations*. In this logical order, it is not the division of labour that pre-exists market trade; on the contrary, the division of labour is the logical consequence of a psychological trait of human nature: 'the propensity to truck, barter, and exchange one thing for another' (Smith, 1976, Vol. I, Book 1, ch. 2, p. 25). Thus it is the market that gives occasion to the division of labour, and, therefore, to the wealth of the nation.

From this logical sequence Smith deduces the central role of the market in the constitution of the social bond and, consequently, the part played by the invisible hand – not only in the market itself, through the gravitation process of market prices around natural prices, but in the society taken as a whole.

This same logical sequence leads Smith – in Chapter 7 of the fourth book of *The Wealth of Nations* – to adopt a double attitude towards the question of colonial trade.

On the one hand, Smith rejects the monopolistic characteristics in colonial trade. These, in his opinion, have three major defects: first, to oppose, through protective duties and restrictions on trade, the doctrine of absolute advantage which he advocates for international trade; secondly to draw capital from all other trades to be employed in that of the colonies; and, thirdly, to raise the rate of profit in some branches of the British foreign trade somewhat higher than it would have been had the general trade with British colonies been ruled by a principle of free trade between them and the rest of the world.[10]

But, on the other hand, Smith recognizes that the colonies of all European nations have undoubtedly provided an extensive market for surplus produce so as to raise its value, and have thereby encouraged their growth.[11]

> By opening a new and inexhaustible market to all the commodities of Europe, [the colonial trade] gave occasion to new divisions of labour and improvement of art, which, in the narrow circle of the ancient commerce, could never have taken place for want of a market to take off the greater part of their produce. The productive powers of labour were improved, and its produce increased in all the different countries of Europe, and together with it the real revenue and wealth of the inhabitants.[12]

According to the same logical order, in which the market determines the division of labour and, consequently, the wealth of nations, Smith states that, through this 'rent for surplus', colonization has widened the market, boosted the industry of all countries, and therefore enriched humanity as a whole. So the existence of colonies is also a factor of growth for the global wealth of Great Britain.

Hence the conclusion:

> We must carefully distinguish between the effects of the colony trade and those of the monopoly of that trade. The former are always and necessarily beneficial; the latter always and necessarily hurtful. But the former are so beneficial that the colony trade, though subject to a monopoly, and notwithstanding the hurtful effects of that monopoly, is still upon the whole beneficial, and greatly beneficial; though a good deal less than it otherwise would be . . . . The natural good effects of the colony trade, however, more than counterbalance to Great Britain the bad effects of the monopoly, so that, monopoly and all together, that trade, even as it is carried on at present, is not only advantageous, but greatly advantageous. The new market and the new employment which are opened by the colony trade, are of much greater extent than the proportion of the old market and of the old employment which is lost by the monopoly . . . . If the colony trade, however, even as it is carried on at present, is advantageous to Great Britain, it is not by the means of the monopoly, but in spite of the monopoly. (Smith, 1976, Vol. II, Book 4, ch. 7, pp. 607–9)

Smith's solution – or 'only expedient' – to the problem of monopoly in colonial trade is therefore different from Turgot's dictum that colonies, like apples, cling to the tree until they are ripe and naturally fall afterwards.[13] Rather, the answer lies in 'some moderate and gradual relaxation of the laws which give to Great Britain the exclusive trade to the colonies, till it is rendered in a great measure free.'[14] Both of Smith's arguments – in favour of colonial trade and against its monopoly characteristics – rest on the same central idea: logically the market trade and hence the size of the market precede the division of labour and the accumulation of wealth.

Bentham's position on colonies and colonial trade is not only more radical than Smith's; it reveals a totally different theoretical base. By the late 1780s Bentham viewed political economy as a branch of the science of legislation,[15] sharing with the other branches the definition of a general aim of society – collective utility – and its 'subordinate ends': subsistence, abundance, security and equality.[16] Within this framework, his call to emancipate colonies combines his concern for a 'universal and perpetual peace' among nations[17] and his work on the principles of political economy. Although he carefully read Smith – and in his early writings called him 'a great master', the 'father of political economy', 'an authority', or 'a writer of consummate genius'[18] – he disagrees with Smith's basic theoretical sequence and clings to the principle that capital stock, and not the extent of the market, is first in the logical order that explains the nature and causes of the wealth of nations: in other words, that 'the quantity of trade a nation can carry on is limited: limited by the quantity of its capital.'[19]

The difference has drastic consequences.[20] The idea that industry and trade are limited by the amount of existing capital – that 'trade is the child of capital' (Bentham, 1793, p. 411) – is expressed in all Bentham's economic writings following the *Defence of Usury*. The demonstration is trivial:

> If I possess a capital of £10 000, and two species of trade, each yielding twenty per cent profit, but each requiring a capital of £10 000 for carrying them on, are proposed to me, it is clear that I may carry on the one or the other with this profit so long as I confine myself to one; but that, in carrying on the one, it is not in my power to carry on the other; and that if I seek to divide my capital between them both, I shall not make more than twenty per cent; but I may make less and even convert a profit into a loss. But if this proposition be true in the case of one individual, it is true for all the individuals in a whole nation. Production is therefore limited by capital.[21]

Conversely, the national stock of capital becomes the centre of Bentham's interest in economic matters, combined with the idea that this stock is linked to private interests.[22] Government intervention – the purpose of which is to maximize social utility – should therefore fulfil two tasks: protect the people and their property (the 'security goal') and limit the evil consequences of individual decisions and actions for social welfare. But government cannot raise the quantity of wealth which is produced.

This position is made clear in *Emancipate Your Colonies!*, a pamphlet sent to the members of the National Convention and privately circulated in 1793: 'Yes; it is *quantity of capital*, not *extent of the market*, that determines the quantity of trade.'[23] This basic principle backs up the whole construction: 'Open a new market, you do not, unless by accident, increase the sum of trade. Shut up an old market, you do not, unless by accident, or for the moment, diminish the sum of trade. In what case, then, is the sum of trade increased by a new market?' (Bentham, 1793, p. 411). In this logic, savings are identical with investments; and these investments, in turn, automatically create new outlets. The quantity of a nation's trade is then strictly determined in proportion to the quantity of capital that has been accumulated.

This first draft of what was to be known later as 'Say's Law' – here strictly interpreted by Bentham[24] – establishes the main argument that Bentham opposes to Smith:

> Give up your colonies, you give up so much of your trade as is carried on with your colonies. No, we do not give up any such thing: we do not give up anything whatsoever. Trade to colonies can not, any more than any where else, be carried on without capital: just so much of our capital as is employed in our trade with the colonies, just so much of it is not employed elsewhere: just so much is either kept or taken from other trades. (Bentham, 1790, p. 215)

The following consequences are clear: if the stock of capital owned by a nation is the limiting factor of trade and industry – and hence of wealth – capital invested in colonies represents a loss of capital for the nation. Therefore, colonial profitability is nothing but an illusion, and the economic utility of the colonies is equal to zero.[25]

By keeping its colonies, France would then commit three 'abominations' (Bentham, 1793, pp. 411–12). First, the principles of liberty, property and equality are violated when colonists are prevented from trading in the more advantageous international market. Secondly, the people of France would be obliged to absorb the cost of maintaining by force the restraints imposed upon the colonists. Thirdly 'abomination', and linked to the century (or more)-old controversy on luxury, the burden of the colonies would fall upon the rich and the poor, but the benefit would be enjoyed exclusively by the rich. Last but not least: Bentham agrees with Smith's argument on the monopolistic character of colonial trade, which, he advocates in *Emancipate Your Colonies*, can 'force down prices', but can never 'keep them down' (Bentham, 1793, p. 413).

The conclusion is thus somewhat different from the one reached by Smith. According to Bentham, 'justice, consistency, policy, economy, honour, generosity', all entail setting free the colonies (Bentham, 1793, p. 408). Such a position was regarded as scandalous on both sides of the

Channel. In England, it contributed to the labelling of Bentham's ideas as 'economic Jacobinism', in spite of his longstanding anti-Jacobin political positions. In France, it was not so much the idea that was shocking; it was the argument based on economic considerations. French partisans of emancipation, by contrast, set forth an argument based on natural law: on the natural rights of the people of the colonies to freedom and property.

In fact Bentham's demonstration in *Emancipate Your Colonies* called for consistency between the necessity to emancipate French colonies and the Declaration of the Rights of Man. 'You abhor tyranny', he exhorted the French Revolutionaries:

> you abhor it in the lump not less than in detail: you abhor the subjection of one nation to another: you call it slavery. You gave sentence in the case of Britain against her colonies: have you so soon forgot that sentence? – have you so soon forgot the school in which you served your apprenticeship to freedom? (Bentham, 1793, p. 408)

The argument is only logical: 'Keep the sugar islands, it is impossible for you to do right; – let go the negroes, you have no sugar, and the reason for keeping these colonies is at an end; keep the negroes, you trample upon the declaration of rights, and act in the teeth of principles' (ibid., p. 416). The conclusion repeats the argument: 'If the happiness of mankind is your object, and the declaration of rights your guide, you will set them [the French colonies] free' (ibid., p. 418).

Lawyer's rhetoric! Bentham strongly opposed the American declarations of rights – particularly those of Virginia and Carolina[26] – and that opposition applied as well to the French *Déclaration des Droits de l'Homme et du Citoyen*. And this leads us to Bentham's second major difference with the Smithian theory and, more broadly, with the natural law tradition.

2. Pandora's box

'Nonsense upon stilts.' Here is the core of Bentham's judgement on the principle of inalienable natural rights. '*Natural rights* is simple nonsense', we can read in his *Anarchical Fallacies*, 'natural and imprescriptible rights, rhetorical nonsense – nonsense upon stilts.'[27] 'I am sorry you have undertaken to publish a Declaration of Rights', he wrote to Brissot in September 1791. 'It is a metaphysical work – the *ne plus ultra* of metaphysics. It may have been a necessary evil, – but it is nevertheless an evil.' And the argument carries on: 'Political science is not far enough advanced for such a declaration. Let the articles be what they may, I will engage they must come under three heads – 1. Unintelligible; 2. False; 3. A mixture of both.'[28]

Bentham, offered the title of French Citizen on 26 August 1792,[29] accepted on the condition that he be authorized to become a citizen of

France in Paris though remaining a citizen of England in London, and to become a republican in Paris though remaining a royalist in London.[30] And in a letter to Wilberforce, who had just received the same title, he observed with amusement 'that were they [the French, ditto *Pandemonians*] to see an *analysis* I have by me of their *favourite Declaration of Rights*, there is not, perhaps, a being upon earth that would be less welcome to them than I could ever hope to be; but there it lies, with so many *other* papers that would be equally obnoxious to them, very quietly upon my shelf.'[31]

The line of argument that Bentham developed against this 'evil' is the same one he had opposed to William Blackstone in his first published book, *A Fragment on Government*.[32] The assault is frontal.

> What I mean to attack is, not the subject or citizen of this or that country – not this or that citizen – not citizen Sieyès or citizen anybody else, but all anti-legal rights of man, all declarations of such rights. What I mean to attack is, not the execution of such a design in this or that instance, but the design itself. (Bentham, 1795a, p. 522)

The attack can be summed up in six points. The natural law tradition relies upon the central notion of an original social contract. And Bentham's first argument consists in rejecting this founding myth of modern societies as a 'fiction'.

> The origination of governments from a contract is a pure fiction, or in other words, a falsehood. It never has been known to be true in any instance . . . . All governments that we have any account of have been gradually established by habit, after having been formed by force . . . . Contracts came from governments, not governments by contracts. (Bentham, 1780, pp. 501–2)

Hence it is the theoretical basis of the natural law tradition which is attacked. Secondly, it is not only the original social contract which is a fiction, but the very notion of natural law. And this, Bentham asserts, because it cannot be related to the 'real entities' that define, in the tradition of David Hume, the bases of all social sciences: individual pleasures and pains. This opposition between 'fictitious' and 'real' entities will have two consequences. One is the distinction between rights and faculties, which gives substance to Bentham's third argument. 'The word right is the name of a fictitious entity; one of those objects the existence of which is feigned for the purpose of discourse.'[33] The distinction is made clear in the *Principes de législation*.

> What is natural in mankind, is means and faculties, but to call those means and those faculties natural rights is to put the language in opposition with itself: because those rights are established in order to assure the exercise of means and faculties; the right is the guarantee, the faculty is what is guaranteed. (Bentham, 1829, Vol. I, p. 47, my translation)

The subject of Bentham's fourth argument arises from the other major consequence of the opposition between 'fictitious' and 'real' entities: as a fiction, natural law will ineluctably lead to anarchy: 'from *real* laws come *real* rights', Bentham proclaims in the conclusion of *Anarchical Fallacies*,

> but from *imaginary* laws, from laws of nature, fancied and invented by poets, rhetoricians, and dealers in moral and intellectual poison, come *imaginary* rights, a bastard brood of monsters, 'gorgons and chimaeras dire'. And thus it is, that from *legal rights*, the offspring of law, and friends of peace, come *anti-legal rights*, the mortal enemies of laws, the subverters of government, and the assassins of security. (Bentham, 1795a, p. 523)

Because it is both laic and scientific, the utilitarian principle is hence the only one able to provide the foundations of a system of positive laws. The fifth argument is a corollary of the previous one: the natural law tradition insists on the necessity of freedom for all individuals within society. But freedom, according to Bentham, cannot be defined as the essence of the law without committing the same logical error with the idea of the law itself. Whereas all rights have to be established in opposition to individual freedom, 'all rights are made at the expense of liberty – all laws by which rights are created or confirmed. No right without a correspondent obligation . . . . All coercive laws, therefore (that is, all laws but constitutional laws, and laws repealing or modifying coercive laws), and in particular all laws creative of liberty, are, as far as they go, abrogative of liberty' (ibid., p. 503). Last but not least, the notion of natural right is a false argument against government tyranny. To the conception that 'the rights of a man anterior to all government, and superior as to their authority to every act of government – these are the rampart, and the only rampart, against the tyrannical enterprises of government', Bentham's answer – and sixth argument – is definitive: 'Not at all – the shadow of a rampart is not a rampart; a fiction proves nothing; from that which is false you can only go on to that which is false.'[34]

This idea of a logical inconsistency between natural rights and positive rights is expressed again in the famous letter to Brissot.

> What then will be the practical evil [of the Declaration of Rights]? Why this: you can never make a law against which it may be not averred, that by it you have abrogated the Declaration of Rights; and the averment will be unanswerable. Thus, you will be compelled either to withdraw a desirable act of legislation – or to give a false colouring (dangerous undertaking!) to the Declaration of Rights. The commentary will contradict the text . . . . The best thing that can happen to the Declaration of Rights will be that it should become a dead letter; and that is the best wish I can breathe for it.[35]

The argument is central to the debate between classical and modern natural law tradition. For the classical natural law tradition,[36] in the line of Aristotle and Thomas Aquinas, the idea of nature – and hence of natural law – refers to the basic Aristotelian cosmology, where the criterion of justice relates not to the subjectivity of individuals but to an objective global order; and where individuals have no existence outside of this natural, harmonious and highly hierarchical order, whose end and significance (*telos*) is by definition metaphysical and, consequently, out of reach of any social thought. As a consequence, the natural rights are necessarily universal – that is to say valid in all times and in all spaces.

The modern natural law tradition – inherited from the continental *jus naturale* school: Grotius, Pufendorf, Barbeyrac, Burlamaqui; and also from Hobbes and Locke – opposes this conception and gives the individual central place in a Galilean, infinite, flat and geometrical universe,[37] where the social bond can be thought of as based on individual autonomy, individual equality and individual property: as 'disenchanted', according to Max Weber.

Here are the propositions with which the continental natural law school prepared the foundations for utilitarianism as well as for political economy: a representation in terms of *societas* instead of *universitas*. The framework rests on eighteenth-century individualism: what Louis Dumont calls 'economic ideology'.[38] But within this common structure, Smith's belief in natural law led him to expect a natural tendency to harmony and order, organized around the market mechanisms: the invisible hand, or, in Elie Halévy's words, the principle of the 'natural identity of interests.'[39] Bentham's analysis of economic matters in terms of individual motives and actions, on the other hand, leads him to suggest that social relationships necessarily carry potential disharmony, so the basic principle of 'the greatest happiness of the greatest number' requires that social utility be achieved not by natural law – as in Helvétius's version of utilitarianism – but by positive law: what Halévy calls an 'artificial identification of interests'. In that way, Bentham's utilitarian position in this discussion goes well beyond the arguments of the eighteenth-century supporters of the classical position. Though highly critical of the Aristotelian cosmology – in the name of the same individualistic *Weltanschauung* as the one put forward by the modern natural law school – he stands for a third position and rejects, in the name of positive law, the notion of natural law forged by Grotius, Pufendorf and Barbeyrac.

It is here that the years of the French Revolution are helpful to the historian of thought. The colonial question gave Bentham the opportunity to re-emphasize his liberal position on economic matters. His opposition to the Declaration of Rights represents the opposite pole, which was authoritarian and based on a fundamental criticism of the natural law tradition.

Here lies, as we have seen, the second opposition to Smith. Bentham's first statement is that capital, not the market, is the starting point of the argument. His other main statement is that the social link is based not on a natural identity of interests but on an artificial one. This proposition leads directly to his conception of the state as a guideline of his entire construction, where the defence of economic liberalism must be submitted to a powerful and extremely centralized administration. 'I have not,' Bentham later wrote in his *Defence of a Maximum*, 'I never had, nor ever shall have, any horror, sentimental or anarchical, of the hand of government. I leave it to Adam Smith, and the champions of the rights of man (for confusion of ideas will jumble together the best subjects and the worst citizens upon the same ground) to talk of invasions of natural liberty' (Bentham, 1801, pp. 257–8).

The visible hand against the invisible hand: here is the distinction between the state 'agenda' and 'non-agenda' that Bentham was to develop later, in his *Method and Leading Features of an Institute of Political Economy*.[40] In the non-agenda, the non-intervention fields, 'the end is promoted by individuals acting for themselves and without any special interference exercised with this special view on the part of government' – what Bentham calls *sponte acta* and recognizes as broadly coinciding with the object of 'what is commonly termed political economy' (Bentham, 1801–4, pp. 323, 324). This non-agenda domain – where synallagmatic contracts are passed between autonomous individuals, free to trade with whomever they desire – excludes all forms of direct state intervention.[41] In a word, '*be quiet* ought to be the motto' (ibid., p. 333). On the other side, Bentham regards intervention as unavoidable in two circumstances: when individuals suffer from a deficiency in inclination, in power or in knowledge with regard to the ends they are pursuing; or when they are not ready to assume, by simply following their own interest, the necessities of the principle of 'the greatest happiness for the greatest number'. Among the state agendas Bentham mentions many items: national security, public health and instruction, market organization, direct and indirect taxation, the establishment of a Sinking Fund, a centralized search for statistics registration and publication (*noscenda*), and, as he suggested to the French Revolutionary government, stocks of agricultural subsidies to avoid famines.

Here we see not only the best illustration of the principle of 'artificial identification of interests', but also the main divergence between Bentham and the French Revolutionaries: in the utilitarian tradition the greatest happiness principle is not necessarily linked to Smithian economic liberalism nor to the founding principles of a political democracy, which the Revolution inherited from the Enlightenment.

3.   'A drawer where devils are locked up'

> My ideas just now are a jumble of architecture, and Lord L., and natural
> philosophy . . .
>
> Jeremy Bentham[42]

The same fundamental opposition between Bentham's economic liberalism
and his civil and political centralism can be found in the proposition that, at
the time, most contributed to his fame as a social reformer: the Panopticon.

The project had major theoretical scope. It intended to transform the
science of utility, based on the *felicific calculus*, into the major means of
social reform. The theme is central to the idea of 'Enlightenment' itself: to
translate – and to transfer – the theoretical transparency of individual
attitudes toward the science of utility into another transparency in the real
world: the social transparency of these individual attitudes towards the
legislator, the inspector of the Panopticon, or, more broadly, the state.

The whole society is concerned. 'If it were possible to find a method of
becoming master of everything which might happen to a certain number of
men', writes Bentham in the opening lines of the French version of the
Panopticon memoir,

> to dispose of everything around them so as to produce on them the desired
> impression, to make certain of their actions, of their connections, and of all the
> circumstances of their lives, so that nothing could escape, nor could oppose the
> desired effect, it cannot be doubted that a method of this kind would be a very
> powerful and a very useful instrument which governments might apply to vari-
> ous objects of the utmost importance. (Bentham, 1977, pp. [3]–[4])

The theoretical principle is well known. Originally, 'a simple idea in architecture' (Bentham, 1791, Letter XXI, p. 66) turns the abstract knowledge of
the individual's calculus of pleasures and pains as perceived by the science
of utility into a more concrete knowledge of the individual's effective acts as
perceived by the central inspector of the Panopticon. This 'simple idea' –
which Bentham compares for simplicity and clarity to the 'old story of
Columbus and his egg' (ibid.) – rests on two circular buildings, embedded
one in another. A circle from four to six floors high defines the circumfer-
ence, where the cells are located, a tower – the 'inspector's lodge' – constitutes the centre. Two sets of windows are opened on each side of the outer
circular building one facing outside, with windows large enough to light the
cells, the other facing inside, toward the inspection tower. The inner circum-
ference of each cell is formed by a light iron grating – 'so light as not to
screen away part of the cell from the inspector's view' (ibid.). In the centre
the inspection tower is surrounded by a gallery, covered with a transparent
blind, through which the inspector, owing to a light effect, can 'reign like a
spirit': see without being seen.

Herein lies the basic principle of what Bentham liked to call his 'haunted house'[43] the apparant omnipresence of the inspector combined with the facility of his real presence. The whole construction is centred around this supposed didactic virtue: 'to be incessantly under the inspector's eyes,' writes Bentham to the French reformers, 'is to lose in effect the power to do evil and almost the thought of wanting to do it.'[44]

France was to be the *locus* of the first Panopticon experiment. To Garran de Coulon, representative for the City of Paris in the Constituent Assembly, a member of the Committee for the Reform of Criminal Laws and chairman of the Supreme Court of Appeal, Bentham petitioned in 1791, 'Would you know how strong my conviction is of the importance of this plan of reform, and the great success which may be anticipated from it? Allow me to construct a prison on this model – I will be the gaoler.'[45] He then adds this extraordinary argument: 'You will see by the memoir that the gaoler will have no salary – will cost nothing to the nation. The more I reflect, the more it appears to me that the execution of the project should be in the hands of the inventor.'[46] Because it will bring to reality the Enlightenment's dream of absolute transparency, the Panopticon is the major tool to reform society as a whole:

> What would you say, if by the gradual adoption and diversified application of this single principle, you should see a new scene of things spread itself over the face of civilized society? – morals reformed, health preserved, industry invigorated, instruction diffused, public burthens lightened, economy seated as it were upon a rock, the gordian knot of the poor-laws not cut but untied – all by a simple idea in architecture? (Bentham, 1791, Letter XXI, p. 66)

Members of the Constituent Assembly welcomed the idea. Both Brissot and Condorcet received a copy of the book. La Rochefoucauld-Liancourt and La Fayette supported the establishment of a prison on Bentham's plan.[47] On 13 December 1791 Garran de Coulon presented Bentham's project (in Dumont's French version) at the Tribune of the National Assembly, whereupon La Rochefoucauld-Liancourt moved that it should be printed and referred to the Committee of Legislation and Succour. 'You have more than shown us, Sir, that you wanted no thanks of ours,' Garran replied to Bentham, 'though these must not be refused to you, to induce you to offer to freedom and humanity some proofs of your zeal and your instruction. The National Assembly has welcomed your tribute as it deserved. It saw in you, according to the expression of one of your great poets, worthy to sing the praise of liberty: *On public virtue, every virtue joined.*'[48] With a proposal from Quatremère de Quincy and with the active support of Talleyrand, Bentham convinced the Directoire du Département de Paris, headed by La Rochefoucauld, to build a Panopticon on municipal land. Never again would the project be so close to achievement. But the pace of political events quickened after 10 August 1792. La Rochefoucauld was murdered and the Panopticon was buried in files. Bentham's 'haunted house' was to stay unbuilt.

This brief analysis of three among the many projects Bentham submitted to the French Revolutionaries presents a portrait of Bentham that contradicts Elie Halévy's observation that 'From the year 1789, in fact, there was as it were a pause in the history of Bentham's thought' (Halévy, 1972, part 2, p. 153). The French Revolution did not bring about such a 'pause'. On the contrary, it led Bentham to work passionately in Lord Lansdowne's 'laboratory of ideas', to sharpen his own thinking, to answer criticisms, to polemicize, to apply his theories to current events – in short, to turn his abstract theory into a broad project of social reform. it is indeed true that the ideas Bentham expressed during that period existed in embryo in his 'Russian works', *Panopticon* and *Defence of Usury*. But the Revolutionary turmoil crystallized the paradoxical encounter between his deep liberal principles and his conception of what a modern state should be.

In that sense, the 1790s were the years during which Bentham both became a philosophical radical and deepened his opposition to the Smithian system. The link is important. From the same starting point – the individualistic ideology inherited from the political philosophy of the Enlightenment – but from opposite views of the theoretical structure of political economy, Smith and Bentham produced two totally different representations of the social bond. When Smith emphasized the market as a condition of the division of labour and thus of the growth of the wealth of nations, he established a consistent link between individual rationality and the notion of the invisible hand as an archetype of all social bonds, moulded on the principle of a 'natural identity of interests'. When Bentham, on the other hand, proposed that capital, and not the market, is first in the logical sequence designed to explain the nature and causes of the wealth of nations he underlined in the same manner the role of private interests – 'the economic psychology put into an imperative' (Halévy, 1972, part 3, p. 478) – but with no social means of coordinating these interests other than state intervention. Hence his defence of positive law as the only means of resolving conflictual private interests and his advocacy of strong government intervention in most parts of social life. Hence also the central part played by the project of the Panopticon in his theoretical system.

The two lines here foreshadowed throw a light on most of the moral and political debate throughout the first half of the nineteenth century: they will carry on as two different philosophical understandings of civil society, through economics or through politics: Smith's science of the legislator versus Bentham's science of legislation.

Notes

1. I am grateful for helpful comments from Bob Coats, André Lapidus, Ezra Suleiman and Karen Vaughn. I alone, of course, am accountable for the contents and errors of this chapter.
2. See his first letters to Mirabeau (trans. John Bowring), in October 1788, in Bentham (1838–43), Vol. XIX, pp. 184–6.
3. Bentham to J. P. Garran de Coulon, 25 November 1791 (trans. John Bowring), in Bentham (1838–43), Vol. XIX, p. 269. For the original French version, see Bentham (1977), p. 2, or Bentham (1981), pp. 340–1.
4. Which was to stay unpublished during his lifetime. For a reproduction, see Halévy (1901), Part I, Appendix IV, pp. 424–39.
5. Bentham to Lord Wycombe, 1 March 1789 (Aet 41), in Bentham (1981), p. 33.
6. 'Je ne pense que de la France, je ne pense que pour la France', Bentham to Mirabeau, no date, quoted in Zagar (1958), p. 294.
7. See Halévy (1972), p. 541.
8. He also had contacts with other French personalities, including Brissot, Condorcet, La Rochefoucauld-Liancourt, Talleyrand, Montmorency, Beaumetz and Lafayette.
9. It is the title of Bentham (1793). See also, on the same subject, Bentham (1787), pp. 202–4, Bentham (1790), and Bentham (1801–4), 'Non-Faciendum the Fourth: Encreasing the Quantity of Land, viz. by Colonization', pp. 352–7.
10. Consequently, writes Smith, 'the industry of the country . . . is thus turned away from a more, to a less advantageous employment, and the exchange value of its annual produce, instead of being increased, according to the intention of the lawgiver, must necessarily be diminished by every such regulation' (Smith, 1976, Vol. I, Book IV, ch. 2, p. 457).
11. 'The general advantages which Europe, considered as one great country, has derived from the discovery and colonization of America consist, first, in the increase of its enjoyments; and, secondly, in the augmentation of its industry' (Smith, 1976, Vol. II, Book IV, ch. 7, p. 591).
12. Ibid., quoted in Winch (1965), p. 9.
13. See ibid., p. 1.
14. This solution is exclusive of an abrupt opening of the trade: 'To open the colony trade all at once,' carries on Smith, 'might not only occasion some transitory inconveniency, but a great permanent loss to the greater part of those whose industry or capital is at present engaged in it' (Smith, 1976, Vol. II, Book IV, ch. 7, p. 606).
15. A branch, which Bentham considered as an *art* and as a *science*: see Bentham (1801–4), p. 318, and, on this general – or rather, in Bentham's words, 'encyclopedical' – classification of sciences, Bentham (1983). For its implications for political economy, see Bentham (1801–4), pp. 307–12, and Bentham (1793–5), pp. 223–5.
16. See Bentham (1793–5), pp. 226–31, and Bentham (1801–4), pp. 308–12.
17. This 'plan for an universal and perpetual peace', which dominates part IV of the *Principles of International Law*, contained two major proposals: 'the reduction and fixation of the force of the several nations that compose the European system', and 'the emancipation of the distant possessions of each state'. See *Pacification and Emancipation* (University College, London, Bentham MSS, Box 25, pp. 26–49) and Bentham (1790). For a comment, see W. Stark, 'Introduction', in Bentham (1952), Vol. I, pp. 46–7, and Winch (1965), p. 26.
18. Bentham (1838–43), Vol. II, pp. 213, 244, 576, Vol. I, p. 400; quoted in Starck, 'Introduction', in Jeremy Bentham (1952), Vol. I, p. 14.
19. Bentham (1790, p. 212). Bentham had already expressed this statement in the 'Preface' and 'Postscript' to the second edition of his *Defence of Usury*: see Bentham (1787), pp. 191–207.
20. For example, the criticism of Smith's central notion of natural prices; see Bentham (1801), pp. 257–63.
21. Bentham (1791), p. 43. See also the 'Postscript' to *Defence of Usury* (Bentham, 1787, p. 201).

22. The point is made particularly clear in the *Manual of Political Economy*, where Bentham views the 'advantageousness of the direction given to a quantity of capital in any instance' as resulting from two types of individual decisions: '1. the choice of the trade itself: 2. the choice of the mode of carrying it on' (Bentham, 1793–5, p. 229). For an exhaustive comment on this point, see Guidi (1990a), pp. 18–21.
23. Bentham (1793), p. 411. This pamphlet remained unpublished until 1830; it was afterwards collected in Bentham's *Works*.
24. See Winch (1965), pp. 32–3 on the part played by this idea in later discussions of colonization and the export of capital.
25. This is the position Bentham held in the 1790s. Donald Winch points out that 'Bentham spent most of his life in the process of revising and occasionally contradicting positions he had reached earlier. His second thoughts on colonial questions can be found in works dealing with other topics and also in his tangled manuscripts. Once these writings have been taken into account, it becomes clear that Bentham had great difficulty in maintaining a consistent anti-colonial position' (Winch, 1965, p. 25).
26. See his codicil to the second edition of *An Introduction to the Principles of Morals and Legislation* (Bentham, 1780, p. 154). These two declarations begin with the idea 'that there are certain natural rights of which men, when they form a social compact, cannot deprive or divest their posterity, among which are the enjoyment of life and liberty, with the means of acquiring, possessing, and protecting property, and pursuing and obtaining happiness and safety' (quoted in Halévy, 1972, Part I, p. 174).
27. Bentham (1795a), p. 501. The formula will give Bentham a title for his *Nonsense Upon Stilts, or Pandora's Box Opened* (Bentham, 1795b).
28. Bentham to Jacques Pierre Brissot de Warville, mid-August, 1789 (Aet 41), in Bentham (1981), pp. 84–5. For the French version, see Halévy (1901), part II, p. 39.
29. Together with Joachim Henry Campe, Thomas Clarkson, Anarchasis Cloots, Joseph Gorani, John Hamilton, F. G. Klopstock, Thadeusz Kosciusko, James Mackintosh, James Madison, Thomas Paine, Cornelius Pauw, Henri Pestalozzi, Joseph Priestley, George Washington, William Wilberforce and David Williams.
30. Bentham to the Minister of the Interior of the French Republic, November 1792, in Bentham (1838–43), Vol. XIX, p. 282.
31. Bentham to Wilberforce, 1 September 1796, ibid., pp. 316–17.
32. Bentham (1776), ch. 1, pp. 261–71; see also his codicil to the second edition of *An Introduction to the Principles of Morals and Legislation* (Bentham, 1780, p. 154).
33. Bentham, 'The Fiction of Right', in Ogden (1932), p. 118.
34. Ibid., p. 121.
35. Bentham to Jacques Pierre Brissot de Warville, mid-August, 1789 (Aet 41), in Bentham (1981), p. 85.
36. For a presentation of this classical tradition, see Strauss (1953); Villey (1975); El Shakankiri (1964; 1970); Derathé (1958); or Barret-Kriegel (1989).
37. On the Renaissance epistemological revolution, see Koyré's important books (1962; 1966).
38. See Dumont, 1977; 1983, Part I, 'Genèse II', pp. 68–114.
39. See Halévy (1972), Part I, ch. 1, pp. 5–35.
40. Bentham (1801–4), pp. 323–77.
41. The argument is somewhat too simple: 'The national wealth is the sum of the particular masses of the matter of wealth, belonging respectively to the several individuals of whom the political community – the nation – is composed. Every atom of that matter, added by any one such individual to his own stock, without being taken from that of another individual, is so much added to the stock of national wealth' (ibid., p. 323).
42. Bentham to Carolina Fox (called 'Miss F.' in Bentham's letters), late February 1791? (Aet 43), in Bentham (1981), p. 255. 'Lord L.' was Lord Lansdowne.
43. 'I do not,' Bentham used to tell John Bowring, 'like to look among the Panopticon papers. It is like opening a drawer where devils are locked up – it is breaking into a haunted house.' Quoted by Bowring, in Bentham (1838–43), Vol. XIX, p. 250.
44. Bentham (1977), p. [8]; my translation. For a theoretical – and historical – analysis of this

'idea in architecture', see Foucault (1975); and Foucault, 'L'oeil du pouvoir', in Bentham (1977), pp. 7–31.

45. Bentham to Jean-Philippe Garran de Coulon, 25 November 1791 (trans. John Bowring), in Bentham (1838–43), Vol. XIX, p. 269. For the original French version, see Bentham (1977), p. [2]; or Bentham (1981), p. 341.
46. Ibid.
47. See Bentham (1838–43), Vol. XIX, pp. 268–70.
48. Jean-Philippe Garran de Coulon to Bentham, 22 December 1791 (trans. John Bowring), ibid. p. 269.

References

Barret-Kriegel, Blandine (1989), *Les droits de l'homme et le droit naturel*, Paris: Presses Universitaires de France.

Baumgart, David (1952), *Bentham and the Ethics of Today. With Bentham Manuscripts Hitherto Unpublished*, Princeton, NJ: Princeton University Press.

Bentham, Jeremy (1776), *A Fragment on Government; or a Comment on the Commentaries: being an Examination of what is Delivered on the Subject of Government Commentaries. With a Preface in which is Given a Critique on the Work at Large*, in Bentham (1838–43), Vol. I, pp. 221–95.

Bentham, Jeremy (1780), *An Introduction to the Principles of Morals and Legislation. With the Last Corrections by the Author and Additions from Dumont's Traités de Législation* (1st edn 1780; 2nd edn 1789), in Bentham (1838–43), Vol. I, pp. 1–154.

Bentham, Jeremy (1787), *Defence of Usury: Shewing the Present Legal Restraints on the Terms of Pecuniary Bargains, in a Series of Letters to a Friend, to which is Added a Letter to Adam Smith, Esq LL.D. on the Discouragements Opposed by the Above Restraints to the Progress of Inventive Industry*, in Bentham (1952), Vol. I, pp. 121–207.

Bentham, Jeremy (1790), *Colonies and Navy, a Fragment* (c. 1790), in Bentham (1952), Vol. 2, pp. 209–18.

Bentham, Jeremy (1791), *Panopticon; or, the Inspection-House: Containing the Idea of a New Principle of Construction Applicable to Any Sort of Establishment, in which Persons of Any Description are to be Kept Under Inspection; and in particular to Penitentiary-Houses, Prisons, Houses of Industry, Workhouses, Poor-Houses, Manufactories, Mad-Houses, Lazarettos, Hospitals, and Schools: with a Plan of Management Applied to the Principle: in a Series of Letters, Written in the Year 1787, from Crecheff in White Russia, to a Friend in England*, in Bentham (1838–43), Vol. III, pp. 37–66.

Bentham, Jeremy (1793), *Emancipate Your Colonies, Addressed to the National Convention of France, Anno 1793. Shewing the Uselessness and Mischievousness of Distant Dependencies to an European State*, in Bentham (1838–43), IV, pp. 408–18.

Bentham, Jeremy (1793–5), *Manual of Political Economy*, in Bentham (1952), Vol. I, pp. 219–73.

Bentham, Jeremy (1795a), *Anarchical Fallacies; being an Examination of the Declarations of Rights Issued during the French Revolution*, in Bentham (1838–43), Vol. VIII, pp. 489–534.

Bentham, Jeremy (1795b), *Nonsense Upon Stilts, or Pandora's Box Opened*, manuscript edited by Dumontin in 1816, after *Tactique des assemblées législatives, suivie d'un Traité des sophismes politiques*, Geneva: Paschoud, 1816.

Bentham, Jeremy (1801), *Defence of a Maximum, Containing a Particular Examination of the Argument on that Head in a Pamphlet of 1800 Attributed to the Late*

Secretary to the Treasury, to which are Subjoined Hints Respecting the Selection of Radical Remedies against Death and Scarcity, in Bentham (1952), Vol. III, pp. 247–302.

Bentham, Jeremy (1801–4), *Method and Leading Features of an Institute of Political Economy (Including Finance) Considered not only as a Science but as an Art*, in Bentham (1952), Vol. III, pp. 305–80.

Bentham, Jeremy (1829), *Oeuvres*, translated by Etienne Dumont, 3 vols, Brussels: Hauman.

Bentham, Jeremy (1838–43), *The Works of Jeremy Bentham, Published under the Superintendence of his Executor, John Bowring*, 21 vols, Edinburgh: Tait.

Bentham, Jeremy (1952), *Economic Writings, Critical Edition Based on his Printed Works and Unpublished Manuscripts*, ed. W. Stark, 3 vols, London: Allen & Unwin for the Royal Economic Society.

Bentham, Jeremy (1977), *Le Panoptique. Précédé de 'L'oeil du pouvoir', entretien avec Michel Foucault*, afterword by Michelle Perrot, Paris: Belfond.

Bentham, Jeremy (1981), *The Correspondence of Jeremy Bentham (The Collected Works of Jeremy Bentham)*, Vol. IV, *October 1788 to December 1793*, ed. Alexander Taylor Milne, London: Athlone Press.

Bentham, Jeremy (1983), *Essay on Nomenclature and Classification*, in M. J. Smith and W. H. Burston (eds), *Chrestomathia*, Oxford: Clarendon Press.

Cot, Annie L. (1991), 'Jeremy Bentham et la Révolution française', *Economies et Sociétés*, 7, 8, 9, 10 *-Oeconomia*, **13**, pp. 472–83.

Cot, Annie L. (1992), *La tradition utilitariste. Bentham, Fisher, Becker*, Paris: Economica (forthcoming).

Cot, Annie L. (1992), 'Jeremy Bentham: un "Newton de la morale"', in A. Béraud, G. Faccarello and A. Lapidus (eds), *Histoire de la pensée économique*, Paris: La Découverte (forthcoming).

Derathé, Robert (1958), *Jean-Jacques Rousseau et la science politique de son temps*, Paris: J. Vrin.

Dumont, Louis (1977), *Homo Aequalis. Genèse et épanouissement de l'idéologie économique*, Paris: Gallimard.

Dumont, Louis (1983), *Essais sur l'individualisme. Une perspective anthropologique sur l'idéologie moderne*, Paris: Le Seuil.

El Shakankiri, Mohamed (1964), 'Jeremy Bentham: critique des droits de l'homme', *Archives de Philosophie du Droit*, **9**, pp. 129–52.

El Shakankiri, Mohamed (1970), *La philosophie juridique de Jeremy Bentham*, Paris: Librairie Générale de Droit et de Jurisprudence.

Foucault, Michel (1975), *Surveiller et punir. Naissance de la prison*, Paris: Gallimard.

Guido, Marco E. L. (1990a), '"Shall the Blind Lead Those who Can See?" Bentham's Theory of Political Economy', in D. E. Moggridge (ed.), *Perspectives on the History of Economic Thought, Selected Papers from the History of Economic Society Conference, 1988*, Vol. III: *Classical, Marxian and Neo-Classical*, Brookfield, Vermont: Edward Elgar for the History of Economics Society, pp. 10–28.

Guidi, Marco E. L. (1990b), 'Le citoyen Bentham, "raisonnable censeur des lois", et l'économie de la Révolution française', *Economie et Sociétés*, History of Economic Thought series, nos 7, 8, 9. 10 *-Oeconomia*, **13**, pp. 485–502.

Halévy, Elie (1901), *La formation du radicalisme philosophique*, Part I: *La jeunesse de Bentham*, Part II: *L'évolution de la doctrine utilitaire de 1789 à 1815*, Paris: Félix Alcan.

Halévy, Elie (1972), *The Growth of Philosophical Radicalism*, trans. Mary Morris, preface by John Plamenatz, London: Faber & Faber.

Harrison, Ross (1983), *Bentham*, London: Routledge & Kegan Paul.

Koyré, Alexandre (1962), *Du monde clos à l'univers infini*, Paris: Gallimard.

Koyré, Alexandre (1966), *Etudes galiléennes*, Paris: Hermann.

Lowry, S. Todd (1981), 'The Roots of Hedonism: an Ancient Analysis of Quantity and Time', *History of Political Economy*, **13** (4), pp. 812–23.

Mack, Mary (1962), *Jeremy Bentham. An Odyssey of Ideas. 1748–1792*, London: Heinemann.

Ogden, C. K. (1932), *Bentham's Theory of Fictions*, New York: Harcourt, Brace.

Pesciarelli, Enzo (1989), 'Smith, Bentham, and the Development of Contrasting Ideas on Entrepreneurship', *History of Political Economy*, **21** (3), pp. 521–36.

Smith, Adam (1976), *An Inquiry into the Nature and Causes of the Wealth of Nations* (1776), R. H. Campbell and A. S. Skinner, general eds; W. B. Todd, textual ed., 2 vols, Oxford: Clarendon Press.

Strauss, Leo (1953), *Natural Right and History*, Chicago: University of Chicago Press.

Villey, Michel (1975), *La formation de la pensée juridique moderne*, Paris: Montchestien.

Winch, Donald (1965), *Classical Political Economy and Colonies*, London: G. Bell & Sons for The London School of Economics and Political Science.

Zagar, Janko (1958), 'Bentham et la France'. Thèse de Doctorat d'Etat ès-Lettres, University of Paris.

6 Rowland Hamilton's neglected contribution on risk, uncertainty and profit*

Anastassios D. Karayiannis

Introduction

Rowland Hamilton – a nineteenth-century British author on the social sciences[1] – published the following works: *The Resources of a Nation: a Series of Essays* (1863); 'General Relations of Employers and Employed' (1873); 'Introductory Observations on Primary Education' (1875); *Money and Value: An Inquiry into the Means and Ends of Economic Production* (1878); and 'Thrift in Great Britain' (1892).

Hamilton's ideas and arguments on the subject of risk, uncertainty and profit are mainly analysed in his 1878 inquiry, though some minor comments are also included in his 1863 and 1873 works.

The main theme of his 1878 inquiry is the function of money and its substantial role in the economy. The anonymous reviewer of his 1878 work in the *British Quarterly Review* writes that,

> Altogether, we are glad to recommend this work very cordially to the attention of those interested in political economy and finance. Mr Hamilton is a clear writer, because he has first of all been a clear thinker; and although the use of technical terms cannot be always avoided, the subject is here dealt with in a luminous style. (Anon., 1878, p. 249)

However, Hamilton completed his inquiry using only a few references to the economic literature of the period. Of the well known economists he referred only to McCulloch (p. 223), J.S. Mill (ibid., pp. 179–80) and Jevons (ibid., p. xxiv).[2]

The classical character of his inquiry is mainly inferred from his treatment of some influential economic subjects. More specifically, he favoured *laissez-faire* (Hamilton, 1863, pp. 91–3), the free trade doctrine (p. 15) and free market competition (pp. 170–1, 277), while he was hostile to any monopolistic situation in the economy (p. 290); he considered that the market price fluctuations tend toward an equilibrium between supply and demand (1863, pp. 131–2; 1971, p. 289); he regarded the supply price as determined by the cost of production and the demand price by utility (1863, pp. 116–17; 1971, pp. xx, 100–1, 124, 276); he recognized the wage fund doctrine (p. 217) and the positive relationship between wage rate and work effort (p. 121). Moreover, he emphasized the extensive division of labour (1863, pp. 18–20; 1971, pp. 66, 135, 149), the efficient combination of the factors of production – mainly capital and skilled labour (1863, p. 23; 1873, p. 502; 1971, pp. 41, 182, 186–9, 195) – the monetary organization (1971, ch. 2), and innovations (1863, p. 119; 1971, pp. 290, 296, 301) as the crucial factors in economic development.

Monetary analysis is the main subject of his work. He analysed the value of metallic money and its function as a medium of exchange, as a standard of value and as a 'reserve of purchasing power' (pp. 7–9, 17, 19–21, 52–3; see also 1863, pp. 249–52). He gave emphasis to the latter fundamental function of money as the one which minimizes the harmful effects caused by any abrupt and unexpected disequilibrium between supply and demand and by ignorance and uncertainty, which accompany the future course of the various economic variables. As Hamilton wrote: 'Their [i.e. the precious metals'] primary use as money is to aid in that redistribution of commodities rendered needful by the inequality and uncertainty of natural production' (p. 133).

By the use of money, some of the economic causes which produce risk and uncertainty are restricted but not eliminated because it is a 'fact that risks and reverses are inseparable from all industrial enterprises' (p. xviii).

Moreover, Hamilton developed the quantity theory of money (pp. 35–6, 75, 104; see also 1863, pp. 270–1); the various substitutes for metallic money and their effectiveness on the economic process (pp. 70–2); and he analytically portrayed the banking system and credit (pp 224–74). Thus the main body of his scientific analysis is focused on the functioning of the monetary economy and only sporadically did he investigate the rate and the variability of some other significant real economic variables.[3]

Hamilton's survey has a positive and normative character (pp. xiv, xviii–xix), while his scope and method of inquiry, as he wrote, 'is not to present an historical sketch, but to deal first with more general principles, and then to proceed to those arising from them which are more liable to casual modification' (p. 26).

On the other hand, the style of his writings is more explanatory than exploratory and strictly scientific. In regard to his methodology, his reviewer comments that, 'He unites the power of distinct observation of the empirical student with the faculty for abstract thought which enables the thinker to suggest hypotheses that express the generalized results of experience in "laws"' (Anon., 1878, p. 249).

Leaving aside all the above economic subjects, in this paper we will analyse the special contribution of Hamilton on the topic of the entrepreneurial function as the bearer of risks and uncertainty, and the receiver of a special reward (i.e. pure profit). His significant and independent (in the sense that there is no trace of theoretical influences upon him by other writers) contribution to this subject is unquestioned as he was a pioneer in relating the existence of uninsured risks and uncertainty to the function and reward of the entrepreneur. Though many classical economists recognized the function of risk-bearing as characteristic of the role of capitalist–entrepreneur (see Karayiannis, 1990, pp. 249–50), none of them (as far as I know) studied the special entrepreneurial function as the one bearing the risk and uncertainty.

The pertinent literature has paid no attention to Hamilton's contribution to the theory of entrepreneurship. It is the purpose of this paper to assess his special contribution to the subject and to attempt to give Hamilton the position he deserves in the history of economic thought and in the history of the special topic of entrepreneurship and profit. The first section (Risk and Uncertainty) outlines what Hamilton has written in regard to the main causes of risk and uncertainty. The next section (Entrepreneurship and Profit) analyses Hamilton's views on entrepreneurial activity, its motive, its ends and its justification as bearing the risk and uncertainty.

By using extensive references (mainly contained in the footnotes) to other authors who developed the same theory, that is, Cantillon and Knight, I will evaluate the independent and significant contribution of Hamilton in my conclusion, as we have no evidence to verify influences among these authors. As is known, Jevons discovered Cantillon's work and published an article on his economic analysis in January 1881, when Hamilton's work had already been published. On the other hand, Knight (based on his doctoral dissertation written between 1914 and 1917 and edited in a new form in 1921) though he devoted about 50 pages of his monumental work to the subject giving an historical sketch of the treatment of entrepreneurship and profit in economic literature, did not make any reference to the works of Cantillon and Hamilton.

Risk and uncertainty
The uncertainty inherent in economic life in regard to the future rate of many economic variables and its unexpected and unknown fluctuations, produces some risks which cannot be measured and insured against. Hamilton has properly distinguished between measurable and non-measurable risk, the latter being that which is produced by uncertainty and which fully justifies the profits of the entrepreneurs.[4] He argues that,

> Deducting wages and interest, there remains an uncertain balance of excess or deficiency in the ultimate reproduction, just as surely uncertain as human knowledge is fallible. Risks there are, it is true, in work of all kinds, but as far as results can be estimated, or special risks provided for by insurance, average rates of production may be assumed, but these must, nevertheless, tell in the final results,

which are further subject in a greater or less degree to special uncertainties, arising from fluctuations of 'supply and demand' to which I need not refer more at length. It is these final results which are commonly spoken of as profits, and much of the work done for profits cannot, in the nature of things, be shared. (1874, p. 509)

Those risks produced by uncertainty, according to Hamilton, are borne by those who want to bear them: 'the risks and uncertainties . . . attend upon all undertakings in a greater or less degree' (p. 162); 'to incur risks is not in itself culpable. On the contrary, some degree of uncertainty waits on all enterprise which depends on future conditions which never can be perfectly anticipated' (pp. 208–9).[5]

Hamilton held that the various risks and uncertainties that existed in the economy originate in the following causes:

1. The imperfect knowledge of agents of the future rate of prices and demand for goods (p. 29; see also 1874, p. 509).
2. Misdirected production (p. 257).
3. The 'uncertain gap between the money in which all importers and wholesale dealers had to pay their longer obligations and that in which their transactions had to be carried out to the end by retailers and consumers' (p. xxviii), that is, by variations in the value of money. An analogous idea was also stressed by Cantillon and Knight.[6]
4. The unexpected and sudden changes in the rate of demand: 'For the demand of the average of mankind is not only capricious, but unintelligent' (p. 30).[7]
5. 'the risk of loss from misadaptation of supply to demand . . . may arise either from error in judgment on the part of the employer, or even from causes impossible for him to foresee and provide against' (p. 214).[8]

The risks and uncertainty occasion the following deleterious effects on the economy – besides those which accompany the entrepreneurial activity (see the following section).

(a) Ignorance and uncertainty make the economic agents reluctant to undertake extensive economic actions (p. 27).
(b) 'The high rate of interest in many new countries does not represent the insecurity of property so much as the risk of failure arising from the difficulty of adapting the new capital to the existing agencies which have to be modified to carry out the work designed' (p. 192, see also p. 218).
(c) 'the wage-earner may be uncertain whether he gets work or not; he does not, having once obtained it, run any further risk as to the ultimate success of the undertaking upon which he is engaged' (p. 213).
(d) 'Holders of "money" do incur one definite risk; no one is obliged to take or to pay them for their money' (p. 220).

Thus, according to Hamilton, on the one hand uncertainty operates as a disincentive to agents, and on the other the labourer is under the burden of finding appropriate employment for himself and the capitalist must find a profitable investment for his capital. This uncertainty assumed by the labourers and the capitalists was not featured by Cantillon and Knight in their treatment of the subject.

Entrepreneurship and profit

Hamilton clearly distinguished between the crucial role of capitalist and that of the entrepreneur (pp. 210–11). In his article of 1873 he argues that, 'the routine headwork of the superintendent; the "abstinence" and the care in selection of the capitalist; the special enterprise and powers of direction of those who take the ultimate control of undertakings, are all clearly distinct functions' (1874, pp. 508–9).[9]

Moreover, he made a strict separation between the gross profits, interest (as a reward of abstinence)[10] and net profits leaving the latter as the sole reward for entrepreneurial activity (pp. 216–17; see also 1863, p. 336).

The entrepreneur, according to Hamilton, is an active factor in the economy, the one who contributes eminently to economic development. Yet the entrepreneur is inspired by two motives. First by the profit motive, and particularly by trying to maximize his expected profit:

> There is . . . in all cases the expectation of profit, as the inducement to undertake the labour and risk [1863, p. 354]. The reasonable desire of those who accept loans [i.e. the entrepreneurs] is to secure to themselves in a larger degree all the more or less of gain which may be derived from their own skill and experience in the management of some special kind of industrial work. Those who grant loans forego this advantage, but are assured of a more certain income. (p. 210; see also pp. 158, 186)

Secondly, the entrepreneur is motivated by the freedom he enjoys in running his own business:[11]

> A love of gain is no doubt a powerful stimulus to exertion, but too much has been made of this motive, and it is moreover one of those which, unbridled, are so apt to o'erleap their own intention. The sense of freedom combined with a sense of a definite sense of responsibility for the use of it, are the most favourable conditions for drawing out the best energies, especially of an enterprising race like our own [i.e. the English]. (pp. 218–19, fn. 1)

The above-mentioned motives operate freely and without restrictions, because 'no power on earth can restrain men from being guided by the practical experiences and by the pressing necessities of life' (pp. 48–9).

The entrepreneurs or 'speculators' or 'adventurers' as Hamilton labelled them (pp. 212, 216), are 'the born pioneers of commercial intercourse' (p. 29), who have voluntarily agreed 'to incur freely the risk of experiments' p. 30). The entrepreneur, according to Hamilton, has the ultimate responsibility of the enterprise, bearing the risks and uncertainties incurred. As he points out:

> If merchants and manufacturers waited for absolute certainty, they would ignore their function in the general economy of life [p. 209]. If the 'adventurer' accepts a loan, he guarantees the lender against loss to the utmost of his resources . . . therefore he bears the first brunt of risk, and it stands to reason that his directions as to the ordering of the labour employed must be supreme within the limits of the undertaking for which he is thus finally responsible . . . his special function is to direct and adjust, and, in the interest of all concerned, he should have fair scope for the exercise of it (p. 216)

If we consider the words of Cantillon and Knight on the same subject, a resemblance among their views can be easily shown:

> All the rest are Undertakers, whether they set up with a capital to conduct their enterprise, or are Undertakers of their own labour without capital, and they may be regarded as living at uncertainty. (Cantillon, 1964, p. 55, see also p. 81)

> The essence of enterprise is the specialization of the function of *responsible direction* of economic life, the neglected feature of which is the inseparability of these two elements, *responsibility and control*. (Knight, 1964, p. 271) The apparent separation between control and risk taken turns out, as predicted, to be illusory. (ibid., p. 297)

However, the valuation of risk and uncertainty is subjected to personal experience and knowledge. In Hamilton's words: 'the sum given for uncertain results is more a matter of individual opinion which must stand or fall by the test of time' (p. 159).[12] So there must be a differential rate of profit among entrepreneurs in relation to their evaluation of the future course of some crucial economic variables.

On the other hand, the entrepreneur, according to Hamilton, acts as an innovator, particularly in creating and promoting new products, in discovering new markets and in organizing the enterprise more efficiently. This fundamental entrepreneurial function, which was developed by Schumpeter almost 40 years later (1978, pp. 132–6; see also Karayiannis, 1990, p. 255), is inevitably accompanied by various risks and uncertainties.[13]

As Hamilton points out:

> No branch of enterprise ever yet was opened up which did not involve some loss and disaster to the early adventurers, and some persistence, in spite of difficulties, may well be urged in favour of attempts to introduce new industries, or a better organization of industries, which may help to develop a wage-earning power, especially among the poorer classes. As far as such industries can acquire the support of this class the fresh wages earned and expenses lessened by improved production are indeed a double gain [pp. 295–6]. To create a demand by affording

a suitable supply is no new thing in commercial enterprise. Those who undertake such ventures often do so on the very imperfectly secured hope that future profits may recompense their first losses. Moreover we have all to buy our experiences and grow wise only by repeated failures . . . the pioneers in this great work may . . . take the first risks, try the first experiments, undergo all the incidental crosses and losses to which all pioneers are subjected, and create the demand by affording the most suitable supply. When this can once be accomplished the field may be left open to those engaged in the ordinary conduct of the trade, and further operations thus become thoroughly self supporting. It is the first steps which are the most difficult and the most costly. (pp. 299–300)[14]

Therefore,

All that I urge is that the capital needed is at hand, ready and waiting to be applied. It is 'mind', not 'matter', that is wanting. It is a problem of life, not of mechanism [p. 295]. The true leaders of men, to patience, experience, and intellectual capacity, must add the courage and resolution which nerves them to undertake the necessary risks of action in doubtful emergencies. (1863, p. 351)

From the previous analysis one may deduce that, according to Hamilton, the active role of the entrepreneur is devoted to the direction, responsibility and control of his enterprise and the introduction of various innovations, while the passive one is the bearing of the ultimate risk and uncertainty.

Hamilton classified the various incomes according to the way they are received. He considered that wage, rent and interest are contractual incomes, while net profit is the only residual of distribution – a classification also introduced by Cantillon (1964, p. 51) and Knight (1964, p. 271).

As Hamilton says:

wages – and in this generic term must be included 'pay', salaries, and all other forms of fixed remuneration – may be disproportionately too high or too low. Profits represent alike the very scanty earnings of the struggling shopkeeper and manufacturer, and the exceptional gains, usually associated with inordinate risks, of the fortunate speculator. (p. 212, see also pp. 215–16)

Again, 'wages as a rule are and must be paid immediately' (p. 214), while 'profits are rather saved out of, than added to, the cost of production' (p. 215).

Profit is the reward for the above-mentioned services supplied by the entrepreneurs. However, Hamilton links this reward much more with the functions of responsibility in directing and controlling the enterprise, and of bearing the risk and uncertainty, than with the innovative activity. He stressed that

The word 'profit' is, in fact, used in two different senses: the first is the excess of production over expenditure; the second (and commoner), the uncertain remuneration of those who undertake, not the superintendence only, but also the risk of employing capital, and who, in a greater or less degree, control the direction and manner in which labour is employed: the expectation of profit and the risk of loss are constantly associated together. (1863, p. 330)

Thus, the market price of goods 'will include the recompense of those on whose responsibility the several undertakings are carried on' (p. 238), and 'Nothing can be more inane and futile than to cry out for special remuneration of any kind without acquiring the skill or undertaking the cares and responsibilities of the work associated with it' (p. 292).

Therefore the uninsured ultimate risks that are assumed by the entrepreneur in running and expanding his enterprise justify his fair reward.[15] As Hamilton put it:

Profit and risk are so inseparably connected, that 'profit and loss' is the appropriate heading of every trader's account which records the success or failure of his several transactions. Indeed, when interest and the wages of superintendence and indemnity against loss are provided for, the final profit may well be termed the remuneration for risk; the risk being of such a kind as, to a greater or less degree, but not altogether, can be provided against by due care, skill, forethought, and good management. (pp. 215–16)[16]

Again, 'The element of risk, however, cannot be wholly eliminated in practice, and is therefore a fair basis for a compensating charge' (p. 218). And as 'profits . . . are often earned under arduous conditions and associated with peculiar risks' (p. 174), 'There is inevitably an uncertain balance of excess or deficiency at the end of every work of reproduction, and it is this resulting risk which is inevitably associated with profit' (p. 215).

Hamilton postulates a proportional relationship between the rate of profit and the rate of risk. He considered that 'the great profits . . . are often associated with great risks, without actual injury to any one' (p. 208). This happens more often in the case of the innovative activity of the entrepreneur, while in the course of things 'Men grow rich by good fortune and industry, or grow poor by thriftlessness and misadventure' (p. 85). A similar argument was put forward by Knight: 'The income of any particular entrepreneur will in general tend to be larger: (1) as he himself has ability, and good luck' (1964, p. 283).

Conclusions

The significant and independent contribution of Hamilton to the theory of entrepreneurship bears a strong resemblance to theories developed by Cantillon and Knight, and could be considered to show that the way is somehow prepared for new ideas and individuals articulate these ideas independently of each other.[17] Hamilton's contribution can be summarized as follows:

1. The various risks and uncertainties inherent in economic life are assumed, though differently, by the labourers, capitalists and entrepreneurs.

2. Most of the risk and uncertainty is assumed by the entrepreneur because: he does not have perfect knowledge of the future rate of economic variables; some variables are influenced by causes out of his control; he has the ultimate responsibility and control of his enterprise; he innovates in various areas and by various means without having a clear perspective on the results of his actions.

3. The entrepreneurial function having the responsibility and control of the enterprise and assuming the risk and uncertainty is justified in receiving a specific economic reward, that is, the pure profit which is the sole residual element of income distribution.

Notes

*   A first draft of this chapter was presented at the History of Economic Thought conference, September 1990, University of East Anglia, Norwich, England. I wish to thank Professor S. Todd Lowry for his suggestions on an earlier draft of this paper.

1. Unfortunately, until now, the only biographical data I have come across while searching in a variety of British reference sources (for example, the biographical sources in the British Library; the index of Macmillan archive in the British Library, Dept. of Manuscripts; the Palmer's index to *The Times*; the Library of the National Institute of Economic and Social Research; and the British Library of Political and Economic Science) is that Hamilton was an Honorary Secretary to the 'Standing Committee on Education' (see Hamilton, 1875, p. 267). He was also a permanent discussant on various subjects of education in the *Transactions of the National Association for the Promotion of Social Science*, at least from 1873 until 1884 (see the various volumes of *Transactions*, 1873–84).

2. All page numbers standing alone in parentheses refer to Hamilton, *Money and Value* (Hamilton, 1971).

3. His anonymous commentator in the *British Quarterly Review* mentions that, 'He [Hamilton] has brought to bear an acute and trained intelligence upon some of the most complex phenomena of our monetary system' (Anon., 1878, p. 249).

4. The same distinction, as is well known, had been drawn also by Knight (1964), pp. 20, 46.

5. Knight stated a similar view: 'Universal foreknowledge would leave no place for an "entrepreneur". His role is to improve knowledge, especially foresight, and bear the incidence of its limitations' (1964, p. lix).

6. As Cantillon wrote: 'many people set up in a City as Merchants or Undertakers, to buy the country produce from those who bring it or to order it to be brought on their account. They pay a certain price following that of the place where they purchase it, to resell wholesale or retail at an uncertain price' (1964, p. 51, see also pp. 47–9, 51–3).

    For Knight, the 'profit arises from the fact that entrepreneurs contract for productive services in advance at fixed rates, and realize upon their use by the sale of the product in the market after it is made' (1964, pp. 197–8).

7. In regard to this cause, Cantillon comments: 'These Undertakers can never know how great will be the demand in their City, nor how long their customers will buy of them since their rivals will try all sorts of means to attract customers from them. All this causes so much uncertainty among these Undertakers that every day one sees some of them become bankrupt' (1964, p. 51).

8. As Cantillon says, 'the price of the Farmer's produce depends naturally upon these unforeseen circumstances, and consequently he conducts the enterprise of his farm at an uncertainty (1964, p. 49).

9. Knight (1964, p. 271), draws the same distinction on the basis that the capitalists and the entrepreneurs not only receive dissimilar types of income, but also play different roles in the economy.
10. He follows (1863, p. 330) Senior's theory on this subject.
11. Cantillon similarly argued: 'It will then come to pass that the Overseers become Undertakers, will be the absolute masters of those who work under them, and will have more care and satisfaction in working on their own account' (1964, p. 61).
12. Similarly, Knight says: 'we judge the future by the past. Experience has taught us that certain time and space relations subsist among phenomena in a degree to be depended upon' (1964, p. 204).
13. The relationship between the entrepreneurial innovative activity and its function as bearing the risk of uncertainty was also recognized by Knight in his latter work on the subject (1942, p. 128).
14. See also his *Essays* for a relevant argument (1863, pp. 341–4, 355).
15. Cantillon had developed a similar justification for the existence of profits by relating the special risks and uncertainties to the entrepreneurial function of bearing them (1964, pp. 49, 51, 55).
16. As Knight wrote: 'The true uncertainty in organized life is the uncertainty in an estimate of human capacity, which is always a capacity to meet uncertainty' (1964, p. 309).
17. I thank Professor C. Jung (University of Richmond) for this comment.

References

Anonymous (1878), comment on Hamilton's *Money and Value: An Inquiry into the Means and Ends of Economic Production* in *The British Quarterly Review*, **68**, July–October, pp. 248–9.

Cantillon, R. (1964), *Essai sur la Nature du Commerce en Général* (1755; ed. with an English trans. by H. Higgs, 1931), New York: A. M. Kelley.

Hamilton, R. (1863), *The Resources of a Nation: a Series of Essays*, London and Cambridge: Macmillan.

Hamilton, R. (1874), 'General Relations of Employers and Employed', in *Transactions of the National Association for the Promotion of Social Sciences*, Norwich meeting 1873, London: Longmans, Green, Reader and Dyer.

Hamilton, R. (1875), 'Introductory Observations on Primary Education', in *Sessional Proceedings, 1874–5*, pp. 267–74.

Hamilton, R. (1892), 'Thrift in Great Britain', *Economic Journal*, **2**, pp. 290–301.

Hamilton, R. (1971), *Money and Value: An Inquiry into the Means and Ends of Economic Production* (1878), New York: A. M. Kelley.

Jevons, W. S. (1881), 'Richard Cantillon and the Nationality of Political Economy', in Cantillon (1964).

Karayiannis, A. D. (1990), 'The Entrepreneurial Function in Economic Literature: A Synoptic Review', *Rivista Internazionale di Scienze Economiche e Commerciali*, **37** (3), pp. 245–68.

Knight, F. (1964), *Risk, Uncertainty and Profit* (1921), New York: A. M. Kelley.

Knight, F. (1942), 'Profit and Entrepreneurial Functions', *Journal of Economic History, Supplement*, **2**, 126–32.

Schumpeter, J. A. (1978), *The Theory of Economic Development* (1911; English trans. 1934), Oxford: Oxford University Press.

7 Léon Walras and the French 'intellectuals' (1896–7)

Pierre Dockès

The third edition of *Eléments d'économie politique pure*[1] appeared in March 1896, and the end of November of that same year saw the publication of *Etudes d'économie sociale*,[2] based on three articles (reprinted in this same volume) which had appeared, also in 1896, in the *Revue Socialiste*.[3] Léon Walras had retired four years previously, and had been replaced by Vilfredo Pareto. At that time, although Walrasian ideas had begun to be known among European and American economists,[4] the great Walrasian themes – mathematical economics, the pure theory of social wealth, and social economics – had caused very little stir in France.

Political economy in France had long been a family affair, in the hands of doctrinaire liberals who had control of the Institute, the main journals (and, to begin with, the *Journal des économistes*) and the teaching centres (among which the most prestigious was the Collège de France). Through his contact with Léon Say, Léon Walras had previously attempted, in a somewhat ambiguous way, to make a place for himself in this milieu. The attempt turned out to be a total failure, though his socialist ideas[5] were only one of the causes of this exclusion. Subsequently, Walras came down as a resolute opponent of this school – and the feeling was mutual!

Since 1877 economics had been taught in law faculties. But although a section of the professorial body was interventionist, critical of ultra-liberalism, even socialist, these professors were generally incapable of understanding Walrasian mathematics. Still, Léon Walras found some support here, and had friends among the socialists. In the first rank of his allies was Charles Gide,[6] who became an important personality in the reforming left. Gide's support (which was sometimes ambiguous)[7] and then, beginning in 1899,[8] that of Charles Rist, with whom Gide worked, played a certain role in the spread of Walras's ideas.[9] The creation, in 1887, in opposition to the *Journal des économistes*, of the *Revue d'économie politique*, by a team gathered around Charles Gide, provided Walras with a small amount of leverage. Let us add moreover that, starting from 1901, he also found support within the law faculty at Lyons, thanks to three young professors, Paul Pic, Charles Brouilhet and Emile Bouvier.[10]

90

Before 1896 what notice had been taken, in France, of Walras's work? The paper he presented to the Académie des Sciences Morales et Politiques[11] in 1873 had been favourably received by Joseph Garnier, chief editor of the *Journal des économistes*,[12] with whom his longstanding relations had however become somewhat strained;[13] but it had been greeted more coolly by Emile Levasseur, Claude Valette and Louis Wolowsky,[14] who were the first to come to the conclusion, which became a veritable leitmotif,[15] that the application of mathematics to economics was designed to put calculation, and thus the state, in the place of the market.

The first edition of the *Eléments* was the subject of very few recensions: an article by Charles Letort in *L'Economiste français* on the application of mathematics to political economy, a 'scientific causerie' in *Le Temps* by Auguste Laigne[16] and, especially, two articles by Charles Renouvier, the well-known philosopher, in his journal *La Critique philosophique*, which moreover supplemented its review with a commentary on the *Recherche de l'Idéal social* (1868). When the *Théorie mathématique de la richesse sociale* appeared, in 1883, Joseph Bertrand raised a certain feeble interest among the mathematical public with his article in the *Journal des savants*.[17] We note the silence of the *Journal des économistes*, which limited itself to a front-page announcement of publication.

The second edition of the *Eléments* achieved real support from the *Revue d'économie politique*, high praise in Charles Gide's 'Chronicle', an article by Anthony Beaujon and one by Ladislas von Bortkiewicz in reply to the critical articles of Francis Y. Edgeworth.[18] But it received a real '17-page slating'[19] in the *Journal des économistes*, at the hands of Auguste Ott. The two articles in the *Revue d'économie politique* were written by a professor in Amsterdam (A. Beaujon) and a Russian economist (L. von Bortkiewicz), with French economists remaining pretty well silent! On the socialist side, Walras could count on Georges Renard, a former *communard* who had been exiled for some time in Lausanne, where the two had become friendly, and whose political and intellectual standing in Paris was of the highest order.[20] In 1893, Renard had written an article on the importance of Walras's work for *La Petite République*, Etienne Millerand's socialist organ,[21] and he readily welcomed Walras's articles in his *Revue socialiste*.

On the engineers' and mathematicians' side,[22] the timid breakthrough made by Walras thanks to Joseph Bertrand's ambiguous article in the *Journal des savants* was not followed up. Walras had received technical support from certain of them,[23] but the second edition of the *Eléments* was given only a mention in the *Bulletin de la société des ingénieurs*,[24] and a brief recension in the *Bulletin des sciences mathématiques* in 1891. As to Hermann Laurent, though he had spoken glowingly of Walras since

1873,[25] and advanced his cause, first at the Cercle, then at the Institut des Actuaires Français and the Ecole des Mines, and had kept up a correspondence with him, during the years 1898 and 1899,[26] on the question of the 'invariable unity of values' and the measurement of utility,[27] he did not succeed – despite the hopes of Walras – in getting the Société des Actuaires interested in mathematical economics.[28] When, finally, in June 1900, Laurent, in a report on the *Etudes d'économie politique appliquée* to the Institut des Actuaires, criticized the Walrasian idea of measuring utility, the break was made in the mind of Walras,[29] who continued to be lenient with Laurent (the latter remaining, for his part, Walrasian) only because he was vice-president of that powerful Institute.

The spread of Walrasian ideas in France at the beginning of the year 1896 can be summed up thus: they were vaguely known to a few rare economists (certain of whom were highly critical), some socialist friends, and a very small group of curious mathematicians and philosophers. Those who had read him could virtually be counted on the fingers of one hand!

Around the time of the publication of the third edition of the *Eléments*, and especially of the *Etudes d'économie sociale*, Léon Walras attempted to effect an opening in the direction of the 'intellectuals'.[30] This typically Parisian milieu, holding leftist ideas, was at the time beginning to acquire a dominant position on the ideological level. The Dreyfus affair led to what was called the 'intellectuals' party' getting off the ground and becoming aware of its strength. The Ecole Normale Supérieure was a citadel at the heart of the network of relations of the Parisian 'intellectuals', who were in any case united by political and social links, and often by family ties. The role of the Parisian salons, for example those of Gustave Lanson, Henri Berr and Xavier Léon, and also that of Georges Renard, with his wife Louise as its guiding light, deserves to be emphasized. X. Léon's salon, for example, attracted all those who occupied an elevated intellectual position at the Sorbonne, the Collège de France and the Ecole Normale Supérieure, with the leading figures in science and philosophy such as Henri Poincaré, Paul Painlevé, Emile Borel, Jean Perrin, Gustave Lanson, Emile Durkheim and Lucien Lévy-Bruhl.[31] Other salons, of a more literary nature, were frequented by writers like, for example, André Gide, Paul Valéry and Pierre Louÿs. The group of young intellectuals at the Ecole Normale Supérieure was the first object of the Walrasian offensive, which was made possible thanks to the intellectual and family ties that existed between Georges Renard and this school, for which Léon Walras had a special fondness due to the fact that his father had passed through it. Walrasian ideas were to attract the attention of Charles Péguy, the future philosopher, writer and poet; and the more literary and artistic section of this intellectual world was not wholly indifferent to them. As a matter of fact, is it not perhaps the most extraordinary thing of all that Paul Valéry, another philosopher, writer and poet, should take an interest in the pure theory of Léon Walras?

1. A strategic citadel, the Ecole Normale Supérieure

In 1895, the Ecole Normale Supérieure celebrated its centenary. The Parisian press followed the proceedings attentively, and published numerous articles on the school,[32] regarding its history, its role, and the political orientation of its teachers and students. With its literary and scientific sections, the Ecole Normale was responsible for the education of a considerable fraction of the French intellectual elite; its only rival, in the scientific domain, being the Ecole Polytechnique.[33] Not only secondary school teachers with the *agrégation*, and a significant proportion of university teachers, but also numerous politicians were graduates of the Ecole Normale. What, then, was the orientation of its teachers and students?

Created in 1795 by the Thermidorian Convention,[34] the Ecole, a century later, still retained certain of the political characteristics of its origin; its republicanism, its political liberalism plus a certain conservatism in social matters, its anti-clericalism, not to say an anti-religious tendency. Normalians came from middle-class backgrounds: the classes which had arisen in the nineteenth-century, liberal professions, the business world, and also that of teaching. Students of families which preferred to have their children educated in Catholic schools sent them to Saint Cyr or to the Ecole Polytechnique (despite the fact that it was more republican). It is to be observed that the number of Protestants and Jews was high among the teachers and students at the Ecole Normale.[35] Deeply attached to intellectual liberty, the Ecole had been dissolved under the Restoration and restored under the July Monarchy in all its glory, under the authority of Victor Cousin, who designed the buildings in the Rue d'Ulm, and also drew up the school's rules to be those of a true 'monastery of liberalism'. Later the Ecole suffered the hostility of the imperial bureaucracy.[36] After the collapse of the Second Empire and the crushing of the Commune, the Ecole appeared at first less than hostile to Adolphe Thiers' 'Conservative Republic'; then, beginning in the years 1879–80, with the reform of higher education, there came into being the grand alliance of the Ecole and the Republic, founded on the sharing of common values – rationalism, neo-Kantianism and positivism in philosophy, anti-clericalism and social conservatism in politics, liberalism in economics – and on the growing power of former Normalians, with their conquest of the main intellectual positions against clerical influences, and their advancement in the state apparatus. It was a real symbiosis, typical of the Third Republic from Jules Ferry to Edouard Herriot.

However, the Ecole was far from homogeneous! The students were divided between the Catholic 'talas'[37] and the 'anti-talas'. Within the professorial body, if one looks at the instances of ideological opposition that occurred between 1880 and 1895, one sees that the history section was dominated by positivists of free-thinking, liberal or leftist tendencies, from Ernest Lavisse to Gabriel Monod, but that philosophy remained dominated by the spiritualistic current, with the highly clericalist and highly reactionary Léon Ollé-Laprune, and the neo-spiritualistic grand master, Emile Boutroux, who was succeeded by Henri Bergson who, in his turn, carried on along the path of anti-rationalism, and even anti-intellectualism. In the domain of literary criticism, Ferdinand Brunetière, who was Catholic, neo-spiritualistic and conservative, though influenced by evolutionism and positivism, became an assistant professor at the Ecole Normale in 1886.

This ideological opposition should not mask another dividing line, namely the one which existed between the 'anciens', who favoured a certain literary formalism, and the 'modernes', reformers who, in the disciplines of history and philosophy, wanted to use methods which were then considered scientific.[38] On the side of the 'reformers' were Monod and Boutroux.

Positivism was at the time often confused with the wish to achieve scientificity by imitating what was imagined to be the method of the natural sciences, by making the fact sovereign, and by applying a rigorous critique of sources, particularly texts, in the case of historians. It was a 'progressive' form of positivism, effectively permitting an in-depth transformation of the Ecole Normale, first the disciplines where positivism and 'critical method' dominated (i.e. history and, though less clearly, literary criticism), but also in philosophy. Emile Boutroux brought respectability to a neo-spiritualistic tendency which had nothing to do with the completely devalued 'Cousinism', a philosophy which aspired to being rigorous (Jules Ferry could talk about 'spiritualistic positivism'). Likewise there was the development of a new rationalism, which rejected the old scientism of Taine and Renan, Spencerian evolutionist theories and Wilhelm Wundt's physiological psychology. This current founded *La Revue de métaphysique et de morale* in 1892 (with Célestin Bouglé, Elie Halévy, Emile Chartier, known as Alain, Léon Brunschvicg and Xavier Léon, the only non-Normalian of the group); the review was an organ of the rationalist, anti-clerical left which was close to the radical party and the radical socialists. The positivist method was at the heart of a new school, Emile Durkheim's sociology and François Simiand's sociological economics.[39] It is necessary to insist on the role played by the German model, in history and in philosophy (neo-Kantianism was massively dominant, and Hegel was becoming known), for these reformers who inaugurated the custom of the study voyage to Germany for the best student in each graduating class in literature. After all, was Germany's victory not that of its universities, was it not the victory of science?

And what about socialism at the Ecole?

Socially the Ecole Normale remained mostly conservative. The students came from middle-class backgrounds, those from the working classes or the general population not being very numerous. Its importance in furthering workers' demands was more or less non-existent. Normalians participated in the liberals' struggles during the Restoration, and in the 'Trois Glorieuses' of 1830, but they were scarcely present during the February Revolution of 1848 and, in June 1848, as at the time of the Commune in 1871, they were on the side of 'order', even if they did have a certain interest in socialist doctrines conceived of as very general visions of future society. At the end of the 1880s Boulangism[40] does not seem to have really interested the Normalians, while the rest of the Latin Quarter was largely unfavourable to General Boulanger.[41] Of the years 1889–92, the philosopher Alain (who graduated in 1889) observed: 'I did not know of a single socialist among us'.[42]

Starting in the years 1892–3, the situation changed, however imperceptibly, with regard to both the professors, the 'maîtres de conférences' (assistant professors), the high administrative officials and the students. The two figures of Lucien Herr and Charles Péguy, close friends of long standing, though later opposed to each other, were characteristic of this development. At these two levels, although the leftist liberals were to be in the majority at the Ecole, socialism was in a minority throughout the period that we are considering (indeed it remained so until the 1930s, and even up to 1950).

On the side of the professors and the school's administration, the central figure for socialism was that of the librarian Lucien Herr, who was born in 1864 into a Catholic family in Alsace, but became an atheist, and who arrived at the Ecole in 1883. At the time he was an admirer of Clémenceau and Bismarck,[43] and was on the side of the 'modernes' and of positivism, as well as being a follower of Littré and of the *Revue de philosophie positive* (1867–81); consequently he was a left-wing positivist, while still being influenced by Boutroux.

In 1886 and 1887 Lucien Herr made his study voyage to Germany, trying vainly to obtain access to the early manuscripts of Hegel, whose 'true' thinking he wanted to make known in France,[44] and then prolonged his trip into Russia. Did he meet Russian revolutionaries?[45] It is known only that on his return Herr was close to the socialist-populist Pierre Lavrov.[46]

Most importantly, after his return to Paris at the end of 1887, Lucien Herr obtained the post of librarian, after a struggle. He wanted it, not in order to hold it for a time,[47] but in order to 'immobilize' himself there; which he did, effectively, for 38 years.[48] His objective was to turn this relatively obscure post into a centre of scientific influence, a place from which he could not only write, but also act upon the students, counter the spiritualistic and nationalist revival, promote science and universal values and, in sum, act for socialism – to begin with, very discreetly, then, starting from 1893–4, and especially from the Dreyfus affair[49] (in 1898–9), more openly. In the end, Herr sacrificed his career and his personal work to his other ambitions ('not to arrive' was at the heart of his moral code; it was an idea which he often expressed, and which strongly marked the students). He had a lot of influence, not only on the groups of students and former students by whom he was surrounded, and who shared his ideas, but also, for those who did not share his ideas, by the exemplary nature of his life. The library of the Ecole Normale, especially between 1890 and 1914, was one of the major intellectual centres of Paris.

Herr's interest in socialism was, to begin with, essentially that of an intellectual; it was simply a certain curiosity about socialist doctrines. Interested in the political economy of Bentham and Ricardo, Herr became one of the foremost specialists in Marx's thinking[50] (with his friend Charles Andler). In 1890 he wrote a series of articles in the *Parti ouvrier*,[51] where, under a pseudonym (Pierre Breton), he developed his socialist ideas. Among these we might note, in particular, that of 'value',[52] which appears to be influenced by Marxian theory, and especially by the theses of Anton Menger, the economist who, in *The Right to the Entire Product of Labour* (which Herr and his friend Charles Andler knew well),[53] criticized the Marxist theory of surplus value. Herr was above all highly critical of liberalism, of what he called the pseudo-natural laws of economics and the selfish society which always favoured the same small number of men to the detriment of the majority.[54]

Lucien Herr was to play an essential role in French socialism.[55] Although, starting from 1888, he became a militant for the 'possibilist party'[56] because of his wish to remain close to the working class, he was essentially the ideologist, the universally respected sage and 'man of influence' of democratic, reformist, parliamentary socialism, highly opposed to Jules Guesde's narrow Marxism and to all forms of authoritarian socialism. He struggled for the unity of the different socialist currents, and also took a leading role, along with Jaurès, his group and then his party, in the foundation (in 1904) of *L'Humanité*. He had introduced socialism to Jaurès, at the time when the former Normalian (an 1878 graduate) and *agrégé* in philosophy returned to the Ecole Normale library to write his theses,[57] including one on the 'philosophical origins of German socialism'. Up to the death of Jaurès, in 1914, his links with Lucien Herr remained very strong. It was also Herr who converted Léon Blum to socialism.

Besides Herr, socialism at the Ecole Normale could count firstly on his friend Charles Andler (an 1884 graduate), appointed in 1894 as an assistant professor of German. True, he was not a professor of philosophy, but it was through Andler that German philosophy, socialism and Marxism entered the school's teaching programme,[58] even though, despite his deep knowledge of Marx, he was not a Marxist, and was indeed influenced by Proudhon's ideas. To clearly mark this break which was constituted by his appointment, in 1895, Andler gave a lecture on *Capital* at the Ecole Normale.

Within the teaching body and the administration, two other socialists were to play a role at the Ecole Normale: the assistant director, Paul Dupuy (an 1876 graduate), who was more anarchist,[59] and Gustave Lanson, who worked at *L'Humanité* from 1904 to 1913.

On the students' side, the central figure of Normalian socialism from 1894 onwards was Charles Péguy.[60] It was he, undeniably, who was at the heart of the 'Utopia *turne*', the somewhat mythical high ground of Normalian socialism on the eve of the Dreyfus Affair. A '*turne*', in Ecole Normale jargon, was a study room where the '*co-turnes*', or fellow-students, got together. The 'Utopia *turne*'[61] was that of Charles Péguy, Albert Mathiez,[62] Albert Lévy[63] and Georges Weulersse.[64] Péguy, Mathiez and Lévy were already old friends, having known each other since 1891, when they had been in the preparatory class (for higher education) at the Lycée Lakanal. Péguy had come from the Lycée of Orléans, where his mother worked as an upholsterer; Mathiez, the son of an innkeeper of the Haute-Saône, had been at the Lycée of Vesoul; and Lévy, the son of a rabbi with origins in Alsace, had attended the Lycée of Troyes. Jules Isaac remembered these three older pupils, who were always together, and who used to walk around deep in discussion during recreation periods at Lakanal.[65] Already the three young men appear to have been close to socialism; for example, they took the lead in organizing a collection for the striking miners of Carmaux.[66]

The three friends at Lakanal[67] were reunited during the academic year of 1894–5 at the Ecole, in the Rue d'Ulm, where they became friendly with Georges Weulersse, who was the son of a collector of indirect taxes and had been at the Lycée Charlemagne (Paris). Péguy enrolled in the philosophy section, Mathiez and Weulersse in history and geography, and Lévy in German. The four friends were socialists – militants starting from 1895 – and close to 'the French socialists, whose more or less official organ is the *Petite République*', as Péguy himself wrote in 1895.[68] Weulersse, in particular, thanks to Andler and Herr, became knowledgeable in the thinking of Marx. From that academic year onwards, they tried to convert their fellow Normalians to their way of thinking, but appear to have remained isolated.

Little by little, however, under the influence of the 'Utopian *turne*', on the one hand, and, on the other, that of Charles Andler and Lucien Herr, and of Jean Jaurès, socialist ideas began to acquire some modest importance. In May 1897, under the influence, or with the support, of Lucien Herr, whom he felt close to the time, Péguy founded a socialist study and propaganda circle, whose manifesto proclaimed the need for 'integral scientific socialism', which would be 'national' and 'international',[69] and at the end of the academic year, before definitively leaving the school[70] to set up a socialist bookshop, the Librairie Bellais,[71] Péguy founded a socialist group, *La Recherche de la Vérité*, which was orientated towards the publication of a 'true journal'.[72]

Besides the three friends of the 'Utopia *turne*', what socialists were there at the Ecole Normale at the start of the academic year 1897–8? This date is important, as it marks the beginning of the real Dreyfus affair, with the start of the fight for the reopening of Captain Dreyfus's case.

Lucien Herr, right from the start of that academic year, led the combat.[73] Those who were convinced of Dreyfus's innocence, in the autumn of 1897, were few indeed. Among the intellectuals we might mention, besides Herr, Lucien Lévy-Bruhl, Gabriel Monod and Michel Bréal. Taking advantage of the sympathetic neutrality of the director of the school,[74] Herr led a veritable 'revisionist' campaign. He was soon surrounded by an activist group including Charles Seignobos, Charles Andler, Paul Dupuy and Victor Bérard.[75] They obtained the support of those professors who were liberal, socialist, or close to socialism, in particular Jules Tannery,[76] the historian Gustave Bloch,[77] and Gustave Lanson. The anti-Dreyfusards at the school were the three Catholic professors, Gaston Boissier, Brunetière and Ollé-Laprune. Bergson, who succeeded Ollé-Laprune after the death of the latter in 1898, refused to take sides. Anti-Semitism led certain left-wingers to a position hostile to Dreyfus, as was the case with Romain Rolland.[78]

As regards the students and the former students, Charles Péguy was in the front line, surrounded almost exclusively by his fellow socialists to the point where, for example in Hubert Bourgin's opinion, socialism and Dreyfusism were one and the same thing. Among the graduating class of 1893, there was first of all François Simiand (who was very close to Herr, and who became his library assistant); among that of 1894, Albert Lévy, Mario Roques, Etienne Burnet, Désiré Roustan, Félicien Challaye,[79] Paul Mantoux[80] and Paul Langevin[81] played important roles. Note that Georges Weulersse, who came first in the 1897 history *agrégation*, obtained an Albert Kahn scholarship and made a round the world tour in 1898, and that Albert Mathiez, who passed the *agrégation* the same year, was appointed to a professorship in Montauban. Also to be noted are Adolphe Landry, who was a socialist sympathizer but rapidly became a member of the Radical Party, and who graduated at the same time as Simiand,[82] and also the younger Hubert Bourgin, Jérôme and Jean Tharaud (present out of friendship for Péguy)[83] and Albert Thomas.[84]

To get an idea of the role of the socialists in the Ecole Normale Supérieure during the Dreyfus Affair, one must, as well as considering the young Normalians and their professors, talk about Léon Blum (an 1890 graduate) and Jean Jaurès (1878), who were both converted, or reinforced in their political allegiance, by Lucien Herr, and were then convinced by Herr and Péguy of the innocence of Dreyfus and of the importance of the combat for socialism. The different parties or socialist groups, in fact, generally did not commit themselves – or, if they did, it was only late in the day – to the fight on behalf of Dreyfus. At the beginning, besides the young Normalians grouped around Herr and Péguy, there were only the 'Allemanists' and the anarchists (present on account of their anti-militarism), in particular Sébastien Faure and Bernard Lazare. The main leaders were in favour of neutrality; they refused to commit the working class to a dispute that was internal to the bourgeoisie.[85] Such was the position of Jules Guesde and of Vaillant, of Millerand and Viviani; and, at the beginning, Jean Jaurès himself was hesitant.[86]

In 1898 the library in the Rue d'Ulm, around Herr, and Péguy's Librairie Bellais, became the two poles of Dreyfusard socialism. At the library there were frequent meetings of the '*Syndicat*' of intellectuals who supported Dreyfus, and the Ecole was 'one of the citadels of Dreyfusism'.[87] As to the Librairie Bellais, at the corner of Rue Victor Cousin and Rue Cujas, it was the headquarters, and Péguy the person who took charge of the training,[88] who organized the students and the '*archicubes*'[89] in demonstrations or for the protection of the 'Dreyfusard' professors at the Sorbonne from attacks by right-wing students and anti-Semite gangs, and equally to protect those (less numerous) of the law faculty (in particular Charles Gide, who had just been appointed). François Simiand was his 'young staff officer'.[90]

The name of François Simiand leads us on to discuss the role of the Durkheimian sociologists, and of Emile Durkheim himself (an 1879 graduate),[91] whose prestige and importance soon became considerable, as well as that of the person who was to become at one and the same time his senior, his colleague and his continuator, Lévy-Bruhl (an 1876 graduate), who was very close to Jaurès. *L'Année Sociologique*, whose first issue dates from 1896–7, was the organ for the dissemination of the work of this school, whose members were all left-wingers, sympathizers or militant socialists, all Dreyfusards; and indeed the link between the new sociology, socialism and a commitment to Dreyfusism cannot be overstressed.[92] Let us also note the commitment to the battle shown by Durkheim's disciples in the universities, such as Marcel Mauss,[93] P. Fauconnet, Emmanuel Lévy, and Normalians such as Célestin Bouglé, Hubert Bourgin[94] and Maurice Halbwachs (an 1898 graduate).

The Dreyfus affair did not leave Léon Walras indifferent. Although he may have scribbled some 'ill-humoured notes' of a fairly anti-Semitic nature, in this case he was unambiguous. At the end of 1898, he wrote: 'the anti-Semites are like the anarchists, they are a product of our morbid state'.[95] Six months later, he criticized Gabriel Tarde for having explained[96] that the Dreyfus affair did not prove that there had been any social decomposition in France, since it had been greatly exaggerated by the press. No, said Walras, the social decomposition was clearly visible: over and above the role played by the army, the clergy, the government and the parliament, it was enough to observe how the law crushed the innocent and protected crime. And he hoped that a party might be formed with a programme comprising voting reforms, an honest, reforming government, an army that was not enslaved to clericalism and imperialism, and an independent judiciary, in 'brief, a whole new *society*'.[97]

2.   Léon Walras and the socialists of the Ecole Normale

Georges Renard, an 1867 graduate and a longstanding friend, tried to help Léon Walras to get his theories and ideas accepted among the Normalian socialists, in which activity he was assisted, as indeed he was with regard to the whole of his career, by his wife Louise[98] and her social contacts, through the salon which she kept.[99] Georges Weulersse, who was his nephew, seems to have persuaded his uncle of the existence of a socialist current among the students at the Ecole Normale, and of the importance of Charles Péguy as the leader of this movement.[100]

Léon Walras, who had just published the third edition of the *Eléments* and *Etudes d'économie sociale*, knew that, with regard to the propagation of his theses concerning mathematical economics, and especially his liberal, scientific socialism, he could not count on his adversaries, i.e. the liberals of the orthodox persuasion, and the original and neo-spiritualistic movements. Moreover we know how little impact his ideas had at this time on mathematicians, even though Hermann Laurent, whose role in the Société des Actuaires was important, appreciated his work in pure economics.[101]

Léon Walras needed to increase the modest impact which he had made, thanks to Charles Gide especially, amongst the 'leftist' academics of the law faculties, and to look for new domains in which to spread his ideas. From the end of 1896 on, he hoped to interest the Jaurèsian current of 'French socialism'.

And to begin with, the politicians. He sent his *Etudes d'économie sociale* to Jean Jaurès and to Etienne Millerand, with a laudatory letter of accompaniment,[102] hoping to convince them; but it does not seem as though this initiative had any effect. The fact that he tried it in no way signifies that he was close to Jaurès's or Millerand's ideas. In a letter to his childhood friend, Gustave Maugin,[103] he talked about the three articles which he had just recently brought out in the *Revue Socialiste*, adding:

> one thing which leads me to believe that I have in fact remained on the straight and narrow is that they didn't at all please the socialists of the *Revue*, Deputies Jaurès, Millerand, Rouanet, and others; you know the kind of socialism they practise. But then who in heaven's name *will* they please? Well, my friend, they'll please people abroad: it's sad to say, but that's the way it is.

Doubtless he was no closer to the socialism of Charles Andler (influenced by Proudhon) or that of Lucien Herr, whether in the latter's 'Allemanist' period or his Jaurèsian, although the 'republican socialist' aspect could be thought to bring them closer together. Naturally Walras's socialism, it hardly needs repeating, is far removed from Marxist or authoritarian socialism, or from that of a Jules Guesde or a Vaillant.

But it was above all a question of getting the interest of the socialist academics.

First, the professors of economics in the faculties of law. Charles Gide, though he had brought Walras into the *Revue d'économie politique* as a collaborator, published a valiant and severe review there,[104] despite some friendly, if ambiguous,[105] comments. He begins by explaining that the work is made up of papers which are often old, and without much interconnection, so that Gide himself had to reconstitute the theory. He insisted on the Walrasian idea of leaving to the individual his personal faculties and the wealth deriving from them, and to the society the social wealth (the land and mines, but also certain natural monopolies and public services). Gide showed the connection that Walras made between this allocation, Walras's proposed solution of the social problem i.e. the nationalization of land, and his theory of value (the value of the land is founded on final utility, not on labour). He questioned the practical efficacy of Walras's plan, insisting on Walras's reluctance to expropriate the landowners, and on a fair price being paid for the land. But what would be the interest of the state, in this case? Even if it were a possible solution in the abstract and if, in a remote future, the state finished making profits thanks to the increasing surplus value of rents, no minister of finance would ever take Walras's plan seriously! Gide noted above all that the nationalization of the land would not be a solution to the social question, since the capital would not remain outside such a solution.[106] If Walras rejected the Marxist solution, and considered the cooperativist one as being insufficient, Walras's solution (typically that of a mathematician economist) was inadequate, and did not even resolve the fiscal problem.[107]

Secondly, the literary elites. At the heart of the system was the Ecole Normale Supérieure, with which Walras was all the more familiar given that his father had been one of its graduates. And on this terrain he had the support of Georges Renard, who was at that time looking for a talented analyst. No doubt talked into it by Georges Weulersse, he asked Charles Péguy to write a review of the *Etudes d'économie sociale* for the *Revue socialiste*. On 1 December 1896 Walras wrote to Weulersse[108] to tell him how pleased he was about the fact that the Normalians were taking an interest in his work. Moreover Péguy had to consult a Normalian mathematician 'on a special point'. Let us note, however, that the 'scientists' at the school did not seem really interested, though Péguy made an effort to get his ideas known in this milieu.[109] Walras suggested to Weulersse that, as a historian, he complete this jury and give 'his opinion on my system of historical evolution of property'.[110] Walras also sent Weulersse his *Théorie géométrique de la détermination des prix* and a voucher on his Parisian publisher[111] for two copies of the *Etudes*, recommending Weulersse to perhaps give one 'on my behalf to M. Herr for the Ecole's library', where Charles Péguy borrowed the *Eléments* on 16 December 1896, and Georges Weulersse the *Etudes* on 31 December 1896.[112] They both returned the books on 24 March 1897.[113] Péguy eventually wrote an article in which he brought together the analysis of the *Eléments* and that of the *Etudes d'économie sociale*, entitled 'Un économiste socialiste, Monsieur Léon Walras':[114] a remarkable article, to which we shall return in the next section since it constitutes no doubt the only serious attempt, at the time, to arrive at a comprehension of Walras's overall system. There followed an exchange of letters between Péguy and Walras.[115] In fact, between December 1896 and April 1897 almost all the members of the 'Utopia turne' were interested in Walrasian ideas: Péguy sent the manuscript of the article he had just written to Albert Lévy, who was then travelling in Germany.[116] It is true that Péguy's socialism was not that of Walras. Péguy was deeply marked by a certain Fourierism, his vision was utopian, the opposite of all 'economism', and was founded on a generous belief in solidarity among men. However, at the end of 1896 what appears to have interested him above all in Walras's writings was the possibility of using mathematical economics to understand society and to construct a 'scientific' socialism, to provide a rigorous base for a non-Marxian form of socialism.

Georges Weulersse, for his part, wrote a brief review[117] of the *Etudes d'économie sociale*, which is interesting to the extent that it shows the gap that existed between Walras's socialist conceptions and those of another member of the 'Utopia *turne*', doubtless more impregnated than he was himself with Marxist culture. After paying homage to Walras's decisive role in the foundation of mathematical economics 'which exists today in the same way that mathematical physics exists', Weulersse noted, essentially, four points. First that Walras 'unveils the poverty of orthodox political economy'.[118] After reading Walras, he explained, the contradictions, the variations, in a word the absence of scientificity of the orthodox system stood out clearly. Moreover, was it not the case that the true heirs of Turgot, Smith and Ricardo were the dissident economists and the socialists? Secondly, Walras criticized 'fiscal radicalism', in the sense intended by the radical party of the time. And in this respect also, Weulersse appreciated his ideas: progressive taxation was only a half of what justice should be, a timid and inconsequential measure, a *de facto* injustice which was less concerned with liberty than real socialism would be. The third point is more interesting. Weulersse was well acquainted with Marx's thought, especially his theory of value, and also with the Physiocrats and the classical economists. He had indeed presented a dissertation at the Ecole Normale on 'Les rapports entre les formules économiques de Marx (in *Capital*, Vol. I) et les formules des Economistes', and he had previously studied, for a lesson, 'La Richesse dans ses rapports avec la Justice sociale'.[119] He noted that Walras, though undeniably a socialist, and certainly a collectivist with regard to redistribution and to the production of social wealth (since he favoured the buying back of land by the state, and demanded the state's intervention in the constitution and regulation of monopolies), was a critic without much sympathy for Marxist collectivism, since he could not admit that all value came from labour. And Weulersse noted that, contrary to what Walras appeared to think, this principle was in no way aimed at 'spiritualizing' political economy, and still less at 'justifying' the existing society, unlike certain authors, such as Bastiat, who '*appeared* to support it before him': Bastiat had never said that all value came from labour, but from a service, which was not the same thing! On the other hand Marx was no doubt alone in maintaining all along, and with rigour, this theory of labour value.

Finally, what did Weulersse think of Walras's socialism, this synthesis of communism (to the extent that he demanded equality of conditions) and individualism (to the extent that he accepted inequality of position among individuals)? Certainly Walras did not resolve the social question, but he helped to resolve it. And

> this propitious conception would be more logical if M. Walras had added – which is no doubt in his thinking – that thanks to equality of conditions, inequality of position will unceasingly continue to decrease, and especially if M. Walras had drawn out all the consequences of his principle of equality of conditions, which implies . . . equality of starting point for all children.

After the philosopher Charles Péguy and the historian Georges Weulersse, might Walrasian theories interest a third element of Normalian socialism, the Durkheimian sociology branch, and thus, for economics, François Simiand and the new economic sociology? The first volume of *L'Année sociologique* contained an article by Simiand on Walras's *Etudes d'économie sociale*,[120] but Simiand was content to give a rapid description of the content of the work – explaining that Walras had to give up the publication of the *Eléments d'économie sociale* and the *Etudes d'économie politique appliquée* in order simply to recommence, order and complete his previous studies – and reserved for later his judgement on the totality of Walras's work. Simiand published two other recensions, one for the *Etudes d'économie politique appliquée*, the other for the fourth edition of the *Eléments*.[121] In the end he was by no means convinced by Walrasian theory, which he criticized severely, or by Walrasian method, which was poles apart from his own, being a positive method founded on the facts, intending to be exclusively inductive, aimed at the construction of an economic sociology; nor was he convinced by his approach to socialism.[122] Simiand, in effect, being a socialist also, very close to L. Herr and to Jaurès, and also eager to construct a *scientific* form of socialism, wanted to do so on an entirely different basis, that of '*positive* socialism'. It remains the case that, given the obscurity in which economists maintained the works of Walras at the time, Simiand's recensions in a new review which served as a landmark for the new sociologists and, more generally, for the young leftist intellectuals of the time, were far from negligible. It is to be noted that G. Weulersse also appeared very close to the ideas of Durkheimian sociology. Writing to Walras in the autumn of 1897, he pointed out that 'the fashion of history for history's sake and of pure erudition is past and gone: it is time for history considered as science, and for history-sociology, whose end, like the end of every science, is to determine the relations which really exist between facts'.[123] This conception was typical of Durkheim's disciples, that is to say typical of a neo-positivist form of sociology which permeated the totality of the social sciences, bringing history down to a form of historical sociology, and economics to economic sociology, as Simiand did. This conception was naturally opposed to Walras's hypothetico-deductive method, which was also the reason for the later criticisms by Simiand and his disciples of the Walrasian school, mathematical economics and, more generally, all deductive approaches; which makes it all the more interesting to note that on the contrary Péguy, in his analysis of Walras's writings, appeared to assert that he saw eye to eye with him.

Another young former Normalian, also a socialist, close to the Renards,[124] and who might equally appear to have been influenced by certain Walrasian ideas, was Adolphe Landry. Utility appeared in effect to be at the centre of his preoccupations. Having read an article by Landry in the *Revue d'économie politique* of May 1897,[125] in which he was quoted on the theory of maximal satisfaction, Walras sent him a copy of the *Etudes d'économie sociale*, and later, in an attempt to convert him, his pamphlet 'Equations de la circulation', then the *Etudes d'économie politique appliquée* (in July 1899), and the fourth edition of the *Eléments*. For his part, Landry sent Walras, in June 1901, his *L'Utilité sociale de la propriété individuelle*, asking him for a critique of it. Naturally, Walras responded and, in his analysis of the cases in which individualism was a cause of diminution of utility, he criticized Landry not only for his German influences (those of Otto Efferts), but especially for not having understood that 'the aim of our efforts' must be, not 'the (absolute) maximum of utility' but 'the (relative) maximum of utility compatible with justice', and for not having tried to give any positive information about the society to be set up, but rather limiting himself to essentially negative criticisms.[126] Landry's reply[127] was typically anti-Walrasian, claiming to be concerned principally with justice, but maintaining also that there could be no conflict between utility and social justice, since justice was only a formal rule which could not be defined except on the basis of utility (in the broad sense). This was a new disappointment for Walras, and also the end of the correspondence between the two economists. We note, however, that in the list of French signatories for Walras's jubilee[128] are to be found, beside the names of Charles Andler and Georges Renard, those of A. Landry and F. Simiand.[129]

A final attempt brings to centre stage once more this little world of ex-Normalians. Gustave Maugin had given a copy of the *Etudes d'économie sociale* to Auguste Penjon, an ex-Normalian,[130] who seemed to have convinced Xavier Léon[131] to publish a report written by Penjon for his *Revue de métaphysique et de morale*. Finally, the only thing that appeared in this review was a bibliographical note on Walras's works and a résumé of the *Etudes*. As to A. Penjon's article, it was published in the *Gazette de Lausanne*.[132]

3.   From Charles Péguy to Paul Valéry

Charles Péguy had not only written the article 'Un économiste socialiste, Monsieur Léon Walras',[133] he had also, for a lecture at the Ecole Normale, prepared a text on mathematical economics (Cournot, Gossen, Jevons and Walras), which has unfortunately been lost.[134] The article from the *Revue socialiste* is all that remains to give us an idea of Péguy's observations on Walrasian economics and socialism.

Péguy, starting from an analysis of the application of mathematics to economics, and from a reflection on mathematical number as opposed to social number, ended up with the idea that social justice and Léon Walras's political economy were finally irreconcilable.

3.1   Léon Walras's method

Walras, applying the mathematical method to economic phenomena 'really instituted a science'. For this science to be possible, it was necessary 'that its object should not be foreign to its methods', and thus that Walras should be able to abstract homogeneous elements from the heterogeneous phenomena given by economics. So that this science might get started, it was necessary to abstract and choose the most simple notions and principles from these complex elements.

Walras's mathematical economics satisfied these conditions. Thus, from competition such as it existed, in a heterogeneous form, he abstracted homogeneous competition, which provided the possibility of obtaining measurements, relations and curves, and 'the economic equilibria acquired will be able to turn themselves into real equations'. In this way Walras abstracted and chose the simplest starting elements, afterwards making them more complex: to study concrete wealth, he considered it as being represented in quantity (if not in fact constituted) by the totality of values.

> To study values as they are, he took it that they are the only variable conditions of exchange, and that consequently, the invariable laws of exchange being known, the calculation of values could be directly deduced from these; to study exchanges, he chose the simplest of all, the bartering of two commodities one for the other. Then and thus could pure political economy begin.

And in the same way, in order to analyse 'society as it should be', he considered it as a legal entity constituted by an ensemble of individuals who are 'so many irreducible moral units. And social economics can then begin.'

Can this mathematical method be criticized? After having rejected the 'naive' criticisms (a superfluous method, too simple, which leads to a neglect of morality and social action), Péguy offered a personal criticism:

Walras should have begun by reflecting on 'the use of mathematical models in economics'. But if mathematical number or line is undefined, social number is defined at each instant; 'from which it follows that the units which constitute this number are not only in solidarity amongst themselves, like the units of ordinary mathematical number ... but are linked together among themselves by a closed, circular solidarity'. This he illustrated by saying that one should not write n men or n francs but (Tm and Tf being respectively the total number of men or francs) n/Tm men and n/Tf francs. From then on, one could not speak of the ownership of a piece of land by a given individual without saying, at the same time, that he dispossessed the state (if one admitted, like Walras, that the state was, by right, the proprietor of the ground).

Walras, who read with attention the young Péguy's work on mathematical economics and the article in the *Revue socialiste*, replied:

> 'mathematics permits us, with three points, to take into account all the men and all the francs. In pure political economy, when I say: take commodities (A), (B), (C), (D) ... and exchangers (1), (2), (3) ... I am considering all the commodities and all the exchangers, without exception. And my considerations in social economics are founded on these considerations of pure political economy.

This may be so, but Péguy, when he talks about 'closed, circular solidarity' in economics, is making reference to the distinction between what we call micro- and macroeconomics: in the latter case, individuals' actions in a sense run up against the framework formed by society, as opposed to the 'ordinary solidarity' of mathematical number. Upon this objection Péguy built his critique of the means that Walras advocated for attaining the social ideal.

For the moment let us note that Péguy, alone among those who reviewed the *Etudes d'économie sociale*, analysed Walras's opposition (given in the chapter 'Théorie de la Propriété') between Jevonian and Gossenian barter as an application of Walrasian scientific method.[135] To study 'wealth such as it is' Walras should, in Péguy's opinion, have supposed that pure economics began with the most simple exchange, the barter of two commodities between two exchangers.

Now whereas, according to Jevons, each of these agents engages in exchanges up to the point of maximizing his satisfaction, and on condition that the one supplies as much of his commodity as the other demands, and vice versa, up to a relative maximum which allows the right to property of each exchanger to continue (he cannot be forced to exchange more than he wants to), according to Gossen the two commodities are shared out to the absolute maximum point of satisfaction of the total utility of the two exchangers without taking account of the property rights of the exchangers (one of them can be obliged to give up more than he wants to); in other words Gossen maximized what could be called social utility, given the total endowments of the individuals when entering the market, irrespective of the initial distribution of their endowments. Walras chose the Jevonsian form of barter for two reasons, as Péguy explained:

1. for a reason of method internal to pure economics: exchangers are proprietors (possessing units) and competitors (competing units). But Gossen's barter affects them as proprietors, reintroducing the heterogeneous; and, as competitors, it supposes that they are not free; but if competition is not perfectly free there is also a return to the heterogeneous;
2. for a 'decisive' reason of relations with another science, 'the "social science" where the law comes into the question': Gossen's form of barter, in not respecting individual property as it is given before the operation, affects 'the natural economic fact' or, as Péguy called it, 'economic being', and, in not respecting individuals' freedom of competition, it affects the economic rights of individuals united in society, i.e. their 'social rights'. And Walras refused any solution which would not respect 'economic being' and 'social rights'.

Jevonian barter was therefore, in Péguy's opinion, the elementary operation which Walras took as his starting point, and from which, by increasing complexity, he arrived at a theory of wealth as it existed, in the *Eléments d'économie politique pure*. It remained for him to calculate, on the one hand, the best social means of maximizing wealth, which was to be the problem in the *Etudes d'économie politique appliquée* and, on the other hand, the best social means of sharing this wealth out justly, which was the subject of the *Etudes d'économie sociale*. And in both cases he used mathematical methods.

Social economics must study 'in exact justice' the distribution of wealth once it has been produced in respect of 'economic being' and of 'social rights' (a reconciliation of vested interests and justice). Walras started with two types of irreducible legal entity: those whose origin was individual (individual persons, families, voluntary associations), and those whose origin was collective (states, districts, communities); or, to simplify, individuals and the society or state. Thus a reduction was carried out to simple, 'irreducible' units.

Walras, according to 'an exact method', had to reason in two stages: first, to define an ideal society which respected economic being and social rights, then to find the best means of arriving at this end.

3.2 From the definition of the social ideal to its realization

As to the first stage, exact justice would be achieved if each person obtained, in the distribution, the share of wealth he had produced with the means that he owned. It remained to be seen who should be the proprietor, and of what. Individuals should be proprietors of the means of production, of their individual faculties, and of the wealth produced or that engendered by their personal faculties. The state should be the proprietor of collective faculties and of the wealth that they produced. And these collective faculties were not only land but also the major means of production, communication and exchange.[136]

From then on, with each enjoying the fruits of his activity, there would be inequality of position, and, society being the proprietor of the land (and of the other principal collective means of production) and enjoying its fruits, there would be equality of conditions.

There remained the second stage: what were the means whereby this social ideal could be realized?

It was a question of doing away with the taxation which was depriving individuals, who were naturally the proprietors of their personal faculties, of their work and its fruits, and of giving the state what belonged to it by right, i.e. the land and the principal means of production, exchange and communication, as well as their produce, which would allow the financing of public expenditure. But how was land to be nationalized without affecting, as Péguy explained it, 'economic being' and 'social rights'?

Walras remarked that in all progressive societies rent was in 'constant surplus value', and that moreover, at that time, the passage from the agricultural age to the industrial and commercial age and to intensive cultivation raised the rate of increase of rents. But as the conditions which caused this surplus value on rents were of social, not individual origin, it would be only in accordance with justice that the surplus value produced in this way should go to society. James Mill thought that the state should then use taxation to recover these surplus values, but for H.H. Gossen the proprietors, having effectively bought, along with their land, the possible surplus value of this land, were its legitimate owners. He considered that the state should buy back the land at current prices, consequently acquiring only the advantages linked to its perpetuity (at the same time it could borrow at better rates, deal in very long-term leases, etc.), which would allow it to borrow money, and so buy up all the land, pay off its debt with its rents, and still cover public expenditure.

Walras did not believe that this would be possible: the state enjoyed these advantages only in relation to speculators with a very short time horizon, and not at all in relation to inheritances. Should the state therefore buy up land, not at the market price, but at a 'present price' (simple capitalization of current rent), without taking account of anticipation of increasing surplus value of rents? This would deprive proprietors of the future surplus value they had bought. Should it buy the land at the 'current price'? According to Péguy, Walras noted that although the present proprietors had been able to buy land at a price that capitalized the anticipated surplus values on the rent, which were due to the existence of a progressive society, surplus values of the second type (which, being linked to the move to intensive cultivation and to the industrial age, could not be anticipated) could not have been capitalized in the price of land when the proprietors bought it. Purchases must therefore take place at a 'real normal price', calculated on the basis of the first type of surplus value alone, and excluding the second. The state would thus buy land at a price below the current price, and would in this way reap the benefit of the subsequent rises in rents which would take place, but which could not have been anticipated. It could then pay off the debt contracted in the buying up of land, and make the interest payments (as was not the case in Gossen's solution). It could then begin to finance its expenditure from its rents.[137]

The operation being terminated, the state would then be the proprietor of all the land, without having infringed the rights of any proprietor, nor affected 'economic being' or 'social rights': 'at the end of m years there would be, so to speak, an intersection of (social) rights, henceforth complete and entire, with (economic) being, still intact'.[138]

3.3 Péguy's criticisms

What is one to think of this plan?

To begin with, noted Péguy, it would take a long time to be able to finance public expenditure out of the income from rents. For the transition period Walras considered that it would be necessary to have recourse to progressive taxation, whose cause he had already, paradoxically, very much weakened by criticizing it so violently!

Above all, was it necessary to respect 'economic being', especially the rights of the landlords? This appeared to Walras to be required by his mathematical method and by his desire not to infringe the economic rights of legal entities. Such was not Péguy's position. We have seen that the units which constituted socioeconomic numbers were linked together by a 'closed, circular solidarity', and that one should never talk about n men or f francs, but n/Tm men or n/Tf francs. From this point on one could not take possession of land as private property without thereby dispossessing the state. In this way economic being, far from being a given that had to be respected, did not even respect itself, and its principles were altered in advance 'because it is composed of elements which are forever irreconcilable with each other'![139]

'After m years', according to Walras's schema, there would be an intersection of economic being and social rights. But this was valid only if one considered these m years as cut out from an infinite expanse of time which was indifferent to the position of the present. However, one was dealing in fact with years constituted in defined series, and positioned with respect to a given present. In the case of the purchase of land by the state, Walras's plan permitted the state, in m years, to achieve a state of 'parity' (it recovered its lands). But should it not already have been, initially, in a state of 'parity'? If such had been the case, the profits it made from the surplus value of rents would have arrived along with the rest, and of this the state was for ever deprived. To put it another way, Walras cannot prevent the state, the society, from suffering injustice today; and justice accomplished tomorrow will never make up this loss. From this point on it is vain to look for a solution which would respect both 'economic being' (i.e. the rights of the landlords) and 'social rights'; if 'a fact, just once, tramples on a right' this will suffice to prevent vested interests and justice from ever being reconciled.

From these remarks Péguy deduced a general criticism of Léon Walras's socialism.

Since 'economic being' was composed of irreconcilable elements, and since, given this, it was in vain to look for a perfect solution that respected both economic being and social justice, it would be preferable to look for the solution which was the least imperfect, and this would not be Walras's solution, since we would have to look for it on the basis of new data, in new conditions. Since we could not reconcile the true, in Walras's sense, with the just, it was best to say that 'the just is just, whatever the economic consequences may be', and he stressed that to prepare future justice out of present injustice was not just. Walras wanted to calculate precisely the ideal meeting point of facts and rights, but he should have reckoned that the calculation itself was often onerous, and that it was a better idea to count on solidarity. Does this indeed not already exist among scholars who work for other ends entirely than material rewards? And the citizens of the future city would profit by the generalization of such a form of solidarity.

This explains Péguy's annoyance when Walras, in a criticism of Marxism, observed that this doctrine implied the disappearance of luxury goods such as Château Lafitte 'when it is for bread and education that the world takes up the social struggle'.

The study of the mathematical method in economics which Charles

Péguy carried out in 1896-7 was, according to Walras himself, the first of this type in France. Here in fact is what he wrote to him:

> I have been informed . . . by G. Renard that you were to give a lecture on the point of departure of mathematical political economy such as Cournot, Gossen, Jevons and I laid it down. I must tell you in confidence that you are already not the only person in France to take an interest in this subject. But I shall not forget that (if I am not mistaken) you were the first; and if your genius and your inclinations maintain you in this path, you may count on me to provide you with any information that may be of use to you.

Besides an acknowledgement of priority, this constituted an offer of support, or even an invitation to become a disciple. But it would have been as easy to hold on to a will-o'-the-wisp!

Why, in the end, did Péguy – and, undoubtedly, the other young Normalians of the 'Utopia *turne*' – become interested, at the end of 1896, in Walras, in his method of mathematical economics and in his scientific socialism? Péguy and his friends were looking for the socialist 'exact method'.[140] And Péguy thought he had found it, perhaps thanks to Walras and his rigorous approach. Péguy then tried to put forward clearly, and then to put down on paper, his ideas on the ideal city, first in an article for the *Revue socialiste*, 'De la cité socialiste',[141] then in *Marcel, Premier dialogue de la cité harmonieuse*.[142] It should be underlined that in these last years of the century Walras and Péguy were not alone in being interested in the socialist city to be constructed, in fact it was a common preoccupation among socialists.[143] This *Premier dialogue* was to be followed by a second, to be entitled *Deuxième dialogue de la cité harmonieuse, De l'action pour la cité harmonieuse* which was never finished (nor perhaps even started).[144] Consequently he took up the plan of Walrasian 'exact method': to define, first of all this ideal city, then the means of achieving it. But, naturally the content of Péguy's ideal city had no connection with Walras's ideas, nor, undoubtedly, with the means of achieving it.

Though Péguy was the first to become interested in mathematical economics, he was already not the only one, as Walras had written to him. Who was the second? It was another young philosopher and poet, Paul Valéry.

3.4 Paul Valéry and mathematical economics

At the end of 1896 Paul Valéry published a review of the third edition of the *Eléments*.[145] One might wonder how the young Valéry (he was 25), the future great poet and essayist, knew about this work, and why he became interested in it. It is possible to imagine a link through Charles Gide. Valéry had done his law studies (between 1888 and 1892) at Montpellier, where Gide was at that time a professor.[146] The Valéry and Gide families had in common not only law, but also Montpellier and its faculty.[147] Further, Paul Valéry was, from December 1890, a very close friend of Charles Gide's nephew, André Gide, the young and already great writer.[148]

But the contingent fashion in which Valéry and the *Eléments* came into contact is not the important thing. It is simply necessary to know that Valéry, in his poetic work, his essays, his dialogues and his notes, was always interested in mental operations and in the play of his intelligence, and that at a very young age he became fascinated by architecture, then by mathematics and physics.[149] His model was Leonardo da Vinci,[150] whom he wanted to emulate in combining art and the scientific spirit. He used mathematics to formalize his intuition about the identity of intellectual phenomena and sensations; for him, finally, everything was mathematics: the title of his letter *Arithmetica Universalis* is revealing.[151]

Through Valéry, Léon Walras's ideas were introduced to a different sector of the intellectual world, which was less orientated towards the 'social sciences' than towards literature, and more artistic. But contacts between the two were numerous, if only via journals like the *Revue blanche*, or men like Léon Blum, who at that time spanned the artistic, Normalian and leftist milieux.[152]

The article on the *Eléments* is very interesting.[153] Valéry begins by way of congratulations: 'M. Walras is among those who think that the domain of mathematical analysis cannot be pushed too far, and that the study of the phenomena of life and of society is in no way incompatible with purely quantitative methods'. Without doubt he was more appreciative of the general orientation of the work, the effort to set up mathematical economics, and the courage of the author (whose speculations implied 'a fine disdain for immediate success: let us not forget that economist-mathematicians are as rare as mathematician-economists, and that a person who founds something is never treated gently') than he was of all the results. Where he found fault with Walras, beyond his ignorance about everything that was not mathematical economics, was in not having begun his work with a general presentation of the physico-mathematical method, and especially a discussion of the theory of *unities*, and he thought that it was wrong 'to have passed over in silence the very important ideas of *continuity* and of the generalization of the concept of *measurement*'. 'A quarrel of form', no doubt, but one which bears upon the most important part of Walras's work: according to Valéry 'the primary analysis of the facts must precede the mathematical analysis. As soon as calculation can be introduced, it may be said that the difficulties are over, and all that then remains to be done is to read the results, or to check them, that is, to compare the new relations produced by the algebra against reality'.

Beyond the interest of the article in itself, it has to be stressed that Valéry and Péguy were almost the only ones who understood the importance of Léon Walras's mathematical economics, and who studied it rigorously. The coming together of these two great names of literature, both of them in their youth, makes it impossible to take these articles as mere intellectual oddities, but shows that in France at that time one had to be an eccentric in political economy, or a visionary poet, to understand the importance of Walras's contribution. Which shows us all the more clearly the theoretical weakness, and sometimes the political blindness, of the professionals in the field of economic science in France! It also shows that the current of social mathematics, so powerful at the time of the Enlightenment and of Condorcet, and which re-emerged particularly with Cournot, had been ignored by French economists, but had continued to be a source of inspiration in philosophy. Cournot, a fellow student of Auguste Walras at the Ecole Normale was a philosopher. And it was as a philosopher that Valéry became interested in social mathematics; it was as a philosopher and a socialist that Péguy became interested in Walras's mathematical economics and 'scientific socialism'; this Walras who, indeed, had to keep repeating that he was neither a philosopher nor a mathematician, but an economist. All the same, the fact that an economist should be applying mathematics to the social sciences – that was the astonishing thing![154]

Notes

1. Léon Walras, *Eléments d'économie politique pure*, in Auguste and Léon Walras, *Oeuvres économiques complètes*, Vol. VIII, Paris: Economica, 1988, 'Histoire des différentes éditions' by Claude Mouchot, p. 808. Cf. The English translation by William Jaffé, *Elements of Pure Economics*, London: Allen & Unwin, 1954, based on the *Edition définitive* (1926).
2. Léon Walras, *Etudes d'économie sociale*, Vol. IX of the *Oeuvres économiques complètes*, Paris: Economica, 1990, Appendix III. The writing of this work was begun in March 1896 and completed between 23 and 26 November 1896 (cf. William Jaffé (ed.), *Correspondence of Léon Walras and Related Papers* (quoted below as *Correspondence*), Amsterdam: North Holland, 1965, Vol. II, p. 704, 11. 1271 to Vilfredo Pareto of 23 November and 1272 to E.R.A. Seligman of 26 November).
3. This review, after the death of Benoit Malon in 1893, was edited by Georges Renard, who preserved its socialist eclecticism.
4. See the recensions of the first two editions of the *Eléments*, of the *Théorie mathématique de la richesse sociale* and of the *Etudes d'économie sociale*, in *Oeuvres économiques complètes*, Vols VIII, IX and XI.
5. 'Socialism is, quite simply, the enemy', for economists like Paul Leroy-Beaulieu, cf. *Etudes d'économie sociale*, p. 424 and n. 42.
6. Charles Gide (1847–1932), professor of economics at the law faculty of Montpellier, was appointed in 1898 to that of Paris. He was a partisan of cooperativist socialism, and founded the 'Nîmes School' on the basis of these ideas.
7. Cf. below, the review in the *Revue d'économie politique*.
8. This was the date when Charles Rist passed the *agrégation* and was appointed to a

post in Montpellier. Unlike Gide, Rist was at that time capable of understanding and appreciating pure Walrasian theory.

9. In the treatise by Charles Gide and Charles Rist, *Histoire des théories économiques des physiocrates jusqu'à nos jours*, Paris: Larose et Tenin, 1909, Walras's contribution was mentioned, pp. 603–6.
10. Cf. his article 'La méthode mathématique en économie politique', *Revue d'économie politique*, 8–9 and 12, August–September and December 1901.
11. 'Principes de la théorie mathématique de l'échange', read on 16 and 23 August 1873.
12. Cf. *Correspondence*, Vol. I, p. 329, 1. 229. Out of this came publication in the *Journal des économistes* in April 1874.
13. Cf. 'Souvenirs du Congrès de Lausanne' in *Etudes d'économie sociale.*
14. Cf. these observations in L. Walras, *Mélanges d'économie politique et sociale*, Vol. VII of the *Oeuvres économiques complètes*, pp. 530 ff.
15. Cf. André Zylberberg, 'The French disciples of Léon Walras before 1914', 14th Annual Meeting of the HES, June 1987.
16. Which in Walras's opinion was 'an article which is worth little in terms of discussion, but which is worth a lot in terms of publicity', *Correspondence*, Vol. I, 1. 320, p. 456, given in Claude Mouchot, 'Histoire des différentes éditions', *Eléments d'économie politique pure*, p. 800, no. 27.
17. September 1883, pp. 499–508. J. Bertrand shows that the equilibrium of production is undetermined in a real market. Cf. Walras's reply in 'Un économiste inconnu: H.-H. Gossen' in *Etudes d'économie sociale.*
18. *Revue d'économie politique*, Vols IX–X 1889, for Gide's column, Vols I–II 1890 for the articles quoted. Edgeworth's articles in *Nature*, 5 and 19 September 1889.
19. *Journal des économistes*, January 1890, series V, **5** (1), pp. 98–114. Cf. *Correspondence*, Vol. II, p. 403, 1. 969 to L. Perozzo of 18 March 1890.
20. They had known each other since 1866. Georges Renard (1847–1930) had at that time been a student at the Ecole Normale, and had been introduced to Walras through A. Noël, Professor of Rhetoric at Bordeaux and a friend of the Walras family, cf. *Correspondence*, Vol. I, pp. 152–3, his letter of 18 November 1866. He remained a professor (of French literature) at Lausanne until 1900 (which did not prevent him being Parisian), at which date he was appointed professor at the Conservatoire des Arts et Métiers (before being given the chair of History of Labour at the Collège de France in 1907).
21. 'Un économiste socialiste', *La Petite République*, 7 November 1893.
22. Cf. André Zylberberg, 'L'Economie mathématique en France au temps de Walras, 1870–1914', doctoral thesis, University of Paris I.
23. L. Walras, *Mélanges* (op. cit. p. 236), and *Etudes d'économie sociale*, in op. cit., p. 312, n. 1 and 4.
24. *Eléments*, p. 818.
25. *Correspondence*, Vol. I, pp. 337–8, 1. 234 from Hyppolite Chardon.
26. *Correspondence*, Vol. III, 11. 1374, 1378, 1379, 1380, 1381, 1385, 1390.
27. To begin with, Laurent, like other actuaries, held a 'vulgar' theory of labor-value, the 'kilogrammetre' being the invariable unit of exchanges. He abandoned this theory thanks to Walras.
28. Walras did however publish an article, his 'Note sur l'équation du revenu net', in the *Bulletin trimestriel de l'Institut des Actuaires Français*, **10**, 1900, pp. 162–4, and became its foreign correspondent. Cf. Zylberberg, op. cit., pp. 141 and 179.
29. Cf. a letter to Emile Bouvier of June 1902, in which Walras repeats what Laurent had dared to say at the time ('How is one to accept that a satisfaction can be measured? No mathematician will allow it'), so as to poke fun at him since, subsequently, Poincaré had given Walras his support (*Correspondence*, Vol. III, p. 113, 1. 1448 and Zylberberg, op. cit., pp. 144–5).
30. Cf. Christian Charles, *Naissance des intellectuels*, Paris: Editions de Minuit, 1990.
31. Cf. Hubert Bourgin, *De Jaurès à Blum*, Paris: Fayard, 1938, p. 223.
32. Forty Paris newspapers carried reports. Cf. Robert J. Smith, 'L'atmosphère politique

à l'école normale supérieure à la fin du XIXe siècle', *Revue d'histoire moderne et contemporaine*, **20**, 1973, pp. 248–68.

33. In the education of the scientific elites, competition between 'Normale Sup' and the Ecole Polytechnique was more or less even up to the 1960s, and the profound devaluation of teaching which developed at that time. Mention should also be made of Saint Cyr, the officers' school which, given that the social role played by the army was considerable, educated a significant proportion of the elites, who often came from military backgrounds, with more conservative schooling, being Catholic and politically conservative.

34. But its effective importance dates from the foundation of the university in 1808, when its essential function was defined, in terms of training secondary school teachers and preparing candidates for the *agrégation* examination.

35. R. J. Smith, op. cit., p. 255.

36. In particular the suspension of the *agrégations* of history and philosophy, the two 'political' disciplines. Cf. Daniel Lindenberg and Pierre-André Meyer, *Lucien Herr, le socialisme et son destin*, Paris: Calmann-Lévy, 1977, p. 26.

37. 'Talas' means 'those who "vont '*t*' à la messe"' (who go to Mass).

38. In 1876 Gabriel Monod founded the *Revue historique* on the basis of the principle that 'history is a positive science'.

39. See below, p. 99, p. 104.

40. In the years 1888–9 the highly popular General Boulanger, a nationalist and advocate of a strong state, along with the large crowds that supported him, put the Republican regime under threat.

41. There were very few Boulangists at the Ecole and, according to Romain Rolland's account, the students were not very active against General Boulanger, cf. Jean-François Sirinelli, *Génération intellectuelle*, Paris: Fayard, 1988, pp. 347–8.

42. Alain, *Histoire de mes pensées*, Paris: Gallimard, p. 38, given in J.-F. Sirinelli, op. cit., p. 345. See also Elie Halévy's account, ibid., p. 348.

43. Charles Andler, *Vie de Lucien Herr*, Paris: Rieder, 1932, p. 27. Cf. also D. Lindenberg and P. A. Meyer, op. cit., H. Bourgin, *De Jaurès à Léon Blum, l'Ecole normale et la politique*, Paris: Fayard, 1938, pp. 104 ff.

44. L. Herr was certainly among those who were best acquainted with Hegel's work at the time. Though he was not able to write his 'great' book on Hegel, he nonetheless left behind him an article entitled 'Hegel', published in *L'Encyclopédie française* in 1890.

45. G. Monod, to whom Herr was very close, married the daughter of Aleksandr Herzen, the Russian revolutionary (died 1870), and perhaps advised Herr to make the trip, besides putting him in contact with this milieu.

46. Ch. Andler wrote that L. Herr, from 1890 onwards, 'lives in intimate contact with Russian revolutionaries', op. cit., p. 96.

47. Three or four years, perhaps, with the intention of writing a thesis there, as appeared normal to the director of the school, M. Perrot, which was why he refused the application made by Herr, who then had to lay siege to Louis Liard, the then director of higher education, who managed to convince Perrot.

48. Lucien Herr died in 1926.

49. Accused of treason and found guilty, Captain Alfred Dreyfus, a Jew, was deported (1894). In 1896 Major Picquart, convinced of the guilt of another officer, Esterhazy, asked that the case be reopened. Esterhazy, summoned before a court martial, was acquitted (January 1898). France was then divided in two: on the one side there were the left-wing 'Dreyfusards' (along with the Human Rights League) and, on the other, the anti-Dreyfusards of the French Fatherland League, the clericals, the anti-Semites and the nationalists. Zola, after publishing his letter 'J'accuse' in *L'Aurore*, was prosecuted. After the discovery of false proofs, fabricated by Colonel Henri (who committed suicide), there was a retrial, but it was only in 1906 that Dreyfus's innocence was fully recognized.

50. It was he who had *Capital* introduced into the library of the Ecole.

51. Journal of the Fédération des Travailleurs Socialistes de France, also called the 'possibilist party'.
52. *Pouvoir ouvrier*, 13 May 1890.
53. Charles Andler prefaced the French edition of 1904.
54. Cf. his review (in *Revue critique*, 1889) of *La Morale économique*, by G. de Molinari.
55. In 1896, in France, there was no unified socialist party (the Parti Socialiste de France, which brought together the socialists of Guesde and Vaillant, along with Jaurès's Parti Socialiste Français, dated from 1901, the SFIO from 1904), but a profusion of parties. The oldest, best structured and most Marxist of these was Guesde's 'Parti Ouvrier Français'. The Blanquist tradition was represented by Edouard Vaillant and his group, the 'Parti Socialiste Révolutionnaire'. A more reformist group broke away from Guesde's party, this being led by Paul Brousse (as the Fédération des Travailleurs Socialistes de France, or 'possibilists'), from which there broke away a faction directed by Jean Allemane (the Parti Ouvrier Socialiste Révolutionnaire, or 'Allemanists'). And most importantly there was the 'Confédération Générale des Socialistes Indépendants' which came together around Jean Jaurès, based on the Saint Mandé programme (after Jaurès's 1896 speech) of the journal *La Petite République* (the other leaders being René Viviani and, up until he became a minister, Etienne Millerand).
56. See above. Afterwards, he remained close to the so-called Allemanist current.
57. Jaurès had just been beaten in the 1889 elections, and was putting his free time to use in writing the two theses that were then necessary for an academic career, of which the one on German socialism was defended in 1892.
58. In 1897 Andler defended a thesis on *Les origines du socialisme d'Etat en Allemagne*.
59. Cf. H. Bourgin, op. cit., pp. 93 ff.
60. Charles Péguy, 1873–1914: a vigorous controversialist, essayist, philosopher and poet. He was a Jaurèsian socialist and an enthusiastic Dreyfusard (see below), who later became harshly critical of Jaurès and of socialism (which appeared to him to have become bogged down in lies and parliamentarism). Starting from 1900, his thought and his poetry were of a more and more Christian and nationalist inspiration, but he kept his distance from Action Française and the traditionalist milieux. He died at the front in 1914. See his *Oeuvres complètes en prose*, prepared by Robert Burac, Paris: Gallimard, La Pléiade collection, Vol. I, 1987.
61. The name 'Utopia' was supposedly cut out by them on the piece of cardboard which masked the glass in the door of this room. Cf. Jérôme and Jean Tharaud, *Notre cher Péguy*, Paris: Plon, 1926, p. 66.
62. Albert Mathiez, 1874–1932, unlike the other members of the 'Utopia turne', does not seem to have been permanently influenced by Péguy (he wanted above all to be a 'Jacobin', and his friends at the Rue d'Ulm called him 'the Citizen'), and remained politically committed. He was above all an academic (after his *agrégation* in 1897 he taught in different provincial secondary schools, at the Lycée Voltaire in Paris, then at the Sorbonne. He was a specialist in the French Revolution, and a great admirer of Robespierre (see his *Etudes sur Robespierre*, Paris, 1958).
63. Albert Lévy, 1874–1929. He took first place in the *agrégation* in German, and taught at Henry IV and Lakanal. After the defence of his theses, he became a professor at the University of Nancy, then at Montpellier. After the war, in which he joined up as a volunteer, he was appointed to Strasbourg, then to Aix. As a socialist he became (like Charles Andler, his master) wary of German nationalism, and above all a patriot.
64. See below, p. 97 and n. 110.
65. Cf. Jules Isaac, *Expérience de ma vie, Péguy*, Paris: Calmann-Lévy, 1959, pp. 46–7.
66. Isaac, op. cit., p. 55, and Félicien Challaye, *Péguy socialiste*, Paris: Amiot-Dumont, 1954. The initiative came no doubt from Mathiez. Péguy himself says a few words about it: *Septième cahier de la Ve série*, in *Oeuvres en prose complètes*, Vol. I, pp. 1258–9.
67. Albert Mathiez and Albert Lévy, after a second year at Lakanal, were accepted by the Ecole Normale Supérieure in 1893 and, after completing their military service, did their first year at the Rue d'Ulm in 1894–5. As to Péguy, after failing in 1892, he opted

to do his military service immediately, and afterwards became a 'khagneux' (which, in student jargon, meant that he was in a preparatory class for the Ecole Nationale Supérieure) at Louis le Grand (and a boarder at Sainte Barbe), and passed in 1894 (cf. Isaac, op. cit.

68. Ibid., p. 88.
69. According to Henri Guillemin, *Charles Péguy*, Paris: Le Seuil, 1981, p. 176, Charles Péguy displayed this manifesto, as he normally did with his 'communiqués', on the refectory door.
70. Without taking the *agrégation* examinations.
71. On 1 May 1898. The bookshop was equally a publishing house and a base for socialist action (in no way a traditional commercial enterprise), and also 'Dreyfusard'. Cf. Isaac, op. cit., pp. 133 ff. From 1899 onwards the Librairie Bellais, which was very badly run, was in difficulty. Péguy called on the help of Lucien Herr, who agreed, along with several friends, to finance the enterprise on the condition that they control its running, Péguy being henceforth only a 'publishing delegate'. At the end of 1899, Péguy, on the one hand, and, on the other, Herr and his friends, who were practically all participants in the 'Société Nouvelle de Librairie et d'Edition', parted company: Péguy moved in the direction of publishing his journal, the *Cahiers de la quinzaine*. He had asked the 'Société Nouvelle de Librairie et d'Edition' to be its publisher, but the board of administrators, Herr and his friends, had refused. After this the breach became increasingly wider, with the affirmation of an ever more parliamentary form of socialism on the part of Herr and his friends, who were close to Jaurès and Millerand, and, on the other side, Péguy's evolution towards a moral, individualistic socialism, not to mention his later evolution towards the exaltation of patriotic, Christian, anti-socialist sentiments. We might add that financial questions were at the centre of the ever more violent quarrel. Péguy, however, always maintained his respect for Herr: 'I have never spoken, and never will speak, of M. Lucien Herr with anything other than extreme respect' (Péguy, 7th notebook, fifth series, 1904, in *Oeuvres*, op. cit., Vol. I, p. 1264), contrary, for example, to what he thought of François Simiand (ibid.).
72. This was to be the *Cahiers de la quinzaine*.
73. On what followed, concerning the Normalians' position at the time of the Dreyfus Affair, see R. J. Smith, op. cit.
74. G. Perrot, who, like his successor Ernest Lavisse, was a 'Dreyfusard in the depths of his soul'; cf. Lindenberg and Meyer, op. cit., p. 147.
75. Victor Bérard became Lucien Herr's collaborator at the *Revue de Paris*.
76. Assistant director of the school, science section.
77. The father of the famous Marc Bloch.
78. To Herr, who tried to persuade him, Rolland gave this reason: 'I do not hide my anti-Semitic feelings from anybody'. Cf. Rolland's letter in R. J. Smith, op. cit.
79. See Bourgin, op. cit., p. 378.
80. Ibid., pp. 489–90.
81. The following is a list of the shareholders of the 'Société Nouvelle de Librairie et d'Edition' in 1899 (year of graduation from the Ecole being given in brackets), with Péguy having just moved away: Charles Andler (1884), Carle Bahon (1893), Léon Blum (1890), Hubert Bourgin (1895), Louis Bourilly (1893), Etienne Burnet (1894), Paul Fauconnet, Lucien Foulet (1895), Jules Isaac, Paul Langevin (1894), Louis Lazard, Albert Lévy (1894), Maurice Loewé, Edgard Milhaud, Albert Monod (1896), Charles Perez (1895), Jean Perrin (1891), Mario Roques (1894), Désiré Roustan (1894), François Simiand (1893), Ernest Tonnelat (1898), Antoine Vacher (1895), according to R. J. Smith (op. cit., p. 261) Georges Weulersse, far from Paris, was not in this group, which he joined afterwards (see the list of shareholders at the time of the dissolution of the Société Nouvelle de Librairie et d'Edition in 1929, in ibid., p. 262). Also to be cited are the students Albert Bayet (graduating class of 1898) and Maurice Halbwachs (same year), Albert Thomas, Lucien Febvre, Henri Wallon and Georges Milhaud (1899).
82. Hubert Bourgin, *De Jaurès à Blum*, p. 366, speaks of a caricature of Simiand.

83. Cf. Jérôme and Jean Tharaud, *Notre cher Péguy*, Paris: Plon, 1926.
84. Albert Thomas, a socialist, became an important politician, in particular as Minister of War in 1915–17. He took several socialist Normalians into his cabinet, in particular F. Simiand.
85. Besides the effect of a certain 'workerism', it has to be said that Dreyfus was Jewish (and the anti-Semitism of the left was very deep-rooted), and that he was a bourgeois and a soldier, which hardly pleaded in his favour with the socialists, and furthermore that he was supported by certain great financiers (in particular Joseph Reinach, whose name evokes the Panama scandal), and was personally not very engaging.
86. Jaurès hesitated to begin with and, even on 19 January, 1898, five days after Zola's article 'J'accuse' in *L'Aurore*, he co-signed, with Guesde, Millerand and Viviani, a manifesto in favour of neutrality. Cf. Lindenberg and Meyer, op. cit., p. 150. Up until then he had made known his doubts in *La Petite République* (at the end of 1897), and was only, finally, totally convinced (by Péguy) at the beginning of 1898. His role then became decisive.
87. Cf. Raoul Blanchard, *Ma Jeunesse sous l'aile de Péguy*, Paris: Fayard, 1961, p. 208.
88. 'At that time I was, so to speak, the military leader of the old Ecole Normale. Or rather, there were two leaders: I was the leader on days *when there was fighting to be done*. Herr was the leader on days *when there wasn't any fighting to be done*', Charles Péguy, in *Oeuvres en prose*, Vol. II, p. 1226.
89. Ecole jargon meaning an ex-student of the Rue d'Ulm.
90. Cf. Bourgin, op. cit., p. 350. Note that F. Simiand was also the author of a Dreyfusard work, *L'Histoire des variations de l'Etat-Major*.
91. He was awarded a chair in pedagogy and social sciences in 1887 at the Faculty of Literature in Bordeaux. In 1902 he was appointed to the Sorbonne. At Bordeaux, Durkheim ran the League of Human Rights, which had just been set up.
92. Cf. Terry N. Clark, *Prophets and Patrons, The French University and the Emergence of the Social Sciences*, Cambridge MA: Harvard University Press, 1973, p. 174.
93. Marcel Mauss was with Lucien Herr and François Simiand at the Société Nouvelle de Librairie et d'Edition, which took over from Péguy's Librairie Bellais. Like Herr and Simiand, he was soon to be against Péguy.
94. Hubert Bourgin left the Ecole Normale in 1899. He had written a volume on Proudhon for the Librairie Bellais and, especially, worked under the direction of François Simiand on various works in sociological economics.
95. Cf. *Correspondence*, Vol. III, p. 54, 1. 1384 of 23 December 1898 to Maurice L. Vernes, a professor of history at the Sorbonne, close to the *Aurore* newspaper.
96. G. Tarde, *Les Transformations du pouvoir*, Paris: Alcan, 1899, pp. 154–5.
97. Cf. *Correspondence*, Vol. III, 11. 1403 to 1405, of 16, 17 and 18 May 1899, between Walras and G. Tarde, who, moreover, explained himself so as to avoid any misunderstanding on such an important question: he was persuaded of the innocence of Dreyfus and of the conspiracy of some officers, journalists and politicians. Finally Walras made it clear that they were in agreement as soon as Tarde ceased to talk about the absence of *national* decomposition; but there was *social* decomposition.
98. She was the author of *Une jeune fille* (Paris: Nathan, 1905).
99. Her salon, in their apartment in Rue Meslay, played an important role in bringing together writers, journalists, politicians and academics; cf. Bourgin, op. cit., p. 173.
100. Cf. R. J. Smith, op. cit., p. 258.
101. See above, pp. 91–2.
102. See *Correspondence*, Vol. III, 11, 1278 and 1279 of 7 December 1896.
103. Ibid., Vol. II, p. 702, 1. 1268 of 11 November 1896. Cf. the editor's notes in the last chapter of *Etudes d'économie sociale*, op. cit., pp. 391–424.
104. *Revue d'économie politique*, **11** (3), March 1897, pp. 301–7. Walras asks for a review in a letter to Charles Gide (W. Jaffé, *Correspondence*, Vol. II, p. 689, 1. 1254, 25 July 1896).
105. 'What appears to us to be most remarkable about this book is some thoughts strewn here and there'.

106. And there was nothing to prove that the nationalization of the land would limit the concentration of capital, as Walras seems to believe.
107. Rent would never be able to finance public expenditure, and the paying of tax was the only form of expression of solidarity between citizens.
108. *Correspondence*, Vol. III, 1. 1274, pp. 706–7.
109. Ibid., Vol. VII, p. 732, 1. 1299 from Péguy: 'I wish to remain, as a philosopher, exactly informed about this science, and, what is much more important, I recommend it to those of my friends and other students who are mathematicians.'
110. For Léon Walras, a historian like G. Weulersse ought to take an interest in the evolution of the system of landed properties in France, with the social and political consequences of these transformations. On 26 September 1897, Weulersse, who had just passed the *agrégation* (in 1897 he came first in the history and geography examinations) wanted to write a doctoral thesis. On the suggestion of G. Renard, the subject he chose was 'The history of the theory of value in France', and he asked Walras for his advice, if only because he was himself 'a fine part of this fine subject'. Walras (see *Correspondence*, Vol. II, p. 758, 1. 1327 of 2 October 1897) advised him against this particular subject, putting forward two objections: one could not study the theory of value for France alone; it would be necessary to take in England, Germany etc.; and furthermore a good knowledge of mathematics would have been necessary, which Weulersse did not have. He advised him, on the contrary, to study *the history of the sales of national property*, which was a real sociopolitical drama for France in that this had been the means of setting up the class with which every French revolution had collided, and it had also been the basis of the alliance between the peasants and the bourgeois which had supported Bonaparte, and which still governed up to that day (with the then ministry of Jules Méline). It is to be noted that Walras recommended that, on this question, Weulersse consult one of his friends, Paul Mantoux (the future author of *La Révolution industrielle au XVIIIe siècle*, Paris: 1905), who was also a Normalian and a socialist (see above): a milieu with which Walras, decidedly, was very familiar! Finally Weulersse wrote two theses: *Le Mouvement physiocratique en France de 1756 à 1770* (Paris: Alcan, 1910) and *Les Manuscrits économiques de F. Quesnay et du marquis de Mirabeau aux Archives Nationales* (Paris: Guethner, 1910). Published after his death were *La Physiocratie sous les ministères de Turgot et de Necker (1774–1781)* (Paris: PUF, 1950) and *La Physiocratie à la fin du règne de Louis XV (1770–1774)* (Paris: PUF, 1959). He was a history and geography teacher in the Lycées of Toulon and of Orléans, then at the Lycée Carnot in Paris, as well as at the Ecole Normale Supérieure of Saint Cloud. He was the pre-eminent specialist on the Physiocrats, and his work remains essential. One should also mention Georges Renard and Georges Weulersse, *Le Travail dans l'Europe moderne* (Paris: Alcan, 1920) in *L'Histoire universelle du travail*, published under the direction of Georges Renard.
111. M. Pichon, bookseller-publisher, 24 Rue Soufflot.
112. Perhaps one of the copies which Walras had had given to him was passed on to Herr, the other being given to Péguy.
113. Cf. the edition of the *Etudes* in *Oeuvres économiques complètes*, Appendix III.
114. *La Revue Socialiste*, **146**, 15 February 1897, pp. 174–86, republished in Péguy, *Oeuvres en prose complètes*, Vol. I, pp. 3–18.
115. See below, the analysis of Péguy's article, and Walras's comments.
116. See Péguy, op. cit., in *Oeuvres en prose complètes*, p. 1545.
117. Walras Collection, Cantonal and University Library of Lausanne, XI, 43c. I have not been able to trace the journal where this review was published.
118. The expression 'poverty of orthodox political economy' is no doubt a reference to Marx's *Poverty of Philosophy*.
119. See *Correspondence*, Vol. II, p. 756, 1. 1326 of 26 September 1897 from G. Weulersse.
120. In *L'Année sociologique*, Vol. 1 (1896–7), pp. 499–500.
121. In *L'Année sociologique*, Vol. III (1898–9), pp. 498–9, and Vol. V (1900–1) respectively, in which he fails to give us the promised analysis, confining himself to a brief overview.

122. See Ludovic Frobert, 'Le Projet de F. Simiand: sociologie économique et méthode positive', dissertation for the Diplôme d'Etudes Approfondies, Université Lyon II, 1989, pp. 34 ff.
123. *Correspondence*, Vol. II, p. 756, 1. 1326 of 26 September 1897.
124. Louise Renard, in a letter written by her to Walras, (and signed in the names of Georges and Louise Renard, cf. *Correspondence*, Vol. III, pp. 146–7, 1. 1481, of 29 March 1901), tells him she knows 'very well' A. Landry, 'a Normalian of the stamp of your nephew' (G. Weulersse). She informs Walras that Bernard Bouvier (a professor at the University of Geneva) asked Georges Perrot (the director of the Ecole Normale) to recommend a young Normalian for the chair of political economy (Pantaléoni's place), and that he recommended Landry. Finally, thanks to Jaurès's support, the person chosen was Edgard Milhaud (a socialist who was also among the group of shareholders around Herr at the New Bookshop and Publishing Company, Péguy's former bookshop).
125. 'La loi de l'offre et de la demande de monnaie', *Revue d'économie politique*, **11** (5), May 1897.
126. *Correspondence*, Vol. III, p. 196, 1. 1521, to A. Landry.
127. Ibid., pp. 197–8, 1. 1522, of 27 February 1902.
128. Ibid., p. 1909, 1. 1745, Appendix.
129. A study of the names of the signatories is very instructive, not for the importance of Walrasianism as a theory but for the networks of support which came into being. One observes, at this time, the role of the Conservatoire des Arts et Métiers, thanks once again to G. Renard. Beside these names are to be found, in effect, those of Emile Levasseur (the former liberal critic of Walras's first dissertation, in 1873, and who had been Georges Renard's professor at the Ecole Normale Supérieure; Renard and he had remained friendly, and became colleagues when the latter was appointed to the Conservatoire des Arts et Métiers as professor of the history of labour: *Correspondence*, Vol. III, p. 242, 1. 1278, to Emile Bouvier of 2 February 1904), Alfred de Foville and André Liesse, who had been, or were, with Renard, professors at this Conservatoire (Simiand was close to Renard – whom he succeeded, first at the Conservatoire des Arts et Métiers, then at the Collège de France – and to A. Liesse, cf. Bourgin, op. cit., p. 361), Clément Colson, professor at the Ecole des Ponts et Chaussées, Ch. Gide and Ch. Rist, the former mainstays of the law faculties at Montpellier and Paris, the cooperativists of the 'Nîmes School', the disciple A. Aupetit, the three Lyonnais Walrasians, P. Pic, Ch. Brouilhet, E. Bouvier, other Parisian academics, A. Souchon, and, from the provinces, Chatelain, Dubois, Sauvaire-Jourdan, and the librarian Bonnet.
130. August Penjon, the French philosopher, born in Valence in 1843. He was a student at the Ecole Normale Supérieure, an *agrégé* in philosophy, then professor at the faculty of literature at Toulouse, and afterwards at Douai and Lille. He wrote *George Berkeley, sa vie, son oeuvre* (Paris, 1878) and a *Précis d'histoire de la philosophique* (Paris: Delaplane, 1896) and did numerous translations, in particular those of Rudolph H. Lotze, *Les Principes généraux de psychologie-physiologique* (2nd edn, Paris, 1881) and of African Spir, *Les Esquisses de philosophi critique* (Paris, 1887).
131. 1868–1935, French philosopher and chief editor of the *Revue de métaphysique et de morale*. He was a left-winger, and played a considerable role in Parisian intellectual circles. His salon was frequented by the elite of Parisian society, in particular by E. Durkheim, G. Lanson, and Louise and Georges Renard. Later (11 April 1898), Walras offered X. Léon an article (his *Esquisse d'une doctrine économique et sociale*), which was refused, and which was finally only published in its entirety in the *Etudes d'économie politique appliquée* (cf. *Correspondence*, Vol. III, 11. 1347, 1349, 1350, 1354 and 1355, of 11 April to 2 May 1898). In November 1904 X. Léon suggested that Walras write an article on Cournot, but he refused (it was A. Aupetit who finally wrote the article in question, for the *Revue de métaphysique et de morale* of May 1905). Cf. L. Walras, 'Cournot et l'économie mathématique', in *Miscellany*, op. cit., pp. 461–6. On

the links between Louise Renard and X. Léon, see *Correspondence*, Vol. III, p. 260, l. 1584: he had even been her escort at a wedding.

132. Supplement to no. 127, 1 June 1897. Cf. Appendix III in *Etudes d'économie sociale.*

133. *La Revue socialiste*, **146**, 15 February 1897. Péguy was anxious that Walras should read the manuscript of this article before publication, which he did, cf. *Correspondence*, Vol. II, p. 717, l. 1287 from G. Renard, and p. 729, l. 1298 to C. Péguy, of 18 February 1897.

134. This lecture was to have taken place in the presence of Georges Lyon, Professor of Philosophy at the Ecole Normale and a specialist in Hobbes. Finally Péguy gave only a brief summary of the text he had prepared, and he handed it over for correction to G. Lyon. Lyon annotated it and gave it back to Péguy, who sent it to L. Walras. Walras told him that he had read it three times, and had found the marginal remarks (by G. Lyon) most judicious. As Péguy remarked in a letter to him, it was a question of 'a philosophical enquiry into mathematical economics, and not a contribution to that science', which was confirmed by Walras's reply, explaining to Péguy that he was an economist, not a philosopher, and that, for him, the legitimacy and the utility of the use of mathematics were demonstrated by its results (as had been the case in physics and astronomy), and that though he was interested by abstract, *a priori* discussions on this theme, he did not have a lot to contribute to them. However he came back to a point in this text in order to criticize it, and in fact this was the only one to be taken up in the article. We will come back to this later. On these points, and on the exchanges of letters between Péguy and Walras, see on the one hand, *Correspondence*, Vol. II. 1298 of 18 February 1897, 1299 of 19 February 1897, 1300 of 21 February 1897, 1301 of 22 February 1897 and 1310 of 31 March 1897, and, on the other hand, Charles Péguy, *Oeuvres en prose complètes*, Vol. I, extracts of this correspondence, and Robert Burac's notes, pp. 1545 ff.

135. See W. Jaffé, 'The Normative Bias of the Walrasian Model: Walras versus Gossen' (1977), in D. A. Walker (ed.), *W. Jaffé's Essays on Walras*, Cambridge: Cambridge University Press, 1983.

136. Péguy, op. cit., p. 178, refers to Walras's note, p. 347 of the *Etudes d'économie sociale*, in the 1896 edition.

137. Péguy's exposition presents a double problem of interpretation: about what he wanted to express and about Walras's plan itself. Let a piece of land belonging to A be worth 1 000 FF today (at t_0). This current price corresponds to: (1) the capitalization of present rents (the 'present price'), and (2) the incorporation of anticipations about future increases in rent (such as the projection of the constant growth rate of the rent, plus, possibly, the passage to an industrial society). Tomorrow (at t_1), rents will have risen more than one could have anticipated at t_0 (rise in the rate of growth, transition to the intensive mode) and, thanks to these increases, it will be possible to keep up the interest payments and pay off the debt on the loan of 1 000 FF taken out by the state to buy the land at its current price – *such is Walras's plan*. But this land was worth 500 FF a century ago (at t_{-1}) when A acquired it. He paid: (1) the rents of that time, capitalized, and (2) what corresponded to possible anticipations (projection of the constant rate of growth, transition to an industrial society). If these anticipations had been correct, the land would be worth only 800 FF, which corresponds to the 'normal price' that the state must pay for the land. There is in effect no reason to pay the additional 200 FF, since: (1) A did not pay this money (the economic being has not been affected) and (2) it was due to collective causes (social rights have to be respected). *Such is the way in which Péguy understands Walras.*

138. Péguy, op. cit., p. 181.

139. Ibid., p. 185.

140. On 12 January 1899 Péguy wrote to E. Millerand (*Oeuvres en prose complètes*, Vol. I, p. liv): 'Monsieur Georges Renard wished to inform you that a certain number of students at the Ecole Normale, along with certain of their friends, had begun to engage in socialist action according to an exact method'.

141. No. 152, 15 August 1897.

142. Published by the Librairie Bellais in June 1898.
143. See in particular Benoit Malon, *Le Socialisme intégral*, 1891; Jean Jaurès, 'L'organisation socialiste', in *La Revue socialiste*, **123, 124, 126, 128, 137**, March to May 1896; Georges Renard, *Le Régime socialiste*, 1897; Eugène Fournière, 'La cité idéale', in *La Revue socialiste* of April 1898.
144. See R. Burac's note in *Oeuvres en prose complètes*, pp. 1560–1.
145. *Revue générale du droit, de la législation et de la jurisprudence*, **20**, November–December 1896, pp. 574–6.
146. In January 1888 Valéry attended a lecture given by Charles Gide.
147. Charles's brother, Paul Gide, the father of André, was a professor of law (he died in 1880 when André, born in 1869, was only 11). Jules Valéry, the brother of Paul, passed his *agrégation* in law in 1893 and was appointed to a professorship at Montpellier.
148. André Gide had already written the *Traité du Narcisse* (1891), dedicated to Valéry, and *Paludes* (1894); he finished *Nourritures terrestres* in 1897.
149. See his *Cahiers* (Paris: CNRS), in particular the one concerning the years 1894–1900, Vol. I, that of 1896 being entitled *Log-Book*.
150. His first book, *L'Introduction à la méthode de L. de Vinci*, was published in 1895.
151. Letter to his friend Gustave Fourment of 4 January 1898, in which he assimilated mental operations and algebraic operations, explaining that he forged instruments out of algebra. At the end of 1896 he published (in the second volume of the review *Le Centaure*) *La soirée avec Monsieur Teste* a personage who represented sublimated intelligence; in April 1897, in a letter to A. Gide (cf. *Correspondance Gide-Valéry*, Paris: Gallimard, 1955, p. 291, line 19, April 1897), he observed that he was studying the mathematics of speech. He was not merely an enlightened amateur: in 1899, for example, he read and annotated G. Cantor's *Fondements de la théorie des ensembles transfinis*, which had just come out.
152. Thus, for example, Blum wrote to Valéry in 1894 to ask him to put one of his unpublished sonnets into the *Revue Blanche*. See Paul Valéry, *Oeuvres*, Paris: Gallimard, 1968, Vol. I, p. 22.
153. As William Jaffé observed in *Correspondence*, Vol. II, p. 730, n. 1, where he reproduced Valéry's article (unfortunately a typographical problem has rendered the beginning incomprehensible). Jaffé also noted that Valéry, almost alone among his contemporaries, saw the importance of the budget equation: a 'remarkable equation', wrote Valéry.
154. Cf. *Correspondence*, Vol. II, p. 742, 1. 1310 to Charles Péguy, 31 March 1897.

8 Schumpeter after Walras: '*économie pure*' or 'stylized facts'?

Richard Arena

As we know, Schumpeter always demonstrated a very high esteem for the contribution of Léon Walras to economics:

> So far as pure theory is concerned, Walras is in my opinion the greatest of all economists. This system of economic equilibrium, uniting, as it does, the quality of 'revolutionary' creativeness with the quality of classic synthesis, is the only work by an economist that will stand comparison with the achievements of theoretical physics. Compared with it, most of the theoretical writings of that period – and beyond – however valuable in themselves and however original subjectively, look like boats beside a liner, like inadequate attempts to catch some particular aspect of Walrasian truth. It is the outstanding landmark on the road that economics travels toward the status of a rigorous or exact science and, though outmoded by now, still stands at the back of much of the best theoretical work of our time. (Schumpeter, 1954, p. 827)

For the historian of economic analysis, this emphasis on the pre-eminence of the Walrasian approach in economics states the ticklish problem of Walras's real influence on the formation of the Schumpeterian system. To put it crudely, may we consider this system as a mere application of the Walrasian research programme in the field of economic dynamics? The answer is far from obvious and economists still disagree today in this respect.[1]

In this regard, we cannot forget that Schumpeter began his academic career as an explicit and strict Walrasian scholar. His first book, *Das Wesen und der Hauptinhalt der Theoretischen Nationalökonomie*, written in 1908, is indeed a statement of the nature and limits of Walras's theory of general economic equilibrium. Although Schumpeter's other works do not exhibit such a proximity to Walras's contribution, they still demonstrate an unquestionable Walrasian fidelity. The preface to the first German edition of the *Theory of Economic Development* (1912) warns the reader about the danger of overestimating the apparent differences with the previous book and emphasizes the reverse way, i.e. the continuity of 'methods and purposes' (Schumpeter, 1935, p. viii). The preface to the Japanese edition of the *Theory of Economic Development* (1937) also stresses what Schumpeter considers an inextinguishable debt to Walrasian economic theory (Schumpeter, 1951, pp. 159–60). *Business Cycles* (1939) does the same, asserting once again that the elaboration of the theory of circular flow was 'definitively achieved by Léon Walras' (Schumpeter, 1939, p. 36).

According to Schumpeter's point of view, this allegiance to the Walrasian approach derives essentially from the acceptance of a specific interpretation of the Walrasian notion of *économie pure*. Schumpeter indeed identifies it with the core of economics and stresses the fact that the Walrasian theory of general economic equilibrium gives an adequate description of its nature. From this point of view, it furnishes the logical foundation of an autonomous economic science. Its method is indeed

> analogous to the method known in mechanics as the method of virtual displacements. What we want to learn before anything else is whether or not the relations known to subsist between the elements of the system are together with the data, sufficient to determine these elements, prices and quantities, uniquely. *For our system is logically self-contained only if this is the case* [my italics]: we can be sure that we understand the nature of economic phenomena only if it is possible to deduce prices and quantities from the data by means of those relations and to prove that no other set of prices and physical quantities is compatible with both the data and the relations. *The proof that this is so is the magna charta of economic theory as an autonomous science, assuring us that its subject matter is a cosmos and not a chaos.* (1939, p. 41)

The fact that economic science is 'self-contained' is first a proof of its scientific nature. This science appears indeed to conform to the hypothetical-deductive scheme of natural sciences. The deductive aspect derives from its logical consistency and is a promise of a sound foundation for a fruitful research programme. That is why Schumpeter stresses the utility of mathematical method in economics, in favour of which he presents a vigorous defence, in his first scientific article (Schumpeter, 1906) as well as in *Dogmengeschichte* (Schumpeter, 1972, para. 28). The hypothetical aspect means that 'in strict logic', hypotheses 'are arbitrary creations of the analyst ... mere instruments or tools framed for the purpose of *establishing* interesting results' (Schumpeter, 1954, p. 15).

Secondly, a 'self-contained' science does not need the help of the methodology and tools of other social sciences, even if, in the process of application, their results can be combined. Thus, in *Das Wesen*, Schumpeter investigates systematically the methods of biology, sociology and psychology and concludes it will not be profitable to import them into the field of economic analysis (1908, pp. 538–9, 543–4). The independence of economics from history is also presented as a necessity and we can therefore understand why a 'self-contained' science is universally applicable to 'primitive, medieval, capitalist as well as socialist economics'.[2]

The methodology of *économie pure* which Schumpeter thought to inherit from Walras was clearly 'individualistic'. According to F. Donzelli (1983, p. 639), Schumpeter was the first writer to introduce the expression 'methodological individualism' into scientific language. So in *Das Wesen* the society is described as a collection of individuals endowed with subjective utility functions and different physical amounts of goods and services. The economic problem is thus typically allocative. It consists in an attempt to discover the social and unique set of equilibrium prices, which corresponds to the network of optimal interindividual transactions. In other words, exchange appears to be the sole social relation between agents and is the pure result of their individual wills and interaction.[3]

All the preceding remarks may contrast with the widely prevalent views, according to which Schumpeter 'was well aware of the intricate patterns of the real world and insisted that sociological and political influences in economics must not be ignored' (Seidl, 1984a, p. 197) or to which 'from the beginning his methodology took the eclectic road of good sense [and] in his view, inductive facts need to interact with simplifying theories'.[4]

These apparent contradictions imply the necessity of a more thorough investigation of the Schumpeterian meaning of the notion of *économie pure*. We are first led to notice an important difference between Walras's and Schumpeter's interpretations. If Walras would certainly have welcomed the idea of an hypothetical-deductive and autonomous economic science, he would have not considered this idea sufficient to characterize the *économie pure*. In Walras's approach, the *économie pure* has to be contrasted with the *économie sociale* and *économie appliquée* and, in this framework, it can be identified with *positive* economic theory. Both later expressions refer to 'morals' and 'art' and represent the *normative* part of economics. Now it is obvious that Schumpeter never identified *économie pure* and economic theory and, moreover, that he was very sceptical about the normative power of economics.[5] A good illustration is precisely provided by economic dynamics, which Schumpeter did not include within the framework of *économie pure* but obviously considered to be a part of positive economic theory.

Secondly, I fully agree with the point of view expressed by L. Costabile (1986) according to which the stress put by Schumpeter on a hypothetical-deductive economic science might be explained by Schumpeter's commitment to criticize the 'essentialist' and 'aprioristic' position that the Austrian School opposed to the Historical School in the famous *Methodenstreit*: 'We do not accept a priori the assumption according to which the economic reality exhibits a consistent regularity and the statement of exact "laws" is therefore possible; those will become such a posteriori' (Schumpeter, 1908, p. 520).

This interpretation seems to be confirmed by the increasing distance with which Schumpeter considered the strict research programme of building an *économie pure*. As early as 1926, in the preface of the second German edition of *The Theory of Economic Development*, he wrote that he 'was now convinced far more than [he] was, about the necessity of a compenetration between facts and theory' (1935, p. ix). Similarly, in one of his last articles he noted that 'economic life is a unique process which takes place in historic time and in a troubled environment. For this reason and for many others, there is a motive for historical or institutional investigation in almost every part of economics' (1949a, p. 308).

These remarks are in perfect harmony with the General Introduction of *History of Economic Analysis*. On the one hand, Schumpeter emphasizes here the interaction of factual and theoretical works in the elaboration of economic analysis (1954, p. 42) and reminds us that hypotheses are suggested by facts (ibid., p. 15). On the other hand he observes that 'economic laws' are historically relative, 'that they work out differently in different institutional conditions, and that neglect of this fact has been responsible for many an aberration' (ibid., p. 35; see also Messori, 1983, pp. 639–42).

All of this is also confirmed by Schumpeter's well balanced and 'tolerant' judgements about the various theoretical approaches investigated in *History of Economic Analysis* as well as in *Dogmengeschichte*. For instance, in opposition to what we might have thought *a priori*, Schumpeter

> believed that [the Historical School] gave economics a perception of reality, that it stressed the unity of social activities and that it identified the place that antirationalism has in the development of societal organization. At its best, it stressed evolution, while the more traditional classical economists focused on statics.[6]

Besides, Schumpeter was not always faithful to methodological individualism.

Describing the circular flow as well as the development of an economy, Schumpeter made room not only for individuals but also for social classes. The existence of these classes played an important part in this flow. As early as the first edition of *The Theory of Economic Development*, Schumpeter renounced the pure microeconomic presentation he adopted in *Das Wesen* in favour of a macroeconomic scheme in which economic relations between social groups (bankers, capitalists, workers, business managers) constituted economic life.[7]

This reference to social classes is also present in the characterization of economic development. A. Dyer (1988) described the theory of economic development as a true 'theory of social order'. In this regard, entrepreneurs appear to be social leaders, whose function is to help capitalism to perform its task, i.e., 'to generate high rates of economic growth by introducing new types of goods, new markets, new forms of industrial organization and new methods of production' (1988, p. 34). This function rests upon a specific institution, seen as an empirical means of differentiating between classes, i.e., credit capital (ibid., pp. 31, 34–5).

Moreover, in many of his writings after *Das Wesen*, Schumpeter noticed that social relations between agents were not limited to pure economic transactions. For instance, in the framework of the circular flow, 'all the preceding periods have ... entangled [the agent] in a net of social and economic connections which he cannot easily shake off. They have bequeathed him definitive means and methods of production. All these hold him in iron fetters fast in his tracks' (Schumpeter, 1934, p. 6).

In *Business Cycles*, these 'iron fetters' are made explicit and described as the 'general business situation' every manager perceives, often comparing his own competitive position to the idea he forms about the 'normal' one. (Schumpeter, 1939, pp. 3–13).

It is clear that Schumpeter's acceptance of the notion of *économie pure* could not be interpreted as a defence of a pure theory without institutions, as it has sometimes tended to become in modern neoclassical general equilibrium theory. It is merely a warning against methodological confusion. Two significant illustrations may be given. The first concerns the influence of 'social power relations' ('Machtverhältnisse') in income distribution (Schumpeter, 1916). The scope of the second is the question of the correspondence between economic and juridical concepts (1917, in Schumpeter, 1983, pp. 47–9). In both cases Schumpeter stressed the absolute necessity of taking into account the presence and influence of institutions in economic analysis. However, the same real institution cannot be considered from the same point of view by the sociologist or the lawyer and the economist. A good example is the constraint of debt payments (ibid., p. 49). Economists cannot ignore it but will not investigate the legal techniques used to enforce these payments; in return they are strongly concerned by the effects this constraint implies upon economic activity.

If the preceding remarks shed some perceptible light on the nature of the influence Walrasian economics exerted on Schumpeter's thought, they are insufficient to bring about convincing and definitive statements. To go further, theory has to replace methodology. Most Schumpeterian themes could have been chosen: the theory of innovation, the theory of the business cycle, the theory of economic policy, etc.[8] Three themes are particularly significant for a further investigation of the nature of Walrasian influence on Schumpeterian economics: economic change, economic behaviour and money.

Time and economic change

The relation of time to economic change has to be investigated in the frameworks of the circular flow and of economic development.

The origin of the notion of circular flow was the Walrasian theory of general and static economic equilibrium. We have already seen how much Schumpeter praised this notion of equilibrium, considered in *Das Wesen* as 'an abstract picture of some economic facts' (1908, p. 527). Schumpeter, however, was much more convinced by the proof of the existence of such an equilibrium than by the Walrasian description of its formation.

In *Das Wesen* Schumpeter offers us a rather laborious statement of Walrasian *tâtonnement* (ibid., pp. 451–95) but asserts its adequacy to the problem of the stability of equilibrium prices. In *The Theory of Economic Development* Schumpeter's opinion has notably evolved:

> If it is to be shown how all the elements of the economic system are determined in equilibrium by one another, this equilibrium system is considered as not yet existing and is built up before our eyes *ab ovo*. This does not mean that its coming into being is genetically explained thereby. Only its existence and functioning are made logically clear by mental dissection. (Schumpeter, 1934, p. 82)

Business Cycles exhibits the long list of the drastic limitations of Walrasian *tâtonnement*: relation with real-world processes; atemporality of Walrasian equilibrium; existence of technological lags or of lags effects; possibility of transactions at false prices; frictions; stickiness of prices; uncertainty; imperfect competition, etc. (1939, pp. 47–67).

At last, in *History of Economic Analysis*, the *tâtonnement* process in a barter economy is asserted to show a 'hopeless discrepancy from any process of real life' (1954, p. 1015), the introduction of money only increasing the existing difficulties (ibid., p. 1025).

This dissatisfaction with the Walrasian theory of *tâtonnement* lead Schumpeter towards an alternative interpretation of the process of formation of general equilibrium prices. His starting point was the rejection of the notion of instantaneous equilibrium founded upon virtual *tâtonnement*. What Schumpeter did was simply to take time and money seriously into account.

In a barter economy production and exchange were confounded because markets for services and markets for products took place simultaneously (1917, in Schumpeter, 1983, p. 42). The introduction of money broke this simultaneity. Before consuming, workers had first to earn wages; before producing, managers had first to buy their inputs (ibid., pp. 43–4).[9] This 'break of the unit process' (ibid., p. 44) transformed a *static* state into a *stationary* one; it introduced a true temporal dimension into the theoretical vision of economic activity.

Schumpeter also rejected the auctioneer trick, which helped Walras to explain the formation of unique and social prices emerging from subjective valuations. Money still appeared and played the part of the auctioneer, in order to fulfil the same purpose (ibid., pp. 43, 44, 46): as a common unit of measure it furnished individuals with a social standard, in which they could express their subjective prices and marginal utilities.

Little by little, Walrasian statics were therefore replaced by a Schumpeterian stationary state. In his comment on the first edition of *The Theory of Economic Development*, E. Böhm-Bawerk immediately took this transformation into account and reproached Schumpeter for his simultaneous utilization of two incompatible notions of statics; one abstract and virtual, and the other adaptive and real (Böhm-Bawerk, 1913, pp. 13–14). In *La pensée économique de J. Schumpeter*, F. Perroux also noticed the substitution of a 'psychologic and sociologic' circular flow for a 'mechanical' one (Perroux, 1965, p. 66). Both Böhm-Bawerk and Perroux were right. Their interpretation was indirectly confirmed by Schumpeter himself, when he identified the circular flow with the real phases of business cycles which precede the 'first wave' of innovations (Schumpeter, 1939, ch. 4); and when he described accurately and systematically all the real economic situations in which a 'static vision of economic life' was prevalent (Schumpeter, 1986, p. 206).[10]

This renewal of the theory of circular flow was, however, too implicit and incomplete. Schumpeter rejected a theoretical scheme which certainly exhibited important limitations yet was logically consistent. He adopted another explanation, which was more suitable to explain some real situations but was clearly insufficient. Schumpeter stopped halfway. He realized that the issue of the *process* of equilibration was more important than the question of the *state* of equilibrium. He ignored how central the problem of acquisition and diffusion of individual knowledge was to the achievement of equilibrium. To refer to the modern Austrian theory of market processes, it could be said that if Schumpeterian individuals exhibit more flesh and blood than their Walrasian cousins, they still remain too omniscient.

When Schumpeter built his theory of economic development, he was clearly conscious of its departure from Walrasian views.

Statics and dynamics are entirely different fields, they not only handle different problems but they also use different methods in different frameworks. They are not so much two chapters of the same theoretical construction as two entirely different constructions . . . . Such a [static] theory is unable to handle all that depends on the phenomenon of development . . . the system of pure economics is indeed essentially deprived of development. (Schumpeter, 1908, p. 509)

Indeed Schumpeter considered neither *tâtonnement* nor balanced economic growth as true dynamic phenomena:

> For it is no part of the system assumptions of 'static' theory that there should be no shifting of the centre of gravity of the economic cosmos. All that is required is that the economic process should adapt itself to such shifting simply by trying to find the new equilibrium of growth or as we prefer – of an equilibrium which, though continually disturbed by growth, tends to be reestablished. (Schumpeter, quoted in Bousquet, 1929, p. 1033)

Now in his *Elements d'économie pure*, Walras saw that true dynamics implied the necessity to take into account variations of the usual static 'fundamental' parameters of general equilibrium theory (technical methods of production; consumers' preferences; individual endowments).[11] Pareto stressed the same necessity in his *Corso di economia politica* and added the possible influence of what we would today call individual overshooting behaviour.[12] However, as a French disciple of Walras, Etienne Antonelli noticed both authors were unable to cope seriously with economic dynamics (Antonelli, 1939, pp. 226–36).

Schumpeter's theory of economic change offers very few analogies with modern temporary or intertemporal equilibrium theories (see Donzelli, 1983, pp. 682–6). Similarly, Schumpeter's theory of business cycles has little in common with modern stochastic recursive models of business cycles, in which entrepreneurs play no prevailing part.[13]

With the introduction of entrepreneurs, Schumpeter assumed firms had the possibility of controlling prices, technical progress and influencing consumers' preferences (Schumpeter, 1939, pp. 73–4). He also described structural change with industries growing at different speeds and discontinuities with which marginal analysis and differential calculus could uneasily cope. (On the creation and disappearance of firms see 1934, p. 66; on productive and technological reorganizations see ibid., p. 71).

This structural change and the introduction of uncertainty had serious consequences on the nature of the Schumpeterian notion of dynamic equilibrium. In some cases, the equilibrium towards which the system might converge was not Walrasian or 'perfect', to use Schumpeter's term (1939, p. 48). In other cases, practical conditions for the realization of an equilibrium were not fulfilled. Then, some situations did not correspond to 'equilibrium points' but to 'ranges within which the system as a whole is more nearly in equilibrium than it is outside of them', i.e., to 'neighborhoods of equilibrium' (ibid., p. 71). The last situations were those in which no equilibrium exists: 'When, for instance, existing states are in the act of being disturbed, say, by a war financed by government fiat, or by a "mania" of railway building, there is very little sense in speaking of an ideal equilibrium coexisting with all that disequilibrium' (ibid., p. 70).

From this perspective, as G. Tichy noted 'the merits of Schumpeter's theory ... are identical with its deficiencies' (in Seidl, 1984b, p. 82). Schumpeter introduced new insights and new problems but he stated them more than he solved them (ibid., pp. 82–6). He investigated complex economic dynamics, which modern theories of structural economic change and of non-linear endogeneous business cycles are only beginning to cope with. We can easily imagine how much more difficult these problems were in Schumpeter's day.

Rationality and economic behaviour

Economic behaviour and economic change are closely related in Schumpeter's theory. This is obviously implied by the part played by entrepreneurs in economic development. However, Schumpeter's contribution to the theory of economic behaviour is not limited to the introduction of entrepreneurs. As Donzelli (1986) accurately noted, the main merit of Schumpeter in this regard is the definition of two opposite types of economic behaviour. The first corresponds to what J. Schumpeter called 'hedonistic egoism' and is predominant in the framework of the circular flow. The second is related to 'energic egoism' and appears with economic development.[14]

In *Das Wesen*, 'hedonistic egoism' is identified with Walrasian rational behaviour. Maximization of utility functions by equalization of relative prices to marginal utilities ratios is the individual rule. In this theoretical framework the use of the term 'hedonism' is the more disputable because Schumpeter supported Walras against the Austrian School in his attempt to expel psychologism from economic theory: 'We have good reasons to be suspicious about sentences which we find everywhere in literature under the name of psychological assertions .... Our examples show us clearly that the reference to psychology of crises does not mean anything but [banality]' (Schumpeter, 1908, p. 545).

Little by little, however, with the successive editions of *The Theory of Economic Development*, a different conception of 'hedonistic egoism' replaced Walrasian rational behaviour, in relation to the substitution of stationary circular flow by static equilibrium. This replacement was rather slow. In the American edition of *The Theory of Economic Development* Schumpeter still maintains the thesis of the compatibility between circular flow individual behaviours and consumers' and producers' micro-equilibria in the Walrasian sense (Schumpeter, 1934, p. 41). This does not yet imply that agents will actually behave as explicit and conscious maximizers:

In this system of values a person's whole economy is expressed, all the relations of his life, his outlook, his method of production, his wants, all his economic combinations. The individual is never equally conscious of all parts of this value system; rather at any moment the greater part of it lies beneath the threshold of consciousness. Also, when he makes decisions concerning his economic conduct he does not pay attention to all the facts given expression to in this value system, but only to certain indices ready at hand. He acts in the ordinary daily round according to the general custom and experience. (Ibid., p. 39)

This experience is the result of the past activity of individuals, which taught them 'sternly what [they had] to do' (ibid., p. 6). In other words, agents might have formed false expectations but, by trial and error, they were able to revise mistaken decisions. Individual behaviour in circular flow appears therefore to be *adaptive* rather than *optimal*. This adaptive behaviour is accurately described in the first pages of *Business Cycles* through the effort of managers to perceive their environment and assign their own place with regard to a social norm, the 'normal business situation'. Here hedonism is the equivalent of routine and adaptive rationality.

On the contrary, 'energic egoism' can be characterized as an active and 'voluntaristic' behaviour adopted by entrepreneurs. In this respect, the Schumpeterian approach contrasts strongly with the Walrasian one. Walras's conception of entrepreneur is considered very weak by Schumpeter. In the Walrasian system, entrepreneurs are pure intermediaries between services and product markets and do not earn any specific income.

Quite the reverse, Schumpeterian entrepreneurs play a central part in economic development. They do not adapt to their environment but adapt the environment to themselves. They shape technical methods of production, endowments as well as consumer preferences, being able to overcome the various resistances (psychological, social, etc.) they meet in order to put their decisions into practice (ibid., pp. 119–24). Their rationality is not compatible with optimization because it excludes what Keynes called 'Benthamite calculation':

Men who created modern industry were 'all of a piece men' and not cheap-jacks who were wondering continuously and with anguish whether every effort they expended promised them a sufficient increment of pleasure. These men were not very preoccupied by the hedonistic fruits of their actions . . . . Such men create because they cannot help but do it (Schumpeter, 1986, pp. 225–6)

It is therefore impossible to convert entrepreneurs' motives into measurable magnitudes. 'The will to found a private Kingdom', 'the will to conquer', or 'the joy of creating' cannot be evaluated or maximized (Schumpeter, 1934, p. 93). Consequently, Schumpeterian entrepreneurs differ drastically from neoclassical ones.

For their success, keenness and rigor, but also a certain narrowness which concentrates on the immediate chances are essential. Schumpeter stresses that, in economic life, decisions must be taken 'without working out all the details' and he is by no means convinced that gathering and exploiting information is essential for the functioning of entrepreneurship! (P. Swoboda, in Seidl, 1984b, p. 18)

Schumpeterian entrepreneurs prefer intuitions to rational calculations (Schumpeter, 1934, p. 85). Innovations make precise calculations impossible (see Egidi, 1981, p. 73). They reinforce uncertainty and oblige decision-makers to face it, sometimes being compelled to 'guess' the future rather than 'predict' it (Schumpeter, 1934, p. 85).

Finally, entrepreneurs are not permanent agents. They are submitted to a real process of selection which eliminates 'losers' to the benefit of 'winners' or 'leaders' (Schumpeter, 1939, pp. 153–5). Moreover, entrepreneurs who cease innovating but survive become mere managers again.

This exhibition of entrepreneurs' specific rationality tends to state the *local* – and not the *universal* – nature of 'hedonistic' rationality and, therefore, of 'static' types of behaviour:

What we are doing amounts to this: we do not attack traditional theory, Walrasian or Marshallian, on its own ground. In particular, we do not take offense at its fundamental assumptions about business behavior – at the picture of prompt recognition of the data of a situation and of rational action in response to them. We know, of course, that these assumptions are very far from reality; but we hold that the logical schema of that theory is yet right 'in principle' and that deviations from it can be adequately taken care of by introducing frictions, lags and so on, and that they are, in fact, being taken care of, with increasing success, by recent work developing from traditional bases. We also hold, however, that this model covers less ground than is commonly supposed and that the whole economic process cannot be adequately described by it or in terms of (secondary) deviations from it . . . . The reasonable thing for us to do, therefore, seems to confine the traditional analysis to the ground on which we find it useful, and to adopt other assumptions . . . for the purpose of describing a class of facts which lies beyond that ground. (Ibid., pp. 98–9)

Schumpeter's contribution to the investigation of economic behaviour can be appraised from two points of view. The first is the stress placed by Schumpeter on the notion of adaptive behaviour. Schumpeter's contribution here converges with the work done today on adaptive economics and their relation to neo-institutionalism (see Day, 1982). The second point of view concerns the nature of 'energic' behaviour. Some economists raised the objection of psychologism, which Schumpeter precisely referred to, against Austrians, in *Das Wesen*. Schumpeter answered in 1926 German edition (1935, pp. 128–9) and 1934 American edition (1934, p. 90) of *The Theory of Economic Development*, arguing roughly that its definition of entrepreneurs was not imported from psychology but from what he called 'economic sociology' in his introduction to the *History of Economic Analysis*. Let us remember that, in this introduction, Schumpeter defined 'economic analysis' as 'dealing with questions of how people behave at any time and the economic effects they produce by so behaving' while 'economic sociology [dealt] with the question of how they come to behave as they do' (1954, p. 21). In this sense, we can thus consider 'economic sociology' as a valuable tool in lending assistance to economists when they try to select what N. Kaldor called 'stylised facts'.

In other ways Schumpeter's analysis of economic behaviour is an amazing prefiguration of some of the major themes of another part of 'new institutionalism', i.e., the evolutionary theory of technical change (Nelson and Winter, 1982); the rejection of the entrepreneur's profit maximization assumption; the introduction of the distinction between routine, imitative and innovative behaviours; the introduction of the concept of selection in the description of competitive processes, and so on.

Money and economic activity

In monetary theory as well as in other areas of economic analysis, the origin of Schumpeterian thought is clearly Walrasian.

In *Das Wesen* Schumpeter identified money with a commodity; its value was nothing but the relative price of this commodity, expressed in another good. According to the marginalist approach, the concept of marginal utility played a central role in the determination of money value and modified the usual precepts of quantity theory (Schumpeter, 1908, p. 293). This first conception of money was still present in the first German edition of the *The Theory of Economic Development*. It was given up in 'Das Sozialprodukt und die Rechenpfennige' (1917), even though this article stresses the fundamental importance of Walras's contribution to the theory of money (in Schumpeter, 1983, p. 40).

In 1917 Schumpeter noticed that the utilization of marginal utilities in order to determine the value of money in another good would lead to 'a vicious circle'. This utilization would imply that

> we obtain goods for money because it has an exchange value, while it would have an exchange value only because we obtain goods for it. But money has no use value and, consequently, it has no exchange value either, in the sense according to which goods have it. (Ibid., p. 56)

The influence of Knapp's nominalist theory of money is here obvious and Schumpeter always maintained from this epoch forward, that 'money not being a commodity, the traditional apparatus of supply and demand cannot be applied to the solution of the problem of money prices of commodities and of the price levels' (1939, p. 547).

The rejection of the concept of money's marginal utility was not the sole disagreement Schumpeter expressed with Walras's theory. Another concerned 'this Walrasian idea of an *encaisse désirée*' which 'is one of the least valuable elements in the great Frenchman's mighty structure' (ibid.). Schumpeter excluded the idea that money could be considered as a store of value.

> This critic led the Austrian author to exclude the function of 'stored value' of money from the definition of proper money: such an assertion would imply a confusion between the concept of money and all the other commodities; secondly, it would break the direct correspondence between the volume of money and the amount of traded goods (Messori, 1983, pp. 662–3)

We also know that the same arguments were directed against Keynes's theory of liquidity preference (ibid., pp. 658, 662, 665, 672–3).

The departure from Walrasian theory could not have prevented Schumpeter from accepting the quantity theory of money. We know, however, that Schumpeter did not make this choice. I will not state in detail the main objections he raised against quantity theory; A. Graziani (1978) and M. Messori (1983; 1984) have already done this accurately. I will only add a reminder that Schumpeter's critique was not superficial but systematic. Our author refused to read *a priori* the quantity equation as a causal influence of money quantity upon prices (1917, in Schumpeter, 1983, pp. 57–9, 83–107). He also supported the idea that it was quite impossible to define money quantity precisely, because of the existence of substitutes and, in particular, of credit and reserves (ibid., pp. 63–75). Moreover, this quantity was not homogeneous and led to the necessity of defining several concepts of velocity of circulation (ibid., pp. 76–83). Money not being a commodity, it had no proper value (ibid., pp. 55–6). Finally, its 'reflected value' was scarcely proportional to the quantity of money because the variation of the latter very often implied relative price variations and redistribution effects (ibid., pp. 88–94; see also Graziani, 1978, p. 92; Messori, 1984, p. 49).

Schumpeter's positive theory of money has to be related to his general theory of economic development. In the circular flow, money is used only for economic transactions. Thus, at the end of the first chapter of his *Theory of Economic Development*, Schumpeter notes:

> We have so far considered money solely as a circulating medium. We have had in view the determination of the value of only those quantities of money which are actually used for the movement of the mass of commodities periodically. Obviously there are also in every economic system, for well known reasons, non-circulating quantities of money, and the determination of their value is not yet explained. For so far we have not learned of any employment of money

which necessitates an accumulation beyond the measure that enables the individual to pay for his current purchases . . . . In the normal circular flow, which we have in view here, no holding of important stocks of money for other purposes would be necessary. (1934, p. 68)

In this framework the practical form of circulating money does not matter: metallic money, papermoney, banknotes, bills of exchange, credit instruments . . . Schumpeter indeed identifies money as 'a general order upon different quantities of goods' (ibid., p. 51), as a 'ticket' (according to J. S. Mill's expression) which is a right to commodities. In other words, in the circular flow the quantity of money is always consistent with the amount of national income; there cannot be too little or too much money (1917, in Schumpeter, 1983, p. 59). Money is here analogous to Tooke's circulating money since it is 'essentially a technical expedient which assists business activity, a simple satellite of commodities, a slave of processes which takes place in the sphere of goods' (ibid., p. 40). In the circular flow, money has no room to exist as a store of value. It can only circulate; there is no financial 'sphere'.

When economic development appears, things become more complex. Two 'spheres' have to be distinguished. The first is the 'sphere of business' (Schumpeter, 1939, p. 124) or 'sphere of goods' (1917, in 1983, p. 40) or 'circulation' (1934, p. 73). This sphere is the place where innovations emerge. To finance them, entrepreneurs demand of the banking system 'credit means of payment, that is means of payment which are created for the purpose and by the act of giving credit' (ibid.).

In general, this new purchasing power is not preceded by any preliminary saving.[15] Banks create money:

> The form [this creation] takes is immaterial. The issue of bank-notes not fully covered by specie withdrawn from circulation is an obvious instance, but methods of deposit banking render the same service, where they increase the sum total of possible expenditure. Or we may think of bank acceptances in so far as they serve as money to make payments in wholesale trade. It is always a question, not of transforming purchasing power which already exists in someone's possession, but of the creation of new purchasing power out of nothing – out of nothing even if the credit contract by which the new purchasing power is created is supported by securities which are not themselves circulating media – which is added to the existing circulation. (Schumpeter, 1934, p. 73)

The introduction of these 'new' means of payment does not change anything for the analysis of the determination of the volume of transaction instruments utilized in the 'sphere of business': this volume still depends on the value of production decided by entrepreneurs. Credit is thus the predominant means of payment (ibid., p. 53) and the supply of means of payment is clearly endogeneous:

> In practice, a boundless credit supply corresponds to a boundless credit demand. The fact that this is still ignored is only due to the presumption that the means of the banks are determined by objective conditions, in particular by saving, and to the ignorance of the phenomenon of money creation . . . . Banks can always allow further loans, as far as incremental outlets correspond to incremental inlets. Credit demand does not only create the conditions of its own existence but also makes possible a corresponding supply, and every supply makes possible a corresponding demand: in this case, supply and demand do not face each other as independent forces. (1917, in Schumpeter, 1983, p. 116)

The question of the measurement of money quantity is obviously compli-cated by this continuous phenomenon of creation and destruction of money. That is why Schumpeter sees in it a supplementary objection against quantity theory (ibid., p. 71).

The 'sphere of business', i.e., the circulation of income, does not cover the complete functions of money. It does not indeed include the 'money market' as such (1934, p. 123). The 'money market' corresponds to both 'spheres' of 'hoarding and reserves' and of 'capital' (1917, in Schumpeter, 1983, p. 72). It can be characterized as the place where assets are exchanged for each other. More precisely, transactions imply 'non-circu-lation money' and 'the sources of income' or 'wealth which yields income' (Schumpeter, 1934, p. 127).

The 'sphere of hoarding and reserves' is the market of the means of payment, i.e. of money and short-term loans. The demand comes gener-ally from entrepreneurs: the 'sphere' provides them with a complement of bank financing. But demanders can also be holders of long-term 'sources of income' or banks looking for liquid assets. Supply includes hoarding, bank cash reserves and provisional deposits (1917, in Schumpeter, 1983, pp. 74–5). The 'sphere of capital' corresponds to 'the market for long-term purchasing power' (1934, p. 124, n. 1) and includes several markets – the markets 'of lands, mortgages, bonds, etc.' (1983, p. 75). The Stock Exchange is obviously the main market in the 'sphere of capital'.

However, for Schumpeter the distinction between both 'spheres' of money market is not important at all.

First, both 'spheres' are not really autonomous, as the simple descrip-tion of their nature has already shown. In particular, the process of financial transformation of short-term saving or hoarding into medium- or long-term investment forbids the real independence of either spheres. For Schumpeter, this process is not 'a mere technique'; it 'is part of the core of the capitalist process' (1939, p. 613). Schumpeter stresses this interdependence.

> We can of course distinguish short and long-term financing and, for purposes of description, can think of the latter as concentrated in a special market, which

we may call as we please – capital market or Stock Exchange, for instance. This special market or rather its component parts are, moreover, obvious realities that raise problems peculiar to themselves and, in particular, produce their own gross rates of interest in the sense that is ordinarily meant when one speaks of the structure of rates. In this sense we shall presently use this distinction, although in doing so we shall merely speak of different sectors of the money market; but no significance deeper than that attaches to it. (Ibid., pp. 612–13)

Emphasizing such a difference between both spheres

easily suggests that money-market transactions [here in the sense of short-term transactions] have little to do with long-term financing and that capital-market transactions never serve the purpose of current business or that the former have only to do with the effecting of payments [*Zählungskredit*] and the latter only with real investment. It need not be emphasized again how wrong all that is. (Ibid., p. 613)

Here one can recognize an echo of Schumpeter's critique of Keynesian theory of liquidity preference. If we accept Schumpeter's conception, it is clear that 'we may hence go so far as to say that there exists no such thing as the long-term rate [of interest] and that, if we nevertheless wish to use the concept, the thing we ought to mean is some kind of "trend value" of short rates' (Schumpeter, 1939, p. 614).

In such a theoretical framework there is little room for speculative behaviour. The sole form of speculation to which Schumpeter refers concerns short-term loans and, from the author's point of view, it is often beneficial to new firms (Schumpeter, 1934). Moreover, if uncertainty stimulates hoarding, its nature is objective rather than behavioural, as in Keynes's theory. Schumpeter refers significantly to 'institutional uncertainty, crises, etc.'.[16]

The main consequence of the preceding remarks is that, in Schumpeter's theory, the fundamental interest rate is the short-term one. Being, in this peculiar respect, in agreement with Keynes, Schumpeter considers that this rate is above all the result of a 'monetary phenomenon' (1939, p. 128). I will not develop this aspect of Schumpeter's theory of money, which is very well known,[17] and was sternly criticized by E. Böhm-Bawerk, as early as 1913. In the determination of the interest rate the money market is influenced by several contingent factors (such as 'all conditions of the national life, all political, economic and natural events': Schumpeter, 1934, p. 126) or psychological ones ('psychological patterns' or 'energic will to go ahead' (1935, p. 191, n. 1). If it is always possible to build supply and demand schedules, their 'value' is, however, 'doubtful' (Schumpeter, 1939, p. 606). Hence, Schumpeter concluded, 'it is necessary to recognize an element of indeterminateness in the problem of interest' (ibid.).[18] Paradoxically, this conclusion coincided with Keynes's observation according to which the level of the interest rate was a 'highly conventional phenomenon', depending on 'mass psychology'.

Schumpeter's theory of money and interest appears to be directly related to his theories of economic change and behaviour. Starting with a Walrasian approach, Schumpeter finally elaborated a conception of money in which credit as a capitalist institution played a central role. Far from being definitively incompatible with Keynesian theory, the Schumpeterian theory of money may indeed be seen today as complementary.[19] To that extent, it is much nearer to monetary theories preoccupied by real world institutions and 'stylized facts' than to neo-Walrasian analysis.

The conclusion of our investigation is obvious. Beginning his career as a Walrasian scholar anxious to extend the scope and field of *économie pure*, Schumpeter in fact built a general theory in which institutions and 'stylized facts' played a central part. Convergences with 'neo-institutionalist'[20] or non-orthodox approaches appear indeed to be numerous: modern Austrian theory of market process; theory of structural change; theory of non-linear endogeneous business cycles; adaptive economics; evolutionary theory of technical change; post-Keynesian theory of money. The length of this list appears to confirm Tichy's remark, quoted earlier about the identity of the 'merits' and 'deficiencies' of Schumpeter's theory.

On the one hand it is clear that the Schumpeterian research programme is in danger of eclecticism. One of the roots of this danger lies undoubtedly in the fact that his explicit research programme never coincided with the real and implicit one: an implicit programme is uneasily worked up. Following Seidl's diagnosis, we may indeed

> consider Walrasian economics to have been Schumpeter's Procrustean bed. Schumpeter admired Walras and had a high esteem for Walrasian economics. It was next to unthinkable to Schumpeter that Walrasian economics could house any major fallacies. So he worked hard ... to enrich the Walrasian system by a dynamic analysis. But he never directed his instruments against the substance of Walrasian economics. Had he come across a contradiction, he would have certainly assumed that he, and not Walras, was wrong. (Seidl, 1984a, p. 197)

On the other hand, we may also consider that Schumpeter's stress on the notion of *économie pure* performed the office of a theoretical parapet and permitted him to avoid the shortcomings of the Historical school. Schumpeter at least inherited scientific rigour from Walras. Hence, if the different aspects of his thought bear the risk of eclecticism taken as a whole, they are scarcely inconsistent when we consider them separately. From this point of view the Schumpeterian approach still remains an extraordinary source of inspiration for those modern economists who are not satisfied with mainstream economics.

Notes

1. See, for instance, the divergent conceptions of Graziani (1978) and Schefold (1986).
2. Schefold (1986), p. 93, refers in this respect to Schumpeter (1913).
3. Akerman (1955), also stresses Schumpeter's characteristic 'atomistic theory' and pretends it is incompatible with structural economics.
4. P. Samuelson in Frisch (1982), p. 4.
5. 'Economists indulged their strong propensity to dabble in politics, to peddle political recipes, to offer themselves as philosophers of economic life, and in doing so neglected the duty of stating explicitly the value judgements that they introduced into their reasoning' (Schumpeter, 1954, p. 19).
6. M. Perlman, in Frisch (1982), pp. 148–9.
7. Graziani (1978) observes the same tendency in Schumpeter's *Treatise on Money*.
8. See Sylos-Labini (1954) and (1977).
9. I cannot help thinking here about R. Clower's hypothesis of 'dual decision'.
10. In this edition (1912) Schumpeter noticed that in the real world static situations were more widespread than dynamic ones (p. 204).
11. Walras (1900), 35ème leçon: 'Du marché permanent'.
12. Pareto (1943), ch. 1 ('Principi generali dell'evoluzione sociale') and ch. 4 ('Le crisi economiche'), of Book 2.
13. Arena (1988); analogies might be more convincing, if we compared Schumpeterian dynamics with the so-called '"new" growth theory' (Aghion and Howitt, 1990; Romer, 1986; 1990).
14. This opposition is present in *Das Wesen* and in the first German edition of *The Theory of Economic Development*.
15. The restriction implied by 'in general' derives from the following possible situation: when the demand for means of payment is not fully satisfied by banks, entrepreneurs can use a preliminary saving, their own past profits being the source of self-financing or the money market replacing bank creation of money (see Schumpeter, 1934, pp. 199–200).
16. Schumpeter (1917, in Schumpeter, 1983, p. 106). To that extent, in another contribution (Arena, 1985, pp. 64–5), I certainly overemphasized similarities between Keynes's and Schumpeter's analysis of financial markets.
17. See Graziani (1978), Messori (1984) and Arena (1985), pp. 63–4.
18. For a more thorough analysis, see Messori (1984).
19. I agree with Messori (1983) in this respect.
20. I will not choose here between A. Gruchy's characterization of 'neo-institutionalism' (Gruchy, 1982, pp. 25–6) and R. Langlois's conception of 'new institutional economics' (Langlois, 1986, pp. 2–4). They share the will to replace dd institutionalism by an *economic theory* taking institutions into account.

References

Aghion, P. and Howitt, P. (1990), 'A Model of Growth through Creative Destruction', MIT Working Paper.

Akerman, J. (1955), *Structures et cycle économique*, Paris: PUF.

Antonelli, E. (1939), *L'économie pure du capitalisme*, Paris: Librairie des Sciences Politiques et Sociales, Marcel Rivière et Cie.

Arena, R. (1985), 'Circulations, revenu et capital: théorie monétaire et tradition non quantitative', in R. Arena, A. Graziani and I. Kregel (eds), *Monnaie, production et circulation*, PUF, Paris.

Arena, R. (1988), 'Keynes après Lucas: quelques enseignements récents de la macroéconomie monétaire', *Cahiers de l'ISMEA*, 'Monnaie' series.

Böhm-Bawerk, E. (1913), 'Eine "dynamische" Theorie des Kapitalzinses', *Zeitschrift für Volkswirtschaft, Sozialpolitik und Verwaltung*, **22**.

Bousquet, G. H. (1929), 'Joseph Schumpeter', *Revue d'Economie Politique*.

Costabile, L. (1986), 'Metodo della scienza e teoria economica in Schumpeter, Note, sur l'*Essenza e i principi dell'economia teorica*', *Studi Economici*, **29**.

Day, R. (1982), 'Orthodox Economists and Existential Economics', in W. Samuels (ed.), *The Methodology of Economic Thought*, New Brunswick, NJ: Transaction Books.

Donzelli, F. (1983), 'Schumpeter e la teoria economica neoclassica', *Ricerche Economiche*, **37** (4).

Donzelli, F. (1986), *Il concetto di equilibrio nella teoria economica neoclassica*, Rome: Nuova Italia Scientifica.

Dyer, A. (1988), 'Schumpeter as an Economic Radical: an Economic Sociology Assessed', *History of Political Economy*, **20** (1), Spring.

Egidi, M. (1981), *Schumpeter lo sviluppo come transformazione morfologica*, Milan: Etas Libà.

Frisch, H. (ed.) (1982), *Schumpeterian Economics*, New York: Praeger.

Graziani, A. (1978), 'Il Trattato sulla Moneta di J. A. Schumpeter', *Note Economiche*, **1**.

Gruchy, A. (1982), 'Neoinstitutionalism and the Economics of Dissent', in W. Samuels (ed.), *The Methodology of Economic Thought*, New Brunswick, NJ and London: Transaction Books.

Langlois, R. (ed.) (1986), *Economics as a Process – Essays in the New Institutional Economics*, Cambridge: Cambridge University Press.

Messori, M. (1983), 'Storia e teoria economica: Schumpeter, Keynes e il ciclo del capitale', in N. Tranfaglia, *Il mondo contemporaneo questioni di metodo*, Florence: Feltrinelli.

Messori, M. (1984), 'Introduzione' to J. Schumpeter, *Antologia di scritti*, ed. M. Messori, Bologna: Il Mulino.

Nelson, R. and Winter, S. (1982), *An Evolutionary Theory of Economic Change*, Cambridge, MA and London: Belknap Press of Harvard University Press.

Pareto, V. (1943), *Corso di economia politica*, 2 vols, Turin: Einaudi.

Perlman, M. (1982), 'Schumpeter as an Historian of Economic Thought', in Frisch (1982).

Perroux, F. (1965), *La pensée économique de J. Schumpeter. Les dynamiques du capitalisme*, Genève: Joseph Droz.

Romer, P. (1986), 'Increasing Returns and Long-run Growth', *Journal of Political Economy*, October.

Romer, P. (1990), 'Endogeneous Technological Change', *Journal of Political Economy*.

Samuelson, P. (1982), 'Schumpeter as an Economic Theorist', in Frisch (1982).

Schefold, B. (1986), 'Schumpeter as a Walrasian Austrian and Keynes as a classical Marshallian', in H. Wagener and J. Drukker (eds), *The Economic Laws of Motion of Modern Society*, Cambridge: Cambridge University Press.

Schumpeter, J. (1906), 'Uber die Mathematische Methode der Theoretischen Okonomie', *Zeitschrift für Volkswirtschaft, Sozialpolitik and Verwaltung*, **15**.

Schumpeter, J. (1908), *Das Wesen und der Hauptinhalt der Theoretischen Nationalökonomie*, Leipzig: Duncker & Humbolt.

Schumpeter, J. (1913), 'Eine "dynamische" Theorie des Kapitalzinses: eine Entgegnung', *Zeitschrift für Volkswirtschaft, Sozialpolitik und Verwaltung*, **22**.

Schumpeter, J. (1916), 'Das Grundprinzip der Verteilungslehre, *Heidelberg Archiv*, **42**.

Schumpeter, J. (1934), *The Theory of Economic Development*, Cambridge, MA: Harvard University Press.

Schumpeter, J. (1935), *Théorie de l'Evolution Economique*, Paris: Dalloz. [This French translation of the second German edition also includes the preface of the first edition (pp. vii–viii)].

Schumpeter, J. (1939), *Business Cycles: a Theoretical Historical and Statistical Analysis of the Capitalist Process*, 2 vols, New York: McGraw-Hill.

Schumpeter, J. (1949a), 'Historical Approach to the Analysis of Business Cycles', in Conference on Business Cycles, New York: NBER.

Schumpeter, J. (1949b), 'Science and Ideology', *American Economic Review*, **39**.

Schumpeter, J. (1951), *Essays on Economic Topics*, ed. R. V. Clemence, Port Washington, NY: Kennikat Press.

Schumpeter, J. (1954), *History of Economic Analysis*, London: Allen & Unwin.

Schumpeter, J. (1972), *Esquisse d'une histoire de la science économique des origines au début du XXe siècle*, Paris: Dalloz.

Schumpeter, J. (1983), *Stato e inflazione*, Turin: Boringhini. [This volume includes the Italian translation of Schumpeter (1917): 'Das Sozial Produkt und die Rechenpfennige: Glossen und Beiträge zur Geld-Theorie von Heute', *Archiv für Sozialwissenschaft und Sozialpolitik*, **44**.]

Schumpeter, J. (1986) 'Il capitolo II della teoria di Schumpeter (1912)', in E. Pesciarelli and E. Santarelli (eds), *Quaderni di storia dell'economia politica*, Vol. IV. [This text is the Italian translation of Chapter 2 of the first German edition of the *Theory of Economic Development*.]

Seidl, C. (1984a), 'Joseph Alois Schumpeter: Character, Life and Particulars of his Graz Period', in Seidl (1984b).

Seidl, C. (ed.) (1984b), *Lectures on Schumpeterian Economics*, Berlin: Springer Verlag.

Swoboda, P. (1984), 'Schumpeter's Entrepreneur in Modern Economic Theory', in Seidl (1984b).

Sylos-Labini, P. (1954), 'Problemi dello sviluppo economico in Marx e Schumpeter', in G. U. Papi (ed.), *Teorie dello sviluppo economico*, Milan: Giuffrè.

Sylos-Labini, P. (1977), 'Introduzione' to J. Schumpeter, *Teoria dello sviluppo economico*, Florence: Sansoni.

Tichy, G. (1984), 'Schumpeter's Business Cycle Theory', in Seidl (1984b).

Walras, L. (1900), *Elements d'économie pure*, Paris: Librairie Générale de Droit et de Jurisprudence.

9 Liberalism and economic thought during the French Revolution 1789–94

J.-Michel Servet

Léon Walras in his *Etudes d'économie sociale* asserts: 'Revolution is a memorable date: it is that of the end of a world and the beginning of another . . . . It is up to us, its sons, to defend it against its adversaries; but it is above all up to us to continue it in pursuing truth and social justice among all the problems of philosophy and science.'[1] The stance Léon Walras inherited from the French Revolution does not correspond very well either to the ideology usually attributed to the author of *Eléments d'économie politique pure* or to the general reading of the economic conceptions of French Revolutionaries. Thus it must make us wonder about the nature of Walras's 'liberal socialism' as well as about the economic ideology prevailing in France at the end of the eighteenth century whose 'son' he can claim to be. We are going to deal more particularly with the nature of the economic doctrines practised in France in the years 1789–94.[2]

This period, 1789–94,[3] in France is particularly favourable to economic debates. Economically it is marked[4] less by the emigration which hit luxury activities and certain domestic services[5] than by the gap of the war, which is felt more or less rapidly according to region and the type of activities. The expansion of exterior trade opened by the trade treaty with England in 1786 halts at the end of 1792, after a period of brisk dynamism in business in 1789–90. The Atlantic front rapidly underwent the setback of the slave rising in the West Indies in 1791 whereas Marseilles was affected in April 1793 only, and the hinterland of the Rhône valley was only affected very markedly in the following summer and with the federalist risings and the Lyons revolt.

Beyond the account of these events, rumours and clamours, the press, the printed opinions of the deputies, the speeches in the assemblies and clubs, the committee reports and the ministerial circulars were brimming with practical questions which were then, as many other controversial issues with an economic purport, immediate or indirect, to be solved urgently or in the future. Some examples were the direct or indirect taxes and the debt of the kingdom, the penury of money and the issue of assignats, the right of ownership (for example of mines, feudal rights, communal lands, its hereditary transmission, even the right of ownership of the swarm leaving the hive), the freedom of internal and external exchanges, the fixing of prices, the crisis of supplies and requisitions, the corporate organization of work and the interdiction of workmen's associations, slavery in the colonies, the financing of the war and the poor relief. Previous to the successive political crises of the period, the almost daily worries about the supply of bread, its price and more generally the economic outlook punctuated the Revolutionary movement and its successive popular risings.

However much certain economic events of the period have been dissected and commented upon (too often, it is true, in the context of more political than economic distinctions), the economic thought has practically been erased by political ideologies to the extent that we may wonder if there was economic thought in those days which were so rich in facts and ideas of all sorts in other fields. Adolphe Blanqui in his *Histoire de l'Economie politique*, a work published in 1837 and republished throughout the nineteenth century, asserts that there was 'nothing new in science from 1789 to 1814, except the experience of accomplished facts and the facility to draw the consequences to go forward and complete the work of our fathers'.[6] The contemporary textbooks about the history of economic thought are silent about the state of economic doctrines in France during the final two decades of the eighteenth century. The parsimonious allusions in the works of historians about the influence of the agricultural system of the Physiocrats and the liberalism of Adam Smith or A.R. Turgot on such or such a decision are insufficient.[7] More surely, reading the numerous monographs devoted to such and such a hero of the Revolutionary epic, it is possible to discover the analysis or the description of his economic concepts.[8] The celebration of the bicentenary of the French Revolution was the occasion to re-evaluate the period from which we can draw some teachings.

We shall consider why French economic thought in the years 1789–94 was ignored, then we shall examine the nature of the economic ideas in the period.

The reasons why the economic thought of the years 1789–94 was overshadowed

Three factors at least can account for the overshadowing of economic thought during the Revolutionary years:

a generation gap;
the domination of the political and factual history;

above all, the difficulty of integrating the representations of the revolutionary actors into our own political-ideological patterns.

A generation gap

If the appearance on the French public scene of a new generation, or more exactly its coming into power, constitutes one of the remarkable elements of the Revolutionary years in the political field, in the field of economic thought the disappearance of the French 'great authors' of the eighteenth century a few years before the collapse of the *ancien régime* is the first 'fact' which must be noted. François Quesnay, the father of Physiocracy, died in 1774 at the age of 80; Condillac in 1780 aged 66, Turgot in 1781 aged 54. The Marquess of Mirabeau, the father of the most famous orator of the Revolution who popularized the Physiocratic chart and wrote *l'Ami des hommes*, died in 1789 at 74, Jean-Joseph Graslin in 1790 at 63, Nicolas Baudeau in 1792 at 62, and so on. We could multiply the examples which illustrate an undeniable generation gap. The same takes place simultaneously in Great Britain, where James Stewart died in 1780 at 78 and Adam Smith ten years later, at 67. Contrary to the political realm in France and in Great Britain, the history of political economy was not marked by a new generation of economists at the end of the eighteenth century: twenty years elapsed between the disappearance of the old masters and the first writings, of, say, David Ricardo.

Was it so in France because silence was necessary either for the assimilation and maturation of the works of the founders, or for the introduction of new ideas? Adam Smith was translated into French by 1778–9[9] and his works were published repeatedly, in pirated editions as well; James Stewart in 1789–90 (under the influence of Vandermonde),[10] Jeremy Bentham in 1789, William Godwin in 1792, an undeniable sign of the diffusion of English social sciences in France. But how many readers did the English economists find in France, and how many readers assimilated the novelty of their writings?

Lawyers and barristers were most numerous in Revolutionary assemblies. Philosophical encyclopaedism however allowed the layman to speak with knowledge of economic facts and Adam Smith was repeatedly quoted by Revolutionary orators. Can we believe that all the authors that we nowadays consider as having written economic works before 1789 and who were still alive during the Revolution stopped writing after the fall of the Bastille? Let us recall a few names: the encyclopaedist l'abbé Morellet[11] died in 1819, François Veron de Forbonnais in 1800,[12] Pierre Mercier de la Rivière in 1801,[13] Achylle Nicolas Isnard and Gabriel Senac de Meilhan in 1803, and Pierre Samuel Dupont de Nemours in 1817. Though the names of P.S. Dupont de Nemours or F. Veron de Forbonnais are better known today than the preceding names, we may wonder why their writings of the Revolutionary period are now generally ignored. Why is Germain Garnier generally known only for his translation of Adam Smith,[14] and why are such authors as P.L. Roederer and above all Condorcet still waiting for the economist who will give them the position they deserve in the pantheon of the founders of political economy?[15] These references contradict the hypothesis that there was a lack of economists in France at the end of the eighteenth century (we give economists the broad meaning attributed to this word from the sixteenth to the eighteenth centuries).

Why was a genuine economic idea ignored?

The domination of political and factual events
A second argument that comes spontaneously to mind to justify the concealment of Revolutionary economic thought is the influence of factual and political events.

One of the main difficulties in grasping the period's economic thought comes from the fact that economy and politics were not yet generally apprehended in France as two essential elements of society. While mercantilists had broken away from Scholastics and severed the bond between economics and morals, politics was a prevailing aspect[16] of economic writings, and remained so until the end of the eighteenth century. The political upheavals between 1789 and 1794 were not an incentive to the emancipation of a specific economic thought and the Revolution created a strong revival of politics and morals.

Moreover, the pressure of economic problems to be solved (price rises, corn storage, tax sharing, financing of the war) may lead us to think that the elites' day-by-day reactions did not proceed from theoretical concepts, but came from preoccupations and ideologies that were immediately political. They would be politicans before being theoreticians. Auguste Cochin saw in this the outcome of the decay of philosophy in the course of the eighteenth century: philosophers, then economists, then politicians.[17] This obliteration of economists by politicians appears to uphold the preceding argument based on the passing at the end of the eighteenth century from one generation to another of 'great' economists.

Should one conclude from the domination of the political and the pressure of events that it is ill advised to look for economic thought fit for a Revolutionary period in general, and for this one in particular?

Undoubtedly, economy was a skill in an elitist ideology and this revolution was regarded first as a *popular* movement. I entirely dismiss the idea of considering only the parliamentary debates of the Revolution, along with the government committees, and of denying the strength of the rebels who did not act (with due respect to the conservative or revisionist historians) out of blind bestiality in favour of strictly immediate interests or under the pressure of corrupt ringleaders. The 'mob' did think, and asserted its rights not for a political economy, but for an economic policy which preserved its immediate interests. The various social groups, with complex hierarchies and frail borders, were ideologically permeable. It is a fact that lawyers and barristers were over-represented amongst the Revolutionaries and that most of the 89 men probably had not read Quesnay, Smith or Turgot.[18] Even among the contemporaries who, through the encyclopaedic spirit of the time, did read them – or pretended to, by quoting them – how many understood the radical innovation brought into social sciences by *The Wealth of Nations*, for instance?[19]

In a general way, for the diffusion of new ideas, the 'societies of thought', clubs, lodges, patriotic societies, and so on,[20] played an essential part; but it is perhaps contrary to the earlier assertion of previous intellectual influences that the Revolution itself afterwards partly gave a considerable intellectual radiance, a sort of justification, to some writers and a new reason for the events. The movement of ideas and the disruption of institutions went side by side. The birth of political economy as a discipline different from the other branches of learning and the 1789 Revolution were in France on the scale of centuries, contemporary facts.[21] To search for its influence, it would be particularly interesting to analyse hundred of books of grievance, their criticisms and proposals.[22] It would also be necessary to study the plentiful revolutionary press. The claims, lawful or not, and the interests, real or imaginary, coherent or not, the passions and the beliefs of various pressure groups and social categories exerted different influences on the assembly orators, pamphleteers, and all those who from 'above' gave shape to the ideas, the very ideas being retrieved, transformed, criticized 'at the bottom' (in Paris, of course, but also, too often forgotten, in 'the provinces').[23] How can we understand, without considering these reciprocal influences and the influence of new ideas on money, the will of the sansculottes to eradicate the traditional metal currency and to support the *assignat*, the Revolutionary paper money?

But if we stick to the elitist ideology, the main difficulty in grasping the economic ideas during the Revolution is that the 1789–94 men have not written treatises and syntheses that would enlighten their thought in action. One does not find what will be called at the beginning of the nineteenth century – without giving then to that term a derogatory meaning – a *metaphysical* economy; this leads us to prefer the undoubtedly vague expression of economic *ideas* rather than that surely more conventional term of economic *thought* but these ideas tend to evoke a constituted and structured, even instituted set of *doctrines*. The contemporaries specifically respond to practical questions (reinforced with *ideology*). Their thought and representation system must be reconstructed from texts which account for these immediate problems, and take the form of speeches in clubs and assemblies, committee reports and ministers' circulars, pamphlets and petitions, press articles. We cannot, because of the technical, non-speculative nature of the debates discard them from the field of political economy. What would then become of the works of David Ricardo, Léon Walras, John Maynard Keynes, and still more those of the *monétaristes* of the second half of the sixteenth century minus their writings about *applied* economy?

It is vital to grasp the economic ideas of the Revolutionaries to understand how some abstract principles become institutionalized and implemented, purified, deepened and transformed, that is to say how they become *living images*,[24] how they act in real life and react to the events by adjusting themselves to their social and cultural milieux, how they destroy or assimilate some close or opposite ideas, how, for instance, they underline a contradiction between the concepts of actuality and free property.

The apparent ideological confusion of the Revolutionary period
We meet here a third factor able to explain the opaqueness of economic ideas during the Revolution: the difficulty of fitting it into our own politico-ideological classifications.

Political Manichaeism, in other words, hatred or fascination, encourages the transformation of the French Revolution into a sort of ante-room to socialism, a social organization hated by some and desired by others. It is therefore convenient for both to imagine either an initial liberalism that went astray, or, on the contrary, a liberation from the feudal shackles of institutionalized socialism. Now the whole period, including the years 1793–4 called the Terror, seems to be understandable from a liberal viewpoint. It is impossible to embody the social actors' representation and political economy into actions, into the usual pattern: market economy versus directed economy, and this probably explained in great part the common lack of reflection on economic ideas during the French Revolution.

Florin Aftalion in his *Economie de la Révolution française*[25] states that most Revolutionaries usually acted not out of conviction, but out of demagogy facing 'public opinion' or as representatives of particular economic interests. In other words, Aftalion says that these 'learned persons [who] shared the common economic ideas which came from the Enlightenment Movement, the physiocrats or Adam Smith'[26] mostly acted outside any system of ideas because they lied.

This interpretation looks similar to that of Adolphe Thiers or H. Taine, who believed the motives of corruption and plunder to account for the social movement.[27] Yet, as far as the 'ringleaders' are concerned, unlike H. Taine who described them as 'hollow' heads, outside the 'commonplaces' drawn from Rousseau and Raynal,[28] F. Aftalion holds the view that 'their economic knowledge, already somewhat advanced, was not used wittingly. To enjoy popularity, the most influential revolutionary leaders often chose to ignore their own knowledge. They preferred to satisfy the extreme claims of the opinion whose ignorance was understandable, taking the risk of producing in the long run inextricable difficulties rather than following their own convictions.'[29] But of course, such an approach forbids reflection on economic thought, since the latter would be silenced or concealed. The particular interests (and who could indeed deny that the Revolutionary finances had been an opportunity for dire speculations?), interior trading, and so on, do not forbid public debate and conflictual ideas, selfish arguments.

The liberal foundation of economic ideas under the Revolution
The deliberate liberal interpretation of the whole period which I choose to give agrees with the rejection of a somewhat socio-professional source of the ideologies. Besides, isn't it difficult to believe in a narrow social determinism of prevailing ideas and of their supposed evolution when historians have discovered a strong permanence of the economic elites during these eventful political years, whether among entrepreneurs[30] or financiers and higher officials?[31] At a theoretical level, it seems excessive to assert and impossible to demonstrate that a social group produces an ideology.[32] The development of a system of thought is not identical with the existence of a social group.

This system is first structurally determined as a body of ideas assuring individuals a certain coherence to understand and express their physical and social environment:

by the intuition of every thinker, that is by the internal logic of already acquired systems of ideas, so that any idea cannot be thought at a given time (a global logic which gives a synchronic coherence to the different discourses and a diachronic logic which enables a limited number of transformations);
by the pitfalls of vocabulary which often make one think new thoughts in old terms, and conversely new terms do not offer the certainty of a novelty. The revolutionary fashions are not only in clothing, in hairstyles or in music, words of courtesy, formal forms of address and approach, metaphors, references or turns of speech. A new word is not always the symptom of an adherence to a new idea, but may just as

easily correspond to a process of assimilation-destruction by the pre-vailing ideas.

It seems indispensable for us to understand how a vision of the world and of society, such and such a conception of the production and the circulation of riches in particular, attracts or repels a segment of society and to understand then why an idea develops and abandons old ideas as it does or does not answer superficially or deeply to the momentary interests or objectives of a social group, even its illusions. Economic thought, spread under multiple forms in a period so fraught with conflict, in a time when one died for one's professed or supposed ideas as much as for one's acts, is more than a revealer of society. It is a constituent of its reality which can light up specific decisions and consequently specific events. The ideologies cannot be reduced to the state of more or less distorting mirrors. Let us go further. All the conflicts between the numerous parties, factions and coteries cannot simply be reduced to economic antagonisms between classes: human passions, personal ambitions, pride, the selfish-ness of power and vanity are also powerful actors in the theatre of economic constraints; thus, the theses put forward can be no more than a pretext. This is largely true of the fight between Girondins and Montag-nards.[33]

In fact, the narrative reading of Revolutionary ideas, which is founded on the mechanism of lying or on that of strictly socio-professional mech-anisms and thus ignores the ideologies of the actors, in particular their knowledge of their economic beliefs and the coherence of their arguments, is an incomplete reading and often mainly partial. We must thus 'think the Revolution', that is produce concepts adequate to its interpretation and more precisely in our field, and reconstruct the abstract frame through which its actors lived it, told it, thought it and understood it (or thought they did).

The reconstruction of this Revolutionary thought would entail con-siderable work – reading thousands of pamphlets and newspapers of all sorts – a long and exacting collective historical task.

The reading of a sample of the texts of the period enables us to note a striking identity of the representation of the world among the Revolution-aries and economists (or such) of the middle of the eighteenth century. Alexis de Tocqueville stigmatized it whereas Karl Marx praised it. The economists built a world where the producing individuals are by nature equal and where ownership can be justified by a present or past work.[34] Competition[35] is a principle and private property a fundamental right,[36] both explicitly asserted. So many essential elements seem to illustrate the liberal foundations[37] of economic ideas under the Revolution.

We shall illustrate the liberal foundations with three themes which correspond to stages of the unfolding of the Revolutionary process:

the question of ownership;
the setting up of a new generation of production and exchanges in particular with the suppression of corporations;
by dealing with the war economy at the origin of administrative regulation of the economy, we shall show that the stage of the Terror is consistent with the then dominant liberal ideology.

The question of the right of ownership
This is one of the most debated themes during the Revolutionary period.

Let us recall a few essential facts. At the start of the convening of the Etats Généraux and of the Revolution is the incapacity of the Crown to face its debts, an incapacity which is a translation into economic terms of its intellectual and social immobility towards the clergy and the nobles who attack absolutism in the name of tradition and the reforming forces which propound a unique tax proportional to income. To solve the financial crisis of the realm, the deputies turn first towards the important landed property of the Church and the Crown. The decision to sell the property of the clergy and the Crown is taken very rapidly and we shall see what arguments are put forward; this policy is adopted by the Assembly in November 1789. Acknowledgement of the debts of the state then takes the form of *assignat*, paper money guaranteed by the anticipated sale of the property of the clergy and the Crown. However, these goods are not the only rights of property that are the object of this new expropriation-appropriation. The feudal rights, a set of seignoral prerogatives of all kinds which supplied 20 per cent of the income of the French nobility were considered by their holders as lawful property because they were acquired by inheritance or bought. These are progressively suppressed. The sale of the property of the noblemen who fled from France was decided in summer 1792. Thus 1 200 000 families (out of 7–8 million households) acquired national property. This movement of expropriation affects not only landed property and feudal rights. Freedom of trade and work which, we shall soon see, is proclaimed with the end of corporations, suppressed a great number of charges and functions. These rights too had been bought or inherited.

The deputies decided they must be refunded, but this will be with a totally depreciated money.[38]

Let us see what debates on property accompanied this movement of expropriation. To expropriate the clergy and the nobility, the Revolutionaries had to overcome a formidable contradiction:[39]

how to claim to defend as a principle the right of property and at the same time not to protect feudal and ecclesiastical property and feudal rights;[40]
how to assert that the right of property has a historical character and at the same time not threaten and give a temporal limit to the bourgeois property rights.

To understand how this contradiction is dealt with it is indispensable to distinguish in the midst of the multiple controversies on property during the Revolution, three types of approach to the question: in terms of natural right, social convention, and usurpation.[41]

For the approach in terms of natural right,[42] property stems from the use of man's faculties, irrespective of any form of political association. By their work, people assimilate a portion of the matter which was initially common to all. The social state only confirms what existed beforehand in the state of nature. The right of ownership is then imprescriptible. This conception prevailed in 1789. Upholders of the rights of the Church and the nobility appeal to it, but so do their opponents. The Revolutionaries assert that the property of the nobility and the Church conforms to the natural right (which assumes the freedom of individuals) or no longer answer to the reasons of its constitution and therefore is no longer a property.[43] During the famous night of 4 August, known as the night of the abolition of privileges, a distinction was made by the deputies between two types of feudal right: rights which proceed from an ancient state of slavery are said to be contrary to the rights of man, thus illegitimate, and are suppressed without any compensation; conversely, rights which appear to be an old-time grant of properties are not abolished, are considered as lawful property, and are declared to be redeemable.[44]

The second approach to the right of property is inspired by the texts of Rousseau or Necker in particular.[45] It makes property a social convention. Mirabeau, for example, asserts: 'the right of property as we exercise it is a social creation . . . laws do not only protect property, they breed it in a way'. In this case, individual property is acknowledged as indispensable, but the right of each individual to his property is subordinated to that of the collectivity. This conception in terms of social convention gradually prevailed during the development of the Revolutionary movement. Moreover, according to this conception, the right of property, 'this social institution' as Robespierre called it, must not encroach on the primitive right, which is the right to live.[46] If property interferes with the right to life, this right to property must be restricted. Then the state finds itself sovereign judge of the limits of the right of property. This justifies requisitioning, and the setting up of a progressive tax or taxes on rich people.

The supporters of the natural right to property, a social convention, 'by smashing the shackles of Agriculture', by blowing away 'the feudal rust', have consciously transformed the right of property and the use of the land; the owner can freely dispose of the soil (fence in his lands, cultivate what he wants and dispose of the products when he wants to rent the land, sell it, and so on). However, property stripped of feudal, ecclesiastical, corporative and monarchic rights does not become for all an absolute right which would be an obstacle to the growth of industry and the bourgeoisie; after debates and propositions by Mirabeau, the mineral rights were excluded from the right to property; the state can thus directly cede the concession of the mines to those who hold the capital necessary to their exploitation.

The third approach does not criticize or limit abuses of the right of property. It asserts that property is a usurped right. A scant minority grouped around Babeuf rejected conventional rights to property and asserted that only the state of community is consistent with nature.

The great majority of the Revolutionaries rejected 'collectivist ideas'; the left and the extreme left of the assemblies, Robespierre or Saint-Just for instance, were fundamentally against the collectivization of the means of production and exchange. The extreme accusation of collectivism is generally used to denounce and eliminate political adversaries, charging them with wanting to derogate from the natural right of societies. This argument is reproduced, and in a way perpetuated, by numerous historians against the Revolutionaries who were content with denouncing, with grandiloquence indeed, not the very institution of property but gross social inequalities, often for primarily political reasons, to represent the hope of a better world for advanced elements of the Revolution, even if they did not want to satisfy some popular appetites. Unanimously on 18 March 1793, in order to reassure past and future purchasers of national goods, the Convention decided that anyone who propounded an agrarian law – that is the equal division of the land between the citizens[47] or any other subversive 'law about landed, commercial or industrial properties'[48] would be put to death. Robespierre called the agrarian law 'a ghost created by rogues to frighten fools.'[49] The Assembly's preventive condemnation of collectivist propositions shows first that the idea was circulating in the streets and in the country among certain Revolutionary popular strata,[50] but also that this idea did not penetrate the Revolutionary assemblies where the supporters of private property sat. Even during the phase called the Terror (1793–4) legislators and rulers relied on social convention. However, even among this small number, apart from the Assembly, which proposed an agrarian law,[51] equal sharing of the land questioned the distribution of the land but did not destroy the principle of the right of property; on the contrary, the proposition aimed at giving it a wider social basis.[52] Most of the supporters of private property yearned for the advent of a society of small landowners,[53] for they thought that democracy was incompatible with too large a disproportion in wealth.[54] The sharing of the common land[55] and the end of the birthright partook of the same ideal. It was the same for the sale of split-up national goods and the propositions to consider as heirs only direct descendants and to limit the value of the share of each one, the remainder going to poor families.[56]

If we take stock of the arguments about the right of property we notice that:

> the debates about property are deeper, the arguments richer than those about what is called 'the production and circulation of riches';
> the ideas put forward in the period 1789–94 are not remarkably original compared to texts previously written by Rousseau and Mably, for example.

The originality lies in the fact that what had until then been philosophical speculations and bookish reveries became in France, in the circumstances of the Revolution, a concrete problem to be solved.

The setting up of a new organization of production and exchange

When we read the speeches and pamphlets of the period 1789–92, we notice that a great number of their writers assert that economic freedom is an indispensable condition for conforming individual interests to the collective interest. State intervention creates privileges which hamper the economy. Competition is considered as increasing general prosperity.[57]

We shall deal in turn with several decisions which suppressed the constraints of the *ancien régime* and established a competitive economy: the end of corporations with the d'Allarde law, the interdiction of working men's and employers' associations that might interfere with the free play of the labour market with the Le Chapelier law,[58] and finally the free circulation of grain.

It is interesting to note that if the liberal consensus was widespread, some pressure groups were stronger than others. The declaration of the rights of man and the citizen and the principles of the freedom of work were slow to reach the French colonies. We must wait until February 1794 for the Convention to abolish slavery. Condorcet and Dupont de Nemours putting forward moral reasons and the economic interest of the country contributed greatly to this.[59] Slavery was very soon restored by Napoléon Bonaparte.

The old regime was characterized by a double system in manufactured production: that of corporations, a very regulated and hierarchical system; and that of manufacturers, whom a royal privilege allowed to escape the corporation restraints.

In 1776 Turgot failed in his attempt to abolish the corporative system. Besides, its suppression does not appear in the agenda of the first great Revolutionary days. A law about fiscal reform was voted to enact this abolition as late as 2 March 1791, on Deputy d'Allarde's proposal. When he introduced the bill, d'Allarde asserted that free competition would allow the number of workers to be adapted to the needs of the industry; an improvement in the quality of goods; and a reduction in prices.

These principles were not challenged. The d'Allarde law states that 'all professional privileges whatever they may be called, are suppressed', that 'any person will be free to carry on any trade or craft, art or occupation he thinks desirable', on condition he pays a tax. One can see that the d'Allarde law did not provide either the interdiction or the setting up of workers' or employers' coalitions. Did not Adam Smith criticize in *The Wealth of Nations* the advisability of such interdictions?

In spring 1791, during the weeks that followed the enactment of the d'Allarde law, some Parisian workers (in particular, carpenters) hoped to gather in mutual help societies and achieve minimal wages. Contradictory petitions of masters and workers were put forward. To put an end to this unrest, Deputy Le Chapelier introduced a bill on 14 June 1791. He particularly stated:

> Though all citizens must be allowed to get together, the citizens of some trades must not be allowed to assemble in the pursuit of their alleged common interests. There are only the particular interest of each individual and general interest. Nobody is allowed to inspire the citizens with an immediate interest and to separate them from the common good out of a corporative spirit.

The law was voted unanimously by the Assembly deputies. It forbade any gathering of the masters and workers,[60] and any collective action such as petition or strike. There was no passionate debate before or when the Le Chapelier or d'Allarde laws were voted. Only Jean-Paul Marat, in his daily *l'Ami du Peuple* criticized the law; he did so in the name of the freedom of political association (and not by putting forward any economic argument).

A third aspect of the liberalization of the economy concerns the free interior circulation of gain. In France the old regime was characterized by a long tradition of the control of grain and meal prices and their supply, a tradition neither the Physiocrats nor Turgot managed to put an end to. The freedom of the sale and interior circulation of grain was proclaimed by an Assembly decree as early as 29 August 1789. The communes however were allowed to subsidize the price of bread. During the first years of the Revolution, the same arguments of the old discussions were debated between the supporters and opponents of free circulation:[61]

> between those who thought that an increase in the price would stimulate supply of the market;
> and between those who stated that it was advisable to forbid exportation, to import corn to resell it at a low subsidized price in public granaries, and that it was advisable to fight the 'grabbers' who speculated on the price rise.

There was nothing very new in the statements of both parties, except perhaps that they required and demanded more urgently the control of the grain, meal and bread market.[62]

In November 1792, while the price of cereals rose and supply difficulties became more and more obvious, an important debate started again. Deputy Feraud supported the unlimited freedom of the grain trade. He proposed the death penalty for those who hampered that circulation. Conversely, Deputy Beffroy proposed the fixing of prices by the state and the control of transactions between individuals in order to discover the 'grabbers'. The Assembly then refused to come to a conclusion between the various contradictory proposals. It ordered the printing of all speeches on the subject for the debate to develop. The debate went on, and Saint-Just took part in it. He who, a year later would be one of the leaders of the so-called Terror policy, then declared: 'I dislike violent laws on commerce ... freedom of commerce is the mother of plenty'.[63] This feeling was largely shared by the Assembly. On 8 December 1792 it reaffirmed by a vote the necessity of not interfering with the interior grain trade. This principle would be short-lived for by the spring of 1793 the administrative steps taken to face the war and the price rise would weigh more and more heavily.

Liberalism and terror

From spring 1793 onwards, the Republican government faced a dreadful contradiction. To finance state expenditure, in particular that linked with the foreign war against Bohemia, Hungary, England, Holland and Spain and the interior rebellion of royalist or anti-Parisian regions, the state multiplied the *assignat* issues.[64] At the same time, the quantities of paper money issued during the previous months did not diminish. The army then requisitioned what the speculators stocked. Consequently there existed indisputable pressure for a price rise.[65] To oppose popular claims, the government decided to freeze the prices of numerous goods and services. The level of intervention then entered a spiral which tended to a heavier and heavier control of the economy. As the inefficacy of these measures called for increasingly stricter control, the prices of goods, then of wages, were authoritatively set, public granaries were instituted, ration books were issued, and a decree of 26 June 1794 even provided for an anticipated requisition of the new harvest.

It is difficult in this period to find any economic arguments. Opponents of the regime hid or kept silent, and failures were ascribed to the 'grabbers' who speculated on goods, the 'gamblers' who speculated on the *assignat* fall, 'emigrated aristocrats' and 'foreigners', hence the growing number of suspects and the political repression. A major event of these struggles between rival factions was a coalition of moderates and ultras in July 1794. Its conclusion was the downfall of Robespierre, who did not find in the Parisian population the necessary support because of the discontent caused by the fall in real income.

Neither were there any economic debates, because the decisions were not considered as the choice of a stable, oriented economy but as exceptional measures justified by the state of war. Many historians regard the Terror, out of repulsion or sympathy, as the harbinger of socialism. Let us refrain from any anachronism. To be sure, the war economy decided upon in 1793–4 anticipated some administrative measures that were systematized much later; the same for education projects and schemes to relieve the poor. However, if we stick to the elite ideas concerning the production and circulation of goods, in a word to economic ideas, we are bound to admit that we are nearer to economic ultra-liberalism than to socialism. Decrees against hoarding may look more consistent with the latter than with the former; they are nothing of the kind. Tariffs, requisitions, confiscations of goods and other restraints of individual freedom were exceptional measures justified by contingency and could be legitimized by the subordinate character of the right of ownership. These dictatorial remedies which were economic, political and moral measures, produced by the will to enlist all energies to cope with the war at the borders and rebellion in some regions were deemed to be temporary and were not an ideal model of the working of the economy. Moreover, these laws signified that, on the one hand producing activity rested in private hands; on the other hand, for want of delivery of goods by their owners, the state had the right to force a sale at market prices on a given date. The law determining public control in money markets and wages could be interpreted as a return to the corporation regulations which kept an eye not on the quality but on the price of goods and services.[66] The montagnard economy can be understood as liberalism, temporarily altered by war.[67] The directed economy that was born in spring 1793 had no primary social ends, but military ones, and could be interpreted less as an anticipation of forms, structures and institutions to come as a temporary return to some economic methods, some acts of the old regime absolutism and as a kind of 'war-mercantilism'.[68]

Let us not mistake liberalism and its modern conservative substitute: the unlimited defence of private property and the refusal of any state intervention. A.R. Turgot, who cannot be placed outside the liberal current, already set bounds to private property when he stated: 'the poor man has undeniable rights to the rich man's wealth'.[69]

For the Revolutionaries, goods must circulate even at the price of violence against their owners. The ideal of the Jacobins and even the Hébertistes was not collectivization of means of production and exchange; this is demonstrated by the sale of national goods and the sharing of communal lands. The ideal as regards circulation of goods and services was trade regulation which excluded hoarding practice, for speculating on stocks was an impediment to the free circulation of goods and the fixing of prices[70] and challenged the survival of the poorest. The proposals of Jacobin Anacharsis Clootz,[71] who advocated the unified political organization of mankind, express extreme liberalism:

> We are not free if foreign barriers stop us within ten or twenty leagues of our manor . . . if our trade is interrupted by hostilities, if our industry is confined within the narrow circle of such and such a country . . . . Wherever you will see ports or havens closed to our trade and ways and canals forbidden to us, fight against error, if it is a free country, against the tyrant if it is a despotic country against the aristocrats, if it is an oligarchic country . . . . A part of mankind could not live apart without rebelling . . . . Trade is the main cause of human contentions; now, republics trade more than kingdoms. Don't let us have neighbors if we do not want to have enemies.

When they destroyed the old orders and privileges, the old regime decisions and the mercantile fiscal and social practices linked to them,[72] the Revolutionaries shaped society according to a new norm. In this the Revolutionaries' thought was not only economic but also liberal, since the old obstacles to the free circulation of goods disappeared; the uniformity of weights and measures and the suppression of road and city tolls[73] were necessary corollaries of *laissez passer*. On the other hand, the bulk of administrative measures taken in the field of the production and circulation of wealth and the attempts to cope with poverty by social measures, both recall some pre-capitalist community, corporation or state relationships[74] and various statements by theologians of the Middle Ages statements and foreshadow elements of the socialist economy to come; thus, in the spirit of a period generally liberal as concerns the elites in power, they did not constitute socially 'contradictory' elements but rather, in my opinion, both remnants inherited from past paradigms and the germ of thoughts to come.

A transition period

When one assesses the Revolutionary years 1789–94 in relation to French economic thought, one notices a great continuity with previous liberal ideas. In fact, things appear more complex when one gets away from short-term analysis; the French Revolution is an intellectual turning point in France for political economy between the Physiocrats and J.-B. Say.

The end of the Physiocratic fashion, even before the end of the old regime, was a time favourable to the introduction in France of the English social sciences, in particular with the translations of Smith's, Stewart's, Godwin's or Bentham's works.

In 1794, the so-called 'Auteuil', or ideologues group, a movement in which Jean-Baptiste Say (secretary to the Finance minister Clavière in 1792) and Destutt de Tracy took an active part, and started a review, *La Décade philosophique*, and those who would be called the ideologues contributed to the creation of one of the first political economy courses in France: political economy became an institution.

The political upheavals of the years 1789–94 were not favourable to the emancipation of a specific economic thought. The Revolution gave birth to a powerful comeback of politics and morals. But the backlash after the Revolution and the despotic period that followed were favourable to intellectual autonomization (or rather to the will to carry it out) of civilian society (at the juncture of economics and politics). The distinction largely ignored by the Physiocrats and introduced by Adam Smith and Anne Robert Turgot between politics and economy[75] was achieved in France by Jean-Baptiste Say at the beginning of the nineteenth century. Say forcibly stated:

> politics proper, the science of society organization has often been mistaken for political economy that teaches how the wealth which meets the needs of societies is formed, distributed and consumed. Yet wealth is essentially independent of political organization; a state can thrive under any form of government, if it is properly ruled. We have seen nations grow rich under absolute monarchs, we have seen some ruining themselves under popular rule.[76]

When passions abated the foundations of a genuine economic thought were laid. French political economy after the Revolution went even further than the first Smithian model[77] with P. L. Roederer and Jean-Baptiste Say, who purified it of its institutional elements and reduced the economic agents to supports of economic functions.

Finally some themes disappeared from political economy. The matter of luxury for instance, a central theme in eighteenth-century political economy (see the success of Mandeville's *Fable of the Bees*, the role of consumption of luxuries by the propertied classed in the Physiocrats' works, its criticism by Forbonnais who sees it as a brake to the development of food crops and hence an obstacle to population growth, etc.), no longer appears at the beginning of the nineteenth century, except in a residual fashion in the works of the critics of Jean-Baptiste Say's *loi des débouchés* (for example in Sismonde de Sismondi's work, where sumptuary expenditure spurs on economic activity). Revolutionary morals play in this respect a part comparable to Anglo-Saxon puritanism.

Notes

1. Léon Walras, *Etudes d'économie sociale, Œuvres économiques complètes*, Paris: Economica, Vol. IX, p. 97. See Jérôme Lallement, 'Léon Walras et les idéaux de 1789', a contribution to the conference Economic Thought during the Revolution, Vizille 6–8 September 1989.
2. A train of thought started when we published jointly a book entitled *Idées économiques sous la Révolution* published in April 1989 by the Lyon PUL in its collection 'Analyse, epistemologie, histoire économique' and furthered in the Vizille conference (6–8 September 1989) 'La pensée économique pendant la Révolution française'.
3. I will not discuss here the historical problem of the dates which must be considered as the beginning of the Revolution (1788–9) and its ending (1794–5, end of the Convention), 1799 (Bonaparte's *coup d'état*), even the advent of the Third Republic or, for our subject matter, 1803, the date of publication of the *Traité* by Jean-Baptiste Say. The history of ideas belongs as much to structural studies of a short-term period which in the expression of an ideology studies movements over a long period whose waves penetrate successively and contradictorily the multiple social layers and classes. Florence Gauthier in 'De Mably à Robespierre, un programme économique égalitaire, 1775–1793', *Annales historiques de la Révolution française*, **261**, July –September 1985, pp. 265–89, has for example shown the link between the thought of Robespierre and, a quarter of a century earlier, Mably's criticism in *Du Commerce des grains* of Turgot's policy.
4. On the economic situation in the Revolutionary period, see the special issue of *Revue économique*, **40** (6) November 1989, under the supervision of Jean-Charles Asselain.
5. So true it is that, concerning consumption, by the diversification of products and services one 'aristocracy' can replace another.
6. See the analysis of this passage by G. Faccarello, 'L'évolution de l'économie politique pendant la Révolution: Alexandre Vandermonde ou la croisée des chemins', in *Französische Revolution und Politische Okonomie*, Conference, 27–28 May 1988, Studienzentrum Karl-Marx-Hauss Trier, p. 75ff.
7. Let us cite a brilliant and recent exception, that of François Hincker, *La Révolution française et l'économie*, Paris: Nathan, 1989, more particularly pp. 67–84.
8. Saint-Just was a Revolutionary studied by economists, but Saint-Just was not an economist. See in particular the study by C. A. Michalet (first published in the *Annales de la Révolution française*, 1968, pp. 60–110) and that of Michel Lutfalla, 'Saint-Just, analyste de l'inflation révolutionnaire', *Revue d'histoire économique et sociale*, **2** (1966), pp. 242–55. In addition to the contributions to *Idées économiques sous la Révolution* and to the Vizille convention (note 2), see two articles devoted to Sieyès which unfortunately stop at the 1789 manuscripts: Marcel Dorigny 'La formation de la pensée économique de Sieyès d'après ses manuscrits (1770–1789)', *Annales historiques de la Révolution française*, **271**, January–March 1988, pp. 17–34 and Georges Benrekassz, 'Crise de l'Ancien Régime, crise des idéologies: une année dans la vie de Sieyès', *Annales: E.S.C.*,

January–February 1989, pp. 25–46; Germain and Mireille Sicard, 'Robespierre avait-il une doctrine économique?', in *Mélanges Max Cluseau*, Toulouse Business School/ Toulouse University of Social Sciences: Presses IEP Toulouse, 1985, pp. 635–59; Marcel Dorigny, 'Recherches sur les idées économiques des Girondins', *Actes du Colloques Girondins-Montagnards*, Paris, 1975–80, pp. 79–102; and 'Les Girondins et le droit de propriété', *Bulletin d'histoire économique et sociale de la Révolution française*, 1980–1, pp. 15–31.

    See also the two brief contributions of Ph. Steiner and G. Faccarello to Michel Vovelle (ed.), *L'Etat de la France pendant la Révolution (1789–1799)*, Paris: La Découverte, 1988, pp. 421–7, which offer research paths and succinct bibliographical indications.

9. The first translation into French in book form was published in La Haye in 1778–9 in four volumes; at Yverdon in 1781, another translation in six volumes was published, followed by a new one in 1788. The knowledge of Adam Smith's works had an undeniable influence, for example on l'abbé Sieyès, see Dorigny, op. cit.

10. On Vandermonde, see the works of Alain Alcouffe presented during the Nice conference (September 1987) of the Association Charles Gide pour l'histoire de la pensée économique, and published in the *Annales historiques de le Révolution française* (1988).

11. See the indications given by Edgar Allix, 'La rivalité entre la propriéte foncière et la fortune mobilière sous la Révolution', *Revue d'histoire économique et sociale*, 1912, pp. 291–348.

12. On his action in the Committee of Money during the Revolution, see Guy Thuillier, *La Monnaie en France au début du 19e siècle*, Geneva: Droz, 1938, p. 37ff.

13. His interventions during the Revolution are dealt with by L. P. Lay, *Le Mercier de la Rivière, 1719–1801, aux origines de la science économique*, Paris/Aix-Marseilles: CNRS, 1975, pp. 127–42.

14. For a first approach to his works, read Edgar Allix, 'L'œuvre économique de Germain Garnier, traducteur d'Adam Smith et disciple de Cantillon', *Revue d'histoire des doctrines économiques et sociales*, 1912, pp. 317–42.

15. Let us mention here the Condorcet seminar set up in Paris from 8 to 11 June 1988 by the CNRS team, Epistemological and Historical Researches on Exact Sciences and Scientific Institutions, in particular Gilbert Faccarello's contribution, and for P. L. Roederer, see Jean Rosio's contribution at the symposium on economic thought during the Revolution, Vizille, 6–8 September 1989.

16. See for instance the article 'Economic politique', written by J.-J. Rousseau for *L'Encyclopédie*.

17. About their influence on the start and development of the Revolutionary process, see the denunciation or, in other words, the analysis by Augustin Cochin, *La Révolution et la libre-pensée*, Paris: Plon, 1924, pp. 108–9.

18. For some people, the economists' influence is both indirect and obvious. This is the case for Mirabeau, one of the greatest orators at the beginning of the Revolution, who read speeches prepared by others, in particular in the circles of the Banque Genevoise in Paris, a liberal Genevan milieu, where one will meet Clavière, and therefore young Jean-Baptiste Say; see J. Bénetruy, *L'Atelier de Mirabeau, quatre Genevois dans la tourmente révolutionnaire*, Geneva: Jullien 1962 and Etienne's testimony, *Souvenirs de Mirabeau et sur les deux premières assemblées législatives*, Paris: PUF, 1951.

19. On the acknowledgment of Adam Smith's thought in France, one will read with interest Allix, 'L'œuvre économique de Germain Garnier', op. cit.

20. Cochin, *La Révolution et la libre-pensée*, op. cit., p. 293; *Les Sociétés de pensée et la démocratie moderne, Etudes d'histoire révolutionnaire*, Paris: Plon, 1921.

21. See, in this respect, J. Hecht, 'De la Révolution scientifique à la révolution culturelle: l'enscigment de l'économie politique à l'âge des lumières', in *Idées économiques sous la Révolution*, Lyon: Pul (1989), pp. 35–80.

22. Witold Kula, in *Les Mesures et les Hommes*, Paris: Maison des Sciences de l'Homme, 1984, pp. 170–210, is a very interesting study of the unification of weights and measures in the *Cahiers de doleances* (where the Third State voices its grievances against the state

of the French kingdom). This question holds a very important place in the Tiers Etat books. Before 1789 France's population was divided into three groups: the Nobility, the Clergy and the 'Third State'.

23. See Michel Vovelle, *La Mentalité révolutionnaire: sociéte et mentalité sous la révolution française*, Paris: Editions sociales, 1985, p. 290.

24. Bernard Groethuysen, *Philosophie de la Révolution française*, Paris: Gallimard, 1956, p. 81.

25. F. Aftalion, *L'économie de la Révolution française*, Paris: Hachette, 1987. See particularly pp. 19, 66–9, 88, 145–6, 166–7, 185–6, 190. This book is also particularly interesting as a synthesis of economic facts.

26. Ibid., p. 19.

27. These causes only complete the bloodthirsty beastliness of 'the riff-raff and bobtail'. See H. Taine, *Les origines de la France contemporaine*, Paris: Laffont/club français du livre, 1972 (on 'highway robbery, see pp. 155, 157, 172–5, 178, 183, 201, 393, and on the 'paid mercenaries', pp. 220–1, 330–3, 431); likewise, but in a more subdued manner, see A. Thiers's allusions to 'the hired ruffians' and private speculations (*Histoire de la Révolution française*, Paris: Furne, 1845, Vol. I, pp. 38–9, 120–1, 162, Vol. III, pp. 304–6, Vol. IV, pp. 327, 335–6).

28. Taine, op. cit., p. 206; Taine is much more discerning when he describes the nobility's recklessness and their inability to oppose the Revolution (see particularly op. cit., pp. 54–6, 124).

29. Aftalion, op. cit., p. 66.

30. See Serge Chassagne, *Oberkampf, un entrepreneur capitaliste au Siècle des Lumières*, Paris: Aubier, 1980 and Denis Woronoff, *L'Industrie sidérurgique en France pendant la Révolution et l'Empire*, Paris: Ecole des Hautes Etudes en Sciences Sociales, 1984. On the activities of Dupont de Nemours and more particularly on the printing works he bought in 1781 and which collapsed in 1797, see Marc Bouloiseau, *Bourgeoisie et Révolution, les Dupont de Nemours* (1788–9), *Mémoires et documents* of the Commission d'Histoire Économique et Sociale de la Révolution Française, Vol. XXVII, Paris: Bibliothèque Nationale, 1972, especially pp. 65–8, 76, 84–90, 115–18, 131.

31. Michel Bruguiere, *Gestionnaires et profiteurs de la Révolution*, Paris: Orban, 1986. In the same direction, see François Hincker, 'Les Révolutionnaires et l'économie: idées et pratiques', in *La Révolution française et ses paradoxes*, Seminar DECTA III, 1988–9, Bordeaux, an article which announces the publication of *La révolution française et l'économie: décollage ou catastrophe?* Paris: Nathan, 1989.

32. For a very subtle approach to the notion of reflection-ideology, see, concerning the Revolutionary period E. Guibert, *Voies idéologiques de la Révolution française*, Paris: Ed. Sociales, 1976, in particular p. 13 ff., 155 ff.

33. Jean Jaurès gives a brilliant demonstration of this: 'If the Girondins became an obstacle to the revolutionary development and a peril for the Revolution, it is not because of a theoretical and systematic attachment to federalism but because of a previous infeodation to class interests, a narrow bourgeois egoism .... I know that for those who believe that political events, even in their details, are the immediate reflection of economic phenomena, this explanation is very superficial and frivolous. If we applied rigorously the method of which Marx in his *Histoire du Dix Huit Brumaire* gave an explanation both brilliant and childish, we should find in the terrible conflict of the Gironde and the Montagne the expression of deep class conflicts. But in history, there are not only class struggles, there are party struggles too. I mean that apart from economic affinities and antagonisms, there arise passion groups, interests of pride, domination, which shape history in its making and are a cause of unrest'. J. Jaurès, Histoire socialiste, livre IV, La Convention, Vol. 2, Paris: Rouff, p. 1459, see too pp. 1458–1464.

34. This is underlined by Ph. Steiner, 'Le projet physiocratique: théorie de la propriété et lien social', *Revue économique*, 1987, p. 1111 ff.

35. See in this respect the reaction of the Assembly in March 1792, after the murder by

rioters of Simoneau, a Jacobin and the mayor of Etampes who opposed the popular demand for the taxation of corn.

36. Article XVII of the Declaration of the rights of man and the citizen is quite explicit in this matter: 'property being an inviolable and sacred right, nobody can be deprived of it, except when legally established public necessity obviously demands it and under the condition of a preliminary just indemnity'.

37. This economic liberalism is not *ultra* because it does not exclude the affirmation and the intervention of the state in certain fields such as education or poor relief or the necessary definition of market rules, for example by protectionist measures of the national territory.

38. This vast movement of expropriation is largely characteristic of all important social transformation. We could draw a parallel with the Mexican Revolution in 1917 and the creation of *eridos* (community) by dismembering large estates, with the independence of Algeria in 1962 and the departure of the French *pieds-noirs* or with the previous example of the independence of the United States when the estates of the loyalists fell into the hands of the republicans.

39. Jean Jaurès in Volume I of his *Histoire socialiste* develops this question brilliantly (p. 158 ff.).

40. It is not by chance that the books of the nobility and the clergy stress the absolute respect of properties, of all properties in the name of the right of property. L'abbé Maury says: 'our properties guarantee yours. We are attacked to-day, but do not be mistaken, if we are despoiled, you will be so in your turn.' (Quoted by F. Furet, *La Révolution française*, Paris, 1973, p. 131).

41. We shall not develop here the link between these debates on the right of property and the political opposition between universal suffrage/census suffrage and landed property. According to some landed property binds men to the Nation; according to others, personal estate is a factor of mobility and statelessness.

42. Let us quote two authors who supported this approach inspired by John Locke and taken by the Physiocrats: Germain Garnier, the translator of *The Wealth of Nations* by Smith, in *De la propriété dans ses rapports avec le droit politique* (1792) and l'abbé Morellet in an article in the *Journal de Paris* (May 1792) entitled 'On the Doctrine of Brissot against Property'.

43. The article 'Fondation' in the *Encyclopédie* written by A. R. Turgot could supply the argument concerning this matter (*Encylopédie ou Dictionnaire raisonné des sciences des arts et des métiers*, Paris: Brisasson, 1757, Vol. VII, pp. 72–5) taken up by Mirabeau and Dupont de Nemours (see in *Idées économiques sous la Révolution*, Henri Goutte, 'Economie et transitions: l'oeuvre économique et politique de Pierre Samuel Dupont de Nemours de début de la Révolution française (1789–1792)', pp. 172–8).

44. In fact, the political situation (the peasants burn a certain number of mansions and their title deeds) is such that these rents are no longer paid. A series of decrees in spring 1792 suppressed a great number of so-called redeemable rights, and finally on 17 July 1793, feudal rights were completely abolished without compensation. A social group (the clergy, the nobility, the bourgeoisie who have acquired feudal title deeds) found itself thus dispossessed for the benefit of peasants and bourgeois.

45. See Henri Grange's contribution, 'Necker et l'inégalité sociale', in *Idées économiques sous la Révolution*, pp. 407–19. Morellet calls Necker's conception regarding property 'a popular doctrine against monopolists, the rich and the property owners'. See his *Mémoires*, Paris: Bossange, 1882, quoted by Edgar Allix, 'La rivalité', op. cit., p. 302.

46. 'Thus, the first social law is that which guarantees to all the members of society the means of existing . . . property was instituted or guaranteed only to cement it, it is to live first that we have properties. It is not true that property could ever be in opposition with the subsistence of mankind. All that is indispensable to keep it [life] is a property common to the whole society. Only the surplus is individual property and is abandoned to the industry of tradespeople'. Robespierre, speech of December 1792, quoted by G. and M. Sicard, op. cit., p. 642. We must however compare this proposition with the following assertion: 'the extreme disproportion in wealth is the source of many evils and

many crimes; but we are none the less convinced that equality of goods is a chimera. For my part, I find it less necessary to private happiness than to public bliss: we must make poverty honourable rather than banish opulence' (speech of April 1793, ibid., p. 643).
On the question of the submission of the private spheres, see the political analysis of Lucien Jaume, 'Le public et le privé chez les Jacobins (1789–1794)', *Revue française de science politique*, 1987, pp. 230–48.

47. R. B. Rose, 'The "Red Scare" of the 1790s: the French Revolution and the "Agrarian Law" ', *Past and Present*, **103**, May 1984, pp. 113–30.
48. In order to balance it, on the same day that Barère proposed to organize public relief for the poor and to divide the national goods sold in plots so as to be more accessible to the greater number.
49. Quoted by C. and M. Sicard, op. cit., p. 643.
50. It is not necessary to interpret this claim as an anticipation of socialism, except if we think its roots are the old rural communal rights.
51. Albert Mathiez, *La Vie chère et le mouvement social sous la Terreur*, Paris: Payot, 1973, Vol. I, pp. 87–95.
52. The lawyer of many businessmen, Berryer himself writes in his *Souvenirs de 1774 à 1838* (Paris: Dupont, 1839, pp. 292–3): 'the abundance of the signs of exchange, in which assignats played a useful part during the years 1792 and 1793 . . . amply helped the division of property which is and will always be, whatever we may say, a great social improvement as it interests a greater number of individuals in the defence of property threatened from so many sides'.
53. Thus the model of free competition is not that of a capitalist economy, but that of small commercial production, for reasons which are not economic but fundamentally political.
54. For Necker, 'the wage earners cannot claim more than the vital minimum, but this vital minimum must be guaranteed, at all costs, by the action of the State, the natural defendant of the underprivileged classes' (H. Grange, 'Necker devant la Révolution française, une constitution à l'anglaise et une Société de notables', *Annales historiques de la Révolution française*, **254**, 1983, p. 597. See too, in *Idées économiques sous la Révolution*, H. Grange's article on Necker, pp. 407–19. He raises the same problem; the banker on the banks of the Leman, a minister in France, did not want to question socio-economic inequality and chose political inequality.
55. See Fabre de l'Hérault report of April 1793, the law of 10 June 1793, and its analysis by J. Jaurès, op. cit., Book IV, pp. 1576–82, 1628–30.
56. For example in *Eléments du républicanisme* (1793) by Billaud-Varennes.
57. The exception is external trade, for which protectionist arguments became prevalent: here again political reasons determine the borders of free trade. We shall find later, with the continental blockade, the same consensus on protection of the 'budding' industry and the same economic patriotism. On this continuity, see Pierre Leon (ed.), *Histoire économique et sociale du monde*, Book 3, Paris: Armand Colin, 1978, p. 358.
58. For a more detailed analysis of these two laws, see *Idées économiques sous la Révolution*, Jean-Pierre Potier's contribution, 'L'Assemblée constituante et la question de liberté du travail: un texte méconnu, la loi Le Chapelier', pp. 235–54.
59. See in *Idées économiques sous la Révolution*, Pierre Dockès, 'Condorcet et l'esclavage des nègres ou lesquisse d'une économie politique de l'esclavage à la veille de la Révolution française', pp. 85–123 and Pierre-Henri Goutte, 'Économie et transitions: l'oeuvre économique et politique de Pierre-Samuel Dupont de Nemours au début de la Révolution française (1789–1792)', pp. 145–233.
60. Let us however notice that chambers of commerce that had been spared so far were suppressed by an Assembly vote only on 27 September 1791 after a Commerce and Agriculture Committee recommendation.
61. See P. S. Dupont de Nemours, 'Analyse historique de la législation des grains depuis 1692, à laquelle on a donné la forme d'un rapport à l'Assemblée nationale', quoted in Goutte, op. cit., p. 182.

62. See the popular movements studied for the year 1792 by Michel Vovelle, 'Les taxations populaires de février–mars et novembre–décembre 1792 dans la Beauce et sur ses confins', in *Mémoires et documents de la Commission de recherche et de publication des documents relatifs à la vie économique de la Révolution*, tome XIII, actes du 82e congrès national des sociétés savantes, Paris: Imprimerie nationale, Structures sociales et problèmes économiques (1787–98), pp. 107–59.

  There is an evident contrast between the deputies who make of Simoneau (the mayor of Etampes murdered by rioters while defending the free circulation of grain) a martyr of freedom and l'abbé Dolivier who drew up la pétition de quarante citoyens des communes d'Etampes et de Saint-Sulpice-de-Favières in which he asserted: 'It is the rise of the prise of corn, it is hunger or the fear of hunger which were the only instigators . . . . There is a consideration which must strike you to some extent: that is to accept that foodstuff of first necessity may rise to a price that the poor workman, the day-labourer cannot pay, which means that there is none for him, that is to say that only the rich man, useful or not, has the right of not starving [. . . Simoneau is . . .] a hero for corn traders since he died a victim of their inhuman and selfish speculations.'

63. Louis Antoine de Saint-Just, 'Discours à la Convention sur les subsistances', 29 November 1972 (*Œuvres*, Paris: Prevost, 1834, p. 37).

64. The inability of the Royal Treasury to solve the fiscal crisis (endemic throughout the century and sharp from 1789 onwards) was the reason for the meeting of the Etats Généraux. Quickly, by the creation of *assignats* first (December 1789) in the form of a bond (bearing interest and guarantee through the following sale of the Church and Crown goods), then that of a security circulating as money and a legal tender (April 1790) and without interest rate (September 1790), finally with the issue of small 5-livre notes (May 1791) then of smaller value and the setting up of the compulsory rate (April 1793), the fiscal problem became monetary as well. The quick depreciation of these *assignats* put them at the heart of the Revolutionary debate.

65. One often sees in the works of historians who want to test the *assignat* solidity an attempt to find a relationship between the value of the money issued and its security in national goods. The value – if this expression means anything – of a sign, that is the general level of prices, rather depends on the volume of the payments it must settle.

66. J. Cl. Perrot, 'Voies nouvelles pour l'histoire économique de la Révolution française', in 'Voies nouvelles pour l'historie de la Révolution française', conference, Albert Mathiez-Georges Lefebvre, commission d'histoire économique et sociale de la Révolution française, Mémoire et documents n° XXXV, Paris: Bibliothèque nationale, 1978, p. 136, which underlines the Malthusian character of this regulation since it eliminates all producers whose costs are above the maximum price.

67. 'For Robespierre, private trade remains thus the normal instrument of exchanges' (G. and M. Sicard, op. cit., p. 647).

68. From autumn 1792 to Thermidor, the commerce committees examined more than 120 subsidy petitions for manufactures and distributed abbeys and châteaux for the production of textile, iron, machinery, chemicals, leather, oil, sugar, beer, paper and glass. The committees supervised as well as they could the raw material supplies and man-power permanence, through exemptions, privileges and monopolies, particularly for armaments, army clothing and transports, vital sectors for the nation. The state even assigned foundlings and orphans to private workshops and greatly affected wages downward. J. Cl. Perrot, 'Voies nouvelles', op. cit.

69. Turgot, 'Fondation', in *Encyclopédie ou Dictionnaire raisonné des sciences, des arts et des métiers*, Vol. VII, Paris, 1757, p. 73, col. 1.

70. The criticism of monopolies and the project of a society where equal economic agents would trade, are the reasons why I disagree with Florence Gauthier's anti-liberal though very stimulating interpretation of Maximilien Robespierre's thought: 'De Mably à Robespierre, un programme économique héréditaire, 1775–1793', *Annales historiques de la Révolution française*, **261**, July–September 1985, pp. 265–89.

71. Sitting of the Convention, 26 April 1793. The proposal was developed in *Appel au genre*

humain, Paris: Frimaire An II, and in *Bases constitutionnelles de la République du genre humain*, Paris: Imprimerie Nationale 1793.

72. Witold Kula, *Les Mesures et les hommes*, Paris: Maison des sciences de l'homme, 1984, p. 304.

73. The suppression was carried out in three stages, 15 March 1790, 19 February 1791 and 25 August 1792.

74. See the many state restraints that were a burden before the Revolution in Denis Woronoff, *L'Industrie sidérurgique*, op. cit., pp. 15–19.

75. J.-M. Servet, 'La monnaie contre l'Etat ou la fable du troc', in *Droit et monnaie, Etats et espace monétaire transnational*, Dijon: Université de Bourgogne, Faculté de Droit, institut de Relations Internationales: CREDIMI, 1988, pp. 49–62. See on this point Dupont de Nemours's contribution compared with François Quesnay analysed by Goutte, op. cit.

76. J.-B. Say, *Traité d'économie politique*, 6th edn, Paris: Guillaumin, p. 1.

77. See Jean Rosio, contribution to the conference 'La Pensée économique pendant la Révolution', Vizille, 6–8 September 1989. Serge Latouche, 'Le luxe guillotiné ou comment un concept disparait du discours économique dans la tourmente révolutionnaire', *La Revue du MAUSS* (Paris), 5 (1989), pp. 39–53.

10 The emergence of the economics of the firm in continental Europe during the twenties: *Betriebswirtschaftslehre* and *Economia Aziendale* as methodological revolutions

Arnaldo Canziani and Paolo Rondo Brovetto

1. Introduction: *Betriebswirtschaftslehre* and *Economia Aziendale*

Social sciences differ from other sciences in that they are more complex. This is due to their greater relativism: they have many premises, shadowed or nonexistent boundaries. So 'any account of the changes . . . in the history of economic thought, must take full account of the complexity of the material and of its various kinds of components . . . . A neatly exclusivist or monistic account will not do justice to the . . . actual process' (Hutchison, 1978, p. 317).

Before the Keynesian revolution, capital and income, interest theory, cycles and fluctuations, *Marktformen* and production theory were the main issues of scientific reflection in the field of economics. After 1936, and mainly after the Keynes–Hicks *vulgata*, macroeconomics became the dominating viewpoint of analyses and contributions for some 30 years.

In the same years, however, in two European countries – Germany and Italy – accounting and business studies turned into unified theories of the firm, drawing also on the legacy of Fisher, Pareto and John Stuart Mill. Resulting from a strong methodological turnaround generally based on the critical positivism of Mach, Poincaré and others, these theories – *Betriebswirtschaftslehre* in Germany and *Economia Aziendale* in Italy – adopted a research approach infinitely larger than the two-case study of the firm of the Marshallian tradition. These two disciplines stated, and developed in time, these principles:

the method to be adopted is deductive-inductive, in order to avoid both 'theory without facts' and 'facts without theory';
firms in general – banks and insurance companies included – represent a unity of prices in time: due to this fact, income is the best economic indicator and the basis of every evaluation;
regardless of industry and sector the economics of firms is a synthetic

discipline studying accounting–management–organization (*Economia Aziendale*) or accounting–production–exchange–finance (*Betriebswirtschaftslehre*).

The evolution of the two disciplines (and, later, entire bodies of knowledge) has gradually taken place since the 1920s and 1930s, with greater intensity since the late 1950s: hundreds of books have been written both on the practice and on the theory of the firm. These works are based on the milestones laid in those two decades. The methodological revolution of the early twentieth century makes those rather neglected years highly relevant to the evolution of economic thought. We usually consider them to be a sometimes confused and unimportant period, at least in Europe: only a minor segment of the long path from Marshall to Keynes. In addition we consider them to be an intermediate phase of political and cultural evolution: the transition between the end of *laissez-faire*, World War I, and the new forms of bilateral clearings; as well as the transition from positivism (naturalism) to neo-positivism, the Vienna Circle and Wittgenstein.

Nevertheless, if we look at that period with scientific attention we discover deeply interesting features in that it displays (1) the usual multi-directional confusion of scientific research; (2) the whole set of premises of every Keynesian, anti-Keynesian or a-Keynesian system of thought; (3) last but not least with reference to our issue here, the starting phase of the economics of the firm in continental Europe (*Economia Aziendale* in Italy, *Betriebswirtschaftslehre* in Germany, *Bedrijfsekonomie* in Holland, *Företagsekonomi* in Sweden, *Foretaksøkonomie* in Norway, *Liiketaloustie* in Finland, *Civiløkonome* in Denmark). Although this is not the object of this work, it is worth mentioning here that similar developments took place in Japan, where the *Shogyogaku* (commercial studies) turned into the *Keieikeizaigaku* (economics of the firm) around the same period, also as a consequence of German influence (Mori, 1987).

2.   The evolution of scientific methodology in Europe in the transition phase 1900–1920: the return to 'a priori' reasoning

During the second part of the nineteenth century Europe experienced the development and the triumph of positivism, a philosophical approach attributing an overwhelming importance to facts. 'Scientific' was the adjective deserved by every branch of knowledge, once it had established itself on close attention to the actual facts: so there was 'scientific' medicine, 'scientific' psychology and 'scientific' sociology.

From the beginning of the twentieth century the idea was resumed that, on the contrary, no facts exist without a subjective consideration (this is especially true for *scientific* facts), and that every science has to become metaphysical in order to be able to explore the *problems* expressed by facts. In those earlier years we can observe that the entire and blind attention to facts seemed to be the self-sufficient solution to any scientific and methodological problem.

One of the most important Italian philosophers of our century made the following comments on this situation (Gentile, 1948, pp. 297–8):

> The philosophy of positivism is the product of the historical development of sciences: it has the same object as all other positivistic sciences, from mathematics to sociology (it is simply the sum of all of them) and the same method and experience: 'facts and experience are the very base of the positivistic philosophy'.
>
> This position seems nowadays to have no sense; it is not even worth criticizing. But we must remember the meaning it had in the period of empiric intoxication we faced in Italy for nearly twenty years between 1870 and 1890. In those days everyone believed facts existed as such, and that it was enough to have open eyes to perceive their presence, to see them as they really are, one by one and as a whole, and to build from them a science driven by the facts.
>
> That epistemology was so comfortable! It said: *quot capita, tot sententiae*; as many systems as there are heads. So let's cut all the heads off and leave – what? – facts and experience! This was the answer of thousands of positivistic scholars of every positivistic science.

Through the years however, not to mention Kuhn's evolutions and revolutions, after the time of its triumph the total blind attention given to facts began to find some opponents, to face stronger and stronger opposition. This was due in general to the discontent caused by every scientific revolution as it progressively wins, dominates and becomes dogmatic; and in particular to the excess of pragmatism, the massive *a posteriori* reasoning and the development of 'scientific' theories even where facts were ordinary, fuzzy, badly defined or even wrong.

European positivism was approaching a point of increasing relativism, even on the basis of a positivistic tradition which was 'still influencing every cultural activity' (Spirito, 1974, p. 15).

Due to this development we can say that the last phase of the evolution of positivism took place in the two decades 1900–1920, before the massive return to idealism (Croce and Gentile in Italy), subjectivism (Prichard, Josep, Joachim in England), ontology (Heidegger in Germany), while the US followed in large part, especially in technical studies, the totally different approach of John Dewey on pragmatism and naturalism.

That evolution was confused with the conflictual and overlapping mixture of the continuation of the story in a pure positivistic fashion, the internal criticism of positivism, and the bluntly anti-positivistic ways of reasoning, i.e. those leaning again towards the *a priori* within *theory-building* processes.

I

The continuation (or even the renewal) of the story is obvious in every evolutionary process, where old theories that are attacked are somehow defended, improved and strengthened. In some cases – as a reaction to a reaction – old theories are applied in a formally renewed way, or extended to new and different fields of analysis, which complicates the debate without solving the problems (so that only a revolution will be a solution).

In those years the continuation of the story meant emphasizing the role of facts, the near impossibility of defining any *a priori* framework, an exclusive focus on empirical research and, in the end, a purely empirical degeneration. Within this framework, thinkers, convinced they were not at all philosophers, and not having any methodology but facts, were actually followers of that peculiar epistemological stream that can be called 'integral empiricism' or 'pan-inductivism'.

The situation was quite interesting in the social sciences, and particularly in the field of business studies, where the contents of practice were large and it was very important to define the relationship between practice and theory. In some cases business disciplines were considered to be nothing else but techniques, thus approaching the content and concept of 'art' in the Renaissance sense.

Eugen Schmalenbach, one of the founders of the renewed *Betriebswirtschaftslehre* (see p. 181) belonged to this stream of ideas: in 1912 he wrote 'Die Privatwirtschaftslehre als Kunstlehre' (The Economics of the Firm as a Practical Art).

II

During the last phases of evolution, normally chaotic ones, a typical way of looking for solutions to scientific problems is the so-called 'internal critique', i.e. the continuation of the same story with every possible improvement or modification so as to use better methods without upsetting the old ones.

Between 1900 and 1920 (or 1905–25) continental Europe – France and Italy in particular – experimented with the intense and short-lived flourishing of the so-called 'critical positivism', i.e. a new form of attention to facts, but in a subjective and non-mechanistic way.

This was the great revolution (and way out), which developed after the turn of the century and offered itself to every thinker who, although he had been educated with it, was not content with traditional positivism. For the goals of this paper, that revolution can be summarized by mentioning some of the main models which were proposed in those years: the critical empiricism of Mach, where we have, in addition to facts, the *relations* between elements; the schematism of Boutroux, where scientific laws have no objective value, but only a reference one (they cannot grasp the reality); the conventionalism of Poincaré, where crude facts and their relational structure are transformed into scientific facts by scientific research, which *imposes* its own laws on facts.

This phase of critical positivism is of overwhelming importance because it appears to have been both a junction between positivism and idealism, *a posteriori* and *a priori*, and also a strongly influential factor on European social sciences in general, including law studies.

Gino Zappa, the founder of *Economia Aziendale* in Italy, belongs in this area (see p. 185) where induction and deduction tend to merge in the so-called mixed (deductive-inductive) methodology resembling Ricardo and John Stuart Mill.

III

Lastly, the reaction to positivism, to empiricism, to induction, could have been nothing but the return to idealism, to *a priori*, to *deduction*. This switch back could have been done in a number of ways, and in fact it was. The common ground of the different ways that have been adopted was the existence of *a priori* principles, or *a priori* judgement schemes, or in any case the action of a *subject* in building thought, theory and facts.

The various authors connected themselves with Hegel (the neo-Hegelism of Bradley in Britain, of Croce in Italy, of Royce in the United States) or Kant (the neo-criticism of Renouvier and others in France, of Cohen and Natorp, of Windelband and Rickert, of Husserl in Germany).

Not to mention further evolutions, idealism in its different forms strongly influenced continental Europe, and Germany in particular. In this country Heinrich Nicklisch, one of the other main builders of the scientific *Betriebswirtschaftslehre* was inspired, from the methodological point of view, by Kant and Hegel (see p. 179).

All these influences, although concentrated in two now nearly neglected decades, were also of great importance for the evolution of economic thought in general. This was mainly due to the fact that philosophy, and epistemology in particular, was in fact looking for renewed methodological foundations, and due to the new epistemological bases the two opposite streams of idealism and empiricism were both influencing economic policy as well as business studies.

The average scientific mentality of that time (or better the *Zeitgeist*) gradually led to the sunset of integral positivism and – year after year – to the fast emergence of 'critical positivism' and 'neo-Kantism'. This phase, only an intermediate stage in the path towards subjectivity in science, was also a critical one from the point of view of studies on business and on the firm, especially in Italy and Germany.

A further cause was that industrial revolutions had gradually modified the nature and structure of the economy, the society, the culture and even the landscape; they had also produced a basic influence on the nature and structure of applied studies.

If the answer to the needs of applied disciplines (techniques) were the colleges of technology in Great Britain – which were anyway separated from the academic world; accounting was there considered to be a matter for training and not for education until the early 1960s – in Germany and Italy those same needs gave life to special institutions, the Upper Schools of Commerce (*Handelshochschulen* in Germany, *Scuole Superiori di Commercio* in Italy), which were somehow connected to the university system.

Also for this reason, in two nations the emergence of a system of firms stimulated the development of a new discipline, specifically dedicated to them. This process – obviously a long, difficult and complicated one – is of basic importance for the following reasons:

1. The very centre of the analysis was now the firm, instead of capital or cycles or international trade.
2. The discipline emerged from older business analyses, and therefore needed differentiation but also to find new analytical methods and tools to investigate the new object (the firm) which was perceived as an individual entity.
3. These new disciplines were simultaneously confronted by the problem of finding their object, their methods, their place and space among the other older disciplines, opposing them or trying to find logical connections and affinity in contents.

3. Business studies in Italy and Germany before the methodological revolutions of the 1920s

3.1 The progress of business studies in Italy: Fabio Besta and the evolution of accounting

During the nineteenth century Italian accounting showed different turning points on its road to evolution, mainly in 1860–70 with Giuseppe Cerboni, the Kingdom's General Comptroller of Accounts. Anyway, the real scientific revolution was made by Fabio Besta, who gave accounting new theoretical bases building on philosophical premises as well as historical researches masterly conducted.

By joining the historical method of analysis (as far as bookkeeping and administration were concerned) with Spencerian epistemology (as far as the object, the method and the contents of accounting and auditing were concerned), Besta gave life to a general theory of Accounting which found its own places within the general system of sciences of his age. This method also allowed Besta to solve in renewed ways a number of technical problems.

He distinguished the pure science and its practical side – the art – by stating, along with John Stuart Mill, that they are connected to each other, the art representing the imperative mood of the science, which is the indicative. The art too is a system of ranked and interconnected pieces of knowledge, which are oriented to practice. The field of action of accounting is not mere bookkeeping, but the whole control of the wealth of the firm. Control is in fact achieved by both accounting and management, the former measuring and orienting the latter.

Due to his fame he was also appointed in 1880 to the chair of Accountancy at the Upper School of Commerce in Venice (established in 1872) one of only four upper schools of commerce in Italy (with Genoa, Naples and Bari). Until the late 1930s accounting (and business in general) was taught at academic level only at these upper schools of commerce which, although they remained separated from the universities for quite some time, played a major role in the development of business studies.

Based on the ideas of G.B. Vico, A.E. Schaeffle and Herbert Spencer, he proposed to include Accounting within the system of sciences studying the same phenomena (i.e. Law, Economics, Mathematics). Besta's theory dominated in Italy from the end of the nineteenth century to World War II. The phenomena Besta refers to can be summarized as follows (F. Besta, 1922, Vol. I, pp. 3–35).

> Even if the ultimate goal of working activity is the satisfaction of human needs and the improvement of the single person, men are motivated to work by the search for a 'subjective' good (Aristotle).
>
> For this reason common things become economic goods once they serve subjective goals.
>
> Among different goods the exchangeable ones are wealth, and gaining wealth is therefore the most important part of economic activity; furthermore, it is the very result of working activity (the so-called *production* of wealth of L. Cossa).
>
> The share of wealth that is saved becomes later, through the investment process, 'working wealth' (F. Ferrara, J.-B. Say), or 'intermediate utility' (A.E.F. Schaeffle) to produce new wealth once more.
>
> Due to the complexity of production, people cannot obtain by themselves the largest part of the goods: that is why they form in society in a

'gathering of reciprocal utilities' (G. Vico), which nowadays means production, exchange, consumption and so on.

The economic activities allowed and implied by the gathering of people in human society need, as a basic element to attain their economic objectives, the 'administration' or their 'wise governance'.

The 'administration' immediately recalls to mind the concept of *azienda*, i.e. the sum of facts, relations and affairs concerning a given set of capital goods belonging to a person, a family or to any other subject, from the single company to the state. *Azienda* is therefore not a person nor any other subject (especially in companies with limited liability, where capital is active *per se* and almost a goal in itself and the subject of rights and obligations is merely a juridical person). In Fabio Besta, 'administration' is similar to governance: this means personal actions tending to guide, to manage, to govern for the utility of the subject who holds the capital (no matter if it is an individual or a collective one). The administration is composed of three main elements:

the owners and their authority;
the managers (a group of persons, or an individual, who has the duty of administrating and governing every administrative activity in order to reach the goals of the *azienda* according to the directives of the owners);
organization, the attitudes and strengths of the many or few performers of the administrative work.

Because the goals of different firms are different, administration too is different from firm to firm due to the difference in interests, goals and means. However, since every firm makes use of goods and wealth through economic administration, all firms have some similarity of *functions* and *processes*.

This similarity can be made clear by separating the three typical features of administration in every kind of firm:

governance, which seeks to aim every action at pursuing the firm's goals in the most effective way;
management as such, i.e. the general actions aiming at regulating and giving direction to every kind of specific technical actions;
control, i.e. audit, accounting and control of economic effects/results in order to aim at the predefined goals and to improve governance and management by increased awareness.

Within this system, accounting is an applied or concrete science (in a

Spencerian framework): from the theoretical point of view it studies and defines the laws of economic control within every kind of *azienda*, also deducing the rules that have to be followed to get effective, complete and convincing control; from the practical point of view, it is the correct application of those rules.

3.2   Business studies in Germany: the foundation of the
Handelshochschulen (Upper Schools of Commerce) and the firm as
the object of empirical analysis

In spite of the early development of accounting and business studies in Europe from 1400 to 1800, according to R. Seyffert the nineteenth century was a period of deep decline in this subject in Germany. The attention of scholars was centred on public administration (the 'Kameralistik' discipline) and on public institutions (*Nationalökonomie*); no relevant progress had been made on the business front, not even the mere continuation of former contributions: the Italian Fabio Besta was the acknowledged leader of European business studies in those years.

A new era in the development of business studies in the form of *Betriebswirtschaftslehre* can be traced back to the period 1898–1910, during which the *Handelshochschule* was conceived and the most important of them were actually established (1989 Leipzig; 1900 St Gallen in Switzerland, Vienna and Aachen; 1901 Cologne and Frankfurt am Main; 1906 Berlin; 1907 Mannheim, 1910 Munich, 1915 Königsberg, 1919 Nuremberg).

The establishment of these schools was the response to the slow development of business studies, but especially to the large and powerful process of industrialization Germany had gone through in the second part of the nineteenth century. The *Handelshochschulen* were the answer to the increasing need for executives, i.e. professionally trained managers and technicians who knew law, history, foreign languages, geography, natural sciences and business matters as well.

From the scientific point of view the first decade of our century was characterized by the blossoming of quite a large number of books, mainly concerning the fields of accounting, banking and trade. They were both very specific in their contents and wholly devoted to practice, a sort of 'how-to' books in different management fields: the situation of business studies before 1910 has been considered 'a period of reflection, a starting point at the most' (Leitherer, 1974, col. 696).

In the same period business studies were still separate and distant from the academic world, which was then rather rigid in keeping practice separated from theory (apart from the medical sciences) and rather supercilious as well.

In spite of the fact that F.W. Taylor's *The Principles of Scientific Management* (1911) was translated into German in 1913, the influence of Anglo-Saxon studies in this period is nonexistent. Even later (we could say up to the end of World War II), the influence of American business and management studies on the *Betriebswirtschaftslehre* is practically irrelevant. Many reasons may have caused this, among them (1) the distance between the two cultural traditions; (2) the difference in stages of economic development. One more reason has been suggested, a specific one: the basically *technical* education of American scholars vs. the *economic* education of methodologists and scientists who originated the economics of the firm in Europe and especially in Germany (Leitherer, 1974).

Finally we must remember in this period the works of L. Gomberg, who proposed to use accounting and control to analyse autonomously the results and behaviour of firms, as well as the foundations of the two most important reviews in the field (which still exist under different names): the *Zeitschrift für Handelswissenschaftliche Forschung*, 1906 (Review of Research in Commercial Sciences) and the *Zeitschrift für Handelswissenschaft und Handelspraxis*, 1908 (Review of Commercial Sciences and Practice).

4. The relation to economic studies and their renewal 1900–1920 as an originating factor of the revolution

If it were possible to sum up in a few lines the long and complex evolution of business studies in Italy and Germany until World War I, one should say that in the first nation a major impulse towards the scientific approach to accounting had already been given, even if after Besta it was reduced to the mere reproduction of his principles in a simplified, mechanistic way. In Germany, on the other hand, perhaps as a reaction to the previous situation, at the *Handelshochschulen* business research was boiling away, waiting for a revolutionary result at any moment. Under the pressures of the market and the new and widespread managerial needs, some researchers were trying to find a substantial solution to transform the nature of accounting, banking, business and commercial studies from a practical to a scientific one.

Among the different factors which stimulated such research, apart from personal interest and self-realization, one can mention the widespread debate on philosophical and epistemological problems (in section 2 above), as well as the continuing development of economic studies.

Since the eighteenth century political economy had studied such problems as the production and distribution of wealth, the nature of exchange and prices, the role of gold, money and credit. For this reason, scholars in the business field perceived again – and more intensely than before – both the interest in deepening general economic studies and the possibility that they could contribute to the analysis of economic problems. These could be interpreted and described from *the point of view of the firm*, which had become one of the main actors in markets, prices, income and wealth; at the same time, some of the interpretative lines or frameworks provided by renowned economists could help the construction of business disciplines of a scientific nature.

At the eve of World War I – when Schmalenbach, Nicklisch and Zappa (nobody knows whether independently or not) were placing the first stones of their research constructions – the evolution of political economy was also highly stimulating to scientific reflection.

In continental Europe a scholar wishing to integrate general economy and the economy of the firm would have found himself exposed – apart from the classics as Smith, Galiani, Genovesi, Say, Bastiat, Stuart Mill and Bagehot – to the influence of two different kinds of economic ideas and contributions: the dominant tradition, and the contributions of contemporary scholars.

As far as the first is concerned, we must make a distinction between the modern Anglo-Saxon view ('the greatest figures of this period, Jevons, Marshall, Wicksteed, Walras, Wicksell and Clark . . .'; Blaug, 1985, p. 295) and the actual situation at the time, when in many cases some works exercised a great influence, whether they were milestones or not. While doubts can be raised on the influence of marginalism, both scholars of different nations and authors of standard treatises have to be remembered: Cairnes, Edgeworth and Fetter for works in the English language; Ferrara in Italy; Cournot, Leroy-Beaulieu and Walras in France; Schaeffle, Menger and Schmoller (and Sax and Schomberg and many others) in Germany.

The contributions of contemporary scholars were of major interest too. For the purpose of this chapter these can be divided into the following categories:

1. the contributions of the Italian school, a leading one at that time (Pantaleoni, 1889; Pareto, 1896–7; Ricci, 1910; Barone, 1913; Gobbi, 1919);
2. the milestone contributions of Böhm-Bawerk (1909–12), J. B. Clark (1902), I. Fisher (1906);
3. the monetary studies of Helfferich (1903–10), Fanno (1908), Fisher (1911), Keynes (1913) and Cannan (1918).

In addition, so many contributions were produced in those very years regarding the different profiles of enterprises as a whole.

The seminal work of Paton, *Principles of Accounting* (still a reference in this field) was published in 1921, and almost concluded the whole debate that took place between 1901 and 1920 (from Walsh to Widman) on the notions of income and capital. In the same period many books were published on the economics and management of the firm on the basis of different but comprehensive approaches; these included F.W. Taylor (1911), H.J. Davenport (1913), E.D. Jones (1918), A. Marshall (1919) and T. Veblen (1923), and gave business scholars the model of what they too could prepare on different bases.

On the whole, most of the ingredients for a unitary theory of the firm were at their disposal, and a revolution was truly expected in the field. (The same was to happen some twenty years later, just before the publication of Keynes's *General Theory*).

5. The emergence and nature of the Betriebswirtschaftslehre: H. Nicklisch, E. Schmalenbach and other pioneers

5.1 The philosophical Betriebswirtschaftslehre of H. Nicklisch

Heinrich Nicklisch, who could be called the founder of *Betriebswirts-chaftslehre* as a science, was the most important representative of the normative stream of thought.

Soundly grounded in philosophical studies, he developed his thought – as well as the implementation of his own findings and theories – in different phases of his scientific life which paralleled the epistemological evolution of his time.

The different phases are as follows:

until 1912: the differentiation of *Betriebswirtschaftslehre* from *Nationalökonomie*;

until 1922: the definition of the contents of *Betriebswirtschaftslehre* (the object of scientific research);

until 1927 and thereafter: the development of the 'system' idea.

Until 1912 Both *Nationalökonomie* and *Betriebswirtschaftslehre* study the same economic units: however, the former does it from a *collective* point of view, the latter from the *individual* point of view of the single unit, i.e. from the point of view of the actors inside every unit.

The object of knowledge in the real world is common to both sciences, but the two epistemologies are very different. The goal of *Nationalökonomie* is to investigate the social and economic relationships among all economic units (families, enterprises, households) as a *totality*. *Betriebswirtschaftslehre*, on the other hand, first of all considers an actual object, the firm, whose nature can be easily recognized and understood in practice and from the theoretical point of view as well; secondly, it studies the firm's economic life (later on, speaking of accounting systems, Nicklisch referred to its economic 'Force' – *die Kraft*).

Until 1922 Betriebswirtschaftslehre must study every kind or form of individual economic unit, be it an enterprise (*Unternehmen*) or a household (*Haushalt*): according to Nicklisch, both the production and the consumption of wealth have to be studied through the analysis of the units where these processes typically take place.

However, throughout his life Nicklisch devoted himself only to the study of the economic activity of the enterprise. His position can be summarized as follows:

> The firm is an organic body, whose actions are in large part oriented to its individual interest within a collective economy.
> It needs a combination of capital and labour and its external appearance is a defined juridical and economic form.
> Profit as a goal is only a formal profile of the goal-minded efforts of the firm: its existence is due to its role in the direct or indirect satisfaction of people's needs.

For these reasons (the last one in particular), one of the most important problems to be solved is the production and circulation of wealth. The values by which it is represented have to be adequately measured by proper accounting systems.

Until 1927 and thereafter Starting from accounting, it is now possible to subdivide the 'system of the firm', i.e. the set of connected interactive elements which give it life: labour, fixed and working capital, and equity.

In order to focus on the values of capital and income, it is necessary to define measurement criteria that are suitable both for static values (relative to a moment in time, such as assets and liabilities) and dynamic ones (formed in time intervals of different length – administrative periods – such as costs and revenues; *die Kraft*).

The goal of these accounting systems is in the end to measure the performance of the firm over its entire life (*Betriebsleitstung*), as well as in each period for which measurement is performed.

The complex philosophical nature of Nicklisch's thought can be described as the result of a synthesis he makes between the two dominant cultural streams in Germany during the nineteenth century, idealism and naturalism, whereby the former was underlined.

He derives from Hegel the idea that the spirit (*Geist*) is given to men, and that activities implying in some way the spirit can be studied only by spirit (the famous Hegelian phase, 'everything rational is real, and everything real is rational'); moreover, the Reason is not a static Being, but action and development.

Kant's influence on Nicklisch is at least as significant as Hegel's. Nicklisch adapts to *Betriebswirtschaftslehre* (and economic research in general) the general ideas of freedom, duty, community: the freedom of action of each economic unit in the general system is *natural*; the duty of every unit is to contribute to the general economic result, just like the duty of every man towards the life of the community.

Naturalism too ('everything is nature, is commanded by physical laws, and nothing more' (Nicklisch, 1932, p. 3)) is present in Nicklisch's mental framework. This can be appreciated just by recalling one of his sentences: 'Outside Conscience there is the Matter. Nature is Matter, and as such it is constituted of Force' (ibid.): through force it survives both as a whole and in its every part.

Later on, Nicklisch included naturalism in his own (idealistic) reinterpretation, stating that there is a 'natural order of the world': empirical evidence and truth do not match each other; truth is only what is in harmony with the 'natural order'.

Finally, romanticism too influenced Nicklisch by transmitting to him the concepts of organism and universalism. According to the first, economic units must be studied as single individual entities; according to the second – both for the economy and for the state – the vital connections between the parts promote and improve the whole. This is because he suggests that business scholars should 'live practical experience too and to study not only single units, but mainly the connections among them'.

5.2   The empirical Betriebswirtschaftslehre of E. Schmalenbach

The work of Eugen Schmalenbach belongs to the empirical-realistic stream of thought. However, his role has been so overwhelmingly important that it can be considered to be one of the bases of business studies in Germany, whether they tend towards empiricism or not.

The contrast between his ideas and Nicklisch's has been deeply discussed for decades in Germany and elsewhere, thus reinforcing the system of thought and giving origin to a method (in many cases of the inductive-deductive type) which still characterizes business studies in Western Europe and even in Japan.

Schmalenbach looked at the *Privatwirtschaftslehre* (as opposed to Nicklisch's *Betriebswirtschaftslehre*) as an applied science, obedient to praxis, and limited only to private enterprises. He defined it as 'scientia militans', a serving science, and said 'the praxis is a sort of client for our science, which has therefore the task of giving it the best possible service' (Schmalenbach, 1911–12, pp. 309–10).

So, according to Schmalenbach, the foundation of scientific knowledge is *experience*. What is not concrete, what is not empirically perceptible and cannot be drawn from experience lies outside of knowledge and therefore outside of any positive science.

In this way Schmalenbach denies the possibility of any influence of philosophy on business economics: the latter is not the object of philosophical analysis, i.e. its methods of gaining knowledge cannot be analysed from the theoretical point of view, or on the basis of any *a priori* judgement. As Schmalenbach pointed out, 'what is necessary for praxis is an economic science of a non-abstract and a-philosophical kind', and 'we must look not into the "why" but into the "how" of things' (Schmalenbach, 1911–12, p. 306).

The difference between theoretical and empirical sciences is that the former have ideal elements as an object (the theory), the latter real elements (the empirical world or *realer Tatbestände*). This difference explains the differentiation of *Nationalökonomie* and *Privatwirtschaftslehre*. These two sciences are characterized by two different spirits (*Geist*): the first is the philosophical science, with all its features; the second has the objective and the task of defining optimal behaviours, the best ways to achieve goals, the best rules to be followed.

To the many opponents who doubted the scientific character of Schmalenbach's *Privatwirtschaftslehre* he answered that such problems of definition were not interesting. In his opinion the most important thing was the practical utility of its results: the lack of such utility would annihilate any achievement. And he added in a historicist way that no rule holds general validity: we can only find single solutions for the problems which emerge at different times.

As far as Schmalenbach's personal convictions are concerned, in his opinion the basic motivation of human economic action is *the search for individual advantages* in a world dominated by the confrontation of juxtaposed interests. The market is the symbol of this contrast and the price is the judge of the quality of the economic performance of human activity: without capitalism there would be no motivation for individual economic action and, consequently, no *Privatwirtschaftslehre* at all.

Economic goods gain a price because they include an economic value, stemming both from their scarcity and from their capability to satisfy needs. For these reasons the aim of economic activities is the increased availability of relatively scarce goods.

After these reflections Schmalenbach (formerly a manager and an entrepreneur) considered exchanges as the starting point of his theories (Löffel-holz, 1935, pp. 238–40), to be followed by production and later consumption (partly on the same path as Nicklisch). Contrary to Nicklisch, he believed that those units where consumption prevails (households) should not be an object of analysis. Within enterprises it is extremely important that values be properly (objectively) measured, which is the final stage of Schmalenbach's reflection: the measurement of the creation and destruction of values inside a firm, i.e. the accounting process.

In this light, accounting takes on a totally new role, also from the methodological standpoint, because knowledge is based on the capacity to observe. Accounting is now more the *method* than the instrument of the analysis: it is a closed system, which allows both a self-evaluation of the firm and the analysis of the main factors in its economic dynamics. The scope of accounting is therefore the observation and control of the economic dynamics of the single units which compose the economic system.

Along with these new positions, a revolution is produced in accounting. As early as 1908 Schmalenbach pointed out that the first goal of accounting is the measurement not of capital but of force, and he clarified that force means income as the parameter of long-term profitability. This revolution was finally completed by parallel – and technically excellent – innovations in both double-entry and cost accounting (Schmalenbach, 1926).

5.3.   *Between pioneering and Methodenstreit: further contributions*

Nicklisch and Schmalenbach were by no means the only remarkable scholars active in Germany in the new climate created by the upper schools of commerce. The developments of *Betriebswirtschaftslehre* had been marked – since its early stages – by some multi-level 'dispute on the method', which later became a stable feature of the discipline that has continued until the present.

These disputes, which were typical of a new discipline, allow us to trace (though in a partial way) a number of scholars and contributions. On the one hand they were continuously recreated because of the solution and the setting aside of such scientific problems as induction, deduction, the boundaries of the scientific field, and the notion of firm. On the other hand they went on for years – to mention just a few sociological elements within the evolution of scientific thought – due to the tradition of autonomy of German universities (and the resulting contrasts between them) and the attention paid in that country to clear-cut and scholarly debated scientific concepts.

According to Johann Friedrich Schär (1910), the economics of the firm is only a part of economic science, an area of research whose existence had to be proven by its connection to economics. He affirms the unitary character of economic science by using a common biological metaphor of those days: the firm as the cell of a human body can be the object of research only in a limited way because it belongs to a greater entity, the body, representing the general economy. Firms develop in an orderly way, like cells which interact in the body, through commerce. Commerce is then the basis and the reason of economic action. It should be interpreted not as a profit-seeking activity, but *as the source of the life of economic units*. Profit-seeking *per se* would be unethical, and would not justify the integration of the firm in the general economy.

In speaking of the 'science of the firm', Rudolf Dietrich (1914) states the autonomy of this field of study. The very object of its research is the internal life of the profit-seeking firm, whereas the other type of economic unit, the household, should also be studied by economic sciences. Dietrich points out that technical matters should not interfere with theoretical questions and clearly affirms that the firm is the natural focus of the new discipline.

The 'internal life of the firm' is not an end in itself from the empirical point of view, nor a satisfying concept from the scientific one: economic relations with other units represent a pillar of the discipline.

Friedrich Leitner (1926), a native Austrian, develops a system in which all economic (private and public) units, those which seek profit and those which do not, are the object of analysis. However, he studies only the private, profit-seeking enterprise, and divides his discipline into four parts, related respectively to: (1) the exchange of goods; (2) banking and the exchange of means of payment; (3) communications (railway transport, shipping, distribution of information); and (4) sales. All these subjects belong to special areas, and are subordinated to the general economics of the firm. In this way Leitner criticizes the streams of thought which – as Schmalenbach did – do not make enough effort to define their object of analysis properly and therefore lack scientific soundness.

A strong focus on theory is the main character of Fritz Schmidt (1921). He states from the beginning of his work the priority of theory over practice in studies related to firms: he obviously admits the existence and utilization of induction, but subordinates it to deduction, interpreted as the guideline of any scientific development. As far as research on the firm is concerned, he suggests a two-sided approach: the study of its internal processes and functional relations, and of its connections with the general economic system.

Even more oriented to theory is Wilhelm Rieger (1927), whose approach refers to the private, profit-seeking enterprise as the only object of research. According to Rieger, the central problem of the economics of the firm is *value*, which is expressed and measured by money. Therefore only those units which have the objective of maximizing their own cash flow over the long run deserve scientific attention.

6. The formative phase of Economia Aziendale and the work of G. Zappa 1920–29

Gino Zappa studied in Milan under Professor Bellini, who later introduced him to Fabio Besta, wishing that his best disciple be permitted to study at the side of the most renowned professor of accounting in Italy.

Zappa wrote his first important work during his assistant professorship to Besta (*Le valutazioni*, 1910). Although it resulted in a good contribution to evaluation criteria for financial statements, it was still totally dependent on Besta's system of thought.

Disappointed by the same positivism which he had believed in, in 1911 Zappa started a troubled decade of methodological reflections, also stimulated by the intense philosophical debate which was taking place at that time.

His thought about the problems of accounting – i.e. capital and income, the value of money, production and distribution of wealth – was partly induced by the debate between 1900 and 1910, and by Fisher's work (1906), but he was also struck and challenged by the economic consequences of the war (hyperinflation, for example) as well as by German advances in the field.

As the result of this controversial speculative period he adopted in general the method of 'critical positivism', i.e. the simultaneously deductive-inductive method. No matter from which side one begins, general hypotheses are used to select special, scientific facts (not causal nor common, but similar to other ones in space and time and belonging to series), the analysis of which allows the researcher to correct, modify and specify the hypotheses themselves.

The critical positivism of Gino Zappa goes back to Bacon and Descartes and brings together empiricism and rationalism up to Kant and beyond. It recalls the last contributions of John Stuart Mill (*On the Definition of Economic Policy*) on the mixed *a priori* method of 'induction-reasoning' as well as Ricardo, and concludes with the active role of the scholar and his hypotheses according to Spencer, Mach, Poincaré, Le Roy and others.

By applying his renewed methodology to the study of accounting, Zappa realized (and stated) that *income* is the most important phenomenon in the firm's economy, and that whatever notion of capital one has it must in some way be related back to income.

In addition, the firm's income cannot be measured without a deep knowledge (a 'scientific' one) of its economy in its dynamics, structure and composition: a renewed concept of accounting must be based on an overall science concerning the analysis of the firm as a whole (*Economia Aziendale*).

A summary of the steps which brought Zappa from the critical positivism to the *Economia Aziendale* can be presented as follows (Zappa, 1920, 1929 and 1937).

a. Sciences have to be established on the basis of the selection and observation of a few practical facts, chosen from a quantity on the basis of frequency and similarity. Thus one can go from common facts to homogeneous groups and series, which are set up in a hierarchical order. Through abstraction and generalization we can go from apparently heterogeneous facts to *systems* of facts, which are useful in that truth is a quality of the system rather than of its individual parts.

b. In applied sciences we need both general schemes and the study of specifics. As the firm is a complex organic unit, accounting systems must represent the whole structure of connected, interactive economic phenomena as well as the relations between the whole and its parts (those relations being a character of reality). In short, systems must be studied in a systemic way.

c. Both the goal and the most important fact of the firm is income. For this reason accounting systems have to represent income itself, determining it in accordance with every other phenomenon of the firm in a systemic way.

    The best way to define income is to detect the monetary behaviour of administrative facts: exchanges (purchases and sales) are the best dynamic representation of the formation of income; they are similar for every firm.

d. However, not every administrative fact is an accounting one; at the same time every non-monetary fact gets lost in accounting: for this reason accounting measurements have to be integrated with statistical measurements.

e. Moreover, as method and content cannot be separated, we need to know the dynamic economy of the firm, and the contents of *Economia Aziendale*, in order to build a correct system of accounting and statistical information.

f. The task of accounting is (1) to separate the elements of the organic and unitary life of the firm; (2) to define values; and (3) to rebuild the system of the firm according to the remaining elements (wealth, organization).

g. Within this system, accounting is close to both management and organization. These three disciplines, once unified by science, give life to *Economia Aziendale*. This science unifies not only those branches, but also (and more importantly) the apparently heterogeneous phenomena of the firm: accounting, organization and management in this way become clear to each other and the same happens for the economy of firms under a unitary, synthetic approach.

Sixty years later, one could point out that Zappa's fundamental contributions were the reference to the *economic nature of the firm* (similarly Coase, 1937), which he defined as 'continuing economic coordination' and his proposal of a unitary perspective of studies on the firm.

Along the way, Zappa differentiated himself from both economists and accountants. The former would have studied the 'theory of the firm' at the end, but in continued neoclassical ways; the latter would have studied mainly the firm's functions (accounting, finance, marketing), thus atomizing its economic nature.

In Zappa the firm is a complex economic phenomenon, epitomized by income, a synthesis of external facts and internal acts (the management) which is at the same time a criterion of knowledge and economic thought. In turn, income is also a complex phenomenon, because it derives from never-ending connections of economic processes in space and time.

The study of income proceeded necessarily in two opposite directions, the first internal, the second external: (1) by the renewal of accounting studies, to control the phenomenon of income also through the information system (which had to be reformed; see p. 186); (2) by the proposal for sectorial and industrial studies, to look into how markets, exchange structures and competition could influence the economy of the firm over time (and therefore the income that represents it).

Along the years, while studies in the above-mentioned fields proceeded, further fields were explored. The investigations starting from income, firms and the market led to the study of consumption and demand, investment, financing, loans and savings, interest rates and bank deposits. These studies gradually grew – though always remaining tentatively unitary – to an inquiry into the economic system as a whole, carried out through its unitary components (families, enterprises, public administration) and their mutual relations.

Income, as a unitary expression of knowledge and action (information and management), was also extensively interpreted as the result of processes of production and consumption. Such processes were unitarily tied up in the firms; although special in production firms, they were similar in *all* firms, be they families or public authorities. With such an object of analysis – processes of production and consumption of families, enterprises, and public authorities – the *Economia Aziendale* aimed at the study of the economy of all kinds of firms over time.

In this last evolution, proposed by Zappa in his unfinished *Le Produzioni* (1955–7), the economics of the firm is seen as a global economic science, as an integration – or almost a substitution – of economics. If this attempt has not yet been successful – and some may legitimately doubt its logical possibility – it must be interpreted in the spirit of the time when it originated. In particular:

1. within the crisis of economics in the *entre-deux-guerres* period (Robinson, 1972), a crisis that was solved in continental culture by the *General Theory* only *after* World War II; and by a solution which still placed emphasis on macroeconomics and again left in shadow the economy of the single units of the system;
2. the influence of German theories, among which is Nicklisch's proposal for an organic view of the economy (where firms are the organs of the global body, i.e. the whole economy of a country; in this last concept economic policy would become only one of the forms of the economics of the *Economia Aziendale*: a monistic one, i.e. optimizing and abstract).

After *Il Reddito* Zappa did not publish any other main works except *Le Produzioni* (1955–7), a large and unconcluded treatise of *Economia Aziendale*. In the twenty years 1935–55 he edited a number of contributions dedicated to the application and extension of his principles to different business fields. Financial statements, cost accounting and advanced accounting were carefully studied from a technical point of view. From a more general point of view a series of books concerning commodity markets and specific industries were published by his assistants: both subjects were analysed as a result of choices and interactions of systems of firms.

7. Conclusions

As time passes the role of people, facts and evolution in the making of history tends to become obscured, and our present image of the world is seen in the light of some major turning points, leaders and trends.

The same happens with the history of economics in general, and of economic thought in particular, which in some cases could be defined as ancient history in Voltaire's sense: only accepted tales.

In such a way, if the industrial revolution, protectionism (or *laissez-faire*) and the Great Depression become the few – or even the only –

highlights of the last three centuries, Smith, Marx and Keynes seem to be the only thinkers known or mentioned by non-specialists.

A first evidence of this is the lesser development of studies on the firm until recent years. A further one, both the lower consideration they enjoy and the total separation from economics, apart from some recent approaches (Simon, 1982; Williamson, 1975, 1986).

However, in some European nations studies of the firm were not limited to the technical-practical side. As argued earlier, in Germany and Italy studies tried to base themselves on deep methodological and critical premisses, to arrive at *general* interpretations of the economy of the enterprise.

This revolution, which started within the methodological debate in continental Europe in the two decades from 1900 to 1920, was substantially accomplished in 1940, relatively independently of the sociopolitical changes of that period. It then grew into a second stage after World War II, by completing its methodological premisses on the one hand and practical applications on the other. From the end of the 1960s it has been greatly influenced by the functional approach in the United States of America, and this tendency seems to continue even today, despite 'Fortress Europe'.

References
Barone, E. (1913), *Principi di economia politica*, Roma: Athenaeum.

Besta, F. (1922), *La Ragioneria*, 3 vols., Milano: F. Vallardi.

Blaug, M. (1985), *Economic Theory in Retrospect*, Cambridge: Cambridge University Press.

Böhm-Bawerk, E. v. (1909–1912), *Positive Theorie des Kapitals*, Innsbruck: Verlag der Wagner'schen Universitaets-Buchhandlung.

Cannan, E. (1918), *Money in connection with rising and falling prices*, London: P. S. King & Son.

Canziani, A. (1987), 'Sulle premesse metodologiche della rivoluzione zappiana', in *Scritti in memoria di Lino Azzini*, Milano: Giuffré.

Clark, J. B. (1902), *The distribution of wealth. A theory of wages, interest and profits*, New York: Macmillan & Co.

Coase, R. H. (1937), 'The Nature of the Firm', *Economica*, November, pp. 386–405.

Davenport, H. J. (1913), *The economies of enterprise*, New York: Longmans, Green & Co.

Dietrich, R. (1914), *Betriebs-wissenschaft*, Berlin: Piper.

Fanno, M. (1908), *La moneta, le correnti monetarie, ed il riordinamento della circolazione nei paesi a finanze dissestate*, Roma, Torino, Milano: F.11i Bocca.

Ferraris Franceschi, R. (1978), *L'indagine metodologica in economia aziendale*, Milano: Giuffré.

Fisher, I. (1906), *The nature of capital and income*, New York: The Macmillan Co.

Fisher, I. (1911), *The purchasing power of money*, New York: The Macmillan Co.

Gentile, G. (1948), *Storia della filosofia italiana*, Florence: Sansoni.

Giannessi, E. (1964), *Corso di Economia Aziendale*, Vol. V, '*I precursori*', Pisa: Cursi.

Gobbi, U. (1919), *Trattato di economia*, Milano: Società Editrice Libraria.

Helfferich, K. (1903–10), *Geld und Banken*, 2 vols, Lipsia: Hirschfeld.

Hutchison, T. W. (1978), *On Revolution and Progress in Economic Knowledge*, Cambridge and Melbourne: Cambridge University Press.

Jevons, S. W. (1909), *Elementary lessons in Logic*, London: Macmillan & Co.

Jones, E. D. (1918), *The administration of industrial enterprises*, New York: Longmans Green & Co.

Keynes, J. M. (1913), *Indian currency and finances*, London: Macmillan & Co.

Kruk, M., Potthoff, E. and Sieben, G. (1984), *Eugen Schmalenbach, Der Mann – Sein Werk – Die Wirkung*, Stuttgart: Schäfer.

Leitherer, E. (1974), 'Dogmengeschichte der Betriebswirtschaftslehre', in *Handwörterbuch der Betriebswirtschaft*, Stuttgart: Poeschel.

Leitner, F. (1926), *Wirtschaftslehre der Unternehmung*, Berlin, Drucker & Humblot, 5th printing.

Löffelholz, J. (1935), *Geschichte der Betriebswirtschaft und der Betriebswirtschaftslehre*, Stuttgart: Poeschel.

Marshall, A. (1919), *Industry and trade*, London: Macmillan.

Mori, A. (1987), 'Zum Stand der Betriebswirtschaftslehre in Japan', *Zeitschrift für Betriebswirtschaft*, pp. 921–39.

Nicklisch, H. (1922), *Der wege auf Wärts! Organisation*, Stuttgart: Poeschel.

Nicklisch, H. (1932), *Die Betriebswirtschaft*, Stuttgart: Poeschel.

Pantaleoni, M. (1889), *Principii di economia pura*, Firenze: Barbera.

Pareto, V. (1896–7), *Cours d'économie politique*, Lausanne: Rouge.

Paton, W. A. and Stevenson, R. A. (1921), *Principles of Accounting*, New York: The Macmillan Co.

Ricci, U. (1910), *Il capitale. Saggio di economia teoretica*, Torino, F. lli Bocca.

Rieger, W. (1928), *Einfürung in die Privatwirtschaftslehre*, Nürberg: Krische & Co.

Robinson, J. (1972), 'The Second Crisis in Economic Theory', *American Economic Review Papers and Proceedings*, pp. 1–10.

Schaer, J. F. (1910), *Allgemeine Handelsbetriebslehre*, Leipzig: G. A. Gloeckner.

Schmalenbach, E. (1911–12), 'Die Privatwirtschaftslehre als Kunstlehre', *Zeitschrift für Handelswissenschaftliche Forschung*, pp. 304–16.

Schmalenbach, E. (1926), *Dynamische Bilanz*, Leipzig: G. A. Gloeckner.

Schmidt, F. (1921), *Die organische Bilanz im Rahmen der Wirtschaft*, Berlin: Drucker & Humblot.

Schönpflug, F. (1954), *Betriebswirtschaftslehre, Methoden und Hauptströmungen*, Stuttgart: Poeschel.

Seyffert, R. (1957), *Über Begriff, Aufgaben und Entwicklung der Betriebswirtschaftslehre*, Stuttgart: Poeschel.

Simon, H. A. (1982), *Models of bounded rationality*, 2 vols, Cambridge, MA: The MIT Press.

Spirito, U. (1974), *Dall'attualismo al problematicismo*, Florence: Sansoni.

Stuart Mill, J. (1948), *Essays on some unsettled questions of political economy*, London: London School of Economics and Political Science.

Stuart Mill, J. (1849), *Principles of Political Economy*, London: Parker.

Taylor, F. W. (1911), *The Principles of Scientific Management*, New York: Macmillan.

Veblen, T. (1923), *Absentee ownership and business enterprise in recent times*, London: George Allen & Unwin.

Williamson, O. E. (1975), *Markets and Hierarchies: analysis and anti-trust implications*, New York: The Free Press.

Williamson, O. E. (1986), *Economic Organisation: firms, markets and policy control*, Brighton: Wheatsheaf Books.

Zappa, G. (1910), *Le valutazioni di bilancio con particolare riguardo alle società per azioni*, Milano: Società Editrice Libraria.

Zappa, G. (1920–9, revised edition 1937), *Il reddito di impresa*, Milano: Giuffré.

Zappa, G. (1955–7), *Le produzioni nell'economia delle imprese*, 3 vols, Milano: Giuffré.

11 Reinterpreting Ricardian scarcity

R. S. Hewett

Public interest in natural resources has waxed and waned over the last two centuries. Economic research has generally followed the public interest. Debate over the British Corn Laws prompted the 1815 series of pamphlets on land rent by T.R. Malthus, Edward West, Robert Torrens and David Ricardo. In the United States Lewis Gray's analysis of exhaustible resources came at the height of the first conservation movement early in the twentieth century. The environmental movement and the OPEC oil crisis inspired a deluge of articles in the 1960s and early 1970s on the economics of exhaustible resources. Currently, as the European Green movement takes root in the United States, a revival of interest in natural resource economics is already under way.

The issue of scarcity lies at the heart of public discussions on natural resources. For Ricardo and others in the Corn Laws debate it is scarcity of productive agricultural land. For Gray and Hotelling it is mineral scarcity. In the 1990s it is scarcity of potable water, of space for waste disposal as well as lingering doubts about the adequacy of energy reserves.

There has been much debate among economists regarding the measurement and interpretation of natural resource scarcity. Should natural resources be accorded a separate niche in economic theory, implying that natural resource scarcity is fundamentally distinct from other forms of scarcity? It has been argued that classical economics provides such a niche while neoclassical theory does not. Though this view may put the case too strongly, it is appropriate to note that the classical, chiefly Ricardian, interpretation of resource scarcity is substantively different from the neoclassical interpretation. Unfortunately, the comparison between the two approaches has been made more difficult by concessions which 'defenders' of the Ricardian faith have made to criticism over time. As a result of these concessions the classical position often referred to in modern literature is actually a pastiche of classical, neoclassical and institutional ideas. This paper will retrace the evolution of economic thought on natural resource scarcity, reconstructing a credible classical interpretation to enable a proper comparison between the classical and neoclassical approaches.

Ricardian scarcity

The classical approach to natural resource scarcity derives mainly from the rent theories of Ricardo and Malthus. Rent, for Ricardo, is 'that portion of the produce of the earth, which is paid to the landlord for the use of the original and indestructible powers of the soil' (Ricardo, 1973, Vol. I, p. 67). At other times the definition applies to 'the original and inherent powers' or simply 'the indestructible powers' of the soil (ibid., p. 69). In modern terms, 'rent' appears restricted to payments for non-depletable natural resources. Ricardo claims Adam Smith erred in applying 'rent' to coal mines and stone quarries: compensation in these cases was paid for value 'removed' (ibid., p. 68). Natural resources which are depleted require compensation of some sort, but this payment should not be confused with rent.

Yet Ricardo, also in his *Principles*, attempts to explain the 'rent' of mines as well. 'Indestructibility' in this explanation is no longer considered an essential quality of resources yielding rent. The term rent remains restricted to natural resources, though this circumstance assumes less importance in Ricardo's explanation. Rather, it is differential 'fertility' which is held as the *sine qua non* of rent: 'If there were abundance of equally fertile mines . . . they could yield no rent' (ibid., p. 85). Later, Ricardo adds that location differences may also give rise to rent (ibid., p. 329).

In Ricardo's example, a number of mines of different fertility are in operation. Working each mine with the same quantity of labour, the outputs vary due to differences in fertility. The production of the least fertile mine 'must at least have an exchangeable value' to pay labour costs and ordinary profits (ibid., pp. 85–7). Any surplus created in excess of this amount by more fertile mines is paid to the landlords as rent.

As society progresses, coal demand increases. Less fertile mines are opened. Assuming the new mines are operated with the same 'dose' of capital and labour as the older, more fertile mines, the cost of producing the additional coal would rise, increasing coal prices. These higher coal prices in turn entailed higher rents for the more fertile mines.

Ricardo's treatment of the relation between rent and the extensive margin (the extent to which lower-quality resources are employed) was more complete than his explanation of rent and the intensive margin (the intensity with which doses of capital and labour are employed). In his 1815 essay he noted that output might be increased either by applying another dose of capital and labour to the currently cultivated parcel of land or to another uncultivated plot (ibid., Vol. V, p. 14). In either case the result was the same: the additional dose resulted in a smaller increase in output than occurred from application of the previous dose. If adding

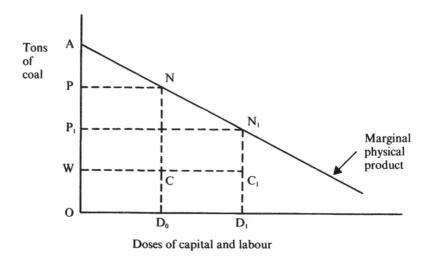

Figure 11.1   Ricardian rent model

the additional dose to the current parcel resulted in a greater increase in output than applying the same dose to a less fertile parcel, the current land would be farmed more intensively. Since the additional dose elicited a smaller increase in output than the previous dose, production costs per unit of output were higher, implying that prices must rise. Thus, an outward shift in the intensive margin of cultivation (or extraction) would create an increase in rent just as an outward shift in the extensive margin.

Ricardo's explanation of rent can be expressed graphically as in Figure 11.1 (Blaug, 1979, p. 91). For simplicity, assume that the coal is of uniform quality and is delivered to one point of sale. Let technology remain constant. Assume as well that the proportion of capital to labour in the doses needed to extract and deliver additional tons of coal from a given stock of reserves is also constant. The quantity of coal produced and delivered is equal to the area under the marginal product curve. If labour's wage is fixed at the subsistence level and the relative value of coal remains constant, labour's share of each additional unit of coal delivered is OW.

If the economy's demand for coal is $OAND_0$, D_0 units of capital and labour are used. Labour's share equals $OWCD_0$. Since the rate of profit is equalized through competition, each coal producer must receive the same increment of profit on his capital advanced during the production period. For all producers, capital is assumed to consist only of wage advances and tools and equipment that will not outlive the production period.[1]

Any differences in fertility or location which make some mine sites more productive than others will generate rent for the landlords. Thus the share of output falling to coal producers is WPNC. The landlord's residual is represented by the triangle APN.

As demand for coal grows, doses of capital and labour are added until D_0 has increased to D_1. Labour, held at a subsistence level, maintains the same coal wage. As a share of marginal output, however, this amount has increased. Similarly, capital's share of the marginal output has decreased. So in general terms, as demand increases, labour's share of output grows as capital's share declines. The matter of rent's share is muddled: it may grow, shrink or stay the same depending on the form of the production function (Blaug, 1979, p. 108).

In light of the subsequent use of the rent concept beyond the field of natural resources, two points should be emphasized. First, Ricardo's equivocation as to the types of return which could be considered rent laid the basis for the later application of 'rent' to a wide variety of returns. Secondly, Ricardo intended his explanation of rent to 'get rid' of the natural resource contribution to value (Ricardo, 1973, Vol. VIII, p. 194). The return on the last dose of capital and labour determined the rate of profit. The return from this marginal dose yielded no rent, permitting Ricardo to focus solely upon the returns to capital and labour. Given that the problem of rent was not Ricardo's main concern, his less than complete analysis of the notion is understandable.

The differences between Malthus and Ricardo are fewer than the similarities. Malthus viewed the earth as composed of 'a great number of machines, all susceptible of continued improvement by the application of capital to them, but yet of very different original qualities and powers' (Malthus, 1969, p. 37). The products of these machines were 'gifts of nature, not the works of man' (ibid., p. 38). Ricardo didn't quarrel with Malthus's characterization of nature's contribution except to mention that the generosity of nature was largely irrelevant in the determination of exchange value.

Malthus attributed the existence of rent to three causes. First, land could be made to yield a surplus over and above the subsistence wages required for the support of the workers. Secondly, 'necessaries of life' would create their own demand (ibid., p. 8). Malthus considered the supply of 'necessaries' as one of the strongest constraints on population; if supply increased, so too would population, leaving per capita demand roughly the same. Lastly, the comparative scarcity of the most fertile land contributed to the existence of rent (ibid.; Ricardo, 1973, Vol. VII, p. 107). Malthus's first explanation, Ricardo argued, was trivially true while his second was patently false. On the third explanation, Malthus and Ricardo were in agreement (Ricardo, 1973, Vol. VII, pp. 107–9).

Malthus viewed a general rise or fall in rents as 'necessarily connected' with the increased or decreased use of 'inferior land' (ibid., Vol. II, p. 161). A change in rents thus implied a change in the pattern of resource extraction as well. Ricardo didn't disagree with Malthus on this issue.

Changes in rents were due, in Malthus's opinion, to changes in 'the expenses of cultivation' and 'the costs of the instruments of production, compared with the price of produce' (ibid., p. 133). Malthus saw four main factors influencing expenses and price: capital accumulation, changes in population, technological change and changes in prices.

As capital accumulated, competition between capitalists would tend to lower profits. With lower profits being the norm, the returns possible from working less fertile land would become acceptable. Consequently, rents on the more fertile land would rise. Ricardo responded that Malthus had reversed the causality: recourse to less fertile land diminished profits and raised rents (ibid., Vol. I, p. 126). An increase, in demand, in turn, was responsible for the employment of less fertile lands.

Changes in population affected rents in much the same manner, according to Malthus. An increase in population increased competition among workers resulting in a decrease in the wage level (ibid., Vol. II, pp. 135–6). Lower labour costs made exploitation of less fertile lands more attractive: the extensive margin of cultivation was extended causing a rise in rents on the more fertile lands.

An increase in population, Ricardo commented, need not imply a fall in wages. '[T]his must depend on the demand for people': if demand grew with population, wages would not fall (ibid., p. 133). Moreover, if wages fell, demand for natural resources would fall as well, implying there could be no need to extend production to less fertile lands.

Improvements in the technology of exploiting natural resources would enable more product to be brought to market at the same cost. Competition would lower the price of the product, but only, Malthus reasoned, in the short run. In the longer run, since the product was one of the 'necessaries of life', prices would rise (ibid., p. 141). Malthus does not specify how high those prices would rise. He does stress, however, that less fertile land will be used as a result of the technological improvement.

Ricardo found Malthus's explanation on this point particularly unsatisfactory. A technological improvement implied that 'with the same quantity of labour a greater quantity of produce can be obtained' (ibid., p. 140). Wage costs would fall and profits would rise but rents would remain unchanged. Less fertile land would *not* be employed *unless* demand had risen.

As for an increase in the real price of a natural resource resulting in an increase in rent, Ricardo agreed with Malthus that this could occur as demand rose. The key, Ricardo claimed, to whether or not those higher prices would endure depended on the necessity of using less fertile lands (ibid., Vol. I, pp. 143–4).

The classical interpretation which coalesced in the writings of Ricardo and Malthus accorded natural resources a separate theoretical treatment. By inference, a scarcity of natural resources was substantively different from a scarcity of labour or capital. While there is ample room for disagreement as to what defines a purely classical interpretation of natural resources, certain distinguishing features of the classical approach emerged with sufficient clarity from the Ricardo–Malthus debate to constitute hallmarks of classical natural resource economic theory.

Reinterpreting Ricardian scarcity

At the Political Economy Club, soon after Ricardo's death, Ricardian economics fell into disrepute; a group normally given to supporting Ricardian theory, Colonel Torrens declared in 1831 'that all the great principles of Ricardo's work had been successively abandoned' (Meek, 1950, p. 56). Among these 'principles' was Ricardo's rent theory, which some held to have been superseded by William Thompson's explanation of rent as a monopoly return (ibid.). Others preferred the explanations of Richard Jones or, later, J.H. von Thunen (Gordon, 1969, p. 379). In no small part the criticism of Ricardo's rent theory reflected opposition to the broader, political implications of Ricardo's theory, particularly as interpreted by the socialist followers of Ricardo (Meek, 1950, pp. 61–2).

Ricardian theory recovered from this attack to emerge as the dominant force in nineteenth-century economics. But, as Ronald Meek has noted, 'it was hardly the Ricardianism of Ricardo' (Meek, 1950, p. 55). Rather, it was the theories of J.S. Mill and Alfred Marshall labelled by their authors as 'Ricardian' which held sway for the remainder of the century (Fetter, 1969, p. 82).

Mill's treatment of natural resources is largely in the tradition of Ricardo. Land is set apart from labour and capital as an 'element of production not susceptible of indefinite increase' (Mill, 1909, p. 176). In emphasizing the differential productivity of land (and mines) as a source of rent and insisting that rent does not enter into the cost of production, Mill was true to his mentor (ibid., pp. 176, 472). However, Mill's Ricardian rent theory coexists uncomfortably with his explanation of the returns to capital and labour as payments for abstinence and productive services respectively (ibid., pp. 405–6). Mill's theories of profits and wages are treated in an almost neoclassical manner while rent is offered in the classical manner.

Superficially, Alfred Marshall's handling of natural resources appears in much the same light as that of Mill. Marshall saw himself as the defender of classical economics, as the latest in an unbroken line of British economists writing in the tradition of Smith and Ricardo. But his defence was largely a matter of semantics: the terminology was classical but the major concepts were neoclassical. The Ricardian ideas are little more than 'heirlooms' in a marginalist structure (Schumpeter, 1981, p. 837).

On the issue of rent, Marshall extended the concept far beyond the bounds suggested by Ricardo. Land rent was 'simply the chief species of a large genus of economic phenomena' (Marshall, 1925, p. 629). Rents and quasi-rents arise, Marshall argued, when the return on a factor of production exceeds that factor's cost of production. If the factor has a short life span and can be reproduced at constant cost, almost no rent will be paid to the factor's owner over the factor's lifetime. If, however, the factor is long lived and limited in supply, the tendency for the return to vary from the cost of production will be substantial (ibid., pp. 412–24). Defined in this manner, rents may arise on any factor of production. Moreover, Marshallian rents may be socially contrived (e.g. rents accruing to artificial monopolies) in addition to originating 'naturally', further alienating the notion of rent from its Ricardian origins.

On natural resources, Marshall thought a 'loose' distinction could be made between 'material things which owe their usefulness to human labor' and those which do not (ibid., p. 144). The former were capital goods, the latter fell under the heading of land. The 'scientific principle underlying the distinction' centred upon the inability of man to reproduce some 'utilities' originally offered 'by nature' (ibid., p. 244).

Marshall added that the fertility of land might be altered through the application of human labour (ibid., p. 147). More importantly, there was 'no absolute measure of the richness or fertility of land' (ibid., p. 157). Changes in demand might rearrange the fertility ranking of parcels of land. Marshall's argument in this case focused upon the different marginal productivity schedules of the land parcels (ibid., pp. 158–61). Changes in production technology might also change the fertility rankings. Thus 'the term fertility has no meaning except with reference to the special circumstances of a particular time and place' (ibid., p. 161). Only with these qualifications did Marshall uphold the Ricardian view that diminishing returns on land would result from increased doses of capital and labour.

Mines, Marshall noted, had to be treated somewhat differently from other categories of land resource. While increasing applications of capital and labour to a particular mine would yield diminishing returns, this decreasing marginal return was fundamentally different from the diminishing return of agriculture. Production in agriculture, Marshall argued, did not decrease the fertility of the soil. Agricultural production was a 'perennial stream' (ibid., p. 167). The produce of mines, however, entailed a net reduction of 'nature's reservoir' (ibid.).

Interestingly, while Marshall reasoned that rent arose in many activities, he also maintained that the return garnered by mine owners typically did not qualify as 'rent'. The difference between the income generated by a mine and the mine's basic production expenses was held by Marshall to be largely a royalty payment for the 'diminution in the value of the mine, regarded as a source of wealth in the future' (ibid., p. 439). Rent might arise in mining, but only where the mine was worked over an extended period of time, an occurrence which could be reduced by mining the resource more intensively. Expressed in this manner, Marshall was able to maintain, with Ricardo, that rent was not a cost of production and at the same time assert that the mine owners' return (now labelled 'royalty') was a production cost.

Much as Marshall focused upon rent as a residual surplus which had been properly defined by Ricardo but improperly restricted to natural resources, W.S. Jevons concentrated upon the diminishing marginal return element in Ricardo's rent theory and found it consistent with a marginalist approach to other aspects of economic theory (Jevons, 1924, p. 214). '[R]ates of wages,' Jevons insisted, 'are governed by the same formal laws as rents' (ibid., p. xlvii). This opinion established Jevons as substantially more radical than Marshall since it implied rejection of the Ricardian tenet that rents are price determined (i.e., are a residue) not price determining.

While Jevons found little difficulty in treating land, labour and capital with the same marginal productivity theory, he did not place them on equal footing in matters of public policy. In *The Coal Question*, Jevons sounded the alarm of natural resource exhaustion. Great Britain, he argued in 1865, would shortly face the dire consequences of coal depletion. Jevons was not worried about a growing worldwide scarcity of coal. His concern lay with the comparative scarcity of coal in Britain which would enable other countries with more abundant resources, such as the United States, to undermine Britain's pre-eminence as an industrial power.

Subsequent British economists slowly dispensed with many of Marshall's Ricardian heirlooms, preferring to argue in the spirit of Jevons that distributive shares of output were 'determined by marginal efficiency . . . when all the factors have received their share in this marginal distribution there is no surplus or residuum at all' (Wicksteed, 1910, p. 550). However, while land as a productive factor did not merit separate theoretical treatment, land resources continued to be treated differently. The arguments presented by Jevons's *Coal Question* continued to hold sway decades after publication (Courtney, 1897).

On the continent the marginalists showed little inclination to tie their theories to the English Ricardian tradition. Ricardo's rent theory was taken by Carl Menger as evidence of a 'methodological blunder' (Menger, 1981, p. 166). The fact that land could not be treated on the same basis as capital and labour was 'telling evidence of the need for reforming' the British theories of economics (ibid.). Writing in the shadow of the influential German historical school of economics, Menger pointedly commented that attempts to separate the 'original powers' of land from the man-made element were 'a hopeless historical investigation, and were in any case irrelevant for economizing men' (ibid., p. 167).

Menger admitted that land had certain identifying characteristics: its supply could not be increased without difficulty, its location was fixed and there were bewildering differences in quality. Yet these characteristics were also present in other goods. In short, 'land occupies no exceptional place among goods' (ibid., p. 165).

Eugen von Böhm-Bawerk made the same point a bit differently. All production, he argued, was a 'purely natural process . . . . Man does not alter that process. He merely guides it' (Böhm-Bawerk, 1959, p. 7). Agricultural production simply requires less 'guiding' than other productive activities. It cannot be distinguished from other pursuits through its strong natural basis since all pursuits, ultimately, have similar bases.

Leon Walras shared Menger's opinion that land merited no special explanation. Additionally, Walras provided a mathematical exposition of Ricardo's rent theory to reveal the implicit restrictive assumptions of the model. In particular, Walras questioned the assumption of constant prices, declaring Ricardo's analysis inappropriate for the dynamic analysis Ricardo intended (Walras, 1954, pp. 404–18).

During the same period in which the marginalist approach was gaining ascendancy, economics was being established as an academic discipline in the United States. Henry George, among the last major non-professional economists, made his mark by accentuating the difference between land and other factors of production.

Land, George argued, is the passive element in production; labour and capital are the active components. Control of this passive element yielded the owner a monopoly return (George, 1914, p. 167). While this approach implied that rent affected the price of land's output, George maintained that he was following the Ricardian approach to rent. The 'law of rent' as bequeathed by Ricardo had 'the self-evident character of a geometric axiom' (ibid., p. 168). Ricardo's failing was excessively narrow restriction of the concept to agriculture and 'all natural agencies such as mines, fisheries etc.' (ibid., p. 166). Manufacturing also demanded land as space and was consequently the cause of location rent.

Rent, George maintained, did not 'arise from the absolute productiveness or utility of land' but from its productivity relative to 'land that can be had for nothing' (ibid.). As Marshall later argued, relative productivity (or fertility) of natural resources was dependent upon demand. Certain physical characteristics may become more or less desirable over time. This was particularly true in the case of location, which figured prominently in George's work.

George's influence on the early generations of American academic economists was at least equalled by the formal instruction many American economists received from German professors of the historical school. Consequently, the deductive Ricardian theory was more subject to question among American economists than among their British colleagues. Richard Ely, whose text became a standard in American universities, is a prime example. Schumpeter described him as 'that excellent German professor in an American skin' (Schumpeter, 1981, p. 874). While early editions of Ely's text treated land in the Ricardian manner, later editions recognized the 'fundamental resemblance between land and capital' (Ely and Hess, 1937, p. 449).

German-trained Frank Taussig held the view that 'rent forms no part of the expenses of production' (Taussig, 1939, Vol. II, p. 96). Taking issue with Marshall's view, Taussig claimed that royalties in well explored areas of mining were simply a part of rent; in less well explored areas they were part of a risk premium which was a production expense (ibid., p. 140). E.R.A. Seligman, in a view similar to Ely's later approach, recognized the similarity of land and capital (Seligman, 1905, p. 300). H. Davenport denied any significant difference between the approaches to land and capital (Davenport, 1913, p. 183).

Marginalist J.B. Clark observed that the traditional approach to land rent had 'become an obstacle to scientific progress' (Clark, 1891, p. 289). Properly treated, however, the notion of differential return underlying the concept of Ricardian rent could offer an explanation of the returns to all factors. As a consequence, natural resources no longer merited a separate theoretical basis. Irving Fisher agreed with Clark, referring derisively to the 'fancied distinction between land and capital' as a simple result of 'confusion' (Fisher, 1919, p. 56).

Frank Fetter (1901) summarized the general feeling at the turn of the century with a somewhat premature obituary on Ricardian rent. Fetter distinguished five concepts underlying the 'failed' theory of rent. In his view a new concept of rent would soon emerge from the work of marginalists such as Clark.

The first concept of rent as arising from a fixed stock of natural resources had two major difficulties. First, it was impossible 'in practice' to distinguish 'accurately between things that are "natural" and things that are produced' (Fetter, 1901, p. 420). Second, natural resources in physical terms may be fixed in supply but in productive use they are variable. Fetter drew this as an implication of Marshall's assertion that land fertility is relative, not absolute (ibid.). This second criticism applied with equal force to the second concept of rent as payment for space: 'No matter what are the "original powers" of land, they have no fixed or predetermined value: they have value only with reference to the social situation, to the needs of men.' (ibid., p. 428). The third and fourth concepts of rent relied upon durability: rent was a surplus accruing to resources fixed in supply for either the long or short term. A less well defined fifth variant also viewed rent as a surplus but for a broader category of rewards achieved without any 'real' sacrifice (ibid., p. 453).

Even though the balance of opinion held that land did not warrant a separate theoretical treatment, many American economists – knowingly or not, following the path of Jevons – provided separate treatment for natural resources in policy matters. Ely in particular was a pioneer in modern land economics, an institutional approach to natural resource economics (Ely and Wehrwein, 1961). Davenport referred to rent as the 'capitalized bounty of nature' and condemned it as 'iniquitous in origin and productive of innumerable abominations' (Davenport, 1911, p. 330). Taussig, in more subdued tones, favoured the public appropriation of land rent (Taussig, 1939, Vol. II, p. 142).

Maintaining this separation between theory and policy was not a simple matter. Difficulty arose particularly in coping with the issue of conservation – a matter of growing interest at the turn of the century. The need for conservation was based upon the 'general recognition' that natural resources were becoming increasingly scarce (Gray, 1913; Smith, 1982). By implication natural resources stood apart from other resources as exhaustible.

Lewis Gray demonstrated this difficulty in 1913 and 1914 with two seminal articles on conservation and natural resource exhaustion. He noted that resource extraction is accelerated by high interest rates and falling prices. Since these actions diminish the present value of resources extracted in the future, he argued that holding the resources in the ground becomes less attractive for the mine owner. Gray felt, though he could not prove it, that the discount rate governing mine owners' resource extraction decisions might not be optimal from society's point of view (Gray,

1913, pp. 518–19). This was a difficulty in other enterprises as well but the problem was particularly 'clear-cut' for exhaustible resources where decisions were irreversible (ibid., p. 501). By implication, natural resources required special treatment but the neoclassical theoretical underpinnings gave little support for Gray's policy recommendations.

The source of rent in Gray's analysis was diminishing returns, not depletion 'royalties'. In this respect Gray was aligned with the more Ricardian opinion of Taussig rather than Marshall on the issue of whether rent was a component of price.[2] For Gray, however, diminishing returns arose as capital and labour were applied to constant units of space and time (Gray, 1914, p. 472). Diminishing increments of output would result from increasing the rate of extraction. This was distinctly different from the diminishing returns specified by Ricardo, which were based on the differential fertility of the plots composing the fixed supply of land. Space appears to be the critical element in Gray's analysis. Time is only significant if the operator encounters difficulty in coordinating increased production or is forced for any other reason to change his technique of production. But in that case the underlying problem is either the supply of homogeneous additional units of labour and capital or the differential fertility of the mine.

While stressing his intellectual debt to Ricardo, Gray expressed much of his argument in modern neoclassical terms. This yielded an uncomfortable combination of neoclassical and classical theoretical approaches to natural resources. The result is an anti-Ricardian conclusion in Ricardian garb: where Ricardo had concluded that diminishing resource productivity would result in falling rates of profit (which, as a return to capital, included interest), Gray reversed the causality and the conclusion by arguing that an increase in profit (interest) caused an increase in extraction and decreasing productivity.

Though Gray's efforts at the turn of the century represented the first comprehensive treatment of natural resources, his influence was overshadowed by the work of Richard Ely. Ely's *Land Economics* stood as the standard work in the field for most of the first half of the century. For many years Ely initiated the land economics round table discussions of the American Economic Association by stressing that his field was primarily concerned with the 'economic relations among men that arise out of the utilization of land' (Ely, 1926; 1928; 1931). As this statement implies, Ely's approach to natural resources was institutional with an emphasis on taxonomy.

The institutional and 'classical' approaches of Ely and Gray were brought together in 1963 with the publication of H. Barnett's and C. Morse's *Scarcity and Growth*. This work is concerned principally 'with economic doctrines of increasing natural resource scarcity and diminishing returns and their relevance in the modern world' (Barnett and Morse, 1963, p. 2). Altering the priorities established by Ely, Barnett and Morse stress the 'quantitative . . . aspects of the natural resource problem' over 'consideration of the social, and more qualitative aspects' (ibid., p. 3). The problem, they assert, lies 'in the realm of historical growth economics, not of static efficiency economics' (ibid.). Their 'framework' of analysis was to be explicitly 'that of the classical economists' (ibid.).

Barnett and Morse identified two basic classical scarcity models: the Malthusian and the Ricardian. The Malthusian model assumes a fixed, 'relatively small', homogeneous resource stock (ibid., p. 106). Malthusian scarcity is, in some sense, an absolute scarcity of a unique resource. Natural resources are free goods until a threshold of usage is reached after which output is progressively constrained by diminishing marginal returns to successive doses of labour and capital. Ricardian or differential scarcity assumes a heterogeneous resource supply which, once again, eventually produces diminishing returns. The difference between the two models has less to do with the composition of the resource stock than with the broader issue of substitution. In the Ricardian model the resource stock is an aggregation of deposits which can be used as substitutes for one another in the production process; resource quality is denoted by each deposit's elasticity of substitution. In the Malthusian model, only capital and labour can function as factor substitutes for natural resources: substitution among natural resources of varying types and qualities is assumed to be infeasible.

To test whether resources are becoming increasingly scarce in either a Malthusian or Ricardian sense, Barnett and Morse defined a unit cost scarcity measure. Real unit cost UC_t is actually a Laspeyres index of capital and labour input per unit of extractive output (Smith, 1980, p. 261).

$$UC_t = \frac{W_B(L_t/Q_t) + r_B(K_t/Q_t)}{W_B(L_B/Q_B) + r_B(K_B/Q_B)}$$

where L_B and K_B are the base levels of labour and capital, Q_B and Q_t are levels of extractive output in constant dollars in the base year and in year t; W_B and r_B are the prices of labour and capital.

On the basis of unit cost strong and weak scarcity hypotheses are developed. The strong scarcity hypothesis is confirmed by rising real unit cost of the extractive output; the weak hypothesis is confirmed by a rise in the unit cost of extractive output relative to the unit cost of non-extractive output.

Barnett's and Morse's empirical results reject both hypotheses for the period from 1870 to 1957 (Barnett and Morse, 1963, pp. 215–16). Extensions of the Barnett and Morse approach have shown the same trends continuing into the late 1960s and early 1970s (Smith, 1979; Johnson and Bennett, 1980).

The Barnett and Morse study raises two major questions. The first concerns the adequacy of unit cost as a Ricardian measure of scarcity. The second involves the measure's accuracy as an indicator of resource scarcity.

In the context of Ricardo's corn model, increasing scarcity is indicated by a rise in labour's share of the resource output or a fall in capital's share. The absolute payment, in units of output, going to rent will rise but as a share of the total output it may rise, fall or stay the same. Putting labour and capital prices in terms of the quantity of the extractive resource they could purchase by multiplying both the numerator and the denominator by the inverse of the price of the output in the base year, unit cost can be expressed as

$$UC_t = \frac{(W'_B L_t + r'_B K_t)/Q_t}{(W'_B L_B + r'_B K_B)/Q_B}$$

Where $W'_B = W_B/P_B$, $r'_B = r_B/P_B$ and P_B is the price of the extractive output. Holding money wages as well as output and capital prices constant, it can be seen from this equation that unit cost reflects the combined share of output falling to labour and capital in year t relative to the base year. Consequently, since unit cost may rise, fall or stay the same as Ricardian scarcity progresses, the measure fails as a Ricardian scarcity index. As was the case in Gray's analysis, the claim of Barnett and Morse to a classical heritage is weak. Nevertheless, in referring to the unit cost measure. Barnett and Morse and others continue to maintain that their approach is 'classical' or 'neo-Ricardian' (Morse, 1976, p. 245; Smith, 1980, p. 261).

Conclusion
It is clear that the classical view of natural resources has been altered by successive reinterpretations over the course of the last two centuries. Moreover, the classical approach, distorted or not, is in large part ignored in the modern literature on natural resources. Modern natural resource economics is essentially a field in applied microeconomics; a field recognizing Harold Hotelling, not David Ricardo, as its primary progenitor. As such, the question of what classical economics might have to say on natural resource scarcity seldom arises.

Neoclassical microeconomics treats natural resource scarcity as it does any other type of scarcity. Natural resources occupy no special niche in standard economic theory, except as an application of the general theory. While classical economics seems to offer such a niche, the boundaries of that niche are not well defined.

Nevertheless, there is a strong case to be made that, in Ricardo's view, natural resource scarcity differs qualitatively from labour or capital scarcity. Natural resource depletion leads to economic stagnation and arguably undesirable changes in the income distribution: rents rise at the expense of profits while wage's share of a slower growing output increases. This causal chain is the hallmark of the classical approach to natural resources.

In classical theory natural resources matter. The policy prescriptions follow naturally, as in the Corn Law debate. In neoclassical theory it is not clear that natural resources matter. The policy prescriptions do not follow unambiguously from the theory. Yet many of the neoclassical school, from Jevons and Gray onwards, often offer policy prescriptions *as if* natural resources mattered. '[T]hese economists,' as Veblen noted, 'are lacking neither in intelligence nor information. They are, indeed, to be credited, commonly, with a wide range of information and an exact control of materials, as well as a very alert interest in what is going on; and apart from their theoretical pronouncements . . . [they] habitually profess the sanest and most intelligent views of current practical questions' (Veblen, 1909, p. 622).

Notes
1. This assumption and that concerning the ratio of capital to labour are typically cited as Ricardian assumptions, though they are not specifically mentioned by Ricardo either in the 1815 essay or in his *Principles*. Ricardo considers buildings and implements in his essay, making no restriction as to their durability. He also states that increasing quantities of labour are required to secure additional output, but this needn't imply constant capital to labour ratios. Ricardo's remark 'that capital and population advance in the proper proportion' (Ricardo, 1973, Vol. IV, p. 12) should perhaps be taken to mean that the capital to labour ratio for corn remains the same as the average for the economy as a whole. This restriction has the impact of holding real wages, measured in corn, constant.
2. This debate continued well into the twentieth century. Other participants in the debate include Orchard (1922), Wolfe (1929) and Roberts (1939). In 1954 Carlisle concluded with little justification that the only valid source of diminishing returns was time. Fine (1982) has offered the most recent contribution framing the dispute as a struggle between proponents of general and partial equilibrium theories.

References
Barnett, H. and Morse, C. (1963), *Scarcity and Growth*, Baltimore, MD: Johns Hopkins University Press for Resources for the Future.

Blaug, Mark (1979), *Economic Theory in Retrospect*, New York: Cambridge University Press.

Böhm-Bawerk, E. (1959), *Capital and Interest*, South Holland, Illinois: Libertarian Press.

Clark, J. B. (1891), 'Distribution as Determined by a Law of Rent', *Quarterly Journal of Economics*, **5**, pp. 289–318.

Courtney, L. H. (1897), 'Jevons' Coal Question 30 Years After', *Journal of the Royal Statistical Society*, **60** (4), pp. 789–810.

Davenport, H. (1911), 'Extent and Significance of Unearned Increment', *Bulletin of the American Economic Association*, Papers and Discussions, April, pp. 322–332.

Davenport, H. (1913), *The Economics of Enterprise*, New York: Macmillan.

Ely, R. T. (1926), 'Round Table Discussions: Land Economics', *American Economic Review*, Supplement (March), **16** (1), pp. 297–9.

Ely, R. T. (1928), 'Round Table Discussions: Land Economics', *American Economic Review*, Supplement (March), **18** (1), p. 5.

Ely, R. T. (1931), 'Round Table Discussions: Land Economics', *American Economic Review*, Supplement (March), **21** (1), pp. 125–33.

Ely, R. T. and Hess, H. (1937), *Outlines of Economics*, New York: Macmillan.

Ely, R. T. and Wehrwein, G. S. (1961), *Land Economics*, Madison, Wisconsin: University of Wisconsin Press.

Fetter, F. (1901), 'The Passing of the Old Rent Concept', *Quarterly Journal of Economics*, **15** (May), pp. 416–55.

Fetter, F. (1969) 'The Rise and Decline of Ricardian Economics', *History of Political Economy*, **1**, 1 (Spring), pp. 67–84.

Fine, B. (1982), 'Landed Property and the Distinction between Royalty and Rent', *Land Economics*, August, pp. 338–50.

Fisher, I. (1919), *The Nature of Capital and Income*, New York: Macmillan.

George, H. (1914), *Progress and Poverty*, New York: Doubleday, Page.

Gordon, B. (1969), 'Criticism of Ricardian Views on Value and Distribution in the British Periodicals, 1820–1850', *History of Political Economy*, **1**, 2 (Fall), pp. 370–87.

Gray, Lewis (1913), 'The Economic Possibilities of Conservation', *Quarterly Journal of Economics*, **27** (May), pp. 497–519.

Gray, Lewis (1914), 'Rent under the Assumption of Exhaustibility', *Quarterly Journal of Economics*, **39** (May), pp. 466–89.

Jevons, W. S. (1866), *The Coal Question*, London: Macmillan.

Jevons, W. S. (1924), *The Theory of Political Economy*, London: Macmillan.

Johnson, M. H. and Bennett, J. T. (1980), 'Increasing Resource Scarcity: Further Evidence', *Quarterly Review of Economics and Business*, **20** (1), Spring, pp. 42–8.

Malthus, T. R. (1969), *An Inquiry into the Nature and Progress of Rent*, New York: Greenwood Press.

Marshall, A. (1925), *Principles of Economics*, 8th edn, London: Macmillan.

Meek, R. L. (1950), 'The Decline of Ricardian Economics in England', *Economica*, **17** (65) (February), pp. 43–62.

Menger, C. (1981), *Principles of Economics*, New York: New York University Press.

Mill, J. S. (1909), *Principles of Political Economy*, ed. W. J. Ashley, London: Longmans, Green.

Morse, C. (1976), 'Depletion, Exhaustibility and Conservation', in *Economics of* the *Mineral Industries*, ed. W. A. Vogely, New York: American Institute of Mining, Metallurgical and Petroleum Engineers.

Orchard, J. E. (1922), 'The Rent of Mineral Lands', *Quarterly Journal of Economics*, **36** (February), pp. 290–318.

Ricardo, D. (1973), *The Works and Correspondence of David Ricardo*, 11 vols, ed. P. Sraffa, London: Cambridge University Press.

Roberts, W. (1939), 'Diminishing Returns in the Mining Industry', *Land Economics*, **2** (39), pp. 21–8.

Schumpeter, J. A. (1981), *History of Economic Analysis*, New York: Oxford University Press.

Seligman, E. R. A. (1905), *Principles of Economics*, New York: Longmans, Green.

Smith, G. A. (1982), 'Natural Resource Economic Theory of the First Conservation Movement (1895–1927)', *History of Political Economy*, **14** (4) (December), pp. 483–95.

Smith, V. K. (1979), 'Natural Resource Scarcity: A Statistical Analysis', *Review of Economic Statistics*, **61** (3) (August), Maryland pp. 423–7.

Smith, V. K. (1980), "The Evaluation of Natural Resource Adequacy: Elusive Quest or Frontier of Economic Analysis?', *Land Economics*, **56** (3) (August), pp. 257–98.

Taussig, F. (1939), *Principles of Economics*, 2 vols, New York: Macmillan.

Veblen, T. (1909), 'The Limitations of Marginal Utility', *Journal of Political Economy*, **17** (9) (November), pp. 620–36.

Walras, L. (1954), *Elements of Pure Economics*, Homewood, Illinois: R. D. Irwin.

Wicksteed, P. H. (1910), *Common Sense of Political Economy*, London: Macmillan.

Wolfe, A. B. (1929), 'Rent under Increasing Returns', *American Economic Review*, **19** (December), pp. 580–604.

12 Pareto's theory of capital rents: a general equilibrium analysis

Ronald Bird and Vincent J. Tarascio

Pareto analysis of rent deserves close examination because it provides an important insight into the economic processes which generate rent. Yet, aside from descriptive examples, to our knowledge no one, including Pareto himself, has published a rigorous analysis of the process underlying rent creation in an economic system under conditions of free competition as described by Pareto. Indeed, as has been shown elsewhere, the concept of 'Paretian' rent as defined by modern writers since 1946 has no basis in Pareto's discussions on this subject, and he has been frequently misinterpreted by modern writers.[1]

To clarify Pareto's theory of rent, a Walrasian–Pareto-type general equilibrium framework will be used. In order to facilitate the discussion the assumptions and relations of the general equilibrium model are specified before the concept of rent is introduced. Although Pareto's theory of rent is general enough to apply to all sources of economic rent, the focus of our analysis will be on capital rents, a subject to which he devoted the greatest attention.

Pareto's example of capital rents

Pareto discussed rent through a series of examples designed to elucidate his understanding of a complex subject. Pareto's central example of rent as found in his *Manual of Political Economy* is as follows:

> Let A be a capital good. As we have seen in sec. 24, the accounts are set up so that it can be assumed that A is used without being consumed, that is simply utilized. Consequently, the entire quantity of A remains after the first time period, not just part of it.
>
> Let us begin by assuming that the rate of net interest on capital is the same in the first period and in the second, and that it is 5 per cent, for example. This means that A, the price of which was 100 in the first time period, yielded 5 net; and that in the second time period having a price of 120, it yields a net interest of 6. [100 and 120 are the prices for which the owner of a unit of A can sell his ownership; 5 and 6 are the net incomes derived from selling the services of a unit of A instead of ownership.]
>
> Conversely, the prices can be deduced from the incomes. Let A be capital that is not produced, ground surface for example. In the first time period it

yielded a net income of 5; we deduce from this that its price must have been 100. In the second time period it gives a net income of 6; we deduce from this that its price has become 120.

That is advantageous to one who possesses A; but if all the other capital goods have increased in price at the same rate there is no advantage in having A rather than B, C . . . If, on the other hand, the prices of all capital goods have not increased at the same rate, the possession of one of them can be more or less advantageous than the possession of another one.

Let us assume that on the average, all the prices of capital goods have increased by 10 percent; the price of A would be 110 instead of 100 and at 5 percent it ought to yield an income of 5.5; consequently, compared to other capital, A yields 0.50 more net income. [Since its income went up to 6 instead of 5.5.] We call this quantity the *rent acquired* in moving from one position to another. (Pareto, 1971, p. 247)

The above serves as a representative example of rent discussions found in Pareto's *Cours d'économie politique* and *Manual*. Our purpose is to examine Pareto's examples in a rigorous manner, in order to gain insights into the process of rent creation in a system of general equilibrium as suggested by Pareto. In what follows, an appropriate model will be developed in order to facilitate the analysis.

The model

The economic environment consists of a collective of autonomous economic units. Each economic unit has at its disposal at any given time a quantity of elementary factors of production – labour and raw materials (including land). There exists a data set indicating the types of consumable goods and services which can be produced and the technological conditions of such production. Each economic unit possesses a preference function indicating its rank ordering of all combinations and quantities of the potential consumption goods. Labour and raw materials are also included in each individual's preference function. Labour and raw materials are not directly consumable, but may be transformed into consumable goods and services. Let (1) U represent an index of utility, (2) L_1 represent quantity of labour transformed, (3) L_2 represent quantity of raw materials transformed, and (4) C_i represent quantity of good i consumed, $i = 1, 2, 3, \ldots, n$. The utility function for an individual economic unit may be written $U = \Psi (L_1, L_2, C_1, C_2, C_3, \ldots, C_n)$, where Ψ is continuous and twice differentiable in all variables. It is assumed that

(1) $\dfrac{\delta U}{\delta L_1} < 0$ and $\dfrac{\delta^2 U}{\delta L^2_1} > 0$

(2) $\dfrac{\delta U}{\delta L_2} < 0$ and $\dfrac{\delta^2 U}{\delta L^2_2} > 0$

(3) $\dfrac{\delta U}{\delta C_i} < 0$ and $\dfrac{\delta^2 U}{\delta C^2_i} < 0$, for all $i = 1, 2, 3, \ldots, n$.

For the present, labour is homogeneous. Later in this paper heterogeneous labour and human capital will be discussed.[2] The inclusion of raw material in the preference function is a way of temporarily ignoring land and other 'gifts of nature'. It is also assumed that for each economic unit

(1) $\displaystyle\lim_{L_1 \to L^*_1} \dfrac{\delta^2 U}{\delta L^2_1} = \infty$

(2) $\displaystyle\lim_{L_2 \to L^*_2} \dfrac{\delta^2 U}{\delta L^2_2} = \infty,$

where L^*_1 and L^*_2 are the quantities of labour and raw materials at the disposal of the economic unit. The quantities of raw materials and labour supplied by each economic unit approach the fixed endowment asymptotically. This device removes the problem of labour and land limitativeness.[3] After the development of the basic analytical framework, labour and land limitativeness will be discussed.

Each economic unit seeks to maximize its own utility. Economic activity occurs whenever two or more economic units find it advantageous to exchange factors and goods. The process of exchange establishes prices for each of the elementary factors of production and consumable goods. These prices may be measured in terms of any one of the goods or factors. Let C_{n+1} be the good which serves as numeraire; the price of C_{n+1} is 1. All other prices $(P_{L1}, P_{L2}, P_{c1}, P_{c2}, \ldots, P_{cn})$, are relative prices measured in terms of numeraire. Money is ignored in this model.

The set of individual preference functions and the set of technological conditions (production functions) for the transformation of elementary factors into consumable goods constitute the conditions of general equilibrium. Given an arbitrary price vector $(P_{L1}, P_{L2}, P_{c1}, P_{c2}, \ldots, P_{cn}, 1)$ utility maximization implies a vector $(L_1, L_2, C_1, C_2, C_3, \ldots, C_n, C_{n+1})$ for each economic unit. This vector indicates the quantities of L_1 and L_2 offered for transformation and the quantities of goods demanded by an economic unit. This vector is determined subject to the constraint

$$P_{L1}L_1 + P_{L2}L_2 = \sum_{i=1}^{n+1} P_{ci}C_i.$$

The vector of aggregate quantities supplied and demanded in response to a given price vector is the summation of all individual quantity vectors.

The aggregate budget constraint is the summation of all individual budget constraints.

For equilibrium it is necessary that the vector of total factor supplies (L_1, L_2) be transformable into the vector of total goods demanded. The transformation must be 'complete' in Pareto's sense. There are three conditions for complete transformation: (1) each good must be produced at minimum cost; (2) no good is produced at a loss, i.e., total revenue cannot be less than total cost; and (3) the aggregate budget constraint must be effective, i.e., $P_{L1}L_1 + P_{L2}L_2 = P_{c1}C_1 + \ldots + P_{cn}C_n + C_{n+1}$. If total revenue exceeds total cost for the production of one type of good, the aggregate budget constraint is satisfied only if there is an offsetting loss in the production of another good. However, no good can be produced at a loss if all transformations are complete. Therefore, there can be no surplus of revenue over cost in equilibrium. This conclusion corresponds to the zero economic profit condition for static competitive equilibrium. The coefficients of production are variable. Determination of equilibrium input ratios is implicit in the cost minimization condition. For one set of prices the given general equilibrium conditions correspond to a vector of factors supplied and a vector of goods demanded which meet the requirements of complete transformation. The equilibrium vectors of prices and quantities describe a general equilibrium position. The cycle of transformation and consumption associated with a specific general equilibrium position constitutes a period of production.

Some consumable goods cannot be produced by the direct transformation of elementary factors. Production of these goods requires the use of specialized, produced factors. Produced factors are the result of prior transformations of elementary factors. The produced factors are combined with units of elementary factors to produce consumption goods. The types of produced factors available and their production functions are included in the technological data of the general equilibrium conditions.

Let K_j $(j = 1, 2, \ldots, m)$ represent total quantity of produced factor $\underline{J}$, and let a_j represent the price of the services of produced factor $\underline{j}$. For an arbitrary price vector $(P_{L1}, P_{L2}, a_1, a_2, \ldots, a_m; P_{c1}, P_{c2}, \ldots, P_{cn}, 1)$, the utility-maximizing decisions of individual economic units imply vectors for the supply of elementary factors and the demand for consumable goods: (L_1, L_2) and $(C_1, C_2, C_3, \ldots, C_n, C_{n+1})$. The technological data specifies a production function for each consumable good: $C_i = C_i(L_1, L_2, K_1, \ldots, K_m)$. Given the factor prices $(P_{L1}, P_{L2}, a_1, a_2, \ldots, a_m)$, application of the cost minimization condition defines the quantities of L_1, L_2, and K_j $(j = 1, \ldots, m)$ necessary to produce C_i $(i = 1, \ldots, n+1)$. Summing these quantities for all $(n + 1)$ consumption goods defines the vector of total quantities $(\bar{L}_1, \bar{L}_2, \bar{K}_1, \bar{K}_2, \bar{K}_3, \ldots, \bar{K}_m)$ necessary to produce the vector of goods (C_1, C_2, C_3, . . ., C_n, C_{n+1}). For each produced factor the technological data specifies a production function $K_j = K_j (L_1, L_2)$. Given the price vector (P_{L1}, P_{L2}) and the desired quantity $\bar{K}_j$ of each produced factor, application of the cost minimization condition to each of the m factor production functions and summation of the results defines a vector ($\hat{L}_1$, $\hat{L}_2$) of total quantities of elementary factors necessary to produce the desired vector of produced goods. The given price vector (P_{L1}, P_{L2}, . . ., P_{cn}, 1) is an equilibrium vector only if $L_1 = \bar{L}_1 + \hat{L}_1$ and $L_2 = \bar{L}_2 + \hat{L}_2$. To attain a position of general equilibrium it is necessary that

$$
\begin{pmatrix} L_1 \\ L_2 \end{pmatrix} \quad \text{transforms} \atop \text{completely} \atop \text{into} \quad \begin{pmatrix} \bar{L}_1 \\ \bar{L}_2 \\ \bar{K}_1 \\ \bar{K}_2 \\ \cdot \\ \cdot \\ \cdot \\ \cdot, \\ K_m \end{pmatrix} \quad \text{and this} \atop \text{transforms} \atop \text{completely} \atop \text{into} \quad \begin{pmatrix} C_1 \\ C_2 \\ C_3 \\ \cdot \\ \cdot \\ \cdot, \\ C_n \\ C_{n+1} \end{pmatrix}
$$

It should be recalled that complete transformation requires: (1) cost minimization in all transformations; (2) no production at a loss; and (3) maintenance of the aggregate budget constraint $P_{L1}L_1 + P_{L2}L_2 = \sum_{i=1}^{n+1} P_{ci}C_i$. This implies that the price of each consumable good and produced factor equals average total cost. The latter conclusion is based on the implicit assumption that all produced factors associated with a particular general equilibrium position are produced and consumed in the immediate period of production corresponding to that equilibrium position. Therefore, no distinction is drawn between the price of the produced factor itself and the price of its services. To enhance the realism of the model this assumption must be eliminated.

The nature of some produced factors, called capital goods, makes it possible for them to be employed throughout several successive periods of production. If allowance is made for perpetual maintenance and insurance, capital goods may be conceived of as being utilized without being consumed. Because of the durability of capital goods, labour and raw materials employed (and generating income) in one period of production may indirectly contribute to production (and generate consumption expenditure) in a future period. The production of capital goods disrupts the intra-period aggregate budget equality by distributing production over time. To restore the intra-period budget equality it is necessary that some income be withheld from consumption expenditure: the current income not spent on current consumption constitutes savings. It is assumed that the quantity of savings is measured in numeraire. The motives for saving are complex and are rooted in the psychological and institutional characteristics of individuals and society. For the present purpose the simplest and most convenient assumption is that savings represent the purchase of a permanent income flow. Pareto referred to the transformation of savings into capital goods (1971, p. 462). A more precise statement is that labour and resources are transformed into capital goods; savings represents the value of the resources transformed into capital goods in a given period of production. The conditions of complete transformation ensure that in equilibrium the prices of capital goods are equal to average cost of production. It is assumed that capital goods are utilized in successive periods of production without being consumed. When resources are transformed into capital goods, a permanent income flow is acquired. The capital good is produced and paid for in the initial period; its services are sold in the present and in successive future periods. When deciding whether or not to purchase a capital good, the individual compares the price of the capital good with the income flow (price) obtainable by selling the capital good's services in future periods. The individual must have some expectation about the size of the future income flow. Assume that the individual transforming resources into capital of type K_j expects the current equilibrium price of its *services* to remain in effect indefinitely. (Even if some other scheme of expectations is adopted, the general principle remains the same.) The individual economic unit is assumed to have perfect knowledge of existing general equilibrium conditions, but perfect knowledge does not imply prescience. Expectations must be based on some sort of evaluation and extrapolation of existing conditions.

Let P_{kj} represent the per unit price of capital good type K_j. Complete transformation implies that $P_{kj} = P_{L1}L_1' + P_{L2}L_2'$. L_1' and L_2' are the quantities of elementary factors used to produce one unit of capital good j. Equilibrium in the current production period requires that all current transformations of resources into capital goods result in the same rate of return, $\dfrac{a_j}{P_{kj}}$. The rate of return for all current transformations of resources into capital is equal to the interest rate.

Assume that there are *no pre-existing capital goods*. For equilibrium within a given period of production, the price vector, $(P_{L1}, P_{L2}; a_1, a_2, \ldots, a_m; P_{k1}, P_{k2}, \ldots, P_{km}; P_{c1}, \ldots, P_{cn}, 1, i)$ must imply quantity vectors such

$$\begin{pmatrix} L_1 \\ L_2 \end{pmatrix} \qquad \begin{pmatrix} L_1 \\ L_2 \\ K_1 \\ \cdot \\ \cdot \\ \cdot \\ K_m \end{pmatrix} \qquad \begin{pmatrix} C_1 \\ C_2 \\ \cdot \\ \cdot \\ C_n \\ C_{n+1} \end{pmatrix}$$

(1)   (2)   (3)

that (1) completely transforms into (2), and (2) completely transforms into (3).[4] It is also necessary that

(1) $P_{L1}L_1 + P_{L2}L_2 + \sum_{j=1}^{m} a_j K_j - S = \sum_{i=1}^{n+1} P_{ci} C_i$

(2) $S = \sum_{j=1}^{m} P_{kj} K_j$

(3) $i = \dfrac{a_j}{P_{kj}}$ for all $j = 1, \ldots, m.$

The durable nature of capital goods implies that at the beginning of a given period of production there may already exist a stock of previously produced capital goods. Production in the current period will involve pre-existing capital goods as well as newly produced capital goods. If in the current period there exists a vector $(\hat{K}_1, \hat{K}_2, \ldots, \hat{K}_m)$ of capital goods produced in previous periods of production, the equilibrium price vector must imply quantity vectors

$$\begin{pmatrix} L_1 \\ L_2 \end{pmatrix} \qquad \begin{pmatrix} \bar{L}_1 \\ \bar{L}_2 \\ K_1 \\ K_2 \\ \cdot \\ \cdot \\ \cdot \\ K_m \end{pmatrix} \qquad \begin{pmatrix} C_1 \\ \cdot \\ \cdot \\ \cdot \\ C_n \\ C_{n+1} \end{pmatrix}$$

(1)   (2)   (3)

such that

$$\begin{pmatrix} L_1 \\ L_2 \end{pmatrix} \begin{array}{c} \text{completely} \\ \text{transforms} \\ \text{into} \end{array} \begin{pmatrix} \bar{L}_1 \\ \bar{L}_2 \\ \mathring{K}_1 \\ \mathring{K}_2 \\ \cdot \\ \cdot \\ \cdot \\ \cdot \\ \mathring{K}_m \end{pmatrix} \text{ and } \begin{pmatrix} \bar{L}_1 \\ \bar{L}_2 \\ \hat{K}_1 \\ \cdot \\ \cdot \\ \cdot \\ K_m \end{pmatrix} + \begin{pmatrix} 0 \\ 0 \\ \hat{K}_1 \\ \hat{K}_2 \\ \cdot \\ \cdot \\ \hat{K}_m \end{pmatrix} = \begin{pmatrix} \bar{L}_1 \\ \bar{L}_2 \\ K_1 \\ K_2 \\ \cdot \\ \cdot \\ K_m \end{pmatrix} \text{, and}$$

(1)   (1a)   (1a)   (2)

$$\begin{pmatrix} \bar{L}_1 \\ \bar{L}_2 \\ K_1 \\ K_2 \\ \cdot \\ \cdot \\ \cdot \\ K_m \end{pmatrix} \begin{array}{c} \text{completely} \\ \text{transforms} \\ \text{into} \end{array} \begin{pmatrix} C^1 \\ C_2 \\ \cdot \\ \cdot \\ \cdot \\ C_n \\ C_{n+1} \end{pmatrix}$$

(2)   (3)

$\mathring{K}_j$ represents the additional quantity of capital type j produced in the current period. The remaining conditions of equilibrium are

$$P_1L_1 + P_2L_2 + \sum_{j=1}^{m} a_jK_j - S = \sum_{i=1}^{n+1} P_{ci}C_i \tag{1}$$

$$S = \sum_{j=1}^{m} P_{kj}\mathring{K}_j \tag{2}$$

$$iK_j = \frac{a_j}{P_{kj}} \mathring{K}_j \text{ for all } j = 1, \ldots, m. \tag{3}$$

The assumption of pre-existing capital means that savings in the current period represent only additions to the capital goods vector (equation 2). The equality of present value of capital goods and the interest rate applies only to new capital goods. Obviously, $\mathring{K}_j$ cannot be negative, but it can be zero for some j.

The rent process
In the model described above, capital goods comprise a vector of specialized factors of production. For any one period of production, a given set of general equilibrium conditions implies an equilibrium vector of capital goods quantities. If the vector of pre-existing capital goods is not equal to

the equilibrium vector of capital goods, then resources are transformed into new units of the various types of capital goods. If, for a given vector of prices, the pre-existing vector of capital goods plus the additional capital goods produced is not sufficient to produce the vector of consumable goods demanded, then changes in relative prices occur. A new price vector is created. This new price vector implies a new vector of consumable goods demanded and a new vector of capital goods demanded. The altered prices have two effects: (1) the quantity of resources transformed into new capital goods changes so that the quantity of capital goods available more nearly meets the requirements of the vector of consumer goods demanded; and (2) the vector of consumer goods demanded is changed so that it more nearly reflects the capabilities of the pre-existing vector of capital goods. As a result of these adjustments, the equilibrium condition $i = \dfrac{a_j}{P_{kj}}$ will apply to all current transformations of savings into capital goods. While the above condition specifies the rate of return to new capital goods, it does not provide any information about the rate of return to pre-existing capital goods. When considering this last question, the concept of rent becomes applicable.

When general equilibrium conditions change and a new equilibrium price vector is determined, three types of change may occur which affect the rate of return of pre-existing capital goods: (1) the interest rate may change, reflecting changes in the costs of production and the service prices of all capital goods relative to the prices of consumption goods, labour and raw materials; (2) the prices of the services of capital goods may change relative to each other; and (3) the costs of production of capital goods may change relative to each other.

In the model presented, capital goods are not a homogeneous mass. As a vector of quantities of different types of specialized, produced factors, the capital stock possesses both size and structure. 'Structure' of the capital stock refers to the relative proportions of each capital type within the total stock. When the economy moves from one position of general equilibrium to another, changes of type (1) above (interest rate variation) are primarily associated with the determination of the equilibrium size of the capital stock; changes of types (2) and (3) (prices and costs of capital goods relative to each other) are associated with the determination of the equilibrium structure of the capital stock.

Rent reflects changes in the flow of income to pre-existing capital goods when the economy moves to a new position of general equilibrium. Let P^1_{kj} represent the price of one unit of capital type j in period t_1; let a^1_j represent the price of type j *services* in period t_1; and let i^1 represent the interest rate in period t_1. Fulfilment of the requirements of general equilibrium in period t_1 implies the following equivalent statements:

(1) $a^1_j - i^1 P^1_{kj} = 0,$

(2) $\dfrac{a^1_j}{i^1} - P^1_{kj} = 0,$ and

(3) $\dfrac{a^1_j}{P^1_{kj}} - i = 0.$

Assume that general equilibrium conditions change. The economic system moves to a new position of general equilibrium in period t_2. Rent accrues to units of capital type j produced in period t_1 if P_{kj}, a_j, or i change as a result of the movement to the new equilibrium position. Let P^2_{kj}, a^2_j, and i^2 represent period t_2 equilibrium values. Rent accruing to units of capital type j produced in period t_1 is the change in income flow

(1) $r = a^2_j - i^2 P^1_{kj},$

This effect of the movement from one equilibrium position to another may also be written in terms of the change in present value

(2) $R = \dfrac{r}{i^2} = \dfrac{a^2_j}{i^2} - P^1_{jk}.$

or in terms of the rate of return

(3) $\rho = \dfrac{r}{P^1_{kj}} = \dfrac{a^2_j}{P^1_{kj}} - i^2.$

Assume that the movement from equilibrium t_1 to t_2 affects the prices of types of capital services relative to each other but does not affect the interest rate ($i^1 = i^2$). This implies that the change is primarily associated with the structure of the capital stock rather than with its size. If $a^2_j > a^1_j$, then $r = a^2_j - i^2 P^1_{kj} > 0$. The movement to a new position of general equilibrium results in a flow of income to the previously produced units of capital type j which is in excess of the expected flow that motivated the original transformation of resources into the capital good. In terms of present value $R = \dfrac{r}{i^2} = \dfrac{a_j}{i^2} - P^1_{kj} > 0$. The movement to a new equilibrium position causes a change in the present value of previously produced units of j, i.e., a capital gain. In terms of rate of return,

$$\rho = \dfrac{r}{P^1_{kj}} = \dfrac{a^2_j}{P^1_{kj}} - i^2 > 0.$$

Units of j produced in period t_2 earn a higher rate of return in period t_2 than can be obtained by new transformations of resources into capital goods in period t_2.

Why is the excess rate of return, capital gain, or rent not eliminated by the production of units of capital type j – increasing the supply and reducing the price of capital type j services? In his discussion of rent, Pareto referred to obstacles which hinder or prevent the transformation of resources into new units of the rent-receiving capital type. From a superficial reading one might interpret 'obstacles' to mean technical or institutional barriers. Although such barriers are not inconsistent with this analysis, it is preferable to define 'obstacles' in the broader sense that Pareto intended; 'obstacles' is a synonym for 'costs'. In period t_2 the average cost of production of new units of capital type j, equal to the price P^2_{kj}, is an obstacle to the transformation of resources into new units of K_j. For any service price a_j^*, such that $\frac{a_j^*}{i^2} - P_{kj} > 0$, there is a tendency for more new units of capital type j to be produced. a_j^* cannot be an equilibrium price. The equilibrium price a^2_j fulfils the condition $\frac{a^2_j}{i^2} - P^2_{kj} = 0$. At this price for type j services an equilibrium quantity $\mathring{K}_j$ of new units is produced in period t_2; to transform resources into more than $\mathring{K}_j$ new units violates the no-loss condition of complete transformation. Production of more than $\mathring{K}_j$ units would cause the price of type j services to fall – making the present value of new units of capital type j less than P^2_{kj}.

If $a^2_j > a^1_j$, then a^2_j can be an equilibrium price for type j services only if $P^2_{kj} > P^1_{kj}$ (still assuming $i^1 = i^2$). The units of capital type j produced in period t_1 maintain their rent share because P^2_{kj} acts as an obstacle to the production of more than $\mathring{K}_j$ new units, i.e., it prevents the price of type j services from falling below a^2_j.

One should not assume from the above discussion that P_{kj} always changes in proportion to a_j. In the general equilibrium model P_{kj} and a_j are determined simultaneously along with all other prices and quantities in the system. But P_{kj} is directly related to the equilibrium prices and quantities of the factors technically required for the production of units of capital type j. Under equilibrium conditions a_j cannot rise in a greater proportion than P_{kj} (assuming i does not change). Any tendency for a_j to rise faster than P_{kj} is counteracted by additional transformations of resources into units of capital type j. But the change in P_{kj} may be proportionately greater than the change in a_j. In this case $\frac{a^2_j}{i^2} - P^2_{kj} < 0$, and no transformations of resources into capital type j occur in period t_2. In the new equilibrium position, P^2_{kj} constitutes an absolute obstacle to transformations and $\mathring{K}_j = 0$ in period t_2. At the same time, pre-existing units of capital type j may receive rent.

Rent and the interest rate

In the preceding discussion the interest rate was assumed to remain constant when the economic system moved to a new general equilibrium position. There is no reason why the interest rate should be unaffected by a change in general equilibrium conditions. To understand the relationship between rent and the interest rate, it is necessary to clarify the role of the interest rate in the general equilibrium model. The interest rate is influenced by the following requirements of general equilibrium:

$$S = \sum_{j=1}^{m} P_{kj}K_j \text{ and } i\mathring{K}_j = \frac{a_j}{P_{kj}} \mathring{K}_j \text{ for all } j = 1, 2, \ldots, m.$$

A given vector of consumable goods and factor prices implies a vector of quantities of consumable goods demanded. The complete transformation condition implies a vector of new units of capital goods ($\mathring{K}_j$, for all $j = 1, 2, \ldots, m$) which must be produced to make production of the consumable goods vector possible. Assume that $S < \sum_{j=1}^{m} P_{kj}\mathring{K}_j$, i.e., total savings available (S) are not sufficient to produce the required new units of capital goods. To attain equilibrium the prices of capital goods services must rise relative to the costs of production of capital goods. When this occurs the relationship $i\mathring{K}_j = \frac{a_j}{P_{kj}} K_j$ (for all $j = 1, 2, \ldots, m$) implies an increase in the rate of interest. The adjustment process has two effects: (1) more savings become available because of the flow of income from capital services rises relative to the cost of capital goods; and (2) the increased prices of capital goods services cause the quantities $\mathring{K}_j$ to be reduced as less capital-intensive methods are used in the production of consumable goods and as income is shifted from consumable goods demanded to savings. The interest rate may be interpreted as an index of the prices of all capital goods services relative to the prices of capital goods (which equal costs of production in equilibrium).

Consider a particular type of capital good, j. P^1_{kj} represents the value of the resources transformable into one unit of j in period t_1; a^1_j represents the price of type j services in period t_1; and i^1 represents the interest rate in period t_1. In period $t_1 \frac{a^1_j}{i^1} - P^1_{kj} = 0$. Assume that a change in general equilibrium conditions occurs so that the interest rate in period t_2 equilibrium is higher than i^1. Let $i^2 = 2i^1$. There are three possible cases.

Case 1. The equilibrium price of type j services is also doubled, i.e., $a^2_j = 2a^1_j$. No rent accrues to units of j produced in period t_1. $r = a^2_j - i^2 p^1_{kj} = 2a^1_j - 2i^1 P^1_{kj} = 2(a^1_j - i^1 P^1_{kj}) = 0$. In this case the rise in the price of type j services is equal to the rise in the general level of the prices of capital goods. The resources transformed into a unit of K_j in period t_1 acquire no income advantage in period t_2 by virtue of being embodied in capital type j rather than being available for transformation in period t_2.

Case 2. The equilibrium price of type j services is more than doubled, i.e., $a^2_j > 2a^1_j$. In period t_2 a positive rent accrues to units of j produced in period t_1, $r = a^2_j - i^2 P^1_{kj} > 2a^1_j - 2i^1 P^1_{kj} = 0$. Note that $P^2_{kj} > P^1_{kj}$.[5] By virtue of having been transformed into a unit of j in period t_1, a quantity of resources valued at P^1_{kj} yields an income which could only be obtained by a larger quantity in period t_2. Rent reflects the advantage which accrues to the capital owner for having transformed resources into j before the change in general equilibrium conditions.

Case 3. The price of type j services does not change, i.e., $a^2_j = a^1_j$. A negative rent accrues to units of type j produced in period t_1. $r = a^2_j - i^2 P^1_{kj} = a^1_j - 2i P^1_{kj} < 0$. The rise in the equilibrium interest rate indicates that the general level of prices of capital services has risen while the costs of production of capital goods (in general) has remained constant. The price (in numeraire) of type j services has remained constant. Therefore, the price of type j services in period t_2 is lower relative to the prices of other capital services than it was in period t_1. The demand for type j services evidently did not keep pace with the demand for other capital goods services when the economy moved from the t_1 equilibrium position to the t_2 equilibrium position. The negative rent accruing to type j units produced in t_1 indicates the disadvantage associated with having transformed resources into j in period t_1. The owner of a unit of j produced in period t_1 would have improved his position if he had either transformed the resources valued at P^1_{kj} into another type of capital in period t_1 or if he had waited until t_2 to engage in a transformation.

Changes in the interest rate produce a (positive) rent effect only if the increase in the general level of capital goods prices is proportionately greater than the increase in the rate of interest. As was demonstrated in note 5, this situation implies that the movement from one equilibrium position to another also causes the general level of capital goods costs to rise. The rent which accrues to units of capital goods produced in previous periods indicates an income advantage of the lower cost of production in the previous periods. (For negative rent, substitute 'decrease' for 'increase'.) If the costs of production of capital goods do not increase when the economy moves to a new equilibrium position, the proportionate increase in the price of capital services cannot exceed the proportionate increase in the interest rate. There is no rent effect, and the explanation is that the conditions of transformation (obstacles or costs) have not changed. No advantage is attached to the transformation of resources into capital in one period rather than another. Except for the case in which a general change in the level of capital in the level of capital costs accompanies the change in the interest rate, rent accruing units of a capital good type is associated with changes in capital goods costs and service prices relative to each other. These changes are associated with adjustment of the capital structure to altered conditions of general equilibrium.

Rent and the growth of factor supplies

As the economic system moves from one general equilibrium position to another, prices of capital services change relative to non-capital prices and relative to prices of other capital goods. These changes are associated with changes in the structure of the equilibrium capital goods vector and reflect the adjustment of the system to new general equilibrium conditions. When preferences shift in favour of some consumer goods and away from others, prices of the favoured goods tend to rise. The price rise is reflected in the market for factors of production and generates a movement of resources into production of the favoured goods. For capital goods, the shift involves a concentration of investment in those types of capital goods especially suited to production of the favoured consumer goods. The structure of the capital goods vector is changed to reflect the altered consumer preferences. The increasing supply of the favoured capital goods and of the consumer goods which they produce generates a counter-acting effect on prices until general equilibrium price and quantity vectors are established. The adjustment process also runs in the opposite direction. If there are obstacles which hinder the supply increasing response in the capital goods vector, the initial tendency for prices to rise will go unchecked (or at least partially unchecked). An increase in the cost of production (price) of a capital good constitutes an obstacle to the expansion of its supply. To the extent that the structure of the capital goods vector fails to be accommodated to the requirements of the new consumer preference pattern, the effect of rising prices will choke off demand for the favoured goods. The vector of consumer goods demanded will be accommodated to the capabilities of the existing structure of the capital goods vector.

Let K_j and K_k represent two types of capital goods which are used (along with other factors) in the production of certain types of consumable goods. In period t_1, $\frac{a^1_k}{i^1} - P_{kk} = 0$ and $\frac{a^1_j}{i^1} - P_{kj} = 0$. In Figure 12.1, it is

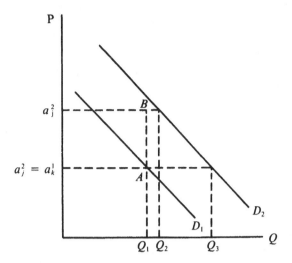

Figure 12.1

assumed that $a^1_k = a^1_j = P_1$ and the quantities $K_k = K_j = Q_1$ in t_1 equilibrium.

Assume that in period t_2 there is a change in general equilibrium conditions. In Figure 12.1 one aspect of this change is represented by a uniform increase in the demand for both K_j and K_k. The resulting tendency for service prices to rise generates an offsetting increase in the supplies of K_j and K_k. The supply increases are accomplished by means of new transformations of savings into units of K_j and K_k. The extent to which the tendency for capital service prices to rise can be offset by new transformations of resources is limited by the obstacle of cost of production. Assume that (1) the elementary factors L_1 and L_2 are used in the production of both K_j and K_k; and (2) the production functions for K_j and K_k differ in at least the following way: the elasticity of substitution for L_1 and L_2 is larger for the production of K_k than for the production of K_j. The assumption of $a^1_k = a^1_j$ in period t_1 contains within it the implicit assumption that $P^1_{kk} = P^1_{kj}$. (This is necessary for the equilibrium conditions to be fulfilled.) In period t_1 equilibrium the average cost of production of K_j is $P^1_{kj} = P^1_{L1}L^{j1}_1 + P^1_{L2}L^{j1}_2$, where P^1_{L1} is the price of a unit of factor L_1 in period t_1, P^1_{L2} is the price of a unit of factor L_2 in period t_1, L^{ji}_1 is the number of units of L_1 used in the production of one unit of j in period t_1. Similarly, $P^1_{kk} = P^1_{L1}L^{k1}_1 + P^1_{L2}L^{k1}_2$. Since $P_{kj} = P_{kk}$ in period t_1 equilibrium, then $L^{k1}_1 = L^{j1}_1$ and $L^{k1}_2 = L^{j1}_2$.

Assume that as a result of the change in general equilibrium conditions in period t_2, the price of factor L_1 rises, i.e., $P^2{}_{L1} > P^1{}_{L1}$ and $P^2{}_{L2} = P^1{}_{L2}$. Recall that the production coefficients ($L^j{}_1$, $L^j{}_2$, $L^k{}_1$, $L^k{}_2$) are not arbitrarily fixed in the general equilibrium; they are determined by cost minimization in the production of K_j and K_k. The increase in the price of L_1 results in the substitution of L_2 for L_1 in each production process. The changes in equilibrium average costs of production of K_j and K_k resulting from the increase in P_{L1} are indicated by

$$\frac{\delta P_{kj}}{\delta P_{L1}} dP_{L1} = L^j{}_1 dP_{L1} + P_{L1} \frac{\delta L^j{}_1}{\delta P_{L1}} dP_{L1} + P_{L2} \frac{\delta L^j{}_2}{\delta P_{L1}} \quad \text{and}$$

$$\frac{\delta P_{KK}}{\delta P_{L1}} dP_{L1} = L^k{}_1 dP_{L1} + P_{L1} \frac{\delta L^k{}_1}{\delta P_{L1}} dP_{L1} + P_{L2} \frac{\delta L^k{}_2}{\delta P_{L1}}.$$

The assumption that the elasticity of substitution is larger in the production of K_k than in the production of K_j implies that, for the given change in P_{L1}

$$\frac{\delta\left(\frac{L^j{}_1}{L^j{}_2}\right)}{\delta P_{L1}} dP_{L1} > \frac{\delta\left(\frac{L^k{}_1}{L^k{}_2}\right)}{\delta P_{L1}} dP_{L1}.$$

This relationship, combined with the assumption that $L^j{}_1 = L^k{}_1$ and $L^j{}_2 = L^k{}_2$ in the initial position (t_1), implies that either

$$\frac{\delta L^j{}_1}{\delta P_{L1}} dP_{L1} > \frac{\delta L^k{}_1}{\delta P_{L1}} dP_{L1}, \quad \text{or}$$

$$\frac{\delta L^j{}_2}{\delta P_{L1}} dP_{L1} < \frac{\delta L^k{}_2}{\delta P_{L1}} dP_{L1}, \quad \text{or both.}$$

The convexity of the production functions for K_j and K_k ensures

$$\frac{\delta L^j{}_1}{\delta P_{L1}} < 0 \text{ and } \frac{\delta L^j{}_2}{\delta P_{L2}} > 0. \quad \text{Therefore,} \frac{\delta P_{kj}}{\delta P_{L1}} dP_{L1} > \frac{\delta P_{kk}}{\delta P_{L1}} dP_{L1}.$$

The preceding discussion can be reduced to one simple statement: an increase in P_{L1} causes P_{kj} to rise more rapidly than P_{kk}. It has been assumed that in period t_1, $P^1{}_{kj} = P^1{}_{kk}$. Therefore, in period t_2, when P_{L1} rises, the equilibrium value of $P^2{}_{kj}$ is greater than the equilibrium value of $P^2{}_{kk}$. In Figure 12.1 it is assumed that $P^2{}_{kk} = P^1{}_{kk}$. An increase in the demand for K_k from D_1 to D_2 results in the transformation of resources into new units of K_k until the condition $\frac{a^2_k}{i} - P^2_{kk} = 0$ is met. Since $P^2_{kk} = P^1_{kk}$, then in equilibrium $a^2_k = a^1_k$ and the quantity of new units of K_k produced in period t_2 is $\overset{\circ}{K}_k = Q_3 - Q_1$. No rent accrues to units of K_k produced in period t_1. Figure 12.1 shows that the demand curve for K_j also moves to D_2 in period t_2. But because of the increase $(P^2_{kj} - P^1_{kj})$ in the cost of producing new units of K_j, the number of new units produced in period t_2 is only $\overset{\circ}{K}_j = Q_2 - Q_1$, and the equilibrium price of K_j services in period t_2 is $a^2_j > a^1_j$. In period t_2, units of K_j produced in period t_1 receive a rent of $r = a^2_j - iP^1_{kj} > 0$. This rent is indicated by the vertical distance AB in Figure 12.1.

The case described above provides a significant insight into the rent-generating process of economic change. A change in general equilibrium conditions raises the level of demand for a certain type of consumable good, C_x. This change results in increased level of demand for all of the factors requisite to the production of C_x. This induces an expansion of the quantities supplies of the affected types of capital goods, i.e. new transformations of savings. But the change in general equilibrium conditions may cause variations in the relative costs of production (prices) of capital goods. In consequence, the available quantities of types of capital goods used in the production of C_x expand at different rates. The prices of these capital *services* change relative to one another. For capital types with relatively slower rates of quantity increase, equilibrium service prices rise relative to the prices of other capital services used in the production of C_x. Rent accrues to those units of the slow growing capital which were produced at lower cost in earlier periods, i.e., produced in response to a different set of general equilibrium conditions.

Rent differences within a capital type

The rents received by units of a particular type of capital good may not be equal. The stock of a type of capital good existing at any time is the summation of quantities produced in a number of previous equilibrium positions. The relative rents received by different units of a capital type are explained in the following illustration.

In period of production t_1 there are no pre-existing units of capital good K_j. The interest rate is $i = 0.05$; the average cost of production of K_j is $P^1_{kj} = \$100$. In equilibrium, enough units of K_j must be produced to bring the price of K_j services to $a^1_j = \$5$. With $i = 0.05$, $P^1_{kj} = \$100$ and $a^1_j = \$5$, the equilibrium condition $\frac{a^1_j}{i} - P_{kj} = 0$ is fulfilled. Resources transformed into K_j earn a return equal to opportunity cost, i.e., the rate return (i) available from alternative transformations.

In period of production t_2 a new set of general equilibrium conditions becomes effective. Compared to the previous set of general equilibrium conditions, preferences have shifted in favour of those goods employing K_j in their production. Also the average cost of production of K_j rises to P_{kj} = \$120 in the new equilibrium position. The interest rate is unchanged; $i = 0.05$. The new equilibrium price is a^2_j = \$6. Units of K_j produced in period t_2 earn a rate of return on the value of resources transformed just equal to the interest rate, i.e., $\dfrac{a^2_j}{P^2_{kj}} = \dfrac{6}{120} = 0.05 = i$. Units of K_j utilized in period t_2 but produced in period t_1 receive a rent, $r = a^2_j - iP^1_{kj} = 6 -$ (0.05)(100) $= 6 - 5 = \$1$. An alternative expression is $R = \dfrac{a^2_j}{i} - P_{kj} =$ \$120 $-$ \$100 $=$ \$20 (the capital gain to owners of the units of K_j produced in t_1).

In period of production t_3 general equilibrium conditions change again. The average cost of production of k_j rises to P^3_{kj} = \$140; the interest rate remains at $i = 0.05$; and the new equilibrium price of K_j services is $P^3_{kj} =$ \$7. For new units of K_j produced in t_3 $\dfrac{a^3_j}{P^3_{kj}} = \dfrac{7}{140} = 0.05 = i$. Previously produced units of K_j receive rents. For those units produced in t_1 but still utilized in t_3 the rent received is $r = 7 - (0.05)(100) = 7 - 5 = \$2$. This rent is composed of two parts: the rent of \$1 associated with the movement from equilibrium position t_1 to t_2 and the rent of \$1 associated with the movement from t_2 to t_3. Each of these increments corresponds to what Pareto called *rent acquired*. Units of K_j produced in period t_2 also receive rent in period t_3. For these units $r = 7 - (0.05)(120) = 7 - 6 = \$1$.

In period t_4 general equilibrium conditions change in such a way that there is a uniform increase in the demand for all types of capital goods. The interest rate rises to $i = 0.10$. The price of K_j services rises to a^4_j = \$14 in the new equilibrium position, while the average cost of production of K_j remains constant, P^4_{kj} = \$140. For new units of K_j produced in period t_4, $\dfrac{a^4_j}{P^4_{kj}} = \dfrac{14}{140} = 0.10 = i$. Those units of K_j utilized in period t_4 which were produced in period t_1 receive rent of $r = 14 - (0.1)(100) = 14 - 10 = \$4$. This represents an additional \$2 rent as a result of the movement from t_3 to t_4. The \$2 *rent acquired* in period t_4 reflects the advantage gained by having transformed a given quantity of resources into capital goods in period t_1, when the costs of production were lower, rather than in period t_4. A unit of K_j produced in period t_2 receives rent of $r = 14 - (0.1)(120)$ $= \$2$. A unit of K_j produced in period t_3 receives no rent, i.e., $r = 14 - (0.1)(140) = 0$. This reflects the fact that \$140 worth of resources can also be transformed into a unit of K_j in period t_4. A capital owner who

Table 12.1   Relative rents by unit age

Period	Basic data			Total rent received by unit produced in					Rent acquired by unit produced in			
	P_{kj}	S_j	i	t_1	t_2	t_3	t_4	t_5	t_1	t_2	t_3	t_4
t_1	$5	$100	0.05	0	–	–	–	–	–	–	–	–
t_2	$6	$120	0.05	1	0	–	–	–	1	–	–	–
t_3	$7	$140	0.05	2	1	0	–	–	1	1	–	–
t_4	$14	$140	0.10	4	2	0	0	–	2	1	0	–
t_5	$16	$160	0.10	6	4	2	2	0	2	2	2	2

transformed resources into K_j in period t_3 acquired no advantage over an individual with resources available for transformation in period t_4.

In period t_5 general equilibrium conditions change in such a way that the price of K_j services rises to $a^5_j = \$16$ in the new equilibrium position; the average cost of production of K_j rises to $P^5_{kj} = \$160$; the interest rate remains at $i = 0.10$. Those units of K_j utilized in period t_5 which were produced in period t_1 receive rent of $r = 16 - (0.1)(100) = \$6$; those units of K_j produced in period t_2 receive rent of $r = 16 - (0.10)(120) = \$4$; those units of K_j produced in either t_3 or t_4 receive rent of $r = 16 - (0.1)(140) = \$2$. The results of these changes in general equilibrium conditions from period t_1 to period t_5 are summarized in Table 12.1.

Land rent
Historically, the theory of rent originated with the investigation of land values. It may seem paradoxical that in this clarification of rent theory land has been ignored. The discussion of rent in this paper has focused on produced capital goods in order to emphasize the relationship between rent and the process of economic change.

Having developed the basic concepts and tools of analysis, land rent can easily be explained as a special case of the general rent phenomenon. As usually described, land differs from capital goods in two respects: (1) the cost of production of the existing units of unimproved land in any period of production is zero; but (2) the total quantity of land available is fixed and cannot be (significantly) increased at any (reasonable) price. Employing the rent definition developed above, $r_{L2} = P_{L2} - 0 = P_{L2}$. Any price greater than zero received for the services of a unit of land constitutes a rent. Assuming that all land is homogeneous and can be employed in production without improvement or modification, then as long as there is a surplus of land, the price of its services is zero. Any change in general equilibrium conditions which increases the demand for land services elicits a proportionate supply response. When the surplus of land is exhausted an increase in the demand for land services elicits a zero supply response; the full effect of the change in demand is translated into a positive price of land services. The price of land services affects quantity demanded so that the equilibrium position of the economy is kept within the production capabilities of the limited quantity of land.

If land must be modified or improved before entering the production process, it is actually a specialized produced factor. Improved land is not essentially different from other capital goods. It has a cost of production determined by the prices of unimproved land, labour, and other capital goods, and the quantities of unimproved land, labour, and other capital goods used to produce each specialized type of improved land. The rent of improved land needs no explanation beyond that given for the rent of capital goods generally.

Heterogeneous lands (including both quality and location differences) fit into the framework already developed if the total stock of land is conceived of as being divided into a number of specialized types of unimproved land. In any productive process the different types of land may be substitutable to some degree, just as labour and capital goods are substitutable for each other and for land. In equilibrium the relative prices of land types reflect their relative marginal productivities. Positive prices for the services of any types of unimproved land constitute rent and reflect the relative scarcity of unimproved land of that type. It is not necessary to modify the rent concept to exclude the rents that could be received from alternative uses of a particular unit. The conundrum of alternative uses, which has confounded economists since the time of J.S. Mill (1857, Vol. II, p. 506), is based on an attempt to separate necessary and unnecessary costs and to achieve a partial equilibrium understanding of a general equilibrium phenomenon. The concept of unnecessary costs has no relevance to general equilibrium. All incomes and payments are mutually determined and in that sense, are equally necessary.

Labour and rent
The concept of rent developed here generally should not be applied to the analysis of labour supply and income. The primary reason for this is that the cost of production of labour cannot be expressed in the same concrete way as the costs of production of capital goods; nor can the supply of labour be conceived of as fixed and imperishable as in the case of land. The obstacles which limit variations in the supply of labour – in general and for specialized types – are embedded in the preference structures of the individual economic units. The concepts of limitativeness and limita-

tionality may be usefully applied to labour problems (Tarascio and Finkel, 1971) in a manner similar to the application to capital and land in this paper. But the fundamental difference between capital costs and labour costs makes the concept of rent inapplicable.

Summary
Rent may be measured in any of three equivalent ways:

1. as a flow of income, $r = a_j - iP_{kj}$,
2. as a change in the present value of transformed savings,

$$R = \frac{a_j}{i} - P_{kj}, \text{ or}$$

3. as a net rate of return,

$$\rho = \frac{a_j}{P_{kj}} - i.$$

Conclusion
Pareto's conception of rent is similar to Ricardo's in that it is a scarcity-related concept, and similar to Marshall's conception in that Pareto included capital goods in his discussion of rent. However, unlike Marshall, he did not limit his discussion of rent to 'quasi-rent of capital goods on the assumption of lengthy time adjustments' alone. Instead he used a broader concept, 'obstacles to transformations', which encompassed not only Marshallian time limitations, but also natural limitations (Ricardo), technological limitations, cost limitations and savings limitations. In other words, Pareto's approach to rent theory was much more general than that of his predecessors, contemporaries and later modern writers.

In this study a general definition of rent was developed based on Pareto's discussion. Rent was described as the result of unresponsiveness of factor supplies to changes in demand conditions. Rent was defined $r = a - iP$, where r is rent, a is the current price of the factor's services, i is the current interest rate, and P is the original value of the resources transformed into the factor. In the case of land, $P = 0$. The total income to land may be defined as rent. However, the application of this definition of rent extends beyond the land case. This definition of rent is applicable to the study of all capital goods. This definition of rent avoids the ambiguities imposed by the existence of alternative uses for a factor. Also, the question of whether or not rent is a real cost, which has plagued most rent discussions, need not arise.

Finally, by following Pareto's insights and examining the rent process in a rigorous manner, we have elucidated the relationship between rent and the interest rate (and the general level of capital goods), rent and the growth of factor supplies (and the structure of capital), and rent differences within a capital type, or to use Pareto's term, 'rent acquired', in addition to land rent normally associated with rent theory.

Notes

1. See Bird and Tarascio for a clarification regarding the modern conception of 'Paretian' rent. For contributors to the discussion of 'Paretian' rent see: Worcester (1946), Wessel (1967), Shepard (1970) and Formby (1972).
2. The treatment of heterogeneous labour will not be examined in depth since the emphasis in this paper is on capital. For a more detailed analysis of heterogeneous labour see Tarascio and Finkel (1971).
3. For a rigorous statement of limitativeness see Georgescu-Roegen (1966), p. 341.
4. The quantities $\bar{L}_1$ and $\bar{L}_2$ in vector (2) are the equilibrium quantities of elementary factors which are used directly in the production of consumption goods. The quantities L_1 and L_2 in vector (1) include $\bar{L}_1$ and $\bar{L}_2$ as well as $\hat{L}_1$ and $\hat{L}_2$: The quantities of elementary factors required to produce the equilibrium quantities of capital goods.
5. The equilibrium condition $i^2 \hat{K}_j = \frac{a^2_j}{P^2_{kj}} \hat{K}_j$ may be rewritten as $i^2 \geq \frac{a^2_j}{P^2_{kj}}$ with equality if $\hat{K}_j > $

   0. Since $i^2 = 2i^1$ and $a^2_j > 2a^1_j$, then by substitution $2i^1 > \frac{2a^1_j}{P^2_{kj}}$ or $i^1 > \frac{a^1_j}{P^2_{kj}}$ but (from period

   t_1 equilibrium conditions) $i^1 = \frac{a^1_j}{P^1_{kj}}$. Therefore, $P^2_{kj} > P^1_{kj}$.

References

Bird, Ronald and Tarascio, Vincent, J. (1990), 'Paretian Rent Theory Versus Pareto's Rent Theory: a Clarification and Correction', *History of Political Economy*, forthcoming.

Formby, John P. (1972), 'A Clarification of Rent Theory', *Southern Economic Journal*, **38** (January), pp. 315–24.

Georgescu-Roegen, Nicholas (1966), *Analytical Economics: Issues and Problems*, Cambridge, MA: Harvard University Press.

Marshall, Alfred (1961), *Principles of Economics*, ed. C. W. Guillebaud, 9th edn, 2 vols, London: Macmillan for the Royal Economic Society (8th edn published in 1920).

Mill, John Stuart (1857), *Principles of Political Economy*, 4th edn, 2 vols, London: John W. Parker & Son.

Pareto, Vilfredo (1961), *Cours d'économie politique*, Paris: Librarie Droz (first published 1897).

Pareto, Vilfredo (1971), *Manual of Political Economy*, ed. Alfred N. Page, trans. Ann S. Schwier, New York: Augustus M. Kelley (first published 1909).

Ricardo, David (1971), *Principles of Political Economy*, ed. R. M. Hartwell (Pelican Classics edn), Baltimore, MD: Penguin Books (first published 1817).

Shepard, A. R. (1970), 'Economic Rent and the Industry Supply Curve', *Southern Economic Journal*, **37** (October), pp. 209–11.

Tarascio, Vincent J. and Finkel, Sidney R. (1971), *Wage and Employment Theory*, New York: Ronald Press.

Wessel, R. H. (1967), 'A Note on Economic Rent', *American Economic Review*, **57** (December), pp. 1221–6.

Worcester, Dean A. (1946), 'A Reconsideration of the Theory of Rent', *American Economic Journal*, **36** (June), pp. 258–77.

13 Keynes on saving, hoarding and finance*
Hansjoerg Klausinger

1. Introduction

In his well-known distinction between 'vision' and 'technique' Schumpeter considered Keynes's work as an excellent example of the overriding importance of the former (cf. Schumpeter, 1952, p. 268; 1954, p. 1171). According to Schumpeter, Keynes's vision is one of stagnation shaped by the conditions of interwar Britain[1] as an 'arteriosclerotic economy whose opportunities for rejuvenating venture decline while the old habits of saving formed in times of plentiful opportunities persist' (Schumpeter, 1954). Therefore not lack but excess of saving must be feared most, and the crucial and possibly damaging feature of the capitalist economy seemingly consists in its failure to coordinate saving with investment.

Consequently, the analysis of the saving-investment process lies at the core of Keynes's major works, the *Treatise on Money* (1930) and the *General Theory* (1936).[2] In both works the lack of an automatic mechanism for transforming additional saving into investment gives rise to processes of price deflation and output contraction, respectively. With regard to the traditional view the question remained to be answered why this coordinating function was not fulfilled by market forces, especially by the rate of interest. This was the main subject of much heated controversy following the publication of both works.

The following study attempts to review both these controversies and especially to highlight Keynes's contributions to it. The next section deals with the critical evaluation of the *Treatise* in the debate on saving and hoarding primarily initiated by Robertson. The third section gives a short sketch of liquidity preference theory, as put forward in the *General Theory*, and the ensuing controversy with adherents to the loanable funds approach. Here Keynes's contribution as regards the so-called 'finance motive' is of central concern. In the concluding section the results are summarized and evaluated from a methodological point of view.

2. The *Treatise on Money*: saving and hoarding

In Keynes's *Treatise on Money* the traditional Cambridge approach to the quantity theory of money is criticized on two accounts, namely that it is ill suited to analysing dynamic adjustments as causal processes and, furthermore, that it illegitimately ignores other motives for holding cash than those directly related to transactions (cf. *TM*, pp. 120 and 198ff.). Keynes's alternative approach attempts not only to correct these analytical deficiencies but also to demonstrate that – in accordance with what was called before his 'vision' – a monetary economy typically lacks an automatic mechanism for balancing saving and investment.

Saving and investment – the independence of price levels

In the following I shall concentrate on instantaneous effects. The analytical means for dealing with them is provided by the famous 'fundamental equations'.[3] They refer to an economy divided into two sectors (for convenience called C- and I-industries) producing consumption and investment goods, where in the very short run outputs of both industries are assumed to be fixed. To each output level corresponds a 'cost of production' paid to households as their 'money income' or 'earnings of factors of production' (*TM*, p. 111); it is defined as including the 'normal remuneration of entrepreneurs' while profits and losses are not counted as income (ibid.). In equilibrium in each sector actual sale proceeds equal cost of production, since in this case entrepreneurs have no incentive 'to increase or decrease their scale of operation' (*TM*, p. 112). Outside equilibrium differences between proceeds and costs create profits or losses[4] by which entrepreneurs are induced to adjust output levels accordingly.

The above relations are transformed by the fundamental equations into those between saving and investment.[5] Hence windfalls accruing to the C-industry correspond to the difference between the cost of production of investment (in the I-industry) and saving, and evidently windfalls in the I-industry equal the difference between the value and cost of its output. So, for cost of production given, the price level of consumption goods is determined by the amount of saving, i.e. the 'excess saving factor', whereas the price level of investment goods is governed by the so-called 'excess bearish factor' (*TM*, p. 130). This establishes a main thesis of the *Treatise*, namely 'that the price level of consumption goods is entirely independent of the price level of investment goods' (*TM*, p. 123) and vice versa.

Consequently, 'a fall in the price of consumption goods due to an excess of saving over investment does not in itself ... require any opposite change in the price of new investment goods' (*TM*, p. 130ff). In the traditional view[6] by lowering the interest rate saving should induce an intertemporal restructuring of the production process, shifting resources from consumption goods to investment goods production. Yet, according to the *Treatise*, an increase in saving only causes a shortage of demand for consumption goods bringing about windfall losses in that industry. As there are no windfall gains in the I-industry capable of counteracting losses in the C-industry or of redirecting resources to the I-industry, on aggregate losses exert their influence on production and, thereby, initiate a deflationary process.

This is true because 'the price level of investment goods . . . depends on a different set of considerations' (*TM*, p. 121), that is on the state of bearishness. In the most highly aggregated version of the financial sector Keynes distinguishes neither between newly produced investment goods and the existing stock of capital (*TM*, p. 128ff.) nor between physical capital goods and the securities by which they are represented. (*TM*, p. 222).[7] Rather all these assets are referred to as 'securities'. Then the demand for securities is analysed by Keynes in the spirit of portfolio theory, i.e. as a decision of what proportion of the existing stock of wealth to hold in the form of securities (*TM*, p. 127).[8] Thus their price is determined by the equilibrium condition for the market for securities as a market for stocks.

As the alternative to holding securities is holding money (in the form of bank deposits) the above result can equivalently be looked at from the perspective of the market for deposits. Deposits are exogenously supplied by the banks.[9] The demand for deposits can roughly be divided into industrial and financial circulation (*TM*, p. 217; cf. also p. 39ff.). Industrial circulation refers, as in the traditional approach, to transactions purposes and is directed towards cash deposits. On the other hand, financial circulation as characterized by the 'excess bearish factor' is a demand for holding money as an asset[10] and it is commonly directed towards savings deposits. Later on, Keynes denoted this desire to hold deposits for portfolio reasons as the 'propensity to hoard' (Keynes, 1931a, p. 413). As the 'distaste for other securities is not absolute and depends on [the] expectations of the future return to be obtained from savings deposits and from securities respectively, which is obviously affected by the price of the latter' (*TM*, p. 127ff.), this propensity gives rise to a 'demand curve for liquid assets', which increases with the price of non-liquid assets (Keynes, 1931a, p. 413). Again the equilibrium price of securities is determined by the condition that the propensity to hoard just absorbs the existing supply of savings deposits which in turn is given by the total quantity of deposits minus the requirements of industrial circulation (see *TM*, p. 132).

Now a change in bearishness (i.e. a shift in the propensity to hoard) will affect only the price of investment goods, i.e. securities, directly,[11] so that – in analogy to what has been said about saving – there is no immediate compensation for windfalls accruing to the I-industry.

Robertson's critique: saving and hoarding
The proposition that changes of saving or investment typically result in a divergence that causes inflationary or deflationary processes was central to the critical discussion of the *Treatise*. The most persistent critique was that of Robertson.[12] He took the traditional Cambridge approach as his starting point and argued that *both* price levels should be analysed by means of flow concepts, i.e. as 'a certain flow of money ... meeting a certain flow of goods in the same time-interval' (Robertson, 1931, p. 401). In his view an increase in saving just means switching some expenditure from consumption to the purchase of securities (ibid., p. 400ff.) so that there cannot be a deflationary effect in the aggregate. Rather the two price levels should move, as Keynes (1931a, p. 414) disapprovingly put it, like 'buckets in a well'.

According to Robertson an increase in saving produces a deflationary effect only when some part of it is hoarded (Robertson, 1931, p. 400), e.g. on its way from households to the capital market. In fact, 'previous writers ... have recognized the possibilities of savings running to waste in a general fall of prices' (ibid., p. 401), yet this should not be considered a necessary consequence of saving but of hoarding.[13] Besides, it is interesting to note that following this tradition Robertson links the possible coordination failure of wasted (or forced) savings to the monetary organization of the saving-investment process.[14]

Unfortunately, as regards clarity of exposition Robertson's definitions of hoarding are found wanting. In his critique of the Treatise 'hoarding' is implicitly defined as 'holding back unspent part of a stream of money which is normally spent' (ibid., p. 400); then in another attempt to clarify the concepts of saving and hoarding 'a man is said to be *hoarding*, if he takes steps to raise the proportion ... between his money stock and his disposable income' (Robertson, 1933, p. 67). Taken literally, this would mean that passively accepting an unchanged cash balance despite a lower income should not be considered as hoarding as long as the person in question has not actively taken steps.[15] As in effect Robertson does count such variations as hoarding (cf. ibid., p. 71), his somewhat clumsy formulation is probably intended to point out that hoarding refers to plans and not to realized behaviour. Indeed, some of Keynes's misinterpretations of this concept are obviously rooted in such a persistent confusion of planned and realized magnitudes. For instance, it is erroneous to identify hoarding as 'an increase of inactive [i.e. savings] deposits' (Keynes, 1931a, p. 416). For hoarding refers to a planned increase in cash holdings, whereas – according to the framework of the *Treatise* – the realized amount of savings deposits is governed by supply decisions of the banking system.

Yet although this terminological confusion, which continued through-out the whole debate, contributed to an omnipresence of communication failures, Robertson's critique was also answered by substantive arguments. To those I shall now turn.

Keynes's counter-critique: windfall effects, stocks and speculation

Keynes's main argument refers to the portfolio effects of windfall losses in the C-industry following an increase in saving.[16] The argument is already present in the *Treatise* (*TM*, p. 156) and is repeated in the reply to Robertson. Accordingly in a first stage following an increase in saving, it 'must necessarily be that the savers find themselves with more [*sic!*] money, and the losers themselves with less money' (Keynes, 1931a, p. 417).[17] Then the losers, i.e. the producers of consumption goods, finance their losses by selling securities, while the savers purchase securities of the same amount so that *ceteris paribus* the price level of securities is left unchanged (ibid.). Looking at the same sequence of events, Robertson recognizes a special type of hoarding, namely 'secondary hoarding' caused by 'distress sales' (Robertson, 1933, p. 77). The relation between cash balances and earnings increases when entrepreneurs in the C-industry fail to adjust their holdings of cash to the decrease in actual earnings. If they had done so, this would have created an excess demand for securities and in turn security prices would have risen.

This in turn may be looked at from the perspective of the market for deposits. Then, according to Robertson, there must be an indirect effect running from lower prices of consumption goods to a decrease in industrial circulation and to an increase in the amount of savings deposits, assuming an unchanged total supply of deposits (cf. Keynes, 1931a, p. 414). With a given propensity to hoard security prices rise. Yet this argument is rejected by Keynes, since this reaction 'is likely ... to be negligible and to belong to the class of the innumerable small' (ibid.).[18]

On this occasion, Keynes is even ready to eliminate any possibility of such a reaction by pointing out that in the *Treatise* he 'was assuming that the quantity of hoards [i.e. savings deposits] was unchanged' (ibid., p. 415). Be that as it may,[19] this calls attention to the vital role played by the banking system in regulating the supply of deposits. In the *Treatise* the supply behaviour of banks is not analysed explicitly (cf. *TM*, pp. 128, 224). The most sensible interpretation as suggested by Miller (1984; 1985) seems to be that Keynes followed contemporary British banking conventions in stipulating equal reserve ratios for cash and savings deposits. Using a money multiplier to derive the supply of deposits (as Keynes did in the *Treatise*, cf. p. 20ff.) leads to a fixed supply of deposits irrespective of its composition between cash and savings deposits. From this the above results follow.

Probably as a consequence of Keynes's confusion between hoarding and the stock of savings deposits he, moreover, falls victim to another misunderstanding. It relates to his identification of a neutral monetary policy (or neutral behaviour of the banking system) as one that keeps 'the excess of the total deposits over the active deposits at a constant rate' (Keynes, 1931a, p. 416).[20] Yet, of course, this is not what neutrality would amount to. Rather such a policy would try to adjust the supply of deposits to fluctuations in financial circulation by providing additional deposits for planned increases of hoards, thereby sheltering industrial circulation from such disturbances.[21] Incidentally, this resembles the kind of banking reform suggested by Keynes (*TM*, II, p. 11ff.), namely to reduce the reserve requirements for saving deposits relative to cash deposits.

After this detour, another Keynesian type of argument will be analysed which would come into play only as a kind of last resort if – for some reason – an increase of saving generated an excess demand for securities despite the need of entrepreneurs to finance their losses.[22] The argument pertains to the fact that the price of securities is determined by evaluating the whole securities stock, relative to which the flow of savings (if any) coming to the market is just a 'trifling proportion' (*TM*, p. 127; cf. also Keynes, 1931a, p. 417ff). Yet this is not sufficient in itself. For saving represents an increase in wealth to be possibly held in the form of securities and, analogously, any increase in the price of securities is just sufficient to enable their owners to hold the existing stock at higher prices. So possibly 'tails may wag dogs', i.e. an additional flow demand for securities may raise the price of stocks to the full amount necessary to compensate for windfall losses. Although Keynes is, of course, correct when pointing to the positively sloping curve of the propensity to hoard, which makes full compensation of windfall losses impossible, the above argument does not constitute an additional reason for such a positive slope.

Some factors that make for a positive slope are already mentioned in the *Treatise* (see p. 31ff.). In an ingenious contribution Robinson (1933) adds another one: the existence of price-stabilizing speculation. Anticipating what was later to become the speculative motive such price-stabilizing behaviour is explained by rigid expectations.[23] This rigidity is considered an essential feature of a speculative security market as otherwise no securities would be traded and their price would fluctuate wildly (ibid., p. 79).[24] Taking such price-stabilizing behaviour for granted, speculators stand ready to absorb any excess demand for securities by exchanging old securities for cash (ibid., p. 78ff). Again there will be no windfall profits in the I-industry following an increase in saving.

Yet it has to be kept in mind that according to Keynes's own dictum the propensity to hoard is *not* absolute. Therefore the amount of new saving would not be completely absorbed by speculation. Nevertheless, the absorption of only part of it suffices to establish Keynes's proposition at least qualitatively so that, as an increase in saving is not transformed into an equal amount of investment, some deflationary pressure still remains. This is evident from the fact that on the one hand if saving raises the price of securities this will increase financial circulation, and that on the other full compensation of windfall losses will leave industrial circulation unchanged. Jointly this is incompatible with a constant supply of deposits.[25]

Whereas Keynes could never be convinced that his arguments might be invalid, Robertson (1983) finally conceded the logic of the above-mentioned result. His concession is reflected by just another amendment in terminology. Now he denotes by propensity to hoard the curve linking the demand for savings deposits to the rate of interest, and by hoarding a point on this curve. Therefore an increase in saving is eventually said to lead to a movement along this curve so that 'there is . . . an increase in hoarding . . . tho the propensity to hoard is unchanged' (ibid., p. 114n.).

Summarizing the debate, the substantive issue of the deflationary effect of saving seems to have been settled as follows: Keynes's original thesis of the *Treatise* – that an increase in saving causes windfall losses in the C-industry which are not compensated at all by a rising price level of investment goods – is only valid in a special case. This special case implies that the whole amount of losses is financed by selling securities or, alternatively, that for some reason the propensity to hoard is absolute. Otherwise there is some compensation from windfall profits in the I-industry, yet this compensation is not complete even if all windfall losses are financed by a reduction in cash balances. So qualitatively Keynes's thesis cannot be refuted. From a methodological point of view it must be noted that Robertson persistently stayed within a flow-of-funds framework which Keynes also used when characterizing saving as a demand and the financing of losses as a supply of securities.[26] However, apart from this argument, Keynes preferred to determine the price of securities by a stock or portfolio approach – either by considering the market for securities or that for deposits.

3.   The *General Theory* and after: saving and finance

The debate on saving and hoarding as reviewed above was revived, if it ever had subsided, by Keynes's *General Theory*. This revival led to the well-known liquidity preference versus loanable funds controversy.[27] Keynes's own contributions to this controversy, especially those dealing with the finance demand for money, are the subject of this section.[28]

The liquidity preference theory of interest determination

Keynes's liquidity preference theory characterizes the interest rate as 'a *monetary* phenomenon' (Keynes, 1937b, p. 245). This contrasts sharply with the 'classical theory of the rate of interest' (*GT*, ch. 14, especially p. 182ff.) according to which the rate of interest is determined by the equality of saving and investment. Thereby, interest reflects only real factors such as time preference and time productivity. In this regard, the classical theory presupposes a state of inessential or neutral money so that theorems derived from (an ideal type of) a real exchange economy can also be applied to a monetary economy.[29] The 'criterion for classicality should be', therefore, 'abstraction . . . from the misbehaviour of money' (Robertson, 1937, p. 435), or 'monetary stability' (Ohlin, 1944, p. 119). As Keynes readily acknowledges, this classical view is *not* implied by the loanable funds approach (cf. *GT*, p. 183; Keynes, 1937b, p. 242n.).

Turning to the *General Theory* there are some striking similarities between liquidity preference theory and the theory expounded in the *Treatise*, on some accounts liquidity preference looking like a mere translation in new terminology. So the direct effect of the propensity to consume (i.e. in the *Treatise* the excess saving factor) is on income (i.e. the price of consumption goods), while there is no effect on the rate of interest (i.e. the price of securities); the latter is in turn determined solely by liquidity preference (i.e. the propensity to hoard) given a constant quantity of money (see *GT*, p. 245ff.).

Of course, the differences are also well known. First, in the *General Theory* there is an explicit role for output adjustment in generating (short-period) equilibrium (cf. Patinkin, 1982, pt. 1) so that a maladjustment of investment to an increase in saving causes a contraction of output. Secondly, physical capital goods are now distinguished analytically from securities such as bonds so that the marginal efficiency of capital becomes a separate entity besides the rate of interest – in consequence fluctuations of marginal efficiency need no longer affect the interest rate directly. Finally, a new terminology is introduced, e.g. by defining saving in a way that makes it always equal to investment;[30] therefore saving in this sense (to be distinguished from the propensity to save) cannot be considered an exogenous ('independent') variable – and an expression like that of 'ex ante saving' becomes devoid of meaning.[31]

Now, changes in saving and investment affect the rate of interest in short-period equilibrium if only as 'repercussions' (*GT*, p. 249). The mechanism by which such repercussions work themselves out is clearly stated (ibid., p. 248ff. and Keynes, 1937a, p. 118). The change in income as determined by the multiplier *ceteris paribus* influences liquidity preference via the transactions demand for cash and, thereby, induces a change in the rate of interest.[32]

Yet the controversial aspect of liquidity preference theory relates again to instantaneous effects. Since the rate of interest depends only on liquidity preference (for convenience the quantity of money is taken as given) fluctuations in saving and investment cannot generate interest rate effects unless income has changed. Therefore, when output is fixed the interest rate is insulated from such shifts. Of course, the thesis that the interest rate depends only on liquidity preference is to some extent tautological, i.e. immune to refutation, if liquidity preference is interpreted with sufficient care.[33] Anyway, the decisive issue is, then, *whether* changes in saving and investment are associated with changes in liquidity preference. It is this substantive question which the following addresses. Moreover, it must be noted that by the adoption of liquidity preference theory Keynes abandons the alternative approach of the *Treatise*, namely interest determination by demand and supply for the stock of securities, in favour of an exclusive money market approach; loanable funds theory, which utilizes flow demand and supply for credit (or securities, respectively), is, of course, rejected outright.

Explicit formulations of the loanable funds approach are to be found, for example, in Robertson (1983, p. 107ff; and especially 1940, p. 2ff.) and Ohlin (1944, p. 111ff.).[34] It differs from the classical approach in not identifying investment and saving with demand and supply of loanable funds but additionally taking into account monetary factors such as hoarding and changes in the money supply. Yet, as investment and saving are still component parts of demand and supply for loanable funds, they will *prima facie* influence the interest rate instantaneously. This result is in obvious opposition to liquidity preference. However, from a methodological point of view adherents to the loanable funds approach do not see it, like Keynes (1937b, p. 241), as 'radically opposed' to liquidity preference but consider them 'alternative methods of procedure . . . either, if carried through consistently, will give the same result as the other' (Robertson, 1938a, p. 317; cf. also 1937, p. 432). From a modern, i.e. general equilibrium, point of view this consistency requirement amounts to a careful specification of budget restraints.[35]

Introducing the finance demand for money
In the following Keynes's reaction to the loanable funds critique will be dealt with (cf. Keynes, 1937b; 1937c; 1938; Ohlin, 1937; Hawtrey, 1937; Robertson, 1937; 1938a; 1938b; 1940, ch. 1; Lerner, 1938; Robinson, 1938). While firmly defending the correctness of the liquidity preference

approach Keynes offers to complement it with another motive for holding cash, namely the 'finance motive'. It is 'due to the fact . . . that an investment decision . . . may sometimes involve a temporary demand for money before it is carried out' (Keynes, 1937b, p. 246), or put differently 'due to the time-lag between the inception and the execution of the entrepreneurs' decisions' (Keynes, 1938, p. 319). Such a finance demand increases liquidity preference and, therefore, raises the rate of interest. In this way an increase in investment may directly influence the interest rate; yet it is not true that an increase in saving is capable of eliminating pressure on the rate of interest: 'The investment market can become congested through shortage of cash. It can never become congested through shortage of saving' (Keynes, 1937c, p. 669). And 'in fact . . . it can only be relieved by an increase of cash' (Keynes, 1938, p. 321).[36]

The finance motive is said to be effective only 'during the interregnum . . . between the date when the entrepreneur arranges his finance and the date when he actually makes his investment' (Keynes, 1937c, p. 665). Specifically, it is generated by 'the transition from a lower to higher scale of activity' (ibid., p. 668; cf. also 1938, p. 319). After this transition is completed finance demand vanishes. When the entrepreneurs execute their decisions, the amount of cash held for finance reasons re-enters the regular circulation of income adequately described by transactions demand. If activity is permanently carried on at a higher scale, liquidity preference will, of course, not fall back to the original level; yet increased liquidity preference is now 'due to the time-lags between the receipt and the disposal of income by the public and also between the receipt by entrepreneurs of their sale-proceeds and the payment by them of wages, etc.' (Keynes, 1938, p. 319). This is just the repercussion effect of investment on liquidity preference and the rate of interest in short-period equilibrium already referred to.

So when Keynes characterizes finance as 'essentially a revolving fund . . . [which is] necessarily "self-liquidating" for the community taken as a whole at the end of the interim period' (1937c, p. 666), he may simply refer to the regular circulation of income which provides for stationary reproduction. Thereby, output decisions based on expectations determine the flow of income from firms to households (and entrepreneurs); in turn expenditure flows are directed towards firms which in stationary conditions would just provide for the finance needed for starting another round of production. Given long-term expectations, this is the situation of short-period equilibrium. If it is disturbed, for example by the decision of firms to increase output or of households to increase expenditure, an additional demand for cash is generated by financial requirements.

Problems of interpretation: liquidation of finance and asymmetry
Yet two problems of interpretation remain. The first one is revealed by
Robertson's (1938a, p. 315) question by what decisions of the entrepreneurs the liquidation of finance is brought about. The textual evidence
permits, in my view, two answers. First, finance may be required for
expenditure so that for example the finance demand for consumption
expenditure is exercised by households; or, secondly, finance may be
required for production so that for example the finance demand for
production of consumer goods is exercised by entrepreneurs.[37] Indeed, it
seems as if Keynes had not been aware of the possibility that these two
versions might constitute alternatives.[38] And, in fact, they coincide if, after
the interim period where finance demand is effective, only the position of
short-period equilibrium is considered, skipping the multiplier process
lying in between.[39]

Another crucial question is whether the finance motive applies symme-
trically to investment and consumption. If it were so, a planned increase in
investment should have the same effect as a planned increase or (with a
negative sign) a decrease in consumption. As the latter is equivalent to
what loanable funds theory describes as an increase in thrift its position
would be vindicated by the symmetry thesis.[40] Yet this latter step was not
accepted by Keynes. Whereas in some places (see note 37) he extended his
argument from investment to consumption he always rejected interest rate
effects of saving.

Now the first version of finance as proposed above will be studied.
According to it, between the planning and the execution of an expenditure
decision finance must be secured (presumably by selling securities) for a
temporary increase of cash balances. With the amount of cash eventually
expended the original level of cash balances is restored. Following Keynes
there is an asymmetry, as additional investment requires finance whereas
additional saving, i.e. a planned decrease of consumption expenditure,
does not generate a supply of finance by lowering liquidity preference. For
savers 'most undoubtedly do not, as a rule, deplete their existing cash well
ahead of their receiving the incomes out of which they propose to save'
(Keynes, 1937c, p. 664)[41] – in contrast to what the symmetry thesis would
imply.

However, the asymmetry proposed by Keynes may lend itself to an
internally consistent reconstruction. Leaving the framework of the
General Theory and anticipating contributions to the microfoundations of
the demand for money by, for example, Baumol (1952), Tobin (1956) and
Clower (1984), transactions costs are taken into account. Then the fact
might become important that probably investment exhibits greater lumpi-
ness than consumption, i.e. on average the relation of a single investment

project to available cash balances exceeds that of a single purchase of consumption goods.[42] If expenditure is constrained by finance, so that the execution of an expenditure decision presupposes disposition over cash, such a demand for finance can be expected with good reason to be more important for investment than consumption.

This argument is strengthened when transactions costs for switching between cash and securities are fixed. Then it may be optimal to desynchronize expenditure decisions from portfolio decisions, especially when the amount by which e.g. consumption fluctuates is minor. In such cases money plays the role of a financial buffer.[43] Fluctuations of expenditure are thereby absorbed by cash holdings diverging temporarily from their target demand – so that no finance demand emerges. Therefore Keynes's asymmetry thesis when applied to saving (and perhaps consumption) may appear as a theoretical possibility.

There remains the second version of finance demand. From an exegetical point of view this version is most convincing as an interpretation of what Keynes said about *ex ante* consumption (cf. Keynes, 1937c, p. 667ff.).[44] Thereby, finance demand arises from entrepreneurs reacting to a planned increase in future (consumption) expenditure by increasing the scale of their output. This necessitates an increased input of factors of production and consequently an increase in factor payments. It is this increase that must be financed. If the planned expenditure is realized such finance is again liquidated as the temporarily held cash balances enter into the regular circulation of income as a revolving fund. Indeed, as Keynes (ibid., p. 668) maintained, this liquidation can only be brought about by consumption and not by saving. (One wonders, however, what the latter argument will prove.)

As a next step, going slightly beyond what Keynes conceded, the results of integrating this second version of finance into a consistent analysis of the multiplier process are examined. Thereby some elements of supply behaviour from the *Treatise* and the *General Theory* are utilized. According to the *Treatise* output adjustment is regulated by windfall gains and losses. Similarly in the *General Theory*:[45] the (representative) firm maximizes profit by choosing output so that expected price is equated to marginal costs; thereby, for the economy as a whole a point on the curve of aggregate supply price is realized. If at the output thus determined the demand price exceeds the expected price (i.e. for the economy as a whole, aggregate demand price exceeds aggregate supply price), windfall gains will be generated. In this way an incentive is provided for raising price expectations for the next period, implying a movement along the (aggregate) supply price curve towards a higher level of output. If the adjustment process is stable (taking the demand curve as fixed), the Keynesian short-period equilibrium of effective demand will be reached. (Moreover, in truly Marshallian fashion profits are pushed to a maximum by this process while windfalls vanish.)[46] For the sake of simplicity it can be assumed that from one period to the next production is adjusted in such a way that the expected increase in the value of (planned) output just matches realized windfalls. Then the planned increase in production generates a demand for finance equal to windfall gains.[47]

However, according to this second version there is no *prima facie* argument in favour of asymmetry. An increase in investment leads to windfall gains in the I-industry just as an increase in saving leads to windfall losses in the C-industry, a situation familiar from the *Treatise*. Yet the former generates a demand for finance by inducing an increase in activity, just as the latter sets some finance free from its revolving fund by inducing a reduction in activity. Thus saving as well as investment may affect the interest rate directly and instantaneously. As at least some textual evidence supports the second version, it must be concluded that, ingenious as most of Keynes's arguments with regard to finance were, even within his own analytical framework he could not establish all the results he believed to be correct. (If the second version might not be supported by textual evidence, its substantive contribution should be evaluated on its own, anyway.)

Furthermore, the arguments used in the saving-and-hoarding debate and those relevant in the above-mentioned second version of finance demand are strikingly similar. When linking the analysis of the *Treatise* to that of the *General Theory* windfalls can be considered as signals for increasing or decreasing production. Therefore we have found – via Keynes's finance demand – good reasons why entrepreneurs should hold windfall profits in the form of cash (and not convert it into securities), namely for the reason of financing increased production. In this regard, this interpretation of finance demand even supports Robertson's critique of the *Treatise*.

4. Conclusion

The analytical results have already been summarized in the preceding sections. Accordingly, the thesis was confirmed that liquidity preference and loanable funds constitute but two different procedures between which choice is just a matter of convenience. With regard to substantive content, though not all of Keynes's theses could be vindicated, none of the propositions advanced by either side could be proved impossible on *a priori* grounds.

Moreover, this uneasy conclusion may hint at a deeper reason why historians have as a rule considered these controversies rather barren.[48]

This might be explained by the vain attempt to reach substantive results, designed to explain the functioning of a real-world economy, by means of *a priori* arguments alone. But obviously this cannot be done. While both Keynesian and orthodox results were shown by model-theoretical reasoning to be logically consistent, their empirical validity cannot be proved in this way. A definite answer, if any, can only be found empirically and not by staying within the boundaries of pure logic. Furthermore, the questions posed by the liquidity preference versus loanable funds controversy are not just resolvable only on empirical grounds, but such empirical answers may also directly be relevant to real-world policy-making decisions e.g. as regards the overshooting property of monetary policy and the usefulness of the interest rate as a monetary indicator (cf. Ferguson and Hart, 1980 and Greenfield and Yeager, 1986).

Notes

* I am grateful to Peter McGregor, Arne Heise and the participants of the Keynes III session for many helpful comments.
1. For a similar interpretation see Dasgupta (1985), ch. 8.
2. These works are cited as *TM* and *GT*; references to the *Treatise* are always to the first volume, if not stated otherwise.
3. Cf. for example Hicks (1967), ch. 11, Patinkin (1976), chs 3ff., Leijonhufvud (1981), ch. 7 and Bridel (1987), ch. 7.
4. These are, occasionally, denoted by Keynes as 'windfalls' (e.g. *TM*, p. 113).
5. There has been some controversy over whether the fundamental equations hold tautologically or conditionally. Anyway, if the amount of saving is exogenous, the first fundamental equation can be interpreted as a reduced form relationship for the price level of consumption goods (cf. also Hicks, 1967, p. 196).
6. Represented most uncompromisingly by Hayek (1931a).
7. Therefore, 'the portfolio-choice model of the *Treatise* is effectively a two-asset one: money and equity securities' (Patinkin, 1976, p. 81).
8. The novelty of this approach consisted in recognizing that wealth and not income constituted the relevant resource constraint, cf. Patinkin (1976), p. 40ff.
9. See also below, p. 236.
10. For the motives of holding money as an asset, see *TM* (p. 31ff.).
11. As an indirect effect, by spending part of their windfall profits entrepreneurs may diminish saving (as defined in the *Treatise*). This is known as the widow's cruse (cf. *TM*, p. 125; Keynes, 1931a, p. 414; see also Kahn's criticism, in Keynes, 1973a, 203ff.).
12. Cf. also his debate with Keynes as documented in Keynes (1973a), p. 275ff.
13. Wicksell (1935), p. 8ff is, of course, a prominent example.
14. Curiously, Robertson (1928, p. 7) describes this metaphorically as the (possibly distorting) 'monetary veil over saving and lending' – quite contrary to the customary use of this metaphor.
15. Cf. Robinson (1978, p. 34) – a 'postscript' added to Robinson (1938).
16. McGregor (1988b) provides a suitable model for analysing such effects.
17. This anticipates the rejection of interest effects of saving according to Keynes's (first version of) demand for finance; see note 41 below.
18. This is true, if industrial circulation strictly depends on income (as defined in the *Treatise*).
19. I believe that no careful reading of the *Treatise* can substantiate this interpretation.
20. Cf. also Keynes (1931b), p. 393 and his correspondence with Hayek as documented in Keynes (1973a), p. 257ff.

21. For a description of such a neutral monetary policy see e.g. Hayek (1931b), ch. 4, especially p. 98ff.; cf. also the 'Say's law policy' more recently proposed by Rose (1985).
22. Both, Keynes (1931a, p. 417) and subsequently Robinson (1933, p. 78ff.), refer to the fiction that – contrary to what they suppose – saving might become effective as demand for securities *before* the additional supply caused by windfall losses comes to the market.
23. In effect, Robinson's argument is valid only if expectations are *absolutely* rigid or – anticipating the terminology of Hicks (1946, p. 205) – *perfectly* inelastic.
24. When concentrating on speculative motives alone this might be true if the commonly held expectations of speculators are unit elastic. Cf. also Keynes on the necessity of 'a *variety* of opinion' (*GT*, p. 172).
25. Evidently this is true whenever industrial circulation is, if only partially, crowded out by financial circulation.
26. In this sense the loanable funds approach is still present in the *Treatise*, see Leijonhuf-vud (1981), p. 160ff.; as it seems, his interpretation owes more to Robinson (1933) than to the *Treatise* itself.
27. For a retrospect on this controversy see Robinson (1951), Johnson (1951), Robertson (1951) and more recently e.g. Patinkin (1965, especially ch. 11), Grossman (1971), Lliang (1984), Bridel (1987), Graziani (1988) and McGregor (1988a). For a fundamentally different perspective see Heise (1990).
28. Controversy also concentrated on more elusive issues, e.g. Keynes's contention that using the concept of marginal efficiency to derive the rate of interest involves circular reasoning (cf. *GT*, pp. 165, 184; Keynes, 1937b, p. 250). Yet these aspects will not be considered here.
29. The term 'neutral money' or 'neutral economy' is often used by Keynes in this sense; see for example *GT* (pp. 183, 243) and Keynes (1973a, p. 420; 1979, p. 78ff, 118ff). For the concept of neutral money see Klausinger (1989).
30. Without, however, sufficiently distinguishing between an equilibrium condition and an accounting identity.
31. Eventually Robertson succeeded in translating his own terms, 'increases in saving' or 'thrift', into the Keynesian one, i.e. 'decrease in the propensity to consume' (Robertson, 1938a, p. 318; 1938b, p. 555). Nevertheless, for the sake of brevity in this section 'increases in saving and investment' will be used as shorthand for 'decrease in propensity to consume and increase in marginal efficiency of capital', thus designating truly independent variables.
32. See above for the analogous indirect effect analysed in the *Treatise*.
33. This is definitely so when the liquidity preference schedule is interpreted as a reduced form relationship linking the equilibrium rate of interest to the quantity of money, cf. *GT* (p. 171ff.) and Hansen (1953), p. 148ff.
34. The origins of this approach may be traced back to the classical monetary theory of Ricardo and Thornton (see Niehans, 1990, ch. 10), and, of course, to Wicksell and Hayek.
35. This was first demonstrated by Hicks (1982), p. 92ff.
36. Therefore the effects of finance demand can be mitigated by the existence of 'unused overdraft facilities' (Keynes, 1937c, p. 669).
37. A few passages will illustrate the dilemma for exegesis: finance is said to be (1) 'required by any *productive process*' (Keynes, 1937b, p. 247); (2) '[finance is exhausted] on paying for . . . *completed investment*' (ibid.); (3) '[finance] is used in the sense of being *expended*' (Keynes, 1937c, p. 666); (4) 'finance required by current ex-ante *output* (. . . true of any *output* which has to be planned ahead)', referring also to 'planned *activity*' (ibid., p. 667); (5) the demand for liquidity increases 'whether the planned *activity* by the *entrepreneur* or the planned *expenditure* by the *public* is directed towards *investment* or towards *consumption*' (ibid.); (6) 'finance required by the increase in planned activity to *produce* consumers' goods' (ibid.); and answering Robertson's explicit question: (7) 'the demand for . . . finance is automatically at an end as soon as finance is *expended*' (Keynes, 1938, p. 320) (my italics throughout). Roughly speaking,

passages (2), (3) and maybe (7) point to the first version, (1), (4) and definitely (6) to the second, and (5) to both at once.

38. These two versions of finance correspond to the distinction between finance and expenditure plans as referring to two different periods – in the first finance demand is for *planned* expenditure, in the second such expenditure is implemented – in both periods output is fixed. See e.g. Hahn (1985), p. 63ff. and for an explicit model McGregor (1988b).
39. This may be due to Keynes's 'logical theory of the multiplier, which holds good continuously, without time-lag, at all moments of time' (*GT*, p. 122).
40. The reinterpretations of finance demand by Davidson (1965) and Tsiang (1980) imply symmetry; for a critique see McGregor (1988a).
41. The formulation in Keynes (1931a, p. 417) quoted above is even more explicit; note that this contradicts the usual results of models dealing with the finance period (cf. McGregor, 1988b, p. 139).
42. This may be more doubtful with regard to durable consumption goods.
43. Cf. Laidler (1984) and Bain and McGregor (1985). See also Hawtrey's criticism of the Robertsonian income-expenditure lag as disregarding the possibility that fluctuations of income are absorbed by cash holdings (Hawtrey, 1933, p. 702).
44. Moreover, Keynes's interpretation of 'ex-ante consumption' or 'income' as used by Ohlin is erroneous; these Swedish concepts do not primarily refer to future variables but to plans relating to the current period. For example, income is an expected variable only in so far as it refers to the expected yield attributable to the current period, cf. Ohlin (1944), p. 96ff, Myrdal (1965), ch. 5, especially 89n., and Lindahl (1970), p. 143ff.
45. Cf. for exegesis and reconstruction Leijonhufvud (1974), Casarosa (1981) and, critically, Patinkin (1982), pt. 2.
46. That is, profits mean expected or normal profits which are (as the *Treatise* says) included in 'normal remuneration' whereas windfalls are unexpected.
47. A model like that of McGregor (1988b) can also be used for analysing this second version of finance demand.
48. Neither are the results concerning instantaneous effects incorporated into standard macroeconomics textbooks; see e.g. Dornbusch and Fischer (1990), p.137ff.

References

Bain, A. D. and McGregor, P. G. (1985), 'Buffer-Stock Monetarism and the Theory of Financial Buffers', *Manchester School*, **53**, pp. 385–403.

Baumol, W. J. (1952), 'The Transactions Demand for Cash: An Inventory Theoretic Approach', *Quarterly Journal of Economics*, **66**, pp. 545–56.

Bridel, P. (1987), *Cambridge Monetary Thought. The Development of Saving-Investment Analysis from Marshall to Keynes*, London: Macmillan.

Casarosa, C. (1981), 'The Microfoundations of Keynes's Aggregate Supply and Expected Demand Analysis', *Economic Journal*, **91**, pp. 188–94.

Clower, R. W. (1984), 'A Reconsideration of the Microfoundations of Monetary Theory' (1967), in D. A. Walker, *Money and Markets. Essays by R. W. Clower*, Cambridge: Cambridge University Press, pp. 81–9.

Dasgupta, A. K. (1985), *Epochs of Economic Theory*, Oxford: Basil Blackwell.

Davidson, P. (1965), 'Keynes's Finance Motive', *Oxford Economic Papers*, **17**, pp. 47–65.

Dornbusch, R. and Fischer, S. (1990), *Macroeconomics*, 5th edn, New York: McGraw-Hill.

Ferguson, J. D. and Hart, W. P. (1980), 'Liquidity Preference and Loanable Funds: Interest Determination in Market Disequilibrium', *Oxford Economic Papers*, **32**, pp. 57–70.

Graziani, A. (1988), 'The Financement of the Economic Activity in Keynes's

Thought', in H. Hagemann and O. Steiger (eds), *Keynes' General Theory nach fünfzig Jahren*, Berlin: Duncker & Humblot, pp. 279–97.

Greenfield, R. L. and Yeager, L. B. (1986), 'Money and Credit Confused. An Appraisal of Economic Doctrine and Federal Reserve Procedure', *Southern Economic Journal*, **53**, pp. 364–73.

Grossman, H. I. (1971), 'Money, Interest, and Prices in Market Disequilibrium', *Journal of Political Economy*, **79**, pp. 943–61.

Hahn, F. H. (1985), 'The Rate of Interest and General Equilibrium Analysis' (1955), in F. H. Hahn, *Money, Growth and Stability*, Oxford: Basil Blackwell, pp. 56–74.

Hansen, A. H. (1953), *A Guide to Keynes*, London: McGraw-Hill.

Hawtrey, R. G. (1933), 'Mr. Robertson on "Saving and Hoarding"', *Economic Journal*, **43**, pp. 701–8.

Hawtrey, R. G. (1937), 'Rejoinder', *Economic Journal*, **47**, pp. 436–43.

Hayek, F. A. (1931a), 'Reflections on the Pure Theory of Money of Mr. J. M. Keynes. Part I', *Economica*, **11**, pp. 270–95.

Hayek, F. A. (1931b), *Prices and Production*, London: Routledge.

Heise, A. (1990), 'Money and Credit Or: A Never-Ending Story', Paper presented at the History of Economics Society Meeting, Lexington VA.

Hicks, J. R. (1946) *Value and Capital*, 2nd edn, Oxford: Oxford University Press (first published 1939).

Hicks, J. R. (1967), *Critical Essays in Monetary Theory*, Oxford: Oxford University Press.

Hicks, J. R. (1982), 'Mr. Keynes' Theory of Employment', (1936) in J. Hicks, *Money, Interest and Wages*, Oxford: Basil Blackwell, pp. 84–99.

Johnson, H. G. (1951), 'Some Cambridge Controversies in Monetary Theory', *Review of Economic Studies*, **20**, pp. 90–104.

Keynes, J. M. (1930), *A Treatise on Money*, 2 vols. Reprinted as *The Collected Writings of John Maynard Keynes* [CWJMK], Vols V and VI. London: Macmillan, 1971.

Keynes, J. M. (1931a), 'Mr. Keynes' Theory of Money. A Rejoinder', *Economic Journal*, **41**, pp. 412–23.

Keynes, J. M. (1931b), 'The Pure Theory of Money. A Reply to Dr. Hayek', in *CWJMK*, Vol. XIII, pp. 243–56.

Keynes, J. M. (1936), *The General Theory of Employment, Interest and Money*, reprinted as *CWJMK*, Vol. VII, London: Macmillan, 1973.

Keynes, J. M. (1937a), 'The General Theory of Employment', reprinted in *CWJMK*, Vol. XIV, pp. 109–23.

Keynes, J. M. (1937b), 'Alternative Theories of the Rate of Interest', *Economic Journal*, **47**, pp. 241–52.

Keynes, J. M. (1937c), 'The "Ex-Ante" Theory of the Rate of Interest', *Economic Journal*, **47**, pp. 663–9.

Keynes, J. M. (1938), 'Comment', *Economic Journal*, **48**, pp. 318–22.

Keynes, J. M. (1973a), *The General Theory and After. Part I: Preparation*, ed. D. Moggridge (*CWJMK*, Vol. XIII), London: Macmillan.

Keynes, J. M. (1973b), *The General Theory and After. Part II: Defence and Development*, ed. D. Moggridge (*CWJMK*, Vol. XIV), London: Macmillan.

Keynes, J. M. (1979), *The General Theory and After. A Supplement*, ed. D. Moggridge (*CWJMK*, Vol. XXIX), London: Macmillan.

Klausinger, H. (1989), 'On the History of Neutral Money', in D. A. Walker (ed.),

Perspectives on the History of Economic Thought, Vol. II, Aldershot: Edward Elgar, pp. 171–86.

Laidler, D. (1984), 'The "Buffer-Stock" Notion in Monetary Economics', *Economic Journal*, **94** (Supplement), pp. 17–34.

Leijonhufvud, A. (1974), 'Comment on "Keynes' Employment Function" by Paul Wells', *History of Political Economy*, **6**, pp. 164–70.

Leijonhufvud, A. (1981), *Information and Coordination. Essays in Macroeconomic Theory*, New York: Oxford University Press.

Lerner, A. P. (1938), 'Alternative Formulations of the Theory of Interest', *Economic Journal*, **48**, pp. 211–29.

Lindahl, E. (1970), *Studies in the Theory of Money and Capital* (1939), New York: Augustus Kelley.

Lliang, M. Y. (1984), 'Keynes's Errors in the Liquidity Preference versus Loanable Funds Controversy', *Journal of Macroeconomics*, **6**, pp. 215–27.

McGregor, P. G. (1988a), 'Keynes on Ex-Ante Saving and the Rate of Interest', *History of Political Economy*, **20**, pp. 107–18.

McGregor, P. G. (1988b), 'The Demand for Money in a Period Analysis Context, the Irrelevance of the "Choice of Market" and the Loanable Funds-Liquidity Preference Debate', *Australian Economic Papers*, **27**, pp. 136–41.

Miller, E. M. (1984), 'Bank Deposits in the Monetary Theory of Keynes', *Journal of Money, Credit and Banking*, **16**, pp. 242–6.

Miller, E. M. (1985), 'Keynesian Economics as a Translation Error: An Essay on Keynes' Financial Theory', *History of Political Economy*, **17**, pp. 265–85.

Myrdal, G. (1965), *Monetary Equilibrium* (1939), New York: Augustus Kelley.

Niehans, J. (1990), *A History of Economic Theory. Classic Contributions, 1720–1980*, Baltimore and London: Johns Hopkins University Press.

Ohlin, B. (1937), 'Rejoinder', *Economic Journal*, **47**, pp. 423–7.

Ohlin, B. (1944), 'Some Notes on the Stockholm Theory of Savings and Investment' (1937), in G. Haberler (ed.), *Readings in Business Cycle Theory*, Homewood, Ill.: Richard D. Irwin, pp. 87–130.

Patinkin, D. (1965), *Money, Interest and Prices*, 2nd edn, New York: Harper & Row.

Patinkin, D. (1976), *Keynes' Monetary Thought*, Durham, NC: Duke University Press.

Patinkin, D. (1982), *Anticipations of the General Theory? And Other Essays on Keynes*, Chicago: Chicago University Press.

Robertson, D. H. (1928), *Money*, 2nd edn, Cambridge: Cambridge University Press.

Robertson, D. H. (1931), 'Mr. Keynes' Theory of Money', *Economic Journal*, **41**, pp. 395–411.

Robertson, D. H. (1933), 'Saving and Hoarding', reprinted in Robertson (1940), pp. 65–82.

Robertson, D. H. (1937), 'Rejoinder', *Economic Journal*, **47**, pp. 428–36.

Robertson, D. H. (1938a), 'Mr. Keynes and "Finance" ', *Economic Journal*, **48**, pp. 314–18.

Robertson, D. H. (1938b), 'Reply', *Economic Journal*, **48**, p. 555ff.

Robertson, D. H. (1940), *Essays on Monetary Theory*, London: Staples Press.

Robertson, D. H. (1951), 'Comments on Mr. Johnson's Notes', *Review of Economic Studies*, **20**, pp. 105–10.

Robertson, D. H. (1983), 'Some Notes on Mr. Keynes' General Theory of

Employment' (1936), in J. C. Wood (ed.), *John Maynard Keynes. Critical Assessments*, Vol. II, London and Canberra: Croom Helm, pp. 99–114.

Robinson, J. (1933), 'A Parable on Savings and Investment', *Economica*, **13**, pp. 75–84.

Robinson, J. (1938), 'The Concept of Hoarding', reprinted with a postscript in Robinson (1978), pp. 29–34.

Robinson, J. (1951), 'The Rate of Interest', reprinted in Robinson (1978), pp. 35–52.

Robinson, J. (1978), *Contributions to Modern Economics*, Oxford: Basil Blackwell.

Rose, H. (1985), 'A Policy Rule for Say's Law in a Theory of Temporary Equilibrium', *Journal of Macroeconomics*, **7**, pp. 1–17.

Schumpeter, J. A. (1952), 'John Maynard Keynes, 1883–1946' (1946), in Schumpeter, *Ten Great Economists*, London: Allen & Unwin, pp. 260–91.

Schumpeter, J. A. (1954), *History of Economic Analysis*, London: Allen & Unwin.

Tobin, J. (1956), 'The Interest-Elasticity of Transactions Demand for Cash', *Review of Economics and Statistics*, **38**, pp. 241–7.

Tsiang, S. C. (1980), 'Keynes's Finance Demand, Robertson's Loanable Funds Theory, and Friedman's Monetarism', *Quarterly Journal of Economics*, **99**, pp. 467–91.

Wicksell, K. (1935), *Lectures on Political Economy. Vol. 2: Money*, London: Routledge & Kegan Paul.

14 Money and equilibrium analysis: Keynes versus Hicks?

*Ivo Maes**

1. Introduction

Equilibrium analysis is one of the fundamental tools of economic theory. As Shackle has remarked, it enables the economist 'to exhibit the economic world as determinate, explicable, calculable, and even predictable' (Shackle, 1982, p. 437). But the method of equilibrium analysis is not without problems. One of the main difficulties concerns the integration of money and equilibrium analysis, a tension which comes clearly to the foreground in the writings of Maynard Keynes.

This ambiguity in the work of Keynes is at the origin of different schools of Keynesianism. Following Coddington (1976), one can distinguish between a fundamentalist and a hydraulic school.[1]

Hydraulic Keynesians, like Alvin Hansen, Paul Samuelson, James Tobin and Franco Modigliani, focus on the macroeconomic aggregates. They assume thereby that there exist stable relationships, which are analysed with the help of macroeconomic equilibrium models.

Fundamentalist Keynesians, like George Shackle and Joan Robinson, perceive Keynes's *General Theory* as posing a fundamental threat to conventional economic theory. For them, a monetary economy is fundamentally characterized by uncertain expectations, 'and uncertain expectation is wholly incompatible and in conflict with the notion of equilibrium' (Shackle, 1982, p. 438).

John Hicks is generally considered as one of the main architects of hydraulic Keynesianism (cf. Coddington, 1979, p. 971). Several economists in the fundamentalist tradition, like Robinson and Shackle, reproach him with initially failing to recognize the importance of uncertain expectations, and with restoring Keynesian economics into an equilibrium system with his IS–LM construction: 'Whenever equilibrium theory is breached, economists rush like bees whose comb has been broken to patch up the damage. J.R. Hicks was one of the first, with his IS–LM, to try to reduce *The General Theory* to a system of equilibrium' (Robinson, 1980, p. 79).

It is the purpose of this paper to analyse the writings of Keynes and

Hicks on the foundations of a monetary economy and their use of equilibrium analysis. This should shed more light on the compatibility of money and equilibrium analysis and can also help to clarify whether the ideas of Keynes and Hicks were really so different after all.

2. Keynes's use of equilibrium analysis

As Keynes learned his economics from Marshall, it is interesting to explore this background, and more specifically Marshall's notion of equilibrium. Marshall uses the equilibrium concept as a kind of artefact. 'Thus it is not descriptive, nor does it deal constructively with real problems. But it sets out the theoretical backbone of our knowledge. . . . It aims not so much at the attainment of knowledge, as at the power to obtain and arrange knowledge' (Marshall, 1969, p. 269).

Equilibrium analysis is closely connected with his *ceteris paribus* method: 'The study of some group of tendencies is isolated by the assumption *other things being equal:* the existence of other tendencies is not denied but their disturbing effect is neglected for a time' (ibid., p. 304). This method was also advocated by Keynes (cf. Keynes, 1976, p. 294).

Marshall admits that the idea of equilibrium is of fundamental importance, and is used throughout his work, to analyse different kinds of problem. One of the difficulties that can be tackled with this concept of equilibrium is the problem of the time horizon of an economy. When analysing the equilibrium of an economy, one can make a distinction between three periods: the ultra-short period (only quantity adjustments through changes in inventories), the short period (changes in production through changes in employment), and the long period (changes in equipment) (Marshall, 1969, p. 274).

How should one situate *The General Theory*? As Don Patinkin remarks, *The General Theory* is also in this respect a rather confusing and muddled book (Patinkin, 1976, pp. 89, 115). But still, one could argue that *The General Theory* contains basically a short period model, something which is naturally in line with Keynes's sensitivity to policy problems. This comes out very clearly in the final chapter of Book IV, 'The General Theory of Employment Re-Stated':

> We take as given the existing skill and quantity of available labour, the existing quality and quantity of available equipment, the existing technique, the degree of competition, the tastes and habits of the consumer, the disutility of different intensities of labour and of the activities of supervision and organisation, as well as the social structure including the forces, other than our variables set forth below, which determine the distribution of the national income. . . . Thus we can sometimes regard our ultimate independent variables as consisting of (1) the three fundamental psychological factors, namely, the psychological propensity to consume, the psychological attitude to liquidity and the psycho-

logical expectation of future yield from capital assets, (2) the wage unit as determined by the bargains reached between employers and employed, and (3) the quantity of money as determined by the action of the central bank; so that, if we take as given the factors specified above, these variables determine the national income (or dividend) and the quantity of employment. But these again would be capable of being subjected to further analysis, and are not, so to speak, our ultimate atomic independent elements. (Keynes, 1976, p. 245)

It is clear then that in Keynes's model the focus is on the factors that determine short-period equilibrium. It is in this context that one can interpret Keynes's claim to have demonstrated the possibility of an 'unemployment equilibrium'. In this unemployment equilibrium there is an equilibrium on the goods markets, as production has adjusted to effective demand. The term equilibrium refers then to a short-period equilibrium on these markets for goods.[2]

One of the ultimate and independent variables, but capable of being subjected to further analysis, in Keynes's model, is expectations, both short period and long period. Short-term expectations are the expected or anticipated values of a variable, especially the price an entrepreneur can get for his finished output. Long-term expectations are the expectations about the future returns of investments (cf. Keynes, 1976, p. 46). Hicks, in his review of *The General Theory*, considers this introduction of expectations into equilibrium analysis as one of the most revolutionary aspects of Keynes's *General Theory* (cf. Hicks, 1936, p. 240).[3]

One can also note here that Keynes's use of an equilibrium framework of analysis in *The General Theory* was rather in contrast to common practice in the 1930s. Most monetary economists used a form of sequence analysis, like the one Keynes himself had applied in his *Treatise on Money* (Keynes, 1971).[4]

So, while Keynes's *General Theory* constituted from the point of view of economic analysis and policy conclusions an attack on 'classical' economic theory, the same cannot be said for methodology. On the contrary, from a methodological point of view, his *General Theory* marked a break with most cycle methodology and a return to a more Marshallian type of analysis, as Hicks remarked in his first review: 'The technique of the work is on the whole conservative: more conservative than in *The General Theory*. It is the technique of Marshall. . . . Thus we have to change, not so much our methods of analysis, as some important elements in the outlook which we have inherited from the classics' (Hicks, 1936, p. 253).

3. Hicks's notion of intertemporal equilibrium
Hicks was less happy with Marshall's 'rigid' tripartite division of the time horizon of an economy (ultra-short period, short period, long period). His

criticism was directed at the partial equilibrium nature of Marshall's construction, 'The categories are suitable enough for Marshall's isolated market, but they hardly fit the analysis of the whole system' (Hicks, 1946, p. 122). For Hicks, the speed of adjustment, and thus the time dimension, differs from market to market. Consequently Marshall's tripartite division is less appropriate for a general equilibrium analysis of the whole economy.

In his thinking on money and equilibrium Hicks was heavily influenced by the Austrians, especially Friedrich Hayek. In those days, Hayek was still an adherent of general equilibrium theory.[5] Hayek would typically set up an intertemporal equilibrium, an equilibrium of an economy with different moments in time (cf. Hayek, 1928). It is Hicks's purpose in 'Equilibrium and the Trade Cycle' (Hicks, 1980) to extend the Paretian system, which is also the basis of Hayek's theory, to incorporate the analysis of production in time. In that case, the behaviour of the economic agents is determined by both present and future prices.

Hicks's approach to this problem of price determination is to divide the whole period into subperiods, which are so short that price changes in these subperiods can be neglected.[6] Taking n present prices and t subperiods, one has nt prices to be determined, and nt demand and supply equations to determine these prices.[7] But such a system can, according to Hicks, only be in equilibrium if there is perfect foresight:

> however the economic data vary, there will always be a set of prices which, if it is foreseen, can be carried through without supplies and demands ever becoming unequal to one another and so without expectations ever being mistaken. The condition for equilibrium, in this widest sense, is Perfect Foresight. Disequilibrium is the Disappointment of Expectations. (Hicks, 1980, p. 526)

It is interesting to note here that Hicks has been severely criticized on this point by Morgenstern. Morgenstern argued that perfect foresight leads to a paradox as it implies perfect foresight of the behaviour of all other economic agents, who also dispose of perfect foresight of the behaviour of the other agents, etc. This leads then to 'an endless chain of reciprocally conjectural reactions and counter-reactions' (Morgenstern, 1976, p. 174). Morgenstern concludes then that 'Unlimited foresight and economic equilibrium are thus irreconcilable with one another' (ibid.). Moreover, Morgenstern also criticized Hicks for his assertion that the presence of as many equations as unknowns is sufficient for the determination of a (unique) equilibrium.[8]

4. Money and equilibrium analysis

Until now, Hicks has been in line with Hayek. But where Hayek now starts with monetary disturbances and their influence on the structure of production, Hicks asks a preliminary question about the nature of money in this construction. He notes that

> Money as a medium of indirect exchange plays no part in the Lausanne equilibrium. . . the tacit assumption of perfect foresight deprives the *numéraire* of any monetary function. . . . It is only for future payments that one needs to hold a stock of money. But it must be noticed that it is only to meet uncertain future payments that a stock of money is necessary . . . thus we cannot escape the conclusion that if the future course of economic data (and the corresponding future course of prices) were exactly foreseen, there would be no demand to hold money as money. People would lend out all their money holdings (Hicks, 1980, p. 527)

It is clear then that the holding of money becomes intimately connected with uncertainty and the possibility of disappointment of expectations.

Hicks is very much in line with Keynes, who stressed in *The General Theory* that 'money enters into the economic scheme in an essential and peculiar manner' (Keynes, 1976, p. xxii). Also for Keynes a monetary economy is characterized by uncertainty and the possibility of disappointment of expectations: 'A monetary economy, we shall find, is essentially one in which changing views about the future are capable of influencing the quantity of employment and not merely its direction' (ibid.).[9] So both for Hicks and Keynes a monetary economy is inherently an economy where uncertainty plays an important role.[10] Consequently, the function of money as a store of value is emphasized.

5. Keynes and Hicks on monetary theory

Keynes and Hicks, in the mid-1930s, also held very similar views on the backbone of monetary theory:

- They both used a balance-sheet approach to monetary theory, regarding money as one of the assets in which an individual can hold his wealth.
- They both identified the issue of why people hold money, an asset that yields no return, as the crucial question of monetary theory.
- They both advanced transaction costs and uncertainty as the fundamental reasons for holding money.

Hicks developed his ideas on monetary theory in 'A Suggestion for Simplifying the Theory of Money'. In this article Hicks pleads for a 'marginal' revolution in monetary theory. He conceives money as one of the assets of the community and he applies choice analysis to investigate the portfolio composition of the community: 'Our method of analysis, it will have appeared, is simply an extension of the ordinary method of value theory ... but this time not of an income account, but of a capital account, a balance-sheet' (Hicks, 1967a, p. 74).[11]

The questions which then have to be resolved are: how will people allocate their wealth, and what are the determinants of this allocation? For most assets it is obvious why people like to have them: they give a certain return. But money yields no return or profit: it is barren.

> So long as rates of interest are positive the decision to hold money rather than lend it, or use it pay off old debts, is apparently an unprofitable one. This, as I see it, is really the central issue in the pure theory of money. (Hicks, 1967a, p. 66)

Keynes also conceives of money as a store of wealth. He distinguishes between the decision to save and the decision on the allocation of wealth between different assets (Keynes, 1976, p. 166). He also asks the fundamental question why people hold money when they can get a positive return on other forms of investment:

> For it is a recognised characteristic of money as a store of wealth that it is barren; whereas practically every other form of storing wealth yields some interest or profit. Why should anyone outside a lunatic asylum wish to use money as a store of wealth? (Keynes, 1973b, p. 115)

To answer this question, Hicks introduces two elements: transactions cost (a new element compared to his earlier article) and the risk factor, with risk affecting both the expected period of investment and the expected net yield of the investment. These elements also form the basis of Keynes's well-known motives for the holding of money: the transactions motive, the precautionary motive and the speculative motive. Keynes's innovation was the introduction of the speculative motive, which is grounded in the uncertainty of expectations: 'our desire to hold money as a store of wealth is a barometer of our distrust of our own calculations and conventions concerning the future' (Keynes, 1973b, p. 116).

One can conclude then that, concerning the essence of monetary theory, Hicks and Keynes were very close in the 1930s. This is confirmed by Keynes's reaction to Hicks's simplifying article: 'I like it very much. I agree with you that what I now call "Liquidity Preference" is the essential concept for Monetary Theory' (Postcard from Keynes to Hicks, 24 December 1934, quoted in Hicks, 1977, p. 142).[12]

6. Hicks and *The General Theory*

Hicks's attention to *The General Theory* was stimulated by the fact that he was asked to review Keynes's work for the *Economic Journal*. At the end of his review he concludes that Keynes's main merit is the extension of Marshall's equilibrium analysis to the problems of employment and output: 'The technique of this work is, on the whole, conservative: more conservative than in the *Treatise*. It is the technique of Marshall, but it is applied to problems never tackled by Marshall and his contemporaries' (Hicks, 1936, p. 253).

In his review Hicks first characterizes *The General Theory* as at the same time being a theory of employment, a theory of output as a whole, a theory of shifting equilibrium and a theory of money. He also explains the interrelationships of these different aspects.

> It may be suggested that the relation between these different aspects is as follows. The new theory is a theory of employment, in so far as the problem of employment and unemployment is the most urgent and practical problem to which this sort of theoretical improvement is relevant. It is a theory of output in general vis-à-vis Marshall, who took into account many of the sort of complications which concern M. Keynes, but took them into account only with reference to a single industry. It is a theory of shifting equilibrium vis-à-vis the static or stationary theories of general equilibrium, such as those of Ricardo, Böhm-Bawerk or Pareto. It is a theory of money, in so far as it includes monetary theory, bringing money out of its isolated position as a separate subject into an integral relation with general economics. (Hicks, 1936, p. 238)

Hicks also pays particular attention to Keynes's use of the method of expectations, 'perhaps the most revolutionary thing about this book' (ibid., p. 24).

When analysing a real world economy, equilibrium is not only determined by the tastes and resources of the economic agents but also by the anticipations of the economic agents. By taking expectations as exogeneous, an equilibrium can be determined. Equilibrium analysis can then be used to analyse a world in disequilibrium: 'The point of the method is that it reintroduces determinateness into a process of change. . . . But all that this reasoning gives us is hypothetical results' (ibid., p. 241).

The most important point of disagreement between Keynes and Hicks concerns the determination of the rate of interest. Keynes holds the view that the rate of interest is a money rate of interest, which equilibrates the demand and supply of money. Hicks has no problem in accepting Keynes's view on the determination of the rate of interest, but he thinks there are also other methods to determine this, i.e. by the demand and supply for loans. Hicks's argument is based on his background in general equilibrium theory, which he had already earlier developed in 'Wages and Interest: the Dynamic Problem' (Hicks, 1963), his 'bread paper'.

Hicks argues that in a general equilibrium system all supply and demand equations have a role to play in the determination of any price. But one can construct several theories for approaching the situation, depending on which equation one prefers to drop.

> The ordinary method of economic theory would be to regard each price as determined by the demand and supply equation for the corresponding commodity or factor; the rate of interest as determined by the demand and supply for loans. If we work in this way, the equation for the demand and supply of money is otiose – it follows from the rest; and fortunately, too, it is not wanted, because we have determined the whole price system without it. But we could equally well work in another way. We could allot to each commodity or factor the demand and supply equation for that commodity or factor, as before; but we could allot to the rate of interest the equation for the demand and supply of money. If we do this, the equation for loans becomes otiose, automatically following from the rest. (Hicks, 1936, p. 246)

Keynes did not understand Hicks's argument and in his letters to Hicks he asks repeatedly for more explanation (cf. Keynes, 1973c, pp. 72, 75, 81). Hicks tries to clear things up and goes over the argument again. He concludes by expressing his support for Keynes's basic theoretical position, although insisting on his own freedom and independence. 'I am a convinced liquidity preference man, but I do covet some freedom of choice about the way (or ways) the doctrine shall be expressed' (Letter from J.R. Hicks to J.M. Keynes, 9 April 1937, reprinted in Keynes, 1973c, p. 83).

Keynes then could not really see Hicks's point of view, as he was not so used to general equilibrium analysis. It was not so much Keynes's attitude to think of interrelated markets; he focused on the market in which a good is traded.[13]

After his first review, Hicks remained concerned with *The General Theory* and the break it marked with prevailing theory: 'in some respects Hicks can be said to have been reviewing *The General Theory* (in the sense of placing it in a modern perspective) ever since' (Morgan, 1981, p. 117). The first outcome of this process was his celebrated 'Mr Keynes and the "Classics": a Suggested Interpretation', first presented at a meeting of the Econometric Society at Oxford in September 1936 and published in Econometrica, April 1937 (Hicks, 1967b).[14] It has become the commonly accepted framework for Keynesian economics.[15] As one shrewd observer put it:

> Although most economists would probably resist, and many resent, being labeled 'Keynesians', almost all would agree that there does exist today a recognizable majority view on the theory of income determination and that the

term can reasonably be used to refer to the main outlines of this view. Keynesian economics, in this popular sense, is far from, being a homogeneous doctrine. The common denominator, which lends some justification to the identification of a majority school, is the class of models generally used. These short-run, simultaneous equation models have their prototype in the famous, early 'Keynes and the Classics' paper by Hicks. (Leijonhufvud, 1976, p. 4)

Keynes also read the article and commented very approvingly on Hicks's 'Suggested Interpretation': 'I found it very interesting and really have next to nothing to say by the way of criticism' (Letter from J.M. Keynes to J.R. Hicks, 31 March 1937, reprinted in Keynes, 1973c, p. 79).[16]

7. Conclusion

When analysing the works of Keynes and Hicks in the 1930s, one finds very different notions of equilibrium. Keynes was thinking in terms of the traditional classical and Marshallian concept (equilibrium as characterized by long-run normal conditions). Hicks, on the contrary, was laying the foundations of the modern concept of intertemporal equilibrium. But despite these different notions of equilibrium, they arrived at a very similar characterization of a monetary economy. For both there is a fundamental difference between a monetary economy and a barter economy, whereby uncertain expectations are of crucial importance for a monetary economy. Nevertheless, in spite of the difficulties money and uncertain expectations pose for equilibrium analysis, they applied equilibrium methods in their theoretical writings.

Hicks later, in his *magnum opus, Value and Capital* (Hicks, 1946), further elaborated the notion of intertemporal equilibrium. There he struggled to incorporate money into a general intertemporal equilibrium framework. Further research showed the limitations of this approach: 'monetary theory cannot simply be grafted on the Walrasian Theory with minor modifications. Money is an outward sign that the economy is not adequately described by the pristine construction of Arrow and Debreu' (Hahn, 1988, p. 972).

But besides his work on intertemporal equilibrium, Hicks also participated in the 'Keynesian revolution'. There he applied, like Keynes, a more classical notion of equilibrium, with expectations as an exogenous element in the analysis. Partly this can be explained by the technical problems associated with other approaches (e.g. sequential analysis). But it also illustrates how Keynes and Hicks, while developing new ideas, tried to define these new theories in terms of the traditional equilibrium approach.

So both Keynes and Hicks, being well aware of the fundamental problems that money and uncertain expectations pose for equilibrium analysis, used hydraulic equilibrium models to analyse the determination of output and employment.

Notes

*   I would like to thank B. Bateman, K. Bosman, E. Buyst, M. M. G. Fase, S. T. Lowry, W. Young and the participants of the Séminaire des Salles d'Etudes Economiques et Statistiques, Université de Paris I, Sorbonne, especially A. Barrère and A. Lapidus, for comments on an earlier draft. Naturally, only the author is responsible for the opinions expressed in this paper.

1.   Coddington also distinguishes a 'reconstituted reductionist' variety, with protagonists such as Clower, Leijonhufvud and Malinvaud. As this school is of more recent origin, it falls outside the scope of this paper.

2.   In several places in *The General Theory* Keynes presents a dynamic analysis, for example in Book V, 'Money-wages and Prices', where he investigates the process of how falling wages influence effective demand. This ambivalence was aptly summarized by Leijonhufvud: 'Keynes' theory was dynamic. His model was static' (Leijonhufvud, 1973, p. 299).

3.   Jan Kregel characterizes three models which Keynes 'may have had in mind' in terms of assumptions about expectations, cf. Kregel (1976), p. 214.

4.   Kohn (1986) argues that *The General Theory* was more a revolution in method than in substance. Hansson (1986) links Keynes's change of method to his shift of subject matter, from changes in the price level in the *Treatise* to the determination of the equilibrium level of output and employment in *The General Theory*. But *The General Theory* still contains certain elements of sequential analysis, as emphasized by Dangel (1988).

5.   The modern Austrian school is well known for its criticism of equilibrium conceptions with its emphasis on the market process as a discovery process and the price mechanism as an information-signalling device. Hayek contributed to this view, starting with his paper, 'Economics and Knowledge' (Hayek, 1937). But before that time Hayek was an adherent of general equilibrium theory; see also McCloughry (1984), p. viii.

6.   A method which he would also use in *Value and Capital*; see Hicks (1946), p. 122.

7.   As Murray Milgate remarked, the notion of equilibrium changed quite drastically during the 1930s, in part under the influence of John Hicks; see Milgate (1987). In the classical concept equilibrium was characterized by 'long-run normal conditions' or 'natural conditions' to which market values tend to conform. Intertemporal equilibrium is about the determination of nt market-clearing prices (for n commodities over t time periods).

8.   As stressed by Mahloudji (1985), Hicks has, in his later works, expressed a good deal of ambivalence towards the notion of equilibrium.

9.   The importance of uncertainty is also emphasized by Meltzer (1989), e.g. p. 7.

10. It can be noted that, in the 1930s, Hicks was an adherent of an objective approach to probability; see Hicks (1931), p. 171. This contrasts sharply with Keynes who, with his *Treatise on Probability* (Keynes, 1973a), was known as 'The principal exponent of the logico-subjective theory of probability' (Popper, 1977, p. 149). Later Hicks revised his opinion, arguing that an objective approach to probability is 'not wide enough for economics' (Hicks, 1979, p. 105).

11. This constituted a further abandonment of Hayek's monetary theories. Instead Hicks laid the foundations for modern portfolio theory, as exemplified in the work of James Tobin. For an overview of this development see Maes (1990).

12. It seems to me that Pekkarinen (1986) greatly exaggerates the differences between Keynes and Hicks.

13. It is interesting to note that Hicks agreed on this point with D. H. Robertson. But despite this theoretical agreement, Hicks was in broad sympathy with Keynes.

14. For a detailed analysis of the origins of the IS–LM article see Young (1987).

15. One should also note that Hicks repeatedly stressed that IS-LM is not really his own theory but a representation of Keynes's theory. For an overview of the development of Hicks's thought on IS–LM see Maes (1989).
16. It is noteworthy that there was a little skirmish between Keynes and Hicks on expectations, Keynes reproaching Hicks that he underestimated the relevance of expected income for the inducement to invest. Hicks agreed that 'it is expected income that locically matters', but emphasized the influence of current events on expectations (letter from J. R. Hicks to J. M. Keynes, 9 April 1937, reprinted in Keynes, 1973c, pp. 81–3).

References

Coddington, A. (1976), 'Keynesian Economics: The Search for First Principles', *Journal of Economic Literature*, **14** (December), pp. 1258–73.

Coddington, A. (1979) 'Hicks' Contribution to Keynesian Economics', *Journal of Economic Literature*, **17** (September), pp. 970–88.

Dangel, C. (1988), 'Théorie monétaire de J. M. Keynes: L'hypothèse de séparabilité de la demande de monnaie', *Recherches Economiques de Louvain*, **54** (4), pp. 439–58.

Hahn, F. (1988), 'On Monetary Theory', *Economic Journal*, **98** (December), pp. 957–73.

Hansson, B. (1986), 'Keynes' Shift of Subject Matter and Method Between a Treatise on Money and the General Theory, mimeo.

Hayek, F. A. (1928), 'Das intertemporale Gleichgewichtssystem der Preise und die Bewegungen des Geldwertes', *Weltwirtschaftliches Archiv*, **28**, pp. 3–76.

Hayek, F. A. (1931), *Prices and Production*, London: Routledge.

Hayek, F. A. (1937), 'Economics and Knowledge', *Economica*, **13** (February), pp. 33–54.

Hicks, J. R. (1931), 'The Theory of Uncertainty and Profit', *Economica*, **32** (May), pp. 170–89.

Hicks, J. R. (1936), 'Mr Keynes' Theory of Employment', *Economic Journal*, **46** (June), pp. 238–53.

Hicks, J. R. (1946), *Value and Capital* (1939), Oxford: Oxford University Press.

Hicks, J. R. (1963), 'Wages and Interest: the Dynamic Problem' (1935), in *Theory of Wages*, London: Macmillan, pp. 249–67.

Hicks, J. R. (1967a), 'A Suggestion for Simplifying the Theory of Money' (1935), in *Critical Essays in Monetary Theory*, Oxford: Clarendon, pp. 61–82.

Hicks, J. R. (1967b), 'Mr Keynes and the "Classics": A Suggested Interpretation' (1937), in *Critical Essays in Monetary Theory*, Oxford: Clarendon, pp. 126–42.

Hicks, J. R. (1977), 'Recollections and Documents' (1973), in *Economic Perspectives*, Oxford: Clarendon, pp. 134–48.

Hicks, J. R. (1979), *Causality in Economics*, Oxford: Basil Blackwell.

Hicks, J. R. (1980), 'Equilibrium and the Trade Cycle' (1933), *Economic Inquiry*, **18** (4) (October), pp. 523–34.

Keynes, J. M. (1971), *A Treatise on Money* (1930), 2 vols, London: Macmillan: *Collected Works* Vols V and VI.

Keynes, J. M. (1973a), *A Treatise on Probability* (1921), London: Macmillan: *Collected Works* Vol. VIII.

Keynes, J. M. (1973b), 'The General Theory of Employment' (1937), in *The General Theory and After, Part II Defence and Development*, London: Macmillan: *Collected Works* Vol. XIV, pp. 109–23.

Keynes, J. M. (1973c), *The General Theory and After: Part II Defence and Development*, London: Macmillan: *Collected Works* Vol. XIV.

Keynes, J. M. (1976), *The General Theory of Employment, Interest and Money*, London: Macmillan: *Collected Works* Vol. VII.

Kohn, M. (1986), 'Monetary Analysis, the Equilibrium Method and Keynes' "General Theory"', *Journal of Political Economy*, **96** (4) (December), pp. 1191–224.

Kregel, J. A. (1976), 'Economic Methodology in the Face of Uncertainty', *Economic Journal*, **86** (342) (June), pp. 209–25.

Leijonhufvud, A. (1973), 'Keynes and the Keynesians: a Suggested Interpretation' (1967), in R. W. Clower (ed.), *Monetary Theory*, Harmondsworth: Penguin Books, pp. 298–310.

Leijonhufvud, A. (1976), *On Keynesian Economics and the Economics of Keynes* (1968), New York: Oxford University Press.

McCloughry, R. (1984), 'Editor's Introduction', in F. A. Hayek, *Money, Capital and Fluctuations*, Chicago: University of Chicago Press, pp. vii–xi.

Maes, I. (1989), 'IS-LM: The Hicksian Journey', *De Economist*, **1**, pp. 91–104.

Maes, I. (1990), 'Hayek's Ailing Research Programme: the Case of Hicks' Marginal Revolution in Monetary Theory', in D. Moggridge (ed.), *Perspectives on the History of Economic Thought*, Aldershot: Edward Elgar, pp. 125–36.

Mahloudji, F. (1985), 'Hicks and the Keynesian Revolution', *History of Political Economy*, **17** (2), pp. 287–307.

Marshall, A. (1969), *Principles of Economics* (1890), London: Macmillan.

Meltzer, A. H. (1989), *Keynes's Monetary Theory. A Different Interpretation*, Cambridge: Cambridge University Press.

Milgate, M. (1987), 'Equilibrium: Development of the Concept', in *The New Palgrave*, Vol I, London: Macmillan, pp. 179–83.

Morgan, B. (1981), 'Sir John Hicks' Contributions to Economic Theory', in J. R. Shackleton and G. Locksley (eds), *Twelve Contemporary Economists*, London: Macmillan, pp. 108–40.

Morgenstern, O. (1976), 'Perfect Foresight and Economic Equilibrium' (1935), in A. Schotter (ed.), *Selected Economic Writings of Oskar Morgenstern*, New York: New York University Press, pp. 169–83.

Patinkin, D. (1976), *Keynes' Monetary Thought: a Study of its Development*, Durham, NC: Duke University Press.

Pekkarinen, J. (1986), 'Early Hicks and Keynesian Monetary Theory: Different Views on Liquidity Preference', *History of Political Economy*, **18** (2) (Summer), pp. 335–49.

Popper, K. R. (1977), *The Logic of Scientific Discovery* (1934), London: Hutchinson.

Robinson, J. (1980), 'Keynes and Ricardo' (1978), in J. Robinson (ed.), *Further Contributions to Modern Economics*, Oxford: Blackwell, pp. 78–85.

Shackle, G. L. S. (1982), 'Sir John Hicks' "IS-LM: an Explanation": a Comment', *Journal of Post Keynesian Economics*, **4** (3) (Spring), pp. 435–8.

Young, W. (1987), *Interpreting Mr Keynes: The IS-LM Enigma*, Oxford: Oxford University Press.

Name index

Aftalion, Florin, 149, 150
Albert the Great, 3, 6
Alexander Lombard, 11
Andler, Charles, 96, 97, 98, 101
Antonelli, Etienne, 131
Aquinas, Thomas, 3, 5, 6, 8, 10, 11–15, 70
Aristotle, 15, 49, 70, 174
Ashley, W., 5

Backhouse, Roger E., 19, 20, 21, 31
Baldwin, James, 5–6
Barnett, H., 203–5
Barone, E., 178
Baumol, W. J. 242
Beaudeau, Nicolas, 146
Beaujon, Anthony, 91
Bennett, J. T., 205
Bentham, Jeremy, 61–3, 65–74, 146
Bérard, Victor, 98
Bergson, Henri, 94, 98
Berr, Henri, 92
Bertrand, Joseph, 91
Besta, Fabio, 173–5, 185
Blackstone, William, 68
Blanchard, O., 20
Blanqui, Adolphe, 145
Blaug, Mark, 1, 20, 24, 26, 178, 194
Bloch, Gustave, 98
Blum, Léon, 97, 99, 113
Böhm-Bawerk, Eugen von, 10, 130, 139, 178, 200
Boissier, Gaston, 98
Bonaparte, Napoléon, 155
Borel, Emile, 92
Bortkiewicz, Ladislas von, 91
Bouglé, Célestin, 94, 100
Boulding, K. E., 42
Bourgin, Hubert, 99, 100
Boutroux, Emile, 94
Bouvier, Emile, 90
Bréal, Michel, 98
Brissot, Jacques, 67, 73

Brouilhet, Charles, 90
Brunetière, Ferdinand, 94, 98
Burnet, Etienne, 99

Caldwell, Bruce, 25
Canard, N.-F., 36–7
Cannan, E., 178
Cantillon, R., 82, 83, 84, 85, 87
Cartwright, Nancy, 46
Challaye, Félicien, 99
Chartier, Emile, 94
Clark, J. B., 178, 201
Clootz, Anacharsis, 159
Clower, R. W., 242
Coase, R. H., 187
Cochin, Auguste, 147
Coddington, A., 42, 251
Colander, D., 24–5, 28
Condillac, Etienne, 146
Condorcet, Marie Jean, 73, 147, 155
Cossa, L., 174
Costabile, L., 126
Cot, A. L., 10
Cournot, Augustin, 114
Courtney, L. H., 200
Cousin, Victor, 93
Cross, R., 20

Davenport, H. J., 179, 201, 202
De Roover, Raymond, 2–4, 8, 10
Dietrich, Rudolf, 184
Donzelli, F., 126
Dow, S. C., 25
Dreyfus, Alfred, 96, 98, 99
Dumont, Louis, 70
Duns Scotus, John, 3
Dupont de Nemours, Pierre Samuel, 146, 155
Dupuy, Paul, 97, 98
Durkheim, Emile, 92, 94, 99–100, 104
Dyer, A., 127–8

Easterlin, Richard, 57

263

Subject index

accountancy
  conventions for national income in, 51, 52–5, 57–58–9
  economics of the firm, and 180, 183, 185, 186–7
  evolution of, 173–6
adaptive rationality, 133–4
administration *see* firm, economics of
associations, 156
Austrian School, 126, 132, 254

banking system, 137–8, 234, 236–7
barter, 107–8, 129
bimetallism, 40
business cycles, 51, 56, 130, 131
business studies *see* firm, economics of

canon law, 4, 10, 11
capital: and colonial system, 64, 65–6
capital goods, rent and, 209–20, 222–7
capital market, 139
capitalists, 84
classes, social, 127–8
collectivism, 154
  see also socialism
colonial system, 63–7, 155
competition, 155–6
  imperfect, 20
contracts, 4, 12
  social, 68
conventions, social, 153–4
corporativism, 155–6
credit, 128, 137–8
critical pluralism, 25
critical positivism, 171–3, 185

debt payments, 128
demand
  and market price, 6, 80
  for money, 240–44, 256
  and risk, 83
determinism, 47–8
development, economic, 51, 130–31

Dreyfus Affair, 96, 98, 99
dynamics, economic, 126, 130–32

eclecticism, 25, 140
Ecole Normale Supérieure, 92, 93–100, 102
econometrics, 30, 57
empiricism, 51–9, 126–7, 181–2
entrepreneurship, 82–8, 127–8, 131, 132–5, 137
equilibrium, 251–3, 257–9
  hydraulic metaphors of, 36
  intertemporal, 253–4, 259
  money and, 255, 259
  see also general equilibrium
exchange *see* trade
expectations, 253
  rational, 21

falsificationism, 26
family
  economics of, 20, 180
  exclusion from national income of, 53, 54
felicific calculus, 61
firm, economics of, 168–9, 177–9, 188–9
  in Germany, 176–7, 179–85
  in Italy, 173–6, 185–8
foreign exchange markets, 21
freedom: and natural law, 69
French Revolution
  Bentham's views on, 61–74
  economic thought in, 144, 150–61
  overshadowing of, 145–50

general equilibrium theory, 27, 124–5, 129, 131, 254, 258
  and capital rent, 217–27
  and interest rates, 220–22, 257–8
  geometrical models, 46, 47
  goods market, hydraulic metaphors of, 37, 42

Printed and bound by CPI Group (UK) Ltd, Croydon, CR0 4YY

23/04/2025

14661002-0005